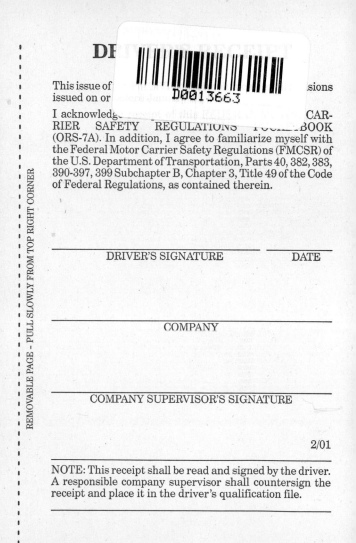

DRIVER'S RECEIPT

This issue of .... ssions
issued on or before Ja.....

I acknowledge ..... receipt of this ISSUE OF ..... CARRIER SAFETY REGULATIONS ..... BOOK (ORS-7A). In addition, I agree to familiarize myself with the Federal Motor Carrier Safety Regulations (FMCSR) of the U.S. Department of Transportation, Parts 40, 382, 383, 390-397, 399 Subchapter B, Chapter 3, Title 49 of the Code of Federal Regulations, as contained therein.

_____   _____
DRIVER'S SIGNATURE   DATE

_____
COMPANY

_____
COMPANY SUPERVISOR'S SIGNATURE

2/01

NOTE: This receipt shall be read and signed by the driver. A responsible company supervisor shall countersign the receipt and place it in the driver's qualification file.

REMOVABLE PAGE - PULL SLOWLY FROM TOP RIGHT CORNER

Reserved

FEDERAL MOTOR CARRIER SAFETY REGULATIONS POCKETBOOK

This issue of the FMCSR Pocketbook includes all revisions issued on or before January 11, 2001. Featured revisions include:

SECTION REVISED	SUBJECT	EFFECTIVE DATE
40	Drug and alcohol testing procedures	1/18/01
382	Random alcohol testing rate	1/1/00
382	Suspension of pre-employment alcohol testing	5/1/95
383	Disqualification for railroad crossing violations	10/4/99
387, 390, 391, 392, 395, 396, 397	Regulatory removals and substantive amendments	7/20/98
390	Motor vehicle marking	7/3/00
390	Motor carrier identification report	12/26/00
390	Passenger-carrying vehicles	2/12/01
391	Revised medical exam form	11/6/00
393	Retroreflective markings, older trailers	6/1/99
393	Rear bumpers	10/1/99

— Includes Appendix G - Minimum Periodic Inspection Standards —

©2001

by: J. J. Keller & Associates, Inc.
Neenah, Wisconsin

LIBRARY OF CONGRESS CATALOG CARD NUMBER — 75-32244
ISBN 0-934674-28-0

7-ORS-A   **2/01**

CONTENTS
Federal Motor Carrier Safety Regulations

SUBJECT INDEX

(Although Parts 325, 350, 385, 386, 388, 389, and 398 are not included in this handbook, index references for these parts are included for further reference.)

A

B

C

D

M

N

O

P

S

PART 382 — CONTROLLED SUBSTANCES AND ALCOHOL USE AND TESTING

AUTHORITY: 49 U.S.C. 31133, 31136, 31301 *et seq.,* 31502; 49 CFR 1.48.

Subpart A — General

§382.101 Purpose.

The purpose of this part is to establish programs designed to help prevent accidents and injuries resulting from the misuse of alcohol or use of controlled substances by drivers of commercial motor vehicles.

§382.103 Applicability.

(a) This part applies to every person and to all employers of such persons who operate a commercial motor vehicle in commerce in any State, and is subject to:

(1) The commercial driver's license requirements of part 383 of this subchapter;

(2) The Licencia Federal de Conductor (Mexico) requirements; or

(3) The commercial driver's license requirements of the Canadian National Safety Code.

(b) An employer who employs himself/herself as a driver must comply with both the requirements in this part that apply to employers and the requirements in this part that apply to drivers. An employer who employs only himself/herself as a driver shall implement a random alcohol and controlled substances testing program of two or more covered employees in the random testing selection pool.

(c) The exceptions contained in §390.3(f) of this subchapter do not apply to this part. The employers and drivers identified in §390.3(f) must comply with the requirements of this part, unless otherwise specifically provided in paragraph (d) of this section.

(d) **Exceptions**. This part shall not apply to employers and their drivers:

(1) Required to comply with the alcohol and/or controlled substances testing requirements of parts 653 and 654 of this title (Federal Transit Administration alcohol and controlled substances testing regulations); or

(2) Who a State must waive from the requirements of part 383 of this subchapter. These individuals include active duty military personnel; members of the reserves; and members of the national guard on active duty, including personnel on full-time national guard duty, personnel on part-time national guard training and national guard military technicians (civilians who are required to wear military uniforms), and active duty U.S. Coast Guard personnel;

(3) Who a State has, at its discretion, exempted from the requirements of part 383 of this subchapter. These individuals may be:

(i) Operators of a farm vehicle which is:

(A) Controlled and operated by a farmer;

(B) Used to transport either agricultural products, farm machinery, farm supplies, or both to or from a farm;

(C) Not used in the operations of a common or contract motor carrier; and

(D) Used within 241 kilometers (150 miles) of the farmer's farm.

(ii) Firefighters or other persons who operate commercial motor vehicles which are necessary for the preservation of life or property or the execution of emergency governmental functions, are equipped with audible and visual signals, and are not subject to normal traffic regulation.

§382.105 Testing procedures.

Each employer shall ensure that all alcohol or controlled substances testing conducted under this part complies with the procedures set forth in part 40 of this title. The provisions of part 40 of this title that address alcohol or controlled substances testing are made applicable to employers by this part.

§382.107 Definitions.

Words or phrases used in this part are defined in §§386.2 and 390.5 of this subchapter, and § 40.3 of this title, except as provided herein—

Alcohol means the intoxicating agent in beverage alcohol, ethyl alcohol, or other low molecular weight alcohols including methyl and isopropyl alcohol.

Alcohol concentration (or content) means the alcohol in a volume of breath expressed in terms of grams of alcohol per 210 liters of breath as indicated by an evidential breath test under this part.

Alcohol use means the consumption of any beverage, mixture, or preparation, including any medication, containing alcohol.

Commerce means:

(1) Any trade, traffic or transportation within the jurisdiction of the United States between a place in a State and a place outside of such State, including a place outside of the United States and

(2) Trade, traffic, and transportation in the United States which affects any trade, traffic, and transportation described in paragraph (1) of this definition.

Commercial motor vehicle means a motor vehicle or combination of motor vehicles used in commerce to transport passengers or property if the motor vehicle—

(1) Has a gross combination weight rating of 11,794 or more kilograms (26,001 or more pounds) inclusive of a towed unit with a gross vehicle weight rating of more than 4,536 kilograms (10,000 pounds); or

(2) Has a gross vehicle weight rating of 11,794 or more kilograms (26,001 or more pounds); or

(3) Is designed to transport 16 or more passengers, including the driver; or

(4) Is of any size and is used in the transportation of materials found to be hazardous for the purposes of the Hazardous Materials Transportation Act and which require the motor vehicle to be placarded under the Hazardous Materials Regulations (49 CFR part 172, subpart F).

Confirmation test for alcohol testing means a second test, following a screening test with a result of 0.02 or greater, that provides quantitative data of alcohol concentration. For controlled substances testing means a second analytical procedure to identify the presence of a specific drug or metabolite which is independent of the screen test and which uses a different technique and chemical principle from that of the screen test in order to ensure reliability and accuracy. (Gas chromatography/mass spectrometry (GC/MS) is the only authorized confirmation method for cocaine, marijuana, opiates, amphetamines, and phencyclidine.)

Consortium means an entity, including a group or association of employers or contractors, that provides alcohol or controlled substances testing as required by this part, or other DOT alcohol or controlled substances testing rules, and that acts on behalf of the employers.

Controlled substances mean those substances identified in §40.21(a) of this title.

Disabling damage means damage which precludes departure of a motor vehicle from the scene of the accident in its usual manner in daylight after simple repairs.

(1) *Inclusions.* Damage to motor vehicles that could have been driven, but would have been further damaged if so driven.

(2) *Exclusions.*

(i) Damage which can be remedied temporarily at the scene of the accident without special tools or parts.

(ii) Tire disablement without other damage even if no spare tire is available.

(iii) Headlight or taillight damage.

(iv) Damage to turn signals, horn, or windshield wipers which make them inoperative.

DOT Agency means an agency (or "operating administration") of the United States Department of Transportation administering regulations requiring alcohol and/or drug testing (14 CFR parts 61, 63, 65, 121, and 135; 49 CFR parts 199, 219, 382, 653 and 654), in accordance with part 40 of this title.

Driver means any person who operates a commercial motor vehicle. This includes, but is not limited to: Full time, regularly employed drivers; casual, intermittent or occasional drivers; leased drivers and independent, owner-operator contractors who are either directly employed by or under lease to an employer or who operate a commercial motor vehicle at the direction of or with the consent of an employer.

Employer means any person (including the United States, a State, District of Columbia, tribal government, or a political subdivision of a State) who owns or leases a commercial motor vehicle or assigns persons to operate such a vehicle. The term employer includes an employer's agents, officers and representatives.

Licensed medical practitioner means a person who is licensed, certified, and/or registered, in accordance with applicable Federal, State, local, or foreign laws and regulations, to prescribe controlled substances and other drugs.

Performing (a safety-sensitive function) means a driver is considered to be performing a safety-sensitive function during any period in which he or she is actually performing, ready to perform, or immediately available to perform any safety-sensitive functions.

Positive rate means the number of positive results for random controlled substances tests conducted under this part plus the number of refusals of random controlled substances tests required by this part, divided by the total of random controlled substances tests conducted under this part plus the number of refusals of random tests required by this part.

Refuse to submit (to an alcohol or controlled substances test) means that a driver:

(1) Fails to provide adequate breath for alcohol testing as required by part 40 of this title, without a valid medical explanation, after he or she has received notice of the requirement for breath testing in accordance with the provisions of this part,

(2) Fails to provide an adequate urine sample for controlled substances testing as required by part 40 of this title, without a genuine inability to provide a specimen (as determined by a medical evaluation), after he or she has received notice of the requirement for urine testing in accordance with the provisions of this part, or

(3) Engages in conduct that clearly obstructs the testing process.

Safety-sensitive function means all time from the time a driver begins to work or is required to be in readiness to work until the time he/she is relieved from work and all responsibility for performing work. Safety-sensitive functions shall include:

(1) All time at an employer or shipper plant, terminal, facility, or other property, or on any public property, waiting to be dispatched, unless the driver has been relieved from duty by the employer;

(2) All time inspecting equipment as required by §§392.7 and 392.8 of this subchapter or otherwise inspecting, servicing, or conditioning any commercial motor vehicle at any time;

(3) All time spent at the driving controls of a commercial mo-

tor vehicle in operation;

(4) All time, other than driving time, in or upon any commercial motor vehicle except time spent resting in a sleeper berth (a berth conforming to the requirements of §393.76 of this subchapter);

(5) All time loading or unloading a vehicle, supervising, or assisting in the loading or unloading, attending a vehicle being loaded or unloaded, remaining in readiness to operate the vehicle, or in giving or receiving receipts for shipments loaded or unloaded; and

(6) All time repairing, obtaining assistance, or remaining in attendance upon a disabled vehicle.

Screening test (also known as initial test) In alcohol testing, it means an analytical procedure to determine whether a driver may have a prohibited concentration of alcohol in his or her system. In controlled substance testing, it means an immunoassay screen to eliminate "negative" urine specimens from further consideration.

Substance abuse professional means a licensed physician (Medical Doctor or Doctor of Osteopathy), or a licensed or certified psychologist, social worker, employee assistance professional, or addiction counselor (certified by the National Association of Alcoholism and Drug Abuse Counselors Certification Commission) with knowledge of and clinical experience in the diagnois and treatment of alcohol and controlled substances-related disorders.

Violation rate means the number of drivers (as reported under §382.305 of this part) found during random tests given under this part to have an alcohol concentration of 0.04 or greater, plus the number of drivers who refuse a random test required by this part, divided by the total reported number of drivers in the industry given random alcohol tests under this part plus the total reported number of drivers in the industry who refuse a random test required by this part.

§382.109 Preemption of State and local laws.

(a) Except as provided in paragraph (b) of this section, this part preempts any State or local law, rule, regulation, or order to the extent that:

(1) Compliance with both the State or local requirement and this part is not possible; or

(2) Compliance with the State or local requirement is an obstacle to the accomplishment and execution of any requirement

in this part.

(b) This part shall not be construed to preempt provisions of State criminal law that impose sanctions for reckless conduct leading to actual loss of life, injury, or damage to property, whether the provisions apply specifically to transportation employees, employers, or the general public.

§382.111 Other requirements imposed by employers.

Except as expressly provided in this part, nothing in this part shall be construed to affect the authority of employers, or the rights of drivers, with respect to the use of alcohol, or the use of controlled substances, including authority and rights with respect to testing and rehabilitation.

§382.113 Requirement for notice.

Before performing an alcohol or controlled substances test under this part, each employer shall notify a driver that the alcohol or controlled substances test is required by this part. No employer shall falsely represent that a test is administered under this part.

§382.115 Starting date for testing programs.

(a) **All domestic employers.** Each domestic-domiciled employer that begins commercial motor vehicle operations will implement the requirements of this part on the date the employer begins such operations.

(b) **Large foreign employers.** Each foreign-domiciled employer with fifty or more drivers assigned to operate commercial motor vehicles in North America on December 17, 1995, must implement the requirements of this part beginning on July 1, 1996.

(c) **Small foreign employers.** Each foreign-domiciled employer with less than fifty drivers assigned to operate commercial motor vehicles in North America on December 17, 1995, must implement the requirements of this part beginning on July 1, 1997.

(d) **All foreign employers.** Each foreign-domiciled employer that begins commercial motor vehicle operations in the United States after December 17, 1995, but before July 1, 1997, must implement the requirements of this part beginning on July 1, 1997. A foreign employer that begins commercial motor vehicle operations in the United States on or after July 1, 1997, must implement the requirements of this part on the date the foreign employer begins such operations.

Subpart B — Prohibitions

§382.201 Alcohol concentration.

No driver shall report for duty or remain on duty requiring the performance of safety-sensitive functions while having an alcohol concentration of 0.04 or greater. No employer having actual knowledge that a driver has an alcohol concentration of 0.04 or greater shall permit the driver to perform or continue to perform safety-sensitive functions.

§382.205 On-duty use.

No driver shall use alcohol while performing safety-sensitive functions. No employer having actual knowledge that a driver is using alcohol while performing safety-sensitive functions shall permit the driver to perform or continue to perform safety-sensitive functions.

§382.207 Pre-duty use.

No driver shall perform safety-sensitive functions within four hours after using alcohol. No employer having actual knowledge that a driver has used alcohol within four hours shall permit a driver to perform or continue to perform safety-sensitive functions.

§382.209 Use following an accident.

No driver required to take a post-accident alcohol test under §382.303 of this part shall use alcohol for eight hours following the accident, or until he/she undergoes a post-accident alcohol test, whichever occurs first.

§382.211 Refusal to submit to a required alcohol or controlled substances test.

No driver shall refuse to submit to a post- accident alcohol or controlled substances test required under §382.303, a random alcohol or controlled substances test required under §382.305, a reasonable suspicion alcohol or controlled substances test required under §382.307, or a follow-up alcohol or controlled substances test required under §382.311. No employer shall permit a driver who refuses to submit to such tests to perform or continue to perform safety-sensitive functions.

§382.213 Controlled substances use.

(a) No driver shall report for duty or remain on duty requiring the performance of safety-sensitive functions when the driver uses any controlled substance, except when the use is pursuant to the instructions of a licensed medical practitioner, as defined in §382.107 of this part, who has advised the driver that the substance will not adversely affect the driver's ability to safely operate a commercial motor vehicle.

(b) No employer having actual knowledge that a driver has used a controlled substance shall permit the driver to perform or continue to perform a safety-sensitive function.

(c) An employer may require a driver to inform the employer of any therapeutic drug use.

§382.215 Controlled substances testing.

No driver shall report for duty, remain on duty or perform a safety-sensitive function, if the driver tests positive for controlled substances. No employer having actual knowledge that a driver has tested positive for controlled substances shall permit the driver to perform or continue to perform safety-sensitive functions.

Subpart C — Tests Required

§382.301 Pre-employment testing.

(a) Prior to the first time a driver performs safety-sensitive functions for an employer, the driver shall undergo testing for alcohol and controlled substances as a condition prior to being used, unless the employer uses the exception in paragraphs (c) and (d) of this section. No employer shall allow a driver, who the employer intends to hire or use, to perform safety-sensitive functions unless the driver has been administered an alcohol test with a result indicating an alcohol concentration less than 0.04, and has received a controlled substances test result from the MRO indicating a verified negative test result. If a pre-employment alcohol test result under this section indicates an alcohol content of 0.02 or greater but less than 0.04, the provision of §382.505 shall apply.

(b) **Exception for pre-employment alcohol testing.** An employer is not required to administer an alcohol test required by paragraph (a) of this section if:

(1) The driver has undergone an alcohol test required by this section or the alcohol misuse rule of another DOT agency under part 40 of this title within the previous six months, with a result indicating an alcohol concentration less than 0.04; and

(2) The employer ensures that no prior employer of the driver of whom the employer has knowledge has records of a violation of this part or the alcohol misuse rule of another DOT agency within the previous six months.

(c) **Exception for pre-employment controlled substances testing.** An employer is not required to administer a controlled substances test required by paragraph (a) of this section if:

(1) The driver has participated in a controlled substances testing program that meets the requirements of this part within the previous 30 days; and

(2) While participating in that program, either

(i) Was tested for controlled substances within the past 6 months (from the date of application with the employer) or

(ii) Participated in the random controlled substances testing program for the previous 12 months (from the date of application with the employer); and

(3) The employer ensures that no prior employer of the driver of whom the employer has knowledge has records of a violation of this part or the controlled substances use rule of another DOT agency within the previous six months.

(d)(1) An employer who exercises the exception in either paragraph (b) or (c) of this section shall contact the alcohol and/or controlled substances testing program(s) in which the driver participates or participated and shall obtain and retain from the testing program(s) the following information:

(i) Name(s) and address(es) of the program(s).

(ii) Verification that the driver participates or participated in the program(s).

(iii) Verification that the program(s) conforms to part 40 of this title.

(iv) Verification that the driver is qualified under the rules of this part, including that the driver has not refused to be tested for controlled substances.

(v) The date the driver was last tested for alcohol or controlled substances.

(vi) The results of any tests taken within the previous six months and any other violations of subpart B of this part.

(2) An employer who uses, but does not employ, a driver more than once a year to operate commercial motor vehicles must obtain the information in paragraph (d)(1) of this section at least once every six months. The records prepared under this paragraph shall be maintained in accordance with §382.401. If the employer cannot verify that the driver is participating in a controlled substances testing program in accordance with this part and part 40, the employer shall conduct a pre-employment alcohol and/or controlled substances test.

(e) Nothwithstanding any other provisions of this subpart, all provisions and requirements in this section pertaining to pre-employment testing for alcohol are vacated as of May 1, 1995.

§382.303 Post-accident testing.

(a) As soon as practicable following an occurrence involving a commercial motor vehicle operating on a public road in commerce, each employer shall test for alcohol and controlled substances each surviving driver:

(1) Who was performing safety-sensitive functions with respect to the vehicle, if the accident involved the loss of human life; or

(2) Who receives a citation under State or local law for a moving traffic violation arising from the accident, if the accident involved:

(i) Bodily injury to any person who, as a result of the injury, immediately receives medical treatment away from the scene of the accident; or

(ii) One or more motor vehicles incurring disabling damage as a result of the accident, requiring the motor vehicle to be transported away from the scene by a tow truck or other motor vehicle.

(3) This table notes when a post-accident test is required to be conducted by paragraphs (a)(1) and (a)(2) of this section.

TABLE FOR §382.303(a)(3)

Type of accident involved	Citation issued to the CMV driver	Test must be performed by employer
Human fatality	YES	YES.
	NO	YES.
Bodily injury with immediate medical treatment away from the scene.	YES	YES.
	NO	NO.
Disabling damage to any motor vehicle requiring tow away.	YES	YES.
	NO	NO.

(b)(1) **Alcohol tests.** If a test required by this section is not administered within two hours following the accident, the employer shall prepare and maintain on file a record stating the reasons the test was not promptly administered. If a test required by this section is not administered within eight hours following the accident, the employer shall cease attempts to administer an alcohol test and shall prepare and maintain the same record. Records shall be submitted to the FHWA upon request of the Associate Administrator.

(2) For the years stated in this paragraph, employers who submit MIS reports shall submit to the FHWA each record of a test required by this section that is not completed within eight hours. The employer's records of tests that are not completed within eight hours shall be submitted to the FHWA by March 15, 1996; March 15, 1997, and March 15, 1998, for calendar years 1995, 1996, and 1997, respectively. Employers shall append these records to their MIS submissions. Each record shall include the following information:

(i) Type of test (reasonable suspicion/post-accident);

(ii) Triggering event (including date, time, and location);

(iii) Reason(s) test could not be completed within eight hours;

(iv) If blood alcohol testing could have been completed within eight hours, the name, address, and telephone number of the testing site where blood testing could have occurred; and

(3) Records of alcohol tests that could not be completed in eight hours shall be submitted to the FHWA at the following address: Attn: Alcohol Testing Program, Office of Motor Carrier Research and Standards (HCS-1), Federal Highway Administration, 400 Seventh Street, SW., Washington, DC 20590.

(4) **Controlled substance tests.** If a test required by this section is not administered within 32 hours following the accident, the employer shall cease attempts to administer a controlled substances test, and prepare and maintain on file a record stating the reasons the test was not promptly administered. Records shall be submitted to the FHWA upon request of the Associate Administrator.

(c) A driver who is subject to post-accident testing shall remain readily available for such testing or may be deemed by the employer to have refused to submit to testing. Nothing in this section shall be construed to require the delay of necessary medical attention for injured people following an accident or to prohibit a driver from leaving the scene of an accident for the period necessary to obtain assistance in responding to the accident, or to obtain necessary emergency medical care.

(d) An employer shall provide drivers with necessary post-accident information, procedures and instructions, prior to the driver operating a commercial motor vehicle, so that drivers will be able to comply with the requirements of this section.

(e)(1) The results of a breath or blood test for the use of alcohol, conducted by Federal, State, or local officials having independent authority for the test, shall be considered to meet the requirements of this section, provided such tests conform to the applicable Federal, State or local alcohol testing requirements, and that the results of the tests are obtained by the employer.

(2) The results of a urine test for the use of controlled substances, conducted by Federal, State, or local officials having independent authority for the test, shall be considered to meet the requirements of this section, provided such tests conform to the applicable Federal, State or local controlled substances testing requirements, and that the results of the tests are obtained by the employer.

(f) **Exception.** This section does not apply to:

(1) An occurrence involving only boarding or alighting from a stationary motor vehicle; or

(2) An occurrence involving only the loading or unloading of cargo; or

(3) An occurrence in the course of the operation of a passenger car or a multipurpose passenger vehicle (as defined in §571.3 of this title) by an employer unless the motor vehicle is transporting passengers for hire or hazardous materials of a type and quantity that require the motor vehicle to be marked or placarded in accordance with §177.823 of this title.

§382.305 Random testing.

(a) Every employer shall comply with the requirements of this section. Every driver shall submit to random alcohol and controlled substance testing as required in this section.

(b)(1) Except as provided in paragraphs (c) through (e) of this section, the minimum annual percentage rate for random alcohol testing shall be 25 percent of the average number of driver positions.*

(2) Except as provided in paragraphs (f) through (h) of this section, the minimum annual percentage rate for random controlled substances testing shall be 50 percent of the average number of driver positions.

(c) The FHWA Administrator's decision to increase or decrease the minimum annual percentage rate for alcohol testing is based on the reported violation rate for the entire industry. All information used for this determination is drawn from the alcohol management information system reports required by §382.403 of this part. In order to ensure reliability of the data, the FHWA Administrator considers the quality and completeness of the reported data, may obtain additional information or reports from employers, and may make appropriate modifications in calculating the industry violation rate. Each year, the FHWA Administrator will publish in the *Federal Register* the minimum annual percentage rate for random alcohol testing of drivers. The new minimum annual percentage rate for random alcohol testing will be applicable starting January 1 of the calendar year following publication.

(d)(1) When the minimum annual percentage rate for random alcohol testing is 25 percent or more, the FHWA Administrator may lower this rate to 10 percent of all driver positions if the FHWA Administrator determines that the data received under the reporting requirements of §382.403 for two consecutive calendar years indicate that the violation rate is less than 0.5 percent.

---

*Editor's Note: The alcohol random testing rate has been set at 10 percent for calendar year 2000.

(2) When the minimum annual percentage rate for random alcohol testing is 50 percent, the FHWA Administrator may lower this rate to 25 percent of all driver positions if the FHWA Administrator determines that the data received under the reporting requirements of §382.403 for two consecutive calendar years indicate that the violation rate is less than 1.0 percent but equal to or greater than 0.5 percent.

(e)(1) When the minimum annual percentage rate for random alcohol testing is 10 percent, and the data received under the reporting requirements of §382.403 for that calendar year indicate that the violation rate is equal to or greater than 0.5 percent, but less than 1.0 percent, the FHWA Administrator will increase the minimum annual percentage rate for random alcohol testing to 25 percent for all driver positions.

(2) When the minimum annual percentage rate for random alcohol testing is 25 percent or less, and the data received under the reporting requirements of §382.403 for that calendar year indicate that the violation rate is equal to or greater than 1.0 percent, the FHWA Administrator will increase the minimum annual percentage rate for random alcohol testing to 50 percent for all driver positions.

(f) The FHWA Administrator's decision to increase or decrease the minimum annual percentage rate for controlled substances testing is based on the reported positive rate for the entire industry. All information used for this determination is drawn from the controlled substances management information system reports required by §382.403 of this part. In order to ensure reliability of the data, the FHWA Administrator considers the quality and completeness of the reported data, may obtain additional information or reports from employers, and may make appropriate modifications in calculating the industry positive rate. Each year, the FHWA Administrator will publish in the *Federal Register* the minimum annual percentage rate for random controlled substances testing of drivers. The new minimum annual percentage rate for random controlled substances testing will be applicable starting January 1 of the calendar year following publication.

(g) When the minimum annual percentage rate for random controlled substances testing is 50 percent, the FHWA Administrator may lower this rate to 25 percent of all driver positions if the FHWA Administrator determines that the data received under the reporting requirements of §382.403 for two consecutive calendar years indicate that the positive rate is less than 1.0 percent. However, after the initial two years of random testing by large employers and the initial first year of testing by small employers under this section, the FHWA Administrator may lower the rate the following calendar year, if the combined positive testing rate is less than 1.0 percent, and if it would be in the interest of safety.

(h) When the minimum annual percentage rate for random controlled substances testing is 25 percent, and the data received under the reporting requirements of §382.403 for any calendar year indicate that the reported positive rate is equal to or greater than 1.0 percent, the FHWA Administrator will increase the minimum annual percentage rate for random controlled substances testing to 50 percent of all driver positions.

(i) The selection of drivers for random alcohol and controlled substances testing shall be made by a scientifically valid method, such as a random number table or a computer-based random number generator that is matched with drivers' Social Security numbers, payroll identification numbers, or other comparable identifying numbers. Under the selection process used, each driver shall have an equal chance of being tested each time selections are made.

(j) The employer shall randomly select a sufficient number of drivers for testing during each calendar year to equal an annual rate not less than the minimum annual percentage rate for random alcohol and controlled substances testing determined by the FHWA Administrator. If the employer conducts random testing for alcohol and/or controlled substances through a consortium, the number of drivers to be tested may be calculated for each individual employer or may be based on the total number of drivers covered by the consortium who are subject to random alcohol and/or controlled substances testing at the same minimum annual percentage rate under this part or any DOT alcohol or controlled substances random testing rule.

(k) Each employer shall ensure that random alcohol and controlled substances tests conducted under this part are unannounced and that the dates for administering random alcohol and controlled substances tests are spread reasonably throughout the calendar year.

(l) Each employer shall require that each driver who is notified of selection for random alcohol and/or controlled substances testing proceeds to the test site immediately; provided, however, that if the driver is performing a safety-sensitive function, other than driving a commercial motor vehicle, at the time of notification, the employer shall instead ensure that the driver ceases to perform the safety-sensitive function and proceeds to the testing site as soon as possible.

(m) A driver shall only be tested for alcohol while the driver is performing safety-sensitive functions, just before the driver is to perform safety-sensitive functions, or just after the driver has ceased performing such functions.

(n) If a given driver is subject to random alcohol or controlled substances testing under the random alcohol or controlled substances testing rules of more than one DOT agency for the same employer, the driver shall be subject to random alcohol and/or controlled substances testing at the annual percentage rate established for the calendar year by the DOT agency regulating more than 50 percent of the driver's function.

(o) If an employer is required to conduct random alcohol or controlled substances testing under the alcohol or controlled substances testing rules of more than one DOT agency, the employer may—

(1) Establish separate pools for random selection, with each pool containing the DOT-covered employees who are subject to testing at the same required minimum annual percentage rate; or

(2) Randomly select such employees for testing at the highest minimum annual percentage rate established for the calendar year by any DOT agency to which the employer is subject.

§382.307 Reasonable suspicion testing.

(a) An employer shall require a driver to submit to an alcohol test when the employer has reasonable suspicion to believe that the driver has violated the prohibitions of subpart B of this part concerning alcohol. The employer's determination that reasonable suspicion exists to require the driver to undergo an alcohol test must be based on specific, contemporaneous, articulable observations concerning the appearance, behavior, speech or body odors of the driver.

(b) An employer shall require a driver to submit to a controlled substances test when the employer has reasonable suspicion to believe that the driver has violated the prohibitions of subpart B of this part concerning controlled substances. The employer's determination that reasonable suspicion exists to require the driver to undergo a controlled substances test must be based on specific, contemporaneous, articulable observations concerning the appearance, behavior, speech or body odors of the driver. The observations may include indications of the chronic and withdrawal effects of controlled substances.

(c) The required observations for alcohol and/or controlled substances reasonable suspicion testing shall be made by a supervisor or company official who is trained in accordance with §382.603 of this part. The person who makes the determination that reasonable suspicion exists to conduct an alcohol test shall not conduct the alcohol test of the driver.

(d) Alcohol testing is authorized by this section only if the observations required by paragraph (a) of this section are made during, just preceding, or just after the period of the work day that the driver is required to be in compliance with this part. A driver may be directed by the employer to only undergo reasonable suspicion testing while the driver is performing safety-sensitive functions, just before the driver is to perform safety-sensitive functions, or just after the driver has ceased performing such functions.

(e)(1) If an alcohol test required by this section is not administered within two hours following the determination under paragraph (a) of this section, the employer shall prepare and maintain on file a record stating the reasons the alcohol test was not promptly administered. If an alcohol test required by this section is not administered within eight hours following the determination under paragraph (a) of this section, the employer shall cease attempts to administer an alcohol test and shall state in the record the reasons for not administering the test.

(2) For the years stated in this paragraph, employers who submit MIS reports shall submit to the FHWA each record of a test required by this section that is not completed within 8 hours. The employer's records of tests that could not be completed within 8 hours shall be submitted to the FHWA by March 15, 1996; March 15, 1997; and March 15, 1998; for calendar years 1995, 1996, and 1997, respectively. Employers shall append these records to their MIS submissions. Each record shall include the following information:

(i) Type of test (reasonable suspicion/post-accident);

(ii) Triggering event (including date, time, and location);

(iii) Reason(s) test could not be completed within 8 hours; and

(iv) If blood alcohol testing could have been completed within eight hours, the name, address, and telephone number of the testing site where blood testing could have occurred.

(3) Records of tests that could not be completed in eight hours shall be submitted to the FHWA at the following address: Attn.: Alcohol Testing program, Office of Motor Carrier Research and Standards (HCS-1), Federal Highway Administration, 400 Seventh Street, SW., Washington, DC 20590.

(4) Notwithstanding the absence of a reasonable suspicion alcohol test under this section, no driver shall report for duty or remain on duty requiring the performance of safety-sensitive functions while the driver is under the influence of or impaired by alcohol, as shown by the behavioral, speech, and performance indicators of alcohol misuse, nor shall an employer permit the driver to perform or continue to perform safety-sensitive functions, until:

(i) An alcohol test is administered and the driver's alcohol concentration measures less than 0.02; or

(ii) Twenty four hours have elapsed following the determination under paragraph (a) of this section that there is reasonable suspicion to believe that the driver has violated the prohibitions in this part concerning the use of alcohol.

(5) Except as provided in paragraph (e)(2) of this section, no employer shall take any action under this part against a driver based solely on the driver's behavior and appearance, with respect to alcohol use, in the absence of an alcohol test. This does not prohibit an employer with independent authority of this part from taking any action otherwise consistent with law.

(f) A written record shall be made of the observations leading to a controlled substance reasonable suspicion test, and signed by the supervisor or company official who made the observations, within 24 hours of the observed behavior or before the results of the controlled substances test are released, whichever is earlier.

§382.309 Return-to-duty testing.

(a) Each employer shall ensure that before a driver returns to duty requiring the performance of a safety-sensitive function after engaging in conduct prohibited by subpart B of this part concerning alcohol, the driver shall undergo a return-to-duty alcohol test with a result indicating an alcohol concentration of less than 0.02.

(b) Each employer shall ensure that before a driver returns to duty requiring the performance of a safety-sensitive function after engaging in conduct prohibited by subpart B of this part concerning controlled substances, the driver shall undergo a return-to-duty controlled substances test with a result indicating a verified negative result for controlled substances use.

§382.311 Follow-up testing.

(a) Following a determination under §382.605(b) that a driver is in need of assistance in resolving problems associated with alcohol misuse and/or use of controlled substances, each employer shall ensure that the driver is subject to unannounced follow-up alcohol and/or controlled substances testing as directed by a substance abuse professional in accordance with the provisions of §382.605(c)(2)(ii).

(b) Follow-up alcohol testing shall be conducted only when the driver is performing safety-sensitive functions, just before the driver is to perform safety-sensitive functions, or just after the driver has ceased performing safety-sensitive functions.

Subpart D — Handling Of Test Results, Record Retention and Confidentiality

§382.401 Retention of records.

(a) **General requirement.** Each employer shall maintain records of its alcohol misuse and controlled substances use prevention programs as provided in this section. The records shall be maintained in a secure location with controlled access.

(b) **Period of retention.** Each employer shall maintain the records in accordance with the following schedule:

(1) **Five years.** The following records shall be maintained for a minimum of five years:

(i) Records of driver alcohol test results indicating an alcohol concentration of 0.02 or greater,

(ii) Records of driver verified positive controlled substances test results,

(iii) Documentation of refusals to take required alcohol and/or controlled substances tests,

(iv) Driver evaluation and referrals,

(v) Calibration documentation,

(vi) Records related to the administration of the alcohol and controlled substances testing programs, and

(vii) A copy of each annual calendar year summary required by §382.403.

(2) **Two years.** Records related to the alcohol and controlled substances collection process (except calibration of evidential breath testing devices).

(3) **One year.** Records of negative and canceled controlled substances test results (as defined in part 40 of this title) and alcohol test results with a concentration of less than 0.02 shall be maintained for a minimum of one year.

(4) **Indefinite period.** Records related to the education and training of breath alcohol technicians, screening test technicians, supervisors, and drivers shall be maintained by the employer while the individual performs the functions which require the training and for two years after ceasing to perform those functions.

(c) **Types of records.** The following specific types of records shall be maintained. "Documents generated" are documents that may have to be prepared under a requirement of this part. If the record is required to be prepared, it must be maintained.

(1) Records related to the collection process:

(i) Collection logbooks, if used;

(ii) Documents relating to the random selection process;

(iii) Calibration documentation for evidential breath testing devices;

(iv) Documentation of breath alcohol technician training;

(v) Documents generated in connection with decisions to administer reasonable suspicion alcohol or controlled substances tests;

(vi) Documents generated in connection with decisions on post-accident tests;

(vii) Documents verifying existence of a medical explanation of the inability of a driver to provide adequate breath or to provide a urine specimen for testing; and

(viii) Consolidated annual calendar year summaries as required by §382.403.

(2) Records related to a driver's test results:

(i) The employer's copy of the alcohol test form, including the results of the test;

(ii) The employer's copy of the controlled substances test chain of custody and control form;

(iii) Documents sent by the MRO to the employer, including those required by §382.407(a).

(iv) Documents related to the refusal of any driver to submit to an alcohol or controlled substances test required by this part; and

(v) Documents presented by a driver to dispute the result of an alcohol or controlled substances test administered under this part.

(vi) Documents generated in connection with verifications of prior employers' alcohol or controlled substances test results that the employer:

(A) Must obtain in connection with the exception contained in §382.301 of this part, and

(B) Must obtain as required by §382.413 of this subpart.

(3) Records related to other violations of this part.

(4) Records related to evaluations:

(i) Records pertaining to a determination by a substance abuse professional concerning a driver's need for assistance; and

(ii) Records concerning a driver's compliance with recommendations of the substance abuse professional.

(5) Records related to education and training:

(i) Materials on alcohol misuse and controlled substance use awareness, including a copy of the employer's policy on alcohol misuse and controlled substance use;

(ii) Documentation of compliance with the requirements of §382.601, including the driver's signed receipt of education materials;

(iii) Documentation of training provided to supervisors for the purpose of qualifying the supervisors to make a determination concerning the need for alcohol and/or controlled substances testing based on reasonable suspicion;

(iv) Documentation of training for breath alcohol technicians as required by §40.51(a) of this title, and

(v) Certification that any training conducted under this part complies with the requirements for such training.

(6) Administrative records related to alcohol and controlled substances testing:

(i) Agreements with collection site facilities, laboratories, breath alcohol technicians, screening test technicians, medical review officers, consortia, and third party service providers;

(ii) Names and positions of officials and their role in the employer's alcohol and controlled substances testing program(s);

(iii) Quarterly laboratory statistical summaries of urinalysis required by §40.29(g)(6) of this title; and

(iv) The employer's alcohol and controlled substances testing policy and procedures.

(d) **Location of records.** All records required by this part shall be maintained as required by §390.31 of this subchapter and shall be made available for inspection at the employer's principal place of business within two business days after a request has been made by an authorized representative of the Federal Highway Administration.

(e)(1) **OMB control number.** The information collection requirements of this part have been reviewed by the Office of Management and Budget pursuant to the Paperwork Reduction Act of 1995 (44 U.S.C. 3501 *et seq.*) and have been assigned OMB control number 2125-0543.

(2) The information collection requirements of this part are found in the following sections: Section 382.105, 382.113, 382.301, 382.303, 382.305, 382.307, 382.309, 382.311, 382.401, 382.403, 382.405, 382.407, 382.409, 382.411, 382.413, 382.601, 382.603, 382.605.

§382.403 Reporting of results in a management information system.

(a) An employer shall prepare and maintain a summary of the results of its alcohol and controlled substances testing programs performed under this part during the previous calendar year, when requested by the Secretary of Transportation, any DOT agency, or any State or local officials with regulatory authority over the employer or any of its drivers.

(b) If an employer is notified, during the month of January, of a request by the Federal Highway Administration to report the employer's annual calendar year summary information, the employer shall prepare and submit the report to the Federal Highway Administration by March 15 of that year. The employer shall ensure that the annual summary report is accurate and received by March 15 at the location that the Federal Highway Administration specifies in its request. The report shall be in the form and manner prescribed by the Federal Highway Administration in its request. When the report is submitted to the Federal Highway Administration by mail or electronic transmission, the information requested shall be typed, except for the signature of the certifying official. Each employer shall ensure the accuracy and timeliness of each report submitted by the employer or a consortium.

(c) **Detailed summary.** Each annual calendar year summary that contains information on a verified positive controlled substances test result, an alcohol screening test result of 0.02 or greater, or any other violation of the alcohol misuse provisions of subpart B of this part shall include the following informational elements:

(1) Number of drivers subject to Part 382;

(2) Number of drivers subject to testing under the alcohol misuse or controlled substances use rules of more than one DOT agency, identified by each agency;

(3) Number of urine specimens collected by type of test (e.g., pre-employment, random, reasonable suspicion, post-accident);

(4) Number of positives verified by a MRO by type of test, and type of controlled substance;

(5) Number of negative controlled substance tests verified by a MRO by type of test;

(6) Number of persons denied a position as a driver following a pre-employment verified positive controlled substances test and/or a pre-employment alcohol test that indicates an alcohol concentration of 0.04 or greater;

(7) Number of drivers with tests verified positive by a medical review officer for multiple controlled substances;

(8) Number of drivers who refused to submit to an alcohol or controlled substances test required under this subpart;

(9)(i) Number of supervisors who have received required alcohol training during the reporting period; and

(ii) Number of supervisors who have received required controlled substances training during the reporting period;

(10)(i) Number of screening alcohol tests by type of test; and

(ii) Number of confirmation alcohol tests, by type of test;

(11) Number of confirmation alcohol tests indicating an alcohol concentration of 0.02 or greater but less than 0.04, by type of test;

(12) Number of confirmation alcohol tests indicating an alcohol concentration of 0.04 or greater, by type of test;

(13) Number of drivers who were returned to duty (having complied with the recommendations of a substance abuse professional as described in §§382.503 and 382.605), in this reporting period, who previously:

(i) Had a verified positive controlled substance test result, or

(ii) Engaged in prohibited alcohol misuse under the provisions of this part;

(14) Number of drivers who were administered alcohol and drug tests at the same time, with both a verified positive drug test result and an alcohol test result indicating an alcohol concentration of 0.04 or greater; and

(15) Number of drivers who were found to have violated any non-testing prohibitions of subpart B of this part, and any action taken in response to the violation.

(d) **Short summary.** Each employer's annual calendar year summary that contains only negative controlled substance test results, alcohol screening test results of less than 0.02, and does not contain any other violations of subpart B of this part, may prepare and submit, as required by paragraph (b) of this section, either a standard report form containing all the information elements specified in paragraph (c) of this section, or an "EZ" report form. The "EZ" report shall include the following information elements:

(1) Number of drivers subject to this Part 382;

(2) Number of drivers subject to testing under the alcohol misuse or controlled substance use rules of more than one DOT agency, identified by each agency;

(3) Number of urine specimens collected by type of test (e.g., pre-employment, random, reasonable suspicion, post-accident);

(4) Number of negatives verified by a medical review officer by type of test;

(5) Number of drivers who refused to submit to an alcohol or controlled substances test required under this subpart;

(6)(i) Number of supervisors who have received required alcohol training during the reporting period; and

(ii) Number of supervisors who have received required controlled substances training during the reporting period;

(7) Number of screen alcohol tests by type of test; and

(8) Number of drivers who were returned to duty (having complied with the recommendations of a substance abuse professional as described in §§382.503 and 382.605), in this reporting period, who previously:

(i) Had a verified positive controlled substance test result, or

(ii) Engaged in prohibited alcohol misuse under the provisions of this part.

(e) Each employer that is subject to more than one DOT agency alcohol or controlled substances rule shall identify each driver covered by the regulations of more than one DOT agency. The identification will be by the total number of covered functions. Prior to conducting any alcohol or controlled substances test on a driver subject to the rules of more than one DOT agency, the employer shall determine which DOT agency rule or rules authorizes or requires the test. The test result information shall be directed to the appropriate DOT agency or agencies.

(f) A consortium may prepare annual calendar year summaries and reports on behalf of individual employers for purposes of compliance with this section. However, each employer shall sign and submit such a report and shall remain responsible for ensuring the accuracy and timeliness of each report prepared on its behalf by a consortium.

§382.405 Access to facilities and records.

(a) Except as required by law or expressly authorized or required in this section, no employer shall release driver information that is contained in records required to be maintained under §382.401.

(b) A driver is entitled, upon written request, to obtain copies of any records pertaining to the driver's use of alcohol or controlled substances, including any records pertaining to his or her alcohol or controlled substances tests. The employer shall promptly provide the records requested by the driver. Access to a driver's records shall not be contingent upon payment for records other than those specifically requested.

(c) Each employer shall permit access to all facilities utilized in complying with the requirements of this part to the Secretary of Transportation, any DOT agency, or any State or local officials with regulatory authority over the employer or any of its drivers.

(d) Each employer shall make available copies of all results for employer alcohol and/or controlled substances testing conducted under this part and any other information pertaining to the employer's alcohol misuse and/or controlled substances use prevention program, when requested by the Secretary of Transportation, any DOT agency, or any State or local officials with regulatory authority over the employer or any of its drivers.

(e) When requested by the National Transportation Safety Board as part of an accident investigation, employers shall disclose information related to the employer's administration of a post-accident alcohol and/or controlled substance test administered following the accident under investigation.

(f) Records shall be made available to a subsequent employer upon receipt of a written request from a driver. Disclosure by the subsequent employer is permitted only as expressly authorized by the terms of the driver's request.

(g) An employer may disclose information required to be maintained under this part pertaining to a driver, the decision-maker in a lawsuit, grievance, or other proceeding initiated by or on behalf of the individual, and arising from the results of an alcohol and/or controlled substance test administered under this part, or from the employer's determination that the driver engaged in conduct prohibited by subpart B of this part (including, but not limited to, a worker's compensation, unemployment compensation, or other proceeding relating to a benefit sought by the driver.)

(h) An employer shall release information regarding a driver's records as directed by the specific, written consent of the driver authorizing release of the information to an identified person. Release of such information by the person receiving the information is permitted only in accordance with the terms of the employee's consent.

§382.407 Medical review officer notifications to the employer.

(a) The medical review officer may report to the employer using any communications device, but in all instances a signed, written notification must be forwarded within three business days of completion of the medical review officer's review, pursuant to part 40 of this title. A legible photocopy of the fourth copy of Part 40 Appendix A subtitled *COPY 4—SEND DIRECTLY TO MEDICAL REVIEW OFFICER—DO NOT SEND TO LABORATORY* of the *Federal Custody and Control Form OMB Number 9999-0023* may be used to make the signed, written notification to the employer for all test results (positive, negative, canceled, etc.), provided that the controlled substance(s) verified as positive, and the MRO's signature, shall be legibly noted in the remarks section of step 8 of the form completed by the medical review officer. The MRO must sign all verified positive test results. An MRO may sign or rubber stamp negative test results. An MRO's staff may rubber stamp negative test results under written authorization of the MRO. In no event shall an MRO, or his/her staff, use electronic signature technology to comply with this section. All reports, both oral and in writing, from the medical review officer to an employer shall clearly include:

(1) A statement that the controlled substances test being reported was in accordance with part 40 of this title and this part, except for legible photocopies of Copy 4 of the Federal Custody and Control Form;

(2) The full name of the driver for whom the test results are being reported;

(3) The type of test indicated on the custody and control form (i.e. random, post-accident, follow-up);

(4) The date and location of the test collection;

(5) The identities of the persons or entities performing the collection, analyzing the specimens, and serving as the medical review officer for the specific test;

(6) The results of the controlled substances test, positive, negative, test canceled, or test not performed, and if positive, the identity of the controlled substance(s) for which the test was verified positive.

(b) A medical review officer shall report to the employer that the medical review officer has made all reasonable efforts to contact the driver as provided in §40.33(c) of this title. The employer shall, as soon as practicable, request that the driver contact the medical review officer prior to dispatching the driver or within 24 hours, whichever is earlier.

§382.409 Medical review officer record retention for controlled substances.

(a) A medical review officer shall maintain all dated records and notifications, identified by individual, for a minimum of five years for verified positive controlled substances test results.

(b) A medical review officer shall maintain all dated records and notifications, identified by individual, for a minimum of one year for negative and canceled controlled substances test results.

(c) No person may obtain the individual controlled substances test results retained by a medical review officer, and no medical review officer shall release the individual controlled substances test results of any driver to any person, without first obtaining a specific, written authorization from the tested driver. Nothing in this paragraph shall prohibit a medical review officer from releasing, to the employer or to officials of the Secretary of Transportation, any DOT agency, or any State or local officials with regulatory authority over the controlled substances testing program under this part, the information delineated in §382.407(a) of this subpart.

§382.411 Employer notifications.

(a) An employer shall notify a driver of the results of a pre-employment controlled substance test conducted under this part, if the driver requests such results within 60 calendar days of being notified of the disposition of the employment application. An employer shall notify a driver of the results of random, reasonable suspicion and post-accident tests for controlled substances conducted under this part if the test results are verified positive. The employer shall also inform the driver which controlled substance or substances were verified as positive.

(b) The designated management official shall make reasonable efforts to contact and request each driver who submitted a specimen under the employer's program, regardless of the driver's employment status, to contact and discuss the results of the controlled substances test with a medical review officer who has been unable to contact the driver.

(c) The designated management official shall immediately notify the medical review officer that the driver has been notified to contact the medical review officer within 24 hours.

§382.413 Inquiries for alcohol and controlled substances information from previous employers.

(a)(1) An employer shall, pursuant to the driver's written authorization, inquire about the following information on a driver from the driver's previous employers, during the preceding two years from the date of application, which are maintained by the driver's previous employers under §382.401(b)(1) (i) through (iii) of this subpart:

(i) Alcohol tests with a result of 0.04 alcohol concentration or greater;

(ii) Verified positive controlled substances test results; and

(iii) Refusals to be tested.

(2) The information obtained from a previous employer may contain any alcohol and drug information the previous employer obtained from other previous employers under paragraph (a)(1) of this section.

(b) If feasible, the information in paragraph (a) of this section must be obtained and reviewed by the employer prior to the first time a driver performs safety-sensitive functions for the employer. If not feasible, the information must be obtained and reviewed as soon as possible, but no later than 14-calendar days after the first time a driver performs safety-sensitive functions for the employer. An employer may not permit a driver to perform safety-sensitive functions after 14 days without having made a good faith effort to obtain the information as soon as possible. If a driver hired or used by the employer ceases performing safety-sensitive functions for the employer before expiration of the 14-day period or before the employer has obtained the information in paragraph (a) of this section, the employer must still make a good faith effort to obtain the information.

(c) An employer must maintain a written, confidential record of the information obtained under paragraph (a) or (f) of this section. If, after making a good faith effort, an employer is unable to obtain the information from a previous employer, a record must be made of the efforts to obtain the information and retained in the driver's qualification file.

(d) The prospective employer must provide to each of the driver's previous employers the driver's specific, written authorization for release of the information in paragraph (a) of this section.

(e) The release of any information under this section may take the form of personal interviews, telephone interviews, letters, or any other method of transmitting information that ensures confidentiality.

(f) The information in paragraph (a) of this section may be provided directly to the prospective employer by the driver, provided the employer assures itself that the information is true and accurate.

(g) An employer may not use a driver to perform safety-sensitive functions if the employer obtains information on a violation of the prohibitions in subpart B of this part by the driver, without obtaining information on subsequent compliance with the referral and rehabilitation requirements of §382.605 of this part.

(h) Employers need not obtain information under paragraph (a) of this section generated by previous employers prior to the starting dates in §382.115 of this part.

Subpart E — Consequences For Drivers Engaging In Substance Use-Related Conduct

§382.501 Removal from safety-sensitive function.

(a) Except as provided in subpart F of this part, no driver shall perform safety-sensitive functions, including driving a commercial motor vehicle, if the driver has engaged in conduct prohibited by subpart B of this part or an alcohol or controlled substances rule of another DOT agency.

(b) No employer shall permit any driver to perform safety-sensitive functions, including driving a commercial motor vehicle, if the employer has determined that the driver has violated this section.

(c) For purposes of this subpart, commercial motor vehicle means a commercial motor vehicle in commerce as defined in §382.107, and a commercial motor vehicle in interstate commerce as defined in Part 390 of this subchapter.

§382.503 Required evaluation and testing.

No driver who has engaged in conduct prohibited by subpart B of this part shall perform safety-sensitive functions, including driving a commercial motor vehicle, unless the driver has met the requirements of §382.605. No employer shall permit a driver who has engaged in conduct prohibited by subpart B of this part to perform safety-sensitive functions, including driving a commercial motor vehicle, unless the driver has met the requirements of §382.605.

§382.505 Other alcohol-related conduct.

(a) No driver tested under the provisions of subpart C of this part who is found to have an alcohol concentration of 0.02 or greater but less than 0.04 shall perform or continue to perform safety-sensitive functions for an employer, including driving a commercial motor vehicle, nor shall an employer permit the driver to perform or continue to perform safety-sensitive functions, until the start of the driver's next regularly scheduled duty period, but not less than 24 hours following administration of the test.

(b) Except as provided in paragraph (a) of this section, no employer shall take any action under this part against a driver based solely on test results showing an alcohol concentration less than 0.04. This does not prohibit an employer with authority independent of this part from taking any action otherwise consistent with law.

§382.507 Penalties.

Any employer or driver who violates the requirements of this part shall be subject to the penalty provisions of 49 U.S.C. section 521(b).

Subpart F — Alcohol Misuse and Controlled Substances Use Information, Training, and Referral

§382.601 Employer obligation to promulgate a policy on the misuse of alcohol and use of controlled substances.

(a) **General requirements.** Each employer shall provide educational materials that explain the requirements of this part and the employer's policies and procedures with respect to meeting these requirements.

(1) The employer shall ensure that a copy of these materials is distributed to each driver prior to the start of alcohol and controlled substances testing under this part and to each driver subsequently hired or transferred into a position requiring driving a commercial motor vehicle.

(2) Each employer shall provide written notice to representatives of employee organizations of the availability of this information.

(b) **Required content.** The materials to be made available to drivers shall include detailed discussion of at least the following:

(1) The identity of the person designated by the employer to answer driver questions about the materials;

(2) The categories of drivers who are subject to the provisions of this part;

(3) Sufficient information about the safety-sensitive functions performed by those drivers to make clear what period of the work day the driver is required to be in compliance with this part;

(4) Specific information concerning driver conduct that is prohibited by this part;

(5) The circumstances under which a driver will be tested for alcohol and/or controlled substances under this part, including post-accident testing under §382.303(d);

(6) The procedures that will be used to test for the presence of alcohol and controlled substances, protect the driver and the integrity of the testing processes, safeguard the validity of the test results, and ensure that those results are attributed to the correct driver, including post-accident information, procedures and instructions required by §382.303(d) of this part;

(7) The requirement that a driver submit to alcohol and controlled substances tests administered in accordance with this part;

(8) An explanation of what constitutes a refusal to submit to an alcohol or controlled substances test and the attendant consequences;

(9) The consequences for drivers found to have violated subpart B of this part, including the requirement that the driver be removed immediately from safety-sensitive functions, and the procedures under §382.605;

(10) The consequences for drivers found to have an alcohol concentration of 0.02 or greater but less than 0.04;

(11) Information concerning the effects of alcohol and controlled substances use on an individual's health, work, and personal life; signs and symptoms of an alcohol or a controlled substances problem (the driver's or a coworker's); and available methods of intervening when an alcohol or a controlled substances problem is suspected, including confrontation, referral to any employee assistance program and or referral to management.

(c) **Optional provision.** The materials supplied to drivers may also include information on additional employer policies with respect to the use of alcohol or controlled substances, including any consequences for a driver found to have a specified alcohol or controlled substances level, that are based on the employer's authority independent of this part. Any such additional policies or consequences must be clearly and obviously described as being based on independent authority.

(d) **Certificate of receipt.** Each employer shall ensure that each driver is required to sign a statement certifying that he or she has received a copy of these materials described in this section. Each employer shall maintain the original of the signed certificate and may provide a copy of the certificate to the driver.

§382.603 Training for supervisors.

Each employer shall ensure that all persons designated to supervise drivers receive at least 60 minutes of training on alcohol misuse and receive at least an additional 60 minutes of training on controlled substances use. The training will be used by the supervisors to determine whether reasonable suspicion exists to require a driver to undergo testing under §382.307. The training shall include the physical, behavioral, speech, and performance indicators of probable alcohol misuse and use of controlled substances.

§382.605 Referral, evaluation, and treatment.

(a) Each driver who has engaged in conduct prohibited by subpart B of this part shall be advised by the employer of the resources available to the driver in evaluating and resolving problems associated with the misuse of alcohol and use of controlled substances, including the names, addresses, and telephone numbers of substance abuse professionals and counseling and treatment programs.

(b) Each driver who engages in conduct prohibited by subpart B of this part shall be evaluated by a substance abuse professional who shall determine what assistance, if any, the employee needs in resolving problems associated with alcohol misuse and controlled substances use.

(c)(1) Before a driver returns to duty requiring the performance of a safety-sensitive function after engaging in conduct prohibited by subpart B of this part, the driver shall undergo a return-to-duty alcohol test with a result indicating an alcohol concentration of less than 0.02 if the conduct involved alcohol, or a controlled substances test with a verified negative result if the conduct involved a controlled substance.

(2) In addition, each driver identified as needing assistance in resolving problems associated with alcohol misuse or controlled substances use,

(i) Shall be evaluated by a substance abuse professional to determine that the driver has properly followed any rehabilitation program prescribed under paragraph (b) of this section, and

(ii) Shall be subject to unannounced follow-up alcohol and controlled substances tests administered by the employer following the driver's return to duty. The number and frequency of such follow-up testing shall be as directed by the substance abuse professional, and consist of at least six tests in the first 12 months following the driver's return to duty. The employer may direct the driver to undergo return-to-duty and follow-up testing for both alcohol and controlled substances, if the substance abuse professional determines that return-to-duty and follow-up testing for both alcohol and controlled substances is necessary for that particular driver. Any such testing shall be performed in accordance with the requirements of 49 CFR part 40. Follow-up testing shall not exceed 60 months from the date of the driver's return to duty. The substance abuse professional may terminate the requirement for follow-up testing at any time after the first six tests have been administered, if the substance abuse professional determines that such testing is no longer necessary.

(d) Evaluation and rehabilitation may be provided by the employer, by a substance abuse professional under contract with the employer, or by a substance abuse professional not affiliated with the employer. The choice of substance abuse professional and assignment of costs shall be made in accordance with employer/driver agreements and employer policies.

(e) The employer shall ensure that a substance abuse professional who determines that a driver requires assistance in resolving problems with alcohol misuse or controlled substances use does not refer the driver to the substance abuse professional's private practice or to a person or organization from which the substance abuse professional receives remuneration or in which the substance abuse professional has a financial interest. This paragraph does not prohibit a substance abuse professional from referring a driver for assistance provided through—

(1) A public agency, such as a State, county, or municipality;

(2) The employer or a person under contract to provide treatment for alcohol or controlled substance problems on behalf of the employer;

(3) The sole source of therapeutically appropriate treatment under the driver's health insurance program; or

(4) The sole source of therapeutically appropriate treatment reasonably accessible to the driver.

(f) The requirements of this section with respect to referral, evaluation and rehabilitation do not apply to applicants who refuse to submit to a pre-employment alcohol or controlled substances test or who have a pre-employment alcohol test with a result indicating an alcohol concentration of 0.04 or greater or a controlled substances test with a verified positive test result.

Reserved

PART 383 — COMMERCIAL DRIVER'S LICENSE STANDARDS; REQUIREMENTS AND PENALTIES

Subpart A — General

Subpart B — Single License Requirement

Subpart C — Notification Requirements and Employer Responsibilities

Subpart D — Driver Disqualifications and Penalties

Subpart E — Testing and Licensing Procedures

Subpart F — Vehicle Groups and Endorsements

Subpart G — Required Knowledge and Skills

Authority: 49 U.S.C. 31136, 31301 *et seq.*, and 31502; and 49 CFR 1.48.

Subpart A — General

§383.1 Purpose and scope.

(a) The purpose of this part is to help reduce or prevent truck and bus accidents, fatalities, and injuries by requiring drivers to have a single commercial motor vehicle driver's license and by disqualifying drivers who operate commercial motor vehicles in an unsafe manner.

(b) This part:

(1) Prohibits a commercial motor vehicle driver from having more than one commercial motor vehicle driver's license;

(2) Requires a driver to notify the driver's current employer and the driver's State of domicile of certain convictions;

(3) Requires that a driver provide previous employment information when applying for employment as an operator of a commercial motor vehicle;

(4) Prohibits an employer from allowing a person with a suspended license to operate a commercial motor vehicle;

(5) Establishes periods of disqualification and penalties for those persons convicted of certain criminal and other offenses and serious traffic violations, or subject to any suspensions, revocations, or cancellations of certain driving privileges;

(6) Establishes testing and licensing requirements for commercial motor vehicle operators;

(7) Requires States to give knowledge and skills tests to all qualified applicants for commercial drivers' licenses which meet the Federal standard;

(8) Sets forth commercial motor vehicle groups and endorsements;

(9) Sets forth the knowledge and skills test requirements for the motor vehicle groups and endorsements;

(10) Sets forth the Federal standards for procedures, methods, and minimum passing scores for States and others to use in testing and licensing commercial motor vehicle operators; and

(11) Establishes requirements for the State issued commercial license documentation.

§383.3 Applicability.

(a) The rules in this part apply to every person who operates a commercial motor vehicle (CMV) in interstate, foreign, or intrastate commerce, to all employers of such persons, and to all States.

(b) The exceptions contained in §390.3(f) of this subchapter do not apply to this part. The employers and drivers identified in §390.3(f) must comply with the requirements of this part, unless otherwise provided in this section.

(c) **Exception for certain military drivers.** Each State must exempt from the requirements of this part individuals who operate CMVs for military purposes. This exception is applicable to active duty military personnel; members of the military reserves; member of the national guard on active duty, including personnel on full-time national guard duty, personnel on part-time national guard training, and national guard military technicians (civilians who are required to wear military uniforms); and active duty U.S. Coast Guard personnel. This exception is not applicable to U.S. Reserve technicians.

(d) **Exception for farmers, firefighters, emergency response vehicle drivers; and drivers removing snow and ice.** A State may, at its discretion, exempt individuals identified in paragraphs (d)(1), (d)(2), and (d)(3) of this section from the requirements of this part. The use of this waiver is limited to the driver's home State unless there is a reciprocity agreement with adjoining States.

(1) Operators of a farm vehicle which is:

(i) Controlled and operated by a farmer, including operation by employees or family members;

(ii) Used to transport either agricultural products, farm machinery, farm supplies, or both to or from a farm;

(iii) Not used in the operations of a common or contract motor carrier; and

(iv) Used within 241 kilometers (150 miles) of the farmer's farm.

(2) Firefighters and other persons who operate CMVs which are necessary to the preservation of life or property or the execution of emergency governmental functions, are equipped with audible and visual signals and are not subject to normal traffic regulation. These vehicles include fire trucks, hook and ladder trucks, foam or water transport trucks, police SWAT team vehicles, ambulances, or other vehicles that are used in response to emergencies.

(3)(i) A driver, employed by an eligible unit of local government, operating a commercial motor vehicle within the boundaries of that unit for the purpose of removing snow or ice from a roadway by plowing, sanding, or salting, if

(A) The properly licensed employee who ordinarily operates a commercial motor vehicle for these purposes is unable to operate the vehicle; or

(B) The employing governmental entity determines that a snow or ice emergency exists that requires additional assistance.

(ii) This exemption shall not preempt State laws and regulations concerning the safe operation of commercial motor vehicles.

(e) **Restricted commercial drivers license (CDL) for certain drivers in the State of Alaska.** (1) The State of Alaska may, at its discretion, waive only the following requirements of this part and issue a CDL to each driver that meets the conditions set forth in paragraphs (e) (2) and (3) of this section:

(i) The knowledge tests standards for testing procedures and methods of subpart H, but must continue to administer knowledge tests that fulfill the content requirements of subpart G for *all* applicants;

(ii) All the skills test requirements; and

(iii) The requirement under §383.153(a)(4) to have a photograph on the license document.

(2) Drivers of CMVs in the State of Alaska must operate exclusively over roads that meet *both* of the following criteria to be eligible for the exception in paragraph (e)(1) of this section:

(i) Such roads are not connected by land highway or vehicular way to the land-connected State highway system; and

(ii) Such roads are not connected to any highway or vehicular way with an average daily traffic volume greater than 499.

(3) Any CDL issued under the terms of this paragraph must carry two restrictions:

(i) Holders may not operate CMVs over roads other than those specified in paragraph (e)(2) of this section; and

(ii) The license is not valid for CMV operation outside the State of Alaska.

(f) **Restricted CDL for certain drivers in farm-related service industries.** (1) A State may, at its discretion, waive the required knowledge and skills tests of subpart H of this part and issue restricted CDLs to employees of these designated farm-related service industries:

(i) Agri-chemical businesses;

(ii) Custom harvesters;

(iii) Farm retail outlets and suppliers;

(iv) Livestock feeders.

(2) A restricted CDL issued pursuant to this paragraph shall meet all the requirements of this part, except subpart H of this part. A restricted CDL issued pursuant to this paragraph shall be accorded the same reciprocity as a CDL meeting all of the requirements of this part. The restrictions imposed upon the issuance of this restricted CDL shall not limit a person's use of the CDL in a non-CMV during either validated or non-validated periods, nor shall the CDL affect a State's power to administer its driver licensing program for operators of vehicles other than CMVs.

(3) A State issuing a CDL under the terms of this paragraph must restrict issuance as follows:

(i) Applicants must have a good driving record as defined in this paragraph. Drivers who have not held any motor vehicle operator's license for at least one year shall not be eligible for this CDL. Drivers who have between one and two years of driving experience must demonstrate a good driving record for their entire driving history. Drivers with more than two years of driving experience must have a good driving record for the two most recent years. For the purposes of this paragraph, the term *good driving record* means that an applicant:

(A) Has not had more than one license (except in the instances specified in §383.21(b));

(B) Has not had *any* license suspended, revoked, or canceled;

(C) Has not had *any* conviction for any type of motor vehicle for the disqualifying offenses contained in §383.51(b)(2);

(D) Has not had *any* conviction for any type of motor vehicle for serious traffic violations; and

(E) Has not had *any* conviction for a violation of State or local law relating to motor vehicle traffic control (other than a parking violation) arising in connection with any traffic accident, and has no record of an accident in which he/she was at fault.

(ii) Restricted CDLs shall have the same renewal cycle as unrestricted CDLs, but shall be limited to the seasonal period or periods as defined by the State of licensure, provided that the total number of calendar days in any 12-month period for which the restricted CDL is valid does not exceed 180. If a State elects to provide for more than one seasonal period, the restricted CDL is valid for commercial motor vehicle operation only during the currently approved season, and must be revalidated for each successive season. Only one seasonal period of validity may appear on the license document at a time. The good driving record must be confirmed prior to any renewal or revalidation.

(iii) Restricted CDL holders are limited to operating Group B and C vehicles, as described in subpart F of this part.

(iv) Restricted CDLs shall not be issued with *any* endorsements on the license document. Only the limited tank vehicle and hazardous materials endorsement privileges that the restricted CDL automatically confers and are described in paragraph (f)(3)(v) of this section are permitted.

(v) Restricted CDL holders may not drive vehicles carrying any placardable quantities of hazardous materials, except for diesel fuel in quantities of 3,785 liters (1,000 gallons) or less; liquid fertilizers (i.e., plant nutrients) in vehicles or implements of husbandry in total quantities of 11,355 liters (3,000 gallons) or less; and solid fertilizers (i.e., solid plant nutrients) that are not transported with any organic substance.

(vi) Restricted CDL holders may not hold an unrestricted

CDL at the same time.

(vii) Restricted CDL holders may not operate a commercial motor vehicle beyond 241 kilometers (150 miles) from the place of business or the farm currently being served.

(g) **Restricted CDL for certain drivers in the pyrotechnic industry.** (1) A State may, at its discretion, waive the required hazardous materials knowledge tests of subpart H of this part and issue restricted CDLs to part-time drivers operating commercial motor vehicles transporting less than 227 kilograms (500 pounds) of fireworks classified as DOT Class 1.3G explosives.

(2) A State issuing a CDL under the terms of this paragraph must restrict issuance as follows:

(i) The GVWR of the vehicle to be operated must be less than 4,537 kilograms (10,001 pounds);

(ii) If a State believes, at its discretion, that the training required by §172.704 of this title adequately prepares part-time drivers meeting the other requirements of this paragraph to deal with fireworks and the other potential dangers posed by fireworks transportation and use, the State may waive the hazardous materials knowledge tests of subpart H of this part. The State may impose any requirements it believes is necessary to ensure itself that a driver is properly trained pursuant to §172.704 of this title.

(iii) A restricted CDL document issued pursuant to this paragraph shall have a statement clearly imprinted on the face of the document that is substantially similar as follows: "For use as a CDL only during the period from June 30 through July 6 for purposes of transporting less than 227 kilograms (500 pounds) of fireworks classified as DOT Class 1.3G explosives in a vehicle with a GVWR of less than 4,537 kilograms (10,001 pounds).

(3) A restricted CDL issued pursuant to this paragraph shall meet all the requirements of this part, except those specifically identified. A restricted CDL issued pursuant to this paragraph shall be accorded the same reciprocity as a CDL meeting all of the requirements of this part. The restrictions imposed upon the issuance of this restricted CDL shall not limit a person's use of the CDL in a non-CMV during either validated or non-validated periods, nor shall the CDL affect a State's power to administer its driver licensing program for operators of vehicles other than CMVs.

(4) Restricted CDLs shall have the same renewal cycle as unrestricted CDLs, but shall be limited to the seasonal period of

June 30 through July 6 of each year or a lesser period as defined by the State of licensure.

(5) Persons who operate commercial motor vehicles during the period from July 7 through June 29 for purposes of transporting less than 227 kilograms (500 pounds) of fireworks classified as DOT Class 1.3G explosives in a vehicle with a GVWR of less than 4,537 kilograms (10,001 pounds) and who also operate such vehicles for the same purposes during the period June 30 through July 6 shall not be issued a restricted CDL pursuant to this paragraph.

§383.5 Definitions.

As used in this part:

Administrator means the Federal Highway Administrator, the chief executive of the Federal Highway Administration, an agency within the Department of Transportation.

Alcohol or "alcoholic beverage" means: (a) Beer as defined in 26 U.S.C. 5052(a), of the Internal Revenue Code of 1954, (b) wine of not less than one-half of one per centum of alcohol by volume, or (c) distilled spirits as defined in section 5002(a)(8), of such Code.

Alcohol concentration (AC) means the concentration of alcohol in a person's blood or breath. When expressed as a percentage it means grams of alcohol per 100 milliliters of blood or grams of alcohol per 210 liters of breath.

Commerce means (a) any trade, traffic or transportation within the jurisdiction of the United States between a place in a State and a place outside of such State, including a place outside of the United States and (b) trade, traffic, and transportation in the United States which affects any trade, traffic, and transportation described in paragraph (a) of this definition.

Commercial driver's license (CDL) means a license issued by a State or other jurisdiction, in accordance with the standards contained in 49 CFR Part 383, to an individual which authorizes the individual to operate a class of a commercial motor vehicle.

Commercial driver's license information system (CDLIS) means the CDLIS established by FHWA pursuant to section 12007 of the Commercial Motor Vehicle Safety Act of 1986.

Commercial motor vehicle (CMV) means a motor vehicle or combination of motor vehicles used in commerce to transport passengers or property if the motor vehicle—

(a) Has a gross combination weight rating of 11,794 kilograms or more (26,001 pounds or more) inclusive of a towed unit with a gross vehicle weight rating of more than 4,536 kilograms (10,000 pounds); or

(b) Has a gross vehicle weight rating of 11,794 or more kilograms (26,001 pounds or more); or

(c) Is designed to transport 16 or more passengers, including the driver; or

(d) Is of any size and is used in the transportation of materials found to be hazardous for the purposes of the Hazardous Materials Transportation Act and which require the motor vehicle to be placarded under the Hazardous Materials Regulations (49 CFR part 172, subpart F).

Controlled substance has the meaning such term has under 21 U.S.C. 802(6) and includes all substances listed on schedules I through V of 21 CFR 1308, as they may be amended by the United States Department of Justice.

Conviction means an unvacated adjudication of guilt, or a determination that a person has violated or failed to comply with the law in a court of original jurisdiction or by an authorized administrative tribunal, an unvacated forfeiture of bail or collateral deposited to secure the person's appearance in court, a plea of guilty or nolo contendere accepted by the court, the payment of a fine or court cost, or violation of a condition of release without bail, regardless of whether or not the penalty is rebated, suspended, or probated.

Disqualification means either:

(a) The suspension, revocation, cancellation, or any other withdrawal by a State of a person's privileges to drive a commercial motor vehicle; or

(b) A determination by the FHWA, under the rules of practice for motor carrier safety contained in part 386 of this title, that person is no longer qualified to operate a commercial motor vehicle under part 391; or

(c) The loss of qualification which automatically follows conviction of an offense listed in §383.51.

Driver applicant means an individual who applies to a State to obtain, transfer, upgrade, or renew a CDL.

Driver's license means a license issued by a State or other jurisdiction, to an individual which authorizes the individual to operate a motor vehicle on the highways.

Driving a commercial motor vehicle while under the influence of alcohol means committing any one or more of the following acts in a CMV: driving a CMV while the person's alcohol concentration is 0.04 percent or more; driving under the influence of alcohol, as prescribed by State law; or refusal to undergo such testing as is required by any State or jurisdiction in the enforcement of §383.51(b)(2)(i)(A) or (B), or §392.5(a)(2).

Eligible unit of local government means a city, town, borough, county, parish, district, or other public body created by or pursuant to State law which has a total population of 3,000 individuals or less.

Employee means any operator of a commercial motor vehicle, including full time, regularly employed drivers; casual, intermittent or occasional drivers; leased drivers and independent, owner-operator contractors (while in the course of operating a commercial motor vehicle) who are either directly employed by or under lease to an employer.

Employer means any person (including the United States, a State, District of Columbia or a political subdivision of a State) who owns or leases a commercial motor vehicle or assigns employees to operate such a vehicle.

Endorsement means an authorization to an individual's CDL required to permit the individual to operate certain types of commercial motor vehicles.

Felony means an offense under State or Federal law that is punishable by death or imprisonment for a term exceeding 1 year.

Foreign means outside the fifty United States and the District of Columbia.

Gross combination weight rating (GCWR) means the value specified by the manufacturer as the loaded weight of a combination (articulated) vehicle. In the absence of a value specified by the manufacturer, GCWR will be determined by adding the GVWR of the power unit and the total weight of the towed unit and any load thereon.

Gross vehicle weight rating (GVWR) means the value specified by the manufacturer as the loaded weight of a single vehicle.

Hazardous materials has the meaning such term has under section 103 of the Hazardous Materials Transportation Act.

Motor vehicle means a vehicle, machine, tractor, trailer, or semitrailer propelled or drawn by mechanical power used on highways, except that such term does not include a vehicle, machine, tractor, trailer, semitrailer operated exclusively on a rail.

Nonresident CDL means a CDL issued by a State to an individual domiciled in a foreign country.

Out-of-service order means a declaration by an authorized enforcement officer of a Federal, State, Canadian, Mexican, or local jurisdiction that a driver, a commercial motor vehicle, or a motor carrier operation, is out-of-service pursuant to §§386.72, 392.5, 395.13, 396.9, or compatible laws, or the North American Uniform Out-of-Service Criteria.

Representative vehicle means a motor vehicle which represents the type of motor vehicle that a driver applicant operates or expects to operate.

Serious traffic violation means conviction, when operating a commercial motor vehicle, of:

(a) Excessive speeding, involving any single offense for any speed of 15 miles per hour or more above the posted speed limit;

(b) Reckless driving, as defined by State or local law or regulation, including but not limited to offenses of driving a commercial motor vehicle in willful or wanton disregard for the safety of persons or property;

(c) Improper or erratic traffic lane changes;

(d) Following the vehicle ahead too closely; or

(e) A violation, arising in connection with a fatal accident, of a State or local law relating to motor vehicle traffic control (other than a parking violation). (Serious traffic violations exclude vehicle weight and vehicle defect violations.)

State means a State of the United States and the District of Columbia.

State of domicile means that State where a person has his/her true, fixed, and permanent home and principal residence and to which he/she has the intention of returning whenever he/she is absent.

Tank vehicle means any commercial motor vehicle that is designed to transport any liquid or gaseous materials within a tank that is either permanently or temporarily attached to the vehicle or the chassis. Such vehicles include, but are not limited to, cargo tanks and portable tanks, as defined in Part 171 of this title. However, this definition does not include portable tanks having a rated capacity under 1,000 gallons.

§383.7

United States the term United States means the 50 States and the District of Columbia.

Vehicle means a motor vehicle unless otherwise specified.

Vehicle group means a class or type of vehicle with certain operating characteristics.

§383.7 [Removed and reserved.]

Subpart B — Single License Requirement

§383.21 Number of drivers' licenses.

No person who operates a commercial motor vehicle shall at any time have more than one driver's license.

§383.23 Commercial driver's license.

(a) **General rule.** (1) Effective April 1, 1992, no person shall operate a commercial motor vehicle unless such person has taken and passed written and driving tests which meet the Federal standards contained in Subparts F, G, and H of this part for the commercial motor vehicle that person operates or expects to operate.

(2) Effective April 1, 1992, except as provided in paragraph (b) of this section, no person shall operate a commercial motor vehicle unless such person possesses a CDL which meets the standards contained in Subpart J of this part, issued by his/her State or jurisdiction of domicile.

(b) **Exception.** If a commercial motor vehicle operator is domiciled in a foreign jurisdiction which, as determined by the Administrator, does not test drivers and issue a CDL in accordance with, or similar to, the standards contained in Subparts F, G, and H of this part, the person shall obtain a Nonresident CDL from a State which does comply with the testing and licensing standards contained in such Subparts F, G, and H[1].

(c) **Learner's permit.** State learner's permits, issued for limited time periods according to State requirements, shall be considered valid commercial drivers' licenses for purposes of behind-the-wheel training on public roads or highways, if the following minimum conditions are met:

(1) The learner's permit holder is at all time accompanied by the holder of a valid CDL; and

(2) He/she either holds a valid automobile driver's license, or has passed such vision, sign/symbol, and knowledge tests as the State issuing the learner's permit ordinarily administers to applicants for automobile drivers' licenses.

---

[1]Effective December 29, 1988, the Administrator determined that commercial drivers' licenses issued by Canadian Provinces and Territories in conformity with the Canadian National Safety Code are in accordance with the standards of this part. Effective November 21, 1991, the Administrator determined that the new Licencias Federales de Conductor issued by the United Mexican States are in accordance with the standards of this part. Therefore, under the single license provision of §383.21, a driver holding a commercial driver's license issued under the Canadian National Safety Code or a new Licencia Federal de Conductor issued by Mexico is prohibited from obtaining nonresident CDL, or any other type of driver's license, from a State or other jurisdiction in the United States.

Subpart C — Notification Requirements and Employer Responsibilities

§383.31 Notification of convictions for driver violations.

(a) Each person who operates a commercial motor vehicle, who has a commercial driver's license issued by a State or jurisdiction, and who is convicted of violating, in any type of motor vehicle, a State or local law relating to motor vehicle traffic control (other than a parking violation) in a State or jurisdiction other than the one which issued his/her license, shall notify an official designated by the State or jurisdiction which issued such license, of such conviction. The notification must be made within 30 days after the date that person has been convicted.

(b) Each person who operates a commercial motor vehicle, who has a commercial driver's license issued by a State or jurisdiction, and who is convicted of violating, in any type of motor vehicle, a State or local law relating to motor vehicle traffic control (other than a parking violation), shall notify his/her current employer of such conviction. The notification must be made within 30 days after the date that the person has been convicted. If the driver is not currently employed, he/she must notify the State or jurisdiction which issued the license according to §383.31(a).

(c) **Notification.** The notification to the State official and employer must be made in writing and contain the following information:

(1) Driver's full name;

(2) Driver's license number;

(3) Date of conviction;

(4) The specific criminal or other offense(s), serious traffic violation(s), and other violation(s) of State or local law relating to motor vehicle traffic control, for which the person was convicted and any suspension, revocation, or cancellation of certain driving privileges which resulted from such conviction(s);

(5) Indication whether the violation was in a commercial motor vehicle;

(6) Location of offense; and

(7) Driver's signature.

§383.33 Notification of driver's license suspensions.

Each employee who has a driver's license suspended, revoked, or canceled by a State or jurisdiction, who loses the right to operate a commercial motor vehicle in a State or jurisdiction for any period, or who is disqualified from operating a commercial motor vehicle for any period, shall notify his/her current employer of such suspension, revocation, cancellation, lost privilege, or disqualification. The notification must be made before the end of the business day following the day the employee received notice of suspension, revocation, cancellation, lost privilege, or disqualification.

§383.35 Notification of previous employment.

(a) Any person applying for employment as an operator of a commercial motor vehicle shall provide at the time of application for employment, the information specified in paragraph (c) of this section.

(b) All employers shall request the information specified in paragraph (c) of this section from all persons applying for employment as a commercial motor vehicle operator. The request shall be made at the time of application for employment.

(c) The following employment history information for the 10 years preceding the date the application is submitted shall be presented to the prospective employer by the applicant:

(1) A list of the names and addresses of the applicant's previous employers for which the applicant was an operator of a commercial motor vehicle;

(2) The dates the applicant was employed by these employers; and

(3) The reason for leaving such employment.

(d) The applicant shall certify that all information furnished is true and complete.

(e) An employer may require an applicant to provide additional information.

(f) Before an application is submitted, the employer shall inform the applicant that the information he/she provides in accordance with paragraph (c) of this section may be used, and the applicant's previous employers may be contacted for the purpose of investigating the applicant's work history.

§383.37 Employer responsibilities.

No employer may knowingly allow, require, permit, or authorize a driver to operate a CMV in the United States:

(a) During any period in which the driver has a CMV driver's license suspended, revoked, or canceled by a State, has lost the right to operate a CMV in a State, or has been disqualified from operating a CMV;

(b) During any period in which the driver has more than one CMV driver's license;

(c) During any period in which the driver, or the CMV he or she is driving, or the motor carrier operation, is subject to an out-of-service order; or

(d) In violation of a Federal, State, or local law or regulation, pertaining to railroad-highway grade crossings.

Subpart D — Driver Disqualifications and Penalties

§383.51 Disqualification of drivers.

(a) **General.** A driver who is disqualified shall not drive a commercial motor vehicle. An employer shall not knowingly allow, require, permit, or authorize a driver who is disqualified to drive a commercial motor vehicle.

(b) Disqualification for driving while under the influence, leaving the scene of an accident, or commission of a felony.

(1) **General rule.** A driver who is convicted of a disqualifying offense specified in paragraph (b)(2) of this section, is disqualified for the period of time specified in paragraph (b)(3) of this section, if the offense was committed while operating a commercial motor vehicle.

(2) **Disqualifying offenses.** The following offenses are disqualifying offenses:

(i) Driving a commercial motor vehicle while under the influence of alcohol. This shall include:

(A) Driving a commercial motor vehicle while the person's alcohol concentration is 0.04 percent or more; or

(B) Driving under the influence of alcohol, as prescribed by state law; or

(C) Refusal to undergo such testing as is required by any State or jurisdiction in the enforcement of §383.51(b)(2)(i)(A) or (B), or §392.5(a)(2).

(ii) Driving a commercial motor vehicle while under the influence of a controlled substance as defined by §383.5 of this part.

(iii) Leaving the scene of an accident involving a commercial motor vehicle;

(iv) A felony involving the use of a commercial motor vehicle, other than a felony described in paragraph (b)(2)(v) of this section; or

(v) The use of a commercial motor vehicle in the commission of a felony involving manufacturing, distributing, or dispensing a controlled substance as defined by §383.5 of this part.

(3) **Duration of disqualification for driving while under the influence, leaving the scene of an accident, or commission of a felony.**

(i) **First offenders.** A driver who is convicted of an offense described in paragraphs (b)(2)(i) through (b)(2)(iv) of this section, is disqualified for a period of one year provided the vehicle was not transporting hazardous materials required to be placarded under the Hazardous Materials Transportation Act (49 U.S.C. 5101 *et seq.*).

(ii) **First offenders transporting hazardous materials.** A driver who is convicted of an offense described in paragraphs (b)(2)(i) through (b)(2)(iv) of this section, is disqualified for a period of three years if the vehicle was transporting hazardous materials required to be placarded under the Hazardous Materials Transportation Act (49 U.S.C. 5101 *et seq.*).

(iii) **First offenders of controlled substance felonies.** A driver who is convicted of an offense described in paragraph (b)(2)(v) of this section, is disqualified for life.

(iv) **Subsequent Offenders.** A driver who is convicted of an offense described in paragraphs (b)(2)(i) through (b)(2)(iv) of this section, is disqualified for life if the driver had been convicted once before in a separate incident of any offense described in paragraphs (b)(2)(i) through (b)(2)(iv) of this section.

(v) Any driver disqualified for life under §383.51(b)(3)(iv) of this paragraph, who has both voluntarily enrolled in and successfully completed, an appropriate rehabilitation program which meets the standards of his/her State's driver licensing agency, may apply to the licensing agency for reinstatement of his/her commercial driver's license. Such applicants shall not be eligible for reinstatement from the State unless and until such time as he/she has first served a minimum disqualification period of 10 years and has fully met the licensing State's standards for reinstatement of commercial motor vehicle driving privileges. Should a reinstated driver be subsequently convicted of another disqualifying offense, as specified in paragraphs (b)(2)(i) through (b)(2)(iv) of this section, he/she shall be permanently disqualified for life, and shall be ineligible to again apply for a reduction of the lifetime disqualification.

(c) **Disqualification for serious traffic violations.**

(1) **General rule.** A driver who is convicted of serious traffic violations is disqualified for the period of time specified in paragraph (c)(2) of this section, if the offenses were committed while operating a commercial motor vehicle.

(2) **Duration of disqualification for serious traffic violations—**

(i) **Second violation.** A driver who, during any 3-year period, is convicted of two serious traffic violations in separate incidents, is disqualified for a period of 60 days.

(ii) **Third violation.** A driver who, during any 3-year period, is convicted of three serious traffic violations in separate incidents, is disqualified for a period of 120 days.

(d) **Disqualification for violation of out-of-service orders.**

(1) **General rule.** A driver who is convicted of violating an out-of-service order while driving a commercial motor vehicle is disqualified for the period of time specified in paragraph (d)(2) of this section. In addition, such driver is subject to special penalties as contained in §383.53(b).

(2) **Duration of disqualification for violation of out-of-service orders.**

(i) **First violation.** A driver is disqualified for not less than 90 days nor more than one year if the driver is convicted of a first violation of an out-of-service order.

(ii) **Second violation.** A driver is disqualified for not less than one year nor more than five years if, during any 10-year period, the driver is convicted of two violations of out-of-service orders in separate incidents.

(iii) **Third or subsequent violation.** A driver is disqualified for not less than three years nor more than five years if, during any 10-year period, the driver is convicted of three or more violations of out-of-service orders in separate incidents.

(iv) **Special rule for hazardous materials and passen-**

ger offenses. A driver is disqualified for a period of not less than 180 days nor more than two years if the driver is convicted of a first violation of an out-of-service order while transporting hazardous materials required to be placarded under the Hazardous Materials Transportation Act (49 U.S.C. 5101 *et seq.*), or while operating motor vehicles designed to transport more than 15 passengers, including the driver. A driver is disqualified for a period of not less than three years nor more than five years if, during any 10-year period, the driver is convicted of any subsequent violations of out-of-service orders, in separate incidents, while transporting hazardous materials required to be placarded under the Hazardous Materials Transportation Act, or while operating motor vehicles designed to transport more than 15 passengers, including the driver.

(e) Disqualification for railroad-highway grade crossing violation—

(1) **General rule.** A driver who is convicted of operating a CMV in violation of a Federal, State, or local law or regulation pertaining to one of the following six offenses at a railroad-highway grade crossing must be disqualified for the period of time specified in paragraph (e)(2) of this section:

(i) For drivers who are not required to always stop, failing to slow down and check that the tracks are clear of an approaching train;

(ii) For drivers, who are not required to always stop, failing to stop before reaching the crossing, if the tracks are not clear;

(iii) For drivers who are always required to stop, failing to stop before driving onto the crossing;

(iv) For all drivers, failing to have sufficient space to drive completely through the crossing without stopping;

(v) For all drivers, failing to obey a traffic control device or the directions of an enforcement official at the crossing;

(vi) For all drivers, failing to negotiate a crossing because of insufficient undercarriage clearance.

(2) **Duration of disqualification for railroad-highway grade crossing violation. — (i) First violation.** A driver must be disqualified for not less than 60 days if the driver is convicted of a first violation of a railroad-highway grade crossing violation.

(ii) **Second violation.** A driver must be disqualified for not less than 120 days if, during any three-year period, the driver is convicted of a second railroad-highway grade crossing violation in separate incidents.

(iii) **Third or subsequent violation.** A driver must be disqualified for not less than 1 year if, during any three-year period, the driver is convicted of a third or subsequent railroad-highway grade crossing violation in separate incidents.

(f) **Substantial compliance by States.**

(1) Nothing in this rule shall be construed to require a State to apply its criminal or other sanctions for driving under the influence to a person found to have operated a commercial motor vehicle with an alcohol concentration of 0.04 percent, except licensing sanctions including suspension, revocation, or cancellation.

(2) A State that enacts and enforces through licensing sanctions the disqualifications prescribed in §383.51(b) at the 0.04 alcohol concentration level and gives full faith and credit to the disqualification of commercial motor vehicle drivers by other States shall be deemed in substantial compliance with section 12009(a)(3) of the Commercial Motor Vehicle Safety Act of 1986.

§383.53 Penalties.

(a) **General rule.** Any person who violates the rules set forth in subparts B and C of this part may be subject to civil or criminal penalties as provided for in 49 U.S.C. 521(b).

(b) **Special penalties pertaining to violation of out-of-service orders.**

(1) **Driver violations.** A driver who is convicted of violating an out-of-service order shall be subject to a civil penalty of not less than $1,000 nor more than $2,500, in addition to disqualification under §383.51(d).

(2) **Employer violations.** An employer who is convicted of a violation of §383.37(c) shall be subject to a civil penalty of not less than $2,500 nor more than $10,000.

(c) **Special penalties pertaining to railroad-highway grade crossing violations.** An employer who is convicted of a violation of §383.37(d) must be subject to a civil penalty of not more than $10,000.

Subpart E — Testing and Licensing Procedures

§383.71 Driver application procedures.

(a) **Initial Commercial Driver's License.** — Prior to obtaining a CDL, a person must meet the following requirements:

(1) A person who operates or expects to operate in interstate or foreign commerce, or is otherwise subject to Part 391 of this title, shall certify that he/she meets the qualification requirements contained in Part 391 of this title. A person who operates or expects to operate entirely in intrastate commerce and is not subject to Part 391, is subject to State driver qualification requirements and must certify that he/she is not subject to Part 391;

(2) Pass a knowledge test in accordance with the standards contained in Subparts G and H of this part for the type of motor vehicle the person operates or expects to operate;

(3) Pass a driving or skills test in accordance with the standards contained in Subparts G and H of this part taken in a motor vehicle which is representative of the type of motor vehicle the person operates or expects to operate; or provide evidence that he/she has successfully passed a driving test administered by an authorized third party;

(4) Certify that the motor vehicle in which the person takes the driving skills test is representative of the type of motor vehicle that person operates or expects to operate;

(5) Provide to the State of issuance the information required to be included on the CDL as specified in Subpart J of this part;

(6) Certify that he/she is not subject to any disqualification, suspension, revocation, or cancellation as contained in §383.51 and that he/she does not have a driver's license from more than one State or jurisdiction.

(7) The applicant shall surrender his/her non-CDL driver's licenses to the State.

(b) **License transfer.** When applying to transfer a CDL from one State of domicile to a new State domicile, an applicant shall apply for a CDL from the new State of domicile within no more than 30 days after establishing his/her new domicile. The applicant shall:

(1) Provide to the new State of domicile the certifications contained in §383.71(a) (1) and (6);

(2) Provide to the new State of domicile updated information as specified in Subpart J of this part;

(3) If the applicant wishes to retain a hazardous materials endorsement, comply with State requirements as specified in §383.73(b)(4); and

(4) Surrender the CDL from the old State of domicile to the new State of domicile.

(c) **License renewal.** When applying for a renewal of a CDL, all applicants shall:

(1) Provide certification contained in §383.71(a)(1);

(2) Provide updated information as specified in Subpart J of this part; and

(3) If a person wishes to retain a hazardous materials endorsement, pass the test for such endorsement as specified in §383.121.

(d) **License upgrades.** When applying to operate a commercial motor vehicle in a different group or endorsement from the group or endorsement in which the applicant already has a CDL, all persons shall:

(1) Provide the necessary certifications as specified in §383.71(a)(1) and (4); and

(2) Pass all tests specified in §383.71(a)(2) and (3) for the new vehicle group and/or different endorsements.

(e) **Nonresident CDL.** When an applicant is domiciled in a foreign jurisdiction, as defined in §383.5, where the commercial motor vehicle operator testing and licensing standards do not meet the standards contained in Subparts G and H of this part, as determined by the Administrator, such applicant shall obtain a Nonresident CDL from a State which meets such standards. Such applicant shall:

(1) Complete the requirements to obtain a CDL contained in §383.71(a); and

(2) After receipt of the CDL, and for as long as it is valid, notify the State which issued the CDL of any adverse action taken by any jurisdiction or governmental agency, foreign or domestic, against his/her driving privileges. Such adverse actions would include but not be limited to license suspension or revocation, or disqualification from operating a commercial motor vehicle for the convictions described in §383.51. Notifications shall be made within the time periods specified in §383.33.

(f) If a State uses the alternative method described in §383.73(i) to achieve the objectives of the certifications in §383.71(a), then the driver applicant shall satisfy such alternative methods as are applicable to him/her with respect to initial licensing, license transfer, license renewal, and license upgrades.

§383.72 Implied consent to alcohol testing.

Any person who holds a CDL shall be deemed to have consented to such testing as is required of him/her by any State or jurisdiction in the enforcement of §383.51(b)(2)(i) and §392.5(a)(2). Consent is implied by driving a commercial motor vehicle.

§383.73 State procedures.

(a) **Initial licensure.** Prior to issuing a CDL to a person, a State shall:

(1) Require the driver applicant to certify, pass tests, and provide information as described in §§383.71(a)(1) through (6);

(2) Check that the vehicle in which the applicant takes his/her test is representative of the vehicle group the applicant has certified that he/she operates or expects to operate;

(3) Initiate and complete a check of the applicant's driving record to ensure that the person is not subject to any disqualification, suspensions, revocations, or cancellations as contained in §383.51 and that the person does not have a driver's license from more than one State. The record check shall include but not be limited to the following:

(i) A check of the applicant's driving record as maintained by his/her current State of licensure, if any;

(ii) A check with the CDLIS to determine whether the driver applicant already has a CDL, whether the applicant's license has been suspended, revoked, or canceled, or if the applicant has been disqualified from operating a commercial motor vehicle; and

(iii) A check with the National Driver Register (NDR), when it is determined to be operational by the National Highway Traffic Safety Administrator, to determine whether the driver applicant has:

(A) Been disqualified from operating a motor vehicle (other than a commercial motor vehicle);

(B) Had a license (other than CDL) suspended, revoked, or canceled for cause in the 3-year period ending on the date of application; or

(C) Been convicted of any offenses contained in section 205(a)(3) of the National Drivers Register Act of 1982 (23 U.S.C. 401 note); and

(4) Require the driver applicant, if he/she has moved from another State, to surrender his/her driver's license issued by another State.

(b) **License transfers.** Prior to issuing a CDL to a person who has a CDL from another State, a State shall:

(1) Require the driver applicant to make the certifications contained in §383.71(a);

(2) Complete a check of the driver applicant's record as contained in §383.73(a) (3);

(3) Request and receive updates of information specified in Subpart J of this part;

(4) If such applicant wishes to retain a hazardous materials endorsement, ensure that the driver has, within the 2 years preceding the transfer, either:

(i) Passed the test for such endorsement specified in §383.121; or

(ii) Successfully completed a hazardous materials test or training that is given by a third party and that is deemed by the State to substantially cover the same knowledge base as that described in §383.121; and

(5) Obtain the CDL issued by the applicant's previous State of domicile.

(c) **License Renewals.** Prior to renewing any CDL, a State shall:

(1) Require the driver applicant to make the certifications contained in §383.71(a);

(2) Complete a check of the driver applicant's record as contained in §383.73(a) (3);

(3) Request and receive updates of information specified in Subpart J of this part; and

(4) If such applicant wishes to retain a hazardous materials endorsement, require the driver to pass the test for such endorsement specified in §383.121.

(d) **License upgrades.** Prior to issuing an upgrade of a CDL, a State shall:

(1) Require such driver applicant to provide certifications and pass tests as described in §383.71(d); and

(2) Complete a check of the driver applicant's record as described in §383.73(a) (3).

(e) **Nonresident CDL.** A State may issue a Nonresident CDL to a person domiciled in a foreign country if the Administrator has determined that the commercial motor vehicle testing and licensing standards in the foreign jurisdiction of domicile do not meet the standards contained in this part. State procedures for the issuance of a nonresident CDL, for any modifications thereto, and for notifications to the CDLIS shall at a minimum be identical to those pertaining to any other CDL, with the following exceptions:

(1) If the applicant is requesting a transfer of his/her Nonresident CDL, the State shall obtain the Nonresident CDL currently held by the applicant and issued by another State;

(2) The State shall add the word "Nonresident" to the face of the CDL, in accordance with §383.153(b); and

(3) The State shall have established, prior to issuing any Nonresident CDL, the practical capability of disqualifying the holder of any Nonresident CDL, by withdrawing, suspending, canceling, and revoking his/her Nonresident CDL as if the Nonresident CDL were a CDL issued to a resident of the State.

(f) **License issuance.** After the State has completed the procedures described in §383.73(a), (b), (c), (d), or (e), it may issue a CDL to the driver applicant. The State shall notify the operator of the CDLIS of such issuance, transfer, renewal, or upgrade within the 10-day period beginning on the date of license issuance.

(g) **Penalties for false information.** If a State determines, in its check of an applicant's license status and record prior to issuing a CDL, or at any time after the CDL is issued, that the applicant has falsified information contained in Subpart J of this part or any of the certifications required in §383.71(a), the State shall at a minimum suspend, cancel, or revoke the person's CDL or his/her pending application, or disqualify the person from operating a commercial motor vehicle for a period of at least 60 consecutive days.

(h) **Reciprocity.** A State shall allow any person who has a valid CDL which is not suspended, revoked, or canceled, and who is not disqualified from operating a commercial motor vehicle to operate a commercial motor vehicle in the State.

(i) **Alternative procedures.** A State may implement alternative procedures to the certification requirements of §383.71(a) (1), (4), and (6), provided those procedures ensure that the driver meets the requirements of those paragraphs.

§383.75 Third party testing.

(a) **Third party tests.** A State may authorize a person (including another State, an employer, a private driver training facility or other private institution, or a department, agency or instrumentality of a local government) to administer the skills tests as specified in Subparts G and H of this part, if the following conditions are met:

(1) The tests given by the third party are the same as those which would otherwise by given by the State; and

(2) The third party as an agreement with the State containing, at a minimum, provisions that:

(i) Allow the FHWA, or its representative, and the State to conduct random examinations, inspections and audits without prior notice;

(ii) Require the State to conduct on-site inspections at least annually;

(iii) Require that all third party examiners meet the same qualification and training standards as State examiners, to the extent necessary to conduct skills tests in compliance with Subparts G and H;

(iv) Require that, at least on an annual basis, State employees take the tests actually administered by the third party as if the State employee were a test applicant, or that States test a sample of drivers who were examined by the third party to compare pass/fail results; and

(v) Reserve unto the State the right to take prompt and appropriate remedial action against the third-party testers in the event that the third-party fails to comply with State or Federal standards for the CDL testing program, or with any other terms of the third-party contract.

(b) **Proof of testing by a third party.** A driver applicant who takes and passes driving tests administered by an authorized third party shall provide evidence to the State licensing agency that he/she has successfully passed the driving tests administered by the third party.

§383.77 Substitute for driving skills tests.

At the discretion of a State, the driving skill test as specified in §383.113 may be waived for a CMV operator who is currently licensed at the time of his/her application for a CDL, and substituted with either an applicant's driving record and previous passage of an acceptable skills test, or an applicant's driving record in combination with certain driving experience. The State shall impose conditions and limitations to restrict the applicants from whom a State may accept alternative requirements for the skills test described in §383.113. Such conditions must require at least the following:

(a) An applicant must certify that, during the two-year period immediately prior to applying for a CDL, he/she:

(1) Has not had more than one license (except in the instances specified in §383.21(b));

(2) Has not had any license suspended, revoked, or canceled;

(3) Has not had any convictions for any type of motor vehicle for the disqualifying offenses contained in §383.51(b)(2);

(4) Has not had more than one conviction for any type of motor vehicle for serious traffic violations; and

(5) Has not had any conviction for a violation of State or local law relating to motor vehicle traffic control (other than a parking violation) arising in connection with any traffic accident, and has no record of an accident in which he/she was at fault; and

(b) An applicant must provide evidence and certify that:

(1) He/she is regularly employed in a job requiring operation of a CMV, and that either:

(2) He/she has previously taken and passed a skills test given by a State with a classified licensing and testing system, and that the test was behind-the-wheel in a representative vehicle for that applicant's driver's license classification; or

(3) He/she has operated, for at least 2 years immediately preceding application for a CDL, a vehicle representative of the commercial motor vehicle the driver applicant operates or expects to operate.

Subpart F — Vehicle Groups and Endorsements

§383.91 Commercial motor vehicle groups.

(a) **Vehicle group descriptions.** Each driver applicant must possess and be tested on his/her knowledge and skills, described in subpart G of this part, for the commercial motor vehicle group(s) for which he/she desires a CDL. The commercial motor vehicle groups are as follows:

(1) Combination vehicle (Group A)—Any combination of vehicles with a gross combination weight rating (GCWR) of 11,794 kilograms or more (26,001 pounds or more) provided the GVWR of the vehicle(s) being towed is in excess of 4,536 kilograms (10,000 pounds).

(2) Heavy Straight Vehicle (Group B)—Any single vehicle with a GVWR of 11,794 kilograms or more (26,001 pounds or more), or any such vehicle towing a vehicle not in excess of 4,536 kilograms (10,000 pounds) GVWR.

(3) Small Vehicle (Group C)—Any single vehicle, or combination of vehicles, that meets neither the definition of Group A nor that of Group B as contained in this section, but that either is designed to transport 16 or more passengers including the driver, or is used in the transportation of materials found to be hazardous for the purposes of the Hazardous Materials Transportation Act and which require the motor vehicle to be placarded under the Hazardous Materials Regulations (49 CFR part 172, subpart F).

(b) **Representative vehicle.** For purposes of taking the driving test in accordance with §383.113, a representative vehicle for a given vehicle group contained in §383.91(a), is any commercial motor vehicle which meets the definition of that vehicle group.

(c) **Relation between vehicle groups.** Each driver applicant who desires to operate in a different commercial motor vehicle group from the one which his/her CDL authorizes shall be required to retake and pass all related tests, except the following:

(1) A driver who has passed the knowledge and skills tests for a combination vehicle (Group A) may operate a heavy straight vehicle (Group B) or a small vehicle (Group C), provided that he/she possesses the requisite endorsement(s); and

(2) A driver who has passed the knowledge and skills tests for a heavy straight vehicle (Group B) may operate any small vehicle (Group C), provided that he/she possesses the requisite endorsement(s).

(d) **Vehicle group illustration.** Figure 1 illustrates typical vehicles within each of the vehicle groups defined in this section.

Figure 1
VEHICLE GROUPS AS ESTABLISHED BY FHWA (SECTION 383.91)

[Note: Certain types of vehicles, such as passenger and doubles/triples, will require an endorsement. Please consult text for particulars.]

Group:	*Description:

A   Any combination of vehicles with a GCWR of 26,001 or more pounds provided the GVWR of the vehicle(s) being towed is in excess of 10,000 pounds. (Holders of a Group A license may, with any appropriate endorsements, operate all vehicles within Groups B and C.)

Examples include but are not limited to:

B   Any single vehicle with a GVWR of 26,001 or more pounds, or any such vehicle towing a vehicle not in excess of 10,000 pounds GVWR (Holders of a Group B license may, with any appropriate endorsements, operate all vehicles within Group C.)

Examples include but are not limited to:

C   Any single vehicle, or combination of vehicles, that does not meet the definition of Group A or Group B as contained herein, but that either is designed to transport 16 or more passengers including the driver, or is placarded for hazardous materials.

Examples include but are not limited to:

*The representative vehicle for the skills test must meet the written description for that group. The silhouettes typify, but do not fully cover, the types of vehicles falling within each group.

§383.93 Endorsements.

(a) **General.** In addition to taking and passing the knowledge and skills tests described in Subpart G of this part, all persons who operate or expect to operate the type(s) of motor vehicles described in paragraph (b) of this section shall take and pass specialized tests to obtain each endorsement. The State shall issue CDL endorsements only to drivers who successfully complete the tests.

(b) **Endorsement descriptions.** An operator must obtain State-issued endorsements to his/her CDL to operate commercial motor vehicles which are:

(1) Double/triple trailers;

(2) Passenger vehicles;

(3) Tank vehicles; or

(4) Required to be placarded for hazardous materials.

(c) **Endorsement testing requirements.** The following tests are required for the endorsements contained in paragraph (b) of this section:

(1) **Double/Triple Trailers** — a knowledge test;

(2) **Passenger** — a knowledge and a skills test;

(3) **Tank vehicle** — a knowledge test; and

(4) **Hazardous Materials** — a knowledge test.

§383.95 Air brake restrictions.

(a) If an applicant either fails the air brake component of the knowledge test, or performs the skills test in a vehicle not equipped with air brakes, the State shall indicate on the CDL, if issued, that the person is restricted from operating a CMV equipped with air brakes.

(b) For the purposes of the skills test and the restriction, air brakes shall include any braking system operating fully or partially on the air brake principle.

Subpart G — Required Knowledge and Skills

§383.110 General requirement.

All drivers of commercial motor vehicles shall have knowledge and skills necessary to operate a commercial motor vehicle safely as contained in this subpart. A sample of the specific types of items which a State may wish to include in the knowledge and skills tests that it administers to CDL applicants is included in the appendix to this Subpart G.

§383.111 Required knowledge.

All commercial motor vehicle operators must have knowledge of the following general areas:

(a) **Safe operations regulations.** Driver-related elements of the regulations contained in 49 CFR Parts 382, 391, 392, 393, 395, 396, and 397, such as: Motor vehicle inspection, repair, and maintenance requirements; procedures for safe vehicle operations; the effects of fatigue, poor vision, hearing, and general health upon safe commercial motor vehicle operation; the types of motor vehicles and cargoes subject to the requirements; and the effects of alcohol and drug use upon safe commercial motor vehicle operations.

(b) **Commercial motor vehicle safety control systems.** Proper use of the motor vehicle's safety system, including lights, horns, side and rear-view mirrors, proper mirror adjustments, fire extinguishers, symptoms of improper operation revealed through instruments, motor vehicle operation characteristics, and diagnosing malfunctions. Commercial motor vehicle drivers shall have knowledge on the correct procedures needed to use these safety systems in an emergency situation, e.g., skids and loss of brakes.

(c) **Safe vehicle control.** (1) **Control systems** — The purpose and function of the controls and instruments commonly found on commercial motor vehicles.

(2) **Basic control** — The proper procedures for performing various basic maneuvers.

(3) **Shifting** — The basic shifting rules and terms, as well as shift patterns and procedures for common transmissions.

(4) **Backing** — The procedures and rules for various backing maneuvers.

(5) **Visual search** — The importance of proper visual search, and proper visual search methods.

(6) **Communication** — The principles and procedures for proper communications and the hazards of failure to signal properly.

(7) **Speed Management** — The importance of understanding the effects of speed.

(8) **Space management** — The procedures and techniques for controlling the space around the vehicle.

(9) **Night operation** — Preparations and procedures for night driving.

(10) **Extreme driving conditions** — The basic information on operating in extreme driving conditions and the hazards that are encountered in extreme conditions.

(11) **Hazard perceptions** — The basic information on hazard perception and clues for recognition of hazards.

(12) **Emergency maneuvers** — The basic information concerning when and how to make emergency maneuvers.

(13) **Skid control and recovery** — The information on the causes and major types of skids, as well as the procedures for recovering from skids.

(d) **Relationship of cargo to vehicle control.** The principles and procedures for the proper handling of cargo.

(e) **Vehicle inspections:** The objectives and proper procedures for performing vehicle safety inspections, as follows:

(1) The importance of periodic inspection and repair to vehicle safety.

(2) The effect of undiscovered malfunctions upon safety.

(3) What safety-related parts to look for when inspecting vehicles.

(4) Pre-trip/enroute/post-trip inspection procedures.

(5) Reporting findings.

(f) **Hazardous materials knowledge, such as:** What constitutes hazardous material requiring an endorsement to transport; classes of hazardous materials; labeling/placarding requirements; and the need for specialized training as a prerequisite to receiving the endorsement and transporting hazardous cargoes.

(g) **Air brake knowledge as follows:**

(1) Air brake system nomenclature;

(2) The dangers of contaminated air supply;

(3) Implications of severed or disconnected air lines between the power unit and the trailer(s);

(4) Implications of low air pressure readings;

(5) Procedures to conduct safe and accurate pre-trip inspections.

(6) Procedures for conducting enroute and post-trip inspections of air actuated brake systems, including ability to detect defects which may cause the system to fail.

(h) **Operators for the combination vehicle group shall also have knowledge of:**

(1) **Coupling and uncoupling** — The procedures for proper coupling and uncoupling a tractor to semi-trailer.

(2) **Vehicle inspection** — The objectives and proper procedures that are **unique** for performing vehicle safety inspections on combination vehicles.

§383.113 Required skills.

(a) **Basic vehicle control skills.** All applicants for a CDL must possess and demonstrate basic motor vehicle control skills for each vehicle group which the driver operates or expects to operate. These skills should include the ability to start, to stop, and to move the vehicle forward and backward in a safe manner.

(b) **Safe driving skills.** All applicants for a CDL must possess and demonstrate the safe driving skills for their vehicle group. These skills should include proper visual search methods, appropriate use of signals, speed control for weather and traffic conditions, and ability to position the motor vehicle correctly when changing lanes or turning.

(c) **Air brake skills.** Except as provided in §383.95, all applicants shall demonstrate the following skills with respect to inspection and operation of air brakes:

(1) **Pre-trip inspection skills.** Applicants shall demonstrate the skills necessary to conduct a pre-trip inspection which includes the ability to:

(i) Locate and verbally identify air brake operating controls and monitoring devices;

(ii) Determine the motor vehicle's brake system condition for proper adjustments and that air system connections between motor vehicles have been properly made and secured;

(iii) Inspect the low pressure warning device(s) to ensure that they will activate in emergency situations;

(iv) Ascertain, with the engine running, that the system maintains an adequate supply of compressed air;

(v) Determine that required minimum air pressure build up time is within acceptable limits and that required alarms and emergency devices automatically deactivate at the proper pressure level; and

(vi) Operationally check the brake system for proper performance.

(2) **Driving skills.** Applicants shall successfully complete the skills tests contained in §383.113 in a representative vehicle equipped with air brakes.

(d) **Test area.** Skills tests shall be conducted in on-street conditions or under a combination of on-street and off-street conditions.

(e) **Simulation technology.** A State may utilize simulators to perform skills testing, but under no circumstances as a substitute for the required testing in on-street conditions.

§383.115 Requirements for double/triple trailersendorsement.

In order to obtain a Double/Triple Trailers endorsement each applicant must have knowledge covering:

(a) Procedures for assembly and hookup of the units;

(b) Proper placement of heaviest trailer;

(c) Handling and stability characteristics including offtracking, response to steering, sensory feedback, braking, oscillatory sway, rollover in steady turns, yaw stability in steady turns; and

(d) Potential problems in traffic operations, including problems the motor vehicle creates for other motorists due to slower speeds on steep grades, longer passing times, possibility for blocking entry of other motor vehicles on freeways, splash and spray impacts, aerodynamic buffeting, view blockages, and lateral placement.

§383.117 Requirements for passenger endorsement.

An applicant for the passenger endorsement must satisfy both of the following additional knowledge and skills test requirements.

(a) **Knowledge test.** All applicants for the passenger endorsement must have knowledge covering at least the following topics:

(1) Proper procedures for loading/unloading passengers;

(2) Proper use of emergency exits, including push-out windows;

(3) Proper responses to such emergency situations as fires and unruly passengers;

(4) Proper procedures at railroad crossings and drawbridges; and

(5) Proper braking procedures.

(b) **Skills test.** To obtain a passenger endorsement applicable to a specific vehicle group, an applicant must take his/her skills test in a passenger vehicle satisfying the requirements of that group as defined in §383.91.

§383.119 Requirements for tank vehicle endorsement.

In order to obtain a Tank Vehicle Endorsement, each applicant must have knowledge covering the following:

(a) Causes, prevention, and effects of cargo surge on motor vehicle handling;

(b) Proper braking procedures for the motor vehicle when it is empty, full and partially full;

(c) Differences in handling of baffled/compartmental tank interiors versus non-baffled motor vehicles;

(d) Differences in tank vehicle type and construction;

(e) Differences in cargo surge for liquids of varying product densities;

(f) Effects of road grade and curvature on motor vehicle handling with filled, half-filled and empty tanks;

(g) Proper use of emergency systems; and

(h) For drivers of DOT specification tank vehicles, retest and marking requirements.

§383.121 Requirements for hazardous materials endorsement.

In order to obtain a Hazardous Material Endorsement each applicant must have such knowledge as is required of a driver of a hazardous materials laden vehicle, from information contained in 49 CFR Parts 171, 172, 173, 177, 178, and 397 on the following:

(a) **Hazardous materials regulations including:**

(1) Hazardous materials table;

(2) Shipping paper requirements;

(3) Marking;

(4) Labeling;

(5) Placarding requirements;

(6) Hazardous materials packaging;

(7) Hazardous materials definitions and preparation;

(8) Other regulated material (e.g., ORM—D);

(9) Reporting hazardous materials accidents; and

(10) Tunnels and railroad crossings.

(b) **Hazardous materials handling including:**

(1) Forbidden Materials and Packages;

(2) Loading and Unloading Materials;

(3) Cargo Segregation;

(4) Passenger Carrying Buses and Hazardous Materials;

(5) Attendance of Motor Vehicles;

(6) Parking;

(7) Routes;

(8) Cargo Tanks; and

(9) "Safe Havens."

(c) **Operation of emergency equipment including:**

(1) Use of equipment to protect the public;

(2) Special precautions for equipment to be used in fires;

(3) Special precautions for use of emergency equipment when loading or unloading a hazardous materials laden motor vehicle; and

(4) Use of emergency equipment for tank vehicles.

(d) **Emergency response procedures including;**

(1) Special care and precautions for different types of accidents;

(2) Special precautions for driving near a fire and carrying hazardous materials, and smoking and carrying hazardous materials;

(3) Emergency procedures; and

(4) Existence of special requirements for transporting Class A and B explosives.

Appendix to Subpart G — Required Knowledge and Skills — Sample Guidelines

The following is a sample of the specific types of items which a State may wish to include in the knowledge and skills tests that it administers to CDL applicants. This appendix closely follows the framework of §§383.111 and 383.113. It is intended to provide more specific guidance and suggestion to States. Additional detail in this appendix is not binding and States may depart from it at their discretion provided their CDL program tests for the general areas of knowledge and skill specified in §§383.111 and 383.113.

Examples of specific knowledge elements

(a) **Safe operations regulations.** Driver-related elements of the following regulations:

(1) Motor vehicle inspection, repair, and maintenance requirements as contained in Parts 393 and 396 of this title;

(2) Procedures for safe vehicle operations as contained in Part 392 of this title;

(3) The effects of fatigue, poor vision, hearing, and general health upon safe commercial motor vehicle operation as contained in Parts 391, 392, and 395 of this title;

(4) The types of motor vehicles and cargoes subject to the requirements contained in Part 397 of this title; and

(5) The effects of alcohol and drug use upon safe commercial motor vehicle operations as contained in Parts 391 and 395 of this title.

(b) **Commercial motor vehicle safety control systems.** Proper use of the motor vehicle's safety system, including lights, horns, side and rear-view mirrors, proper mirror adjustments, fire extinguishers, symptoms of improper operation revealed through instruments, motor vehicle operation characteristics, and diagnosing malfunctions. Commercial motor vehicle drivers shall have knowledge on the correct procedures needed to use these safety systems in an emergency situation, *e.g.*, skids and loss of brakes.

(c) **Safe vehicle control.** (1) **Control systems** — The purpose and function of the controls and instruments commonly found on commercial motor vehicles.

(2) **Basic control** — The proper procedures for performing various basic maneuvers, including:

(i) Starting, warming up, and shutting down the engine;

(ii) Putting the vehicle in motion and stopping;

(iii) Backing in a straight line; and

(iv) Turning the vehicle, *e.g.*, basic rules, off-tracking, right/left turns and right curves.

(3) **Shifting** — The basic shifting rules and terms, as well as shift patterns and procedures for common transmissions, including:

(i) Key elements of shifting, *e.g.*, controls, when to shift and double clutching;

(ii) Shift patterns and procedures; and

(iii) Consequences of improper shifting.

(4) **Backing** — The procedures and rules for various backing maneuvers, including:

(i) Backing principles and rules; and

(ii) Basic backing maneuvers, e.g., straight-line backing, and backing on a curved path.

(5) **Visual search** — The importance of proper visual search, and proper visual search methods, including:

(i) Seeing ahead and to the sides;

(ii) Use of mirrors; and

(iii) Seeing to the rear.

(6) **Communication** — The principles and procedures for proper communications and the hazards of failure to signal properly, including:

(i) Signaling intent, e.g., signaling when changing speed or direction in traffic;

(ii) Communicating presence, e.g., using horn or lights to signal presence; and

(iii) Misuse of communications.

(7) **Speed Management** — The importance of understanding the effects of speed, including:

(i) Speed and stopping distance;

(ii) Speed and surface conditions;

(iii) Speed and the shape of the road;

(iv) Speed and visibility; and

(v) Speed and traffic flow.

(8) **Space management** — The procedures and techniques for controlling the space around the vehicle, including:

(i) The importance of space management;

(ii) Space cushions, e.g., controlling space ahead/to the rear;

(iii) Space to the sides; and

(iv) Space for traffic gaps.

(9) **Night operation** — Preparations and procedures for night driving, including:

(i) Night driving factors, e.g., driver factors, (vision, glare, fatigue, inexperience), roadway factors, (low illumination, variation in illumination, familiarity with roads, other road users, especially drivers exhibiting erratic or improper driving), vehicle factors (headlights, auxiliary lights, turn signals, windshields and mirrors); and

(ii) Night driving procedures, e.g., preparing to drive at night and driving at night.

(10) **Extreme driving conditions** — The basic information on operating in extreme driving conditions and the hazards that are encountered in extreme conditions, including:

(i) Adverse weather;

(ii) Hot weather; and

(iii) Mountain driving.

(11) **Hazard perceptions** — The basic information on hazard perception and clues for recognition of hazards, including:

(i) Importance of hazards recognition;

(ii) Road characteristics; and

(iii) Road user activities.

(12) **Emergency maneuvers** — The basic information concerning when and how to make emergency maneuvers, including:

(i) Evasive steering;

(ii) Emergency stop;

(iii) Off-road recovery;

(iv) Brake failure; and

(v) Blowouts.

(13) **Skid control and recovery** — The information on the causes and major types of skids, as well as the procedures for recovering from skids.

(d) **Relationship of cargo to vehicle control.** The principles and procedures for the proper handling of cargo, including:

(1) The importance of proper cargo handling, e.g., consequences of improperly secured cargo, drivers' responsibilities, Federal/State and local regulations.

(2) Principles of weight distribution.

(3) Principles and methods of cargo securement.

(e) **Vehicle inspections:** The objectives and proper procedures for performing vehicle safety inspections, as follows:

(1) The importance of periodic inspection and repair to vehicle safety and to prevention of enroute breakdowns.

(2) The effect of undiscovered malfunctions upon safety.

(3) What safety-related parts to look for when inspecting vehicles, e.g., fluid leaks, interference with visibility, bad tires, wheel and rim defects, braking system defects, steering system defects, suspension system defects, exhaust system defects, coupling system defects, and cargo problems.

(4) Pre-trip/enroute/post-trip inspection procedures.

(5) Reporting findings.

(f) **Hazardous materials knowledge, as follows:**

(1) What constitutes hazardous material requiring an endorsement to transport; and

(2) Classes of hazardous materials, labeling/placarding requirements, and the need for specialized training as a prerequisite to receiving the endorsement and transporting hazardous cargoes.

(g) **Air brake knowledge as follows:**

(1) General air brake system nomenclature;

(2) The dangers of contaminated air (dirt, moisture and oil) supply;

(3) Implications of severed or disconnected air lines between the power unit and the trailer(s);

(4) Implications of low air pressure readings;

(5) Procedures to conduct safe and accurate pre-trip inspections, including knowledge about:

(i) Automatic fail-safe devices;

(ii) System monitoring devices; and

(iii) Low pressure warning alarms.

(6) Procedures for conducting enroute and post-trip inspections of air actuated brake systems, including ability to detect defects which may cause the system to fail, including:

(i) Tests which indicate the amount of air loss from the braking system within a specified period, with and without the engine running; and

(ii) Tests which indicate the pressure levels at which the low air pressure warning devices and the tractor protection valve should activate.

(h) **Operators for the combination vehicle group shall also have knowledge of:**

(1) **Coupling and uncoupling** — The procedures for proper coupling and uncoupling a tractor to semi-trailer.

(2) **Vehicle inspection** — The objectives and proper procedures that are **unique** for performing vehicle safety inspections on combination vehicles.

Examples of Specific Skills Elements

These examples relate to paragraphs (a) and (b) of §383.113 only.

(a) **Basic vehicle control skills.** All applicants for a CDL must possess and demonstrate the following basic motor vehicle control skills for each vehicle group which the driver operates or expects to operate. These skills shall include:

(1) Ability to start, warm-up, and shut down the engine;

(2) Ability to put the motor vehicle in motion and accelerate smoothly, forward and backward;

(3) Ability to bring the motor vehicle to a smooth stop;

(4) Ability to back the motor vehicle in a straight line, and check path and clearance while backing;

(5) Ability to position the motor vehicle to negotiate and then make left and right turns;

(6) Ability to shift as required and select appropriate gear for speed and highway conditions;

(7) Ability to back along a curved path; and

(8) Ability to observe the road and the behavior of other motor vehicles, particularly before changing speed and direction.

(b) **Safe driving skills.** All applicants for a CDL must possess and demonstrate the following safe driving skills for any vehicle group. These skills shall include:

(1) Ability to use proper visual search methods.

(2) Ability to signal appropriately when changing speed or direction in traffic.

(3) Ability to adjust speed to the configuration and condition of the roadway, weather and visibility conditions, traffic conditions, and motor vehicles, cargo and driver conditions;

(4) Ability to choose a safe gap for changing lanes, passing other vehicles, as well as for crossing or entering traffic;

(5) Ability to position the motor vehicle correctly before and during a turn to prevent other vehicles from passing on the wrong side as well as to prevent problems caused by off-tracking;

(6) Ability to maintain a safe following distance depending on the condition of the road, on visibility, and on vehicle weight; and

(7) Ability to adjust operation of the motor vehicle to prevailing weather conditions including speed selection, braking, direction changes and following distance to maintain control.

Subpart H — Tests

§383.131 Test procedures.

(a) **Driver information manuals.** Information on how to obtain a CDL and endorsements shall be included in manuals and made available by States to CDL applicants. All information provided to the applicant shall include the following:

(1) Information on the requirements described in §383.71, the implied consent to alcohol testing described in §383.72, the procedures and penalties, contained in §383.51(b) to which a CDL holder is exposed for refusal to comply with such alcohol testing, State procedures described in §383.73, and other appropriate driver information contained in Subpart E of this part;

(2) Information on vehicle groups and endorsements as specified in Subpart F of this part;

(3) The substance of the knowledge and skills which drivers shall have as outlined in Subpart G of this part for the different vehicle groups and endorsements;

(4) Details of testing procedures, including the purpose of the tests, how to respond, any time limits for taking the test, and any other special procedures determined by the State of issuance; and

(5) Directions for taking the tests.

(b) **Examiner procedures.** A State shall provide to test examiners details on testing and any other State-imposed requirements in the examiner's manual, and shall ensure that examiners are qualified to administer tests on the basis of training and/or other experience. States shall provide standardized scoring sheets for the skills tests, as well as standardized driving instructions for the applicants. Such examiners' manuals shall contain the following:

(1) Information on driver application procedures contained in §383.71, State procedures described in §383.73, and other appropriate driver information contained in Subpart E of this part;

(2) Details on information which must be given to the applicant;

(3) Details on how to conduct the tests;

(4) Scoring procedures and minimum passing scores;

(5) Information for selecting driving test routes;

(6) List of the skills to be tested;

(7) Instructions on where and how the skills will be tested;

(8) How performance of the skills will be scored; and

(9) Causes for automatic failure of skills tests.

§383.133 Testing methods.

(a) All tests shall be constructed in such a way as to determine if the applicant possesses the required knowledge and skills contained in Subpart G of this part for the type of motor vehicle or endorsement the applicant wishes to obtain.

(b) States shall develop their own specifications for the tests for each vehicle group and endorsement which must be at least as stringent as the Federal standards.

(c) States shall determine specific methods for scoring the knowledge and skills tests.

(d) Passing scores must meet those standards contained in §383.135.

(e) Knowledge and skills tests shall be based solely on the information contained in the driver manuals referred to in §383.131(a).

(f) Each knowledge test shall be valid and reliable so as to assure that driver applicants possess the knowledge required under §383.111.

(g) Each basic knowledge test, i.e., the test covering the areas referred to in §383.111 for the applicable vehicle group, shall contain at least 30 items, exclusive of the number of items testing air brake knowledge. Each endorsement knowledge test, and the air brake component of the basic knowledge test as described in §383.111(g), shall contain a number of questions that is sufficient to test the driver applicant's knowledge of the required subject matter with validity and reliability.

(h) The skills tests shall have administrative procedures, designed to achieve interexaminer reliability, that are sufficient to ensure fairness of pass/fail rates.

§383.135 Minimum passing scores.

(a) The driver applicant must correctly answer at least 80 percent of the questions on each knowledge test in order to achieve a passing score on such knowledge test.

(b) To achieve a passing score on the skills test, the driver applicant must demonstrate that he/she can successfully perform all of the skills listed in §383.113.

(c) If the driver applicant does not obey traffic laws, or causes an accident during the test, he/she shall automatically fail the test.

(d) The scoring of the basic knowledge and skills test shall be adjusted as follows to allow for the air brake restriction (§383.95):

(1) If the applicant scores less than 80 percent on the air brake component of the basic knowledge test as described in §383.111 (g), the driver will have failed the air brake component and, if the driver is issued a CDL, an air brake restriction shall be indicated on the license; and

(2) If the applicant performs the skills test in a vehicle not equipped with air brakes, the driver will have omitted the air brake component as described in §383.113(c) and, if the driver is issued a CDL, the air brake restriction shall be indicated on the license.

Subpart I — [Reserved]

Subpart J — Commercial Driver's License Document

§383.151 General.

The CDL shall be a document that is easy to recognize as a CDL. At a minimum, the document shall contain information specified in §383.153.

§383.153 Information on the document and application.

(a) All CDLs shall contain the following information:

(1) The prominent statement that the license is a "Commercial Driver's License" or "CDL," except as specified in §383.153(b).

(2) The full name, signature, and mailing address of the person to whom such license is issued;

(3) Physical and other information to identify and describe such person including date of birth (month, day, and year), sex, and height;

(4) Color photograph of the driver;

(5) The driver's State license number;

(6) The name of the State which issued the license;

(7) The date of issuance and the date of expiration of the license;

(8) The group or groups of commercial motor vehicle(s) that the driver is authorized to operate, indicated as follows:

(i) A for Combination Vehicle;

(ii) B for Heavy Straight Vehicle; and

(iii) C for Small Vehicle.

(9) The endorsement(s) for which the driver has qualified, if any, indicated as follows:

(i) T for double/triple trailers;

(ii) P for passenger;

(iii) N for tank vehicle;

(iv) H for hazardous materials;

(v) X for a combination of the tank vehicle and hazardous materials endorsements; and

(vi) At the discretion of the State, additional codes for additional groupings of endorsements, as long as each such discretionary code is fully explained on the front or back of the CDL document.

(b) If the CDL is a Nonresident CDL, it shall contain the prominent statement that the license is a "Nonresident Commercial Driver's License" or "Nonresident CDL." The word "Nonresident" must be conspicuously and unmistakably displayed, but may be noncontiguous with the words "Commercial Driver's License" or "CDL."

(c) If the State has issued the applicant an air brake restriction as specified in §383.95, that restriction must be indicated on the license.

(d) Except in the case of a Nonresident CDL:

(1) A driver applicant must provide his/her Social Security Number on the application of a CDL; and

(2) The State must provide the Social Security Number to the CDLIS.

§383.155 Tamperproofing requirements.

States shall make the CDL tamperproof to the maximum extent practicable. At a minimum, a State shall use the same tamperproof method used for noncommercial drivers' licenses.

PART 387 — MINIMUM LEVELS OF FINANCIAL RESPONSIBILITY FOR MOTOR CARRIERS

Subpart A — Motor Carriers of Property

Subpart B — Motor Carriers of Passengers

Subpart C — Surety Bonds and Policies of Insurance for Motor Carriers and Property Brokers

AUTHORITY: 49 U.S.C. 31138 and 31139; and 49 CFR 1.48.

Subpart A — Motor Carriers of Property

§387.1 Purpose and scope.

This subpart prescribes the minimum levels of financial responsibility required to be maintained by motor carriers of property operating motor vehicles in interstate, foreign, or intrastate commerce. The purpose of these regulations is to create additional incentives to motor carriers to maintain and operate their vehicles in a safe manner and to assure that motor carriers maintain an appropriate level of financial responsibility for motor vehicles operated on public highways.

§387.3 Applicability.

(a) This subpart applies to for-hire motor carriers operating motor vehicles transporting property in interstate or foreign commerce.

(b) This subpart applies to motor carriers operating motor vehicles transporting hazardous materials, hazardous substances, or hazardous wastes in interstate, foreign, or intrastate commerce.

(c) **Exception.** (1) The rules in this part do not apply to a motor vehicle that has a gross vehicle weight rating (GVWR) of less than 10,000 pounds. This exception does not apply if the vehicle is used to transport any quantity of a Division 1.1, 1.2, or 1.3 material, any quantity of a Division 2.3, Hazard Zone A, or Division 6.1, Packing Group I, Hazard Zone A, or to a highway route controlled quantity of a Class 7 material as it is defined in 49 CFR 173.403, in interstate or foreign commerce.

(2) The rules in this part do not apply to the transportation of nonbulk oil, nonbulk hazardous materials, substances, or wastes in intrastate commerce, except that the rules in this part do apply to the transportation of a highway route controlled quantity of a Class 7 material as defined in 49 CFR 173.403, in intrastate commerce.

§387.5 Definitions.

As used in this subpart —

Accident — includes continuous or repeated exposure to the same conditions resulting in public liability which the insured neither expected nor intended.

Bodily injury — means injury to the body, sickness, or disease including death resulting from any of these.

Cancellation of insurance — the withdrawal of insurance coverage by either the insurer or the insured.

Endorsement — an amendment to an insurance policy.

Environmental restoration — restitution for the loss, damage, or destruction of natural resources arising out of the accidental discharge, dispersal, release or escape into or upon the land, atmosphere, watercourse, or body of water of any commodity transported by a motor carrier. This shall include the cost of removal and the cost of necessary measure taken to minimize or mitigate damage to human health, the natural environment, fish, shellfish, and wildlife.

Evidence of security — a surety bond or a policy of insurance with the appropriate endorsement attached.

Financial responsibility — the financial reserves (e.g., insurance policies or surety bonds) sufficient to satisfy liability amounts set forth in this part covering public liability.

For-hire carriage means the business of transporting, for compensation, the goods or property of another.

In bulk — the transportation, as cargo, of property, except Division 1.1, 1.2, or 1.3 materials, and Division 2.3, Hazard Zone A gases, in containment systems with capacities in excess of 3,500 water gallons.

In bulk (Division 1.1, 1.2, and 1.3 explosives) — the transportation, as cargo, of any Division 1.1, 1.2, or 1.3 materials in any quantity.

In bulk (Division 2.3, Hazard Zone A or Division 6.1, Packing Group I, Hazard Zone A materials) — the transportation, as cargo, of any Division 2.3, Hazard Zone A, or Division 6.1, Packing Group I, Hazard Zone A material, in any quantity.

Insured and principal — the motor carrier named in the policy of insurance, surety bond, endorsement, or notice of cancellation, and also the fiduciary of such motor carrier.

Insurance premium — the monetary sum an insured pays an insurer for acceptance of liability for public liability claims made against the insured.

Motor carrier means a for-hire motor carrier or a private motor carrier. The term includes, but is not limited to, a motor carrier's agent, officer, or representative; an employee responsible for hiring, supervising, training, assigning, or dispatching a driver; or an employee concerned with the installation, inspection, and maintenance of motor vehicle equipment and/or accessories.

Property damage — means damage to or loss of use of tangible property.

Public liability — liability for bodily injury or property damage and includes liability for environmental restoration.

State — means a State of the United States, the District of Columbia, Puerto Rico, the Virgin Islands, American Samoa, Guam, and the Northern Mariana Islands.

§387.7 Financial responsibility required.

(a) No motor carrier shall operate a motor vehicle until the motor carrier has obtained and has in effect the minimum levels of financial responsibility as set forth in §387.9 of this subpart.

(b)(1) Policies of insurance, surety bonds, and endorsements required under this section shall remain in effect continuously until terminated. Cancellation may be effected by the insurer or the insured motor carrier giving 35 days' notice in writing to the other. The 35 days' notice shall commence to run from the date the notice is mailed. Proof of mailing shall be sufficient proof of notice.

(2) **Exception.** Policies of insurance and surety bonds may be obtained for a finite period of time to cover any lapse in continuous compliance.

(3) **Exception.** Mexican motor carriers may meet the minimum financial responsibility requirements of this subpart by obtaining insurance coverage, in the required amounts, for periods of 24 hours or longer, from insurers that meet the requirements of §387.11 of this subpart. A Mexican motor carrier so insured must have available for inspection in each of its vehicles copies of the following documents:

(i) The Certificate of Registration;

(ii) The required insurance endorsement (Form MCS-90); and

(iii) An insurance identification card, binder, or other document issued by an authorized insurer which specifies both the effective date and the expiration date of the temporary insurance coverage authorized by this exception.

Mexican motor carriers insured under this exception are also exempt from the notice of cancellation requirements stated on Form MCS-90.

(c) Policies of insurance and surety bonds required under this section may be replaced by other policies of insurance or surety bonds. The liability of the retiring insurer or surety, as to events after the termination date, shall be considered as having terminated on the effective date of the replacement policy of insurance or surety bond or at the end of the 35 day cancellation period required in paragraph (b) of this section, whichever is sooner.

(d) Proof of the required financial responsibility shall be maintained at the motor carrier's principal place of business. The proof shall consist of:

(1) "Endorsement(s) for Motor Carrier Policies of Insurance for Public Liability Under Sections 29 and 30 of the Motor Carrier Act of 1980" (Form MCS-90) issued by an insurer(s);

(2) A "Motor Carrier Surety Bond for Public Liability Under Section 30 of the Motor Carrier Act of 1980" (Form MCS-82) issued by a surety; or

(3) A written decision, order, or authorization of the Interstate Commerce Commission authorizing a motor carrier to

self-insure under §1043.5 of this title, provided the motor carrier maintains a satisfactory safety rating as determined by the Federal Highway Administration under Part 385 of this title.

(e) The proof of minimum levels of financial responsibility required by this section shall be considered public information and be produced for review upon reasonable request by a member of the public.

(f) All vehicles operated within the United States by motor carriers domiciled in a contiguous foreign country, shall have on board the vehicle a legible copy, in English, of the proof of the required financial responsibility (Forms MCS-90 or MCS-82) used by the motor carrier to comply with paragraph (d) of this section.

(g) Any motor vehicle in which there is no evidence of financial responsibility required by paragraph (f) of this section shall be denied entry into the United States.

§387.9 Financial responsibility, minimum levels.

The minimum levels of financial responsibility referred to in §387.7 of this subpart are hereby prescribed as follows:

SCHEDULE OF LIMITS
(Public liability)

Type of carriage	Commodity transported	January 1, 1985
(1) For-hire (In inter-state or foreign commerce, with a gross vehicle weight rating of 10,000 or more pounds).	Property (nonhazardous)	$ 750,000
(2) For-hire and Pri-vate (In interstate, foreign, or intra-state commerce, with a gross ve-hicle weight rating of 10,000 or more pounds).	Hazardous substances, as defined in 49 CFR 171.8 transported in cargo tanks, portable tanks, or hopper-type ve-hicles with capacities in excess of 3,500 water gallons; or in bulk Division 1.1, 1.2, and 1.3 materials, Division 2.3, Hazard Zone A, or Division 6.1, Pack-ing Group I, Hazard Zone A material; in bulk Division 2.1 or 2.2; or highway route controlled quantities of a Class 7 material, as defined in 49 CFR §173.403	5,000,000
(3) For-hire and Pri-vate (In interstate or foreign com-merce: in any quantity; or in in-trastate com-merce, in bulk only; with a gross vehicle weight rating of 10,000 or more pounds) .	Oil listed in 49 CFR 172.101; hazardous waste, hazardous materials and haz-ardous substances defined in 49 CFR 171.8 and listed in 49 CFR 172.101, but not mentioned in (2) above or (4) be-low	1,000,000
(4) For-hire and Pri-vate (In interstate or foreign com-merce, with a gross vehicle weight rating of less than 10,000 pounds).	Any quantity of Division 1.1, 1.2, or 1.3 material; any quantity of Division 2.3, Hazard Zone A, or Division 6.1, Pack-ing Group I, Hazard Zone A material; or highway route controlled quanti-ties of a Class 7 material as defined in 49 CFR 173.403	5,000,000

§387.11 State authority and designation of agent.

A policy of insurance or surety bond does not satisfy the financial responsibility requirements of this subpart unless the insurer or surety furnishing the policy or bond is—

(a) Legally authorized to issue such policies or bonds in each State in which the motor carrier operates; or

(b) Legally authorized to issue such policies or bonds in the State in which the motor carrier has its principal place of business or domicile, and is willing to designate a person upon whom process, issued by or under the authority of any court having jurisdiction of the subject matter, may be served in any proceeding at law or equity brought in any State in which the motor carrier operates; or

(c) Legally authorized to issue such policies or bonds in any State of the United States and eligible as an excess or surplus lines insurer in any State in which business is written, and is willing to designate a person upon whom process, issued by or under the authority of any court having jurisdiction of the subject matter, may be served in any proceeding at law or equity brought in any State in which the motor carrier operates.

§387.13 Fiduciaries.

The coverage of fiduciaries shall attach at the moment of succession of such fiduciaries.

§387.15 Forms.

Endorsements for policies of insurance (Illustration I) and surety bonds (Illustration II) must be in the form prescribed by the FHWA and approved by the OMB. Endorsements to policies of insurance and surety bonds shall specify that coverage thereunder will remain in effect continuously until terminated, as required in §387.7 of this subpart. The continuous coverage requirement does not apply to Mexican motor carriers insured under §387.7(b)(3) of this subpart. The endorsement and surety bond shall be issued in the exact name of the motor carrier.

ILLUSTRATION I

Form MCS-90 (3/82)
Form Approved
OMB No. 2125-0074

ENDORSEMENT FOR MOTOR CARRIER POLICIES OF INSURANCE FOR PUBLIC LIABILITY UNDER SECTIONS 29 AND 30 OF THE MOTOR CARRIER ACT OF 1980

Issued to _____

of _____

Dated at _____

this _____ day of _____, 19 _____

Amending Policy No. _____

Effective Date _____

Name of Insurance Company _____

Countersigned by _____

Authorized Company Representative

The policy to which this endorsement is attached provides primary or excess insurance, as indicated by "X", for the limits shown:

( )   This insurance is primary and the company shall not be liable for amounts in excess of $____ for each accident.

( )   This insurance is excess and the company shall not be liable for amounts in excess of $____ for each accident in excess of the underlying limit of $____for each accident.

Whenever required by the FHWA or the ICC the company agrees to furnish the FHWA or the ICC a duplicate of said policy and all its endorsements. The company also agrees, upon telephone request by an authorized representative of the FHWA or the ICC, to verify that the policy is in force as of a particular date. The telephone number to call is:

_____

Cancellation of this endorsement may be effected by the company or the insured by giving (1) thirty-five (35) days notice in writing to the other party (said 35 days notice to commence from the date the notice is mailed, proof of mailing shall be sufficient proof of notice), and (2) if the insured is subject to the ICC's jurisdiction, by providing thirty (30) days notice to the ICC (said 30 days notice to commence from the date the notice is received by the ICC at its office in Washington, D.C.).

DEFINITIONS AS USED IN THIS ENDORSEMENT

Accident includes continuous or repeated exposure to conditions which results in bodily injury, property damage, or environmental damage which the insured neither expected or intended.

Motor Vehicle means a land vehicle, machine, truck, tractor, trailer, or semitrailer propelled or drawn by mechanical power and used on a highway for transporting property, or any combination thereof.

Bodily Injury means injury to the body, sickness, or disease to any person, including death resulting from any of these.

Environmental Restoration means restitution for the loss, damage, or destruction of natural resources arising out of the accidental discharge, dispersal, release or escape into or upon the land, atmosphere, watercourse, or body of water, of any commodity transported by a motor carrier. This shall include the cost of removal and the cost of necessary measures taken to minimize or mitigate damage to human health, the natural environment, fish, shellfish, and wildlife.

Property Damage means damage to or loss of use of tangible property.

Public Liability means liability for bodily injury, property damage, and environmental restoration.

The insurance policy to which this endorsement is attached provides automobile liability insurance and is amended to assure compliance by the insured, within the limits stated herein, as a motor carrier of property, with Sections 29 and 30 of the Motor Carrier Act of 1980 and the rules and regulations of the Federal Highway Administration and the Interstate Commerce Commission (ICC).

In consideration of the premium stated in the policy to

which this endorsement is attached, the insurer (the company) agrees to pay, within the limits of liability described herein, any final judgment recovered against the insured for public liability resulting from negligence in the operation, maintenance or use of motor vehicles subject to the financial responsibility requirements of Sections 29 and 30 of the Motor Carrier Act of 1980 regardless of whether or not each motor vehicle is specifically described in the policy and whether or not such negligence occurs on any route or in any territory authorized to be served by the insured or elsewhere. Such insurance as is afforded, for public liability, does not apply to injury to or death of the insured's employees while engaged in the course of their employment, or property transported by the insured, designated as cargo. It is understood and agreed that no condition, provision, stipulation, or limitation contained in the policy, this endorsement, or any other endorsement thereon, or violation thereof, shall relieve the company from liability or from the payment of any final judgment, within the limits of liability herein described, irrespective of the financial condition, insolvency or bankruptcy of the insured. However, all terms, conditions, and limitations in the policy to which the endorsement is attached shall remain in full force and effect as binding between the insured and the company. The insured agrees to reimburse the company for any payment made by the company on account of any accident, claim, or suit involving a breach of the terms of the policy, and for any payment that the company would not have been obligated to make under the provisions of the policy except for the agreement contained in this endorsement.

It is further understood and agreed that, upon failure of the company to pay any final judgment recovered against the insured as provided herein, the judgment creditor may maintain an action in any court of competent jurisdiction against the company to compel such payment.

The limits of the company's liability for the amounts prescribed in this endorsement apply separately to each accident and any payment under the policy because of any one accident shall not operate to reduce the liability of the company for the payment of final judgments resulting from any other accident.

ILLUSTRATION II

Form MCS-82 (4/83)
(Form approved by Office of Management and Budget under control no. 2125-0075)

MOTOR CARRIER PUBLIC LIABILITY SURETY BOND UNDER SECTIONS 29 AND 30 OF THE MOTOR CARRIER ACT OF 1980

Parties	Surety company and principal place of business address	Motor carrier principal, ICC Docket No. and principal place of business
	_____	_____
	_____	_____
	_____	_____
	_____	_____

Purpose — This is an agreement between the Surety and the Principal under which the Surety, its successors and assignees, agree to be responsible for the payment of any final judgment or judgments against the Principal for public liability, property damage, and environmental restoration liability claims in the sums prescribed herein; subject to the governing provisions and the following conditions.

Governing provisions—(1) Sections 29 and 30 of the Motor Carrier Act of 1980 (49 U.S.C. 10927 note).

(2) Rules and regulations of the Federal Highway Administration.

(3) Rules and regulations of the Interstate Commerce Commission (ICC).

Conditions—The Principal is or intends to become a motor carrier of property subject to the applicable governing provisions relating to financial responsibility for the protection of the public.

This bond assures compliance by the Principal with the applicable governing provisions, and shall inure to the benefit of any person or persons who shall recover a final judgment or judgments against the Principal for public liability, property damage, or environmental restoration liability claims (excluding injury to or death of the Principal's employees while engaged in the course of their employment, and loss of or damage to property of the principal, and the cargo transported by the Principal). If every final judgment shall be paid for such claims resulting from the negligent operation, maintenance, or use of motor vehicles in transportation subject to the applicable governing provisions, then this obligation shall be void, otherwise it will remain in full effect.

Within the limits described herein, the Surety extends to such losses regardless of whether such motor vehicles are specifically described herein and whether occurring on the route or in the territory authorized to be served by the Principal or elsewhere.

The liability of the Surety on each motor vehicle subject to the financial responsibility requirements of Section's 29 and 30 of the Motor Carrier Act of 1980 for each accident shall not exceed $ _____, and shall be a continuing one notwithstanding any recovery hereunder.

The surety agrees, upon telephone request by an authorized representative of the FHWA or the ICC, to verify that the surety bond is in force as of a particular date. The telephone number to call is: _____

This bond is effective from _____(12:01 a.m., standard time, at the address of the Principal as stated herein) and shall continue in force until terminated as described herein. The principal or the Surety may at any time terminate this bond by giving (1) thirty-five (35) days notice in writing to the other party (said 35 day notice to commence from the date the notice is mailed, proof of mailing shall be sufficient proof of notice), and (2) if the Principal is subject to the ICC's jurisdiction, by providing thirty (30) days notice to the ICC (said 30 days notice to commence from the date notice is received by the ICC at its office in Washington, D.C.). The Surety shall not be liable for the payment of any judgment or judgments against the Principal for public liability, property damage, or environmental restoration claims resulting from accidents which occur after the termination of this bond as described herein, but such termination shall not affect the liability of the Surety for the payment of any such judgment or judgments resulting from accidents which occur during the time the bond is in effect.

(AFFIX CORPORATE SEAL)
Date _____
Surety _____
City _____
State _____
By _____

ACKNOWLEDGEMENT OF SURETY

State of _____
County of _____
On this_____day of_____, 19_____, before me
personally came _____, who, being by me duly
sworn, did depose and say that he/she resides in
_____; that he/she is the _____ of
the _____, the corporation described in and
which executed the foregoing instrument; that he/she knows
the seal of said corporation, that the seal affixed to said instrument is such corporate seal, that it was so affixed by order of
the board of directors of said corporation, that he/she signed
his/her name thereto by like order, and he/she duly acknowledged to me that he/she executed the same for and on behalf of said corporation.

(OFFICIAL SEAL)

_____
Title of official administering oath _____
Surety Company file No. _____

§387.17 Violation and penalty.

Any person (except an employee who acts without knowledge) who knowingly violates the rules of this subpart shall be
liable to the United States for civil penalty of no more than
$10,000 for each violation, and if any such violation is a contin-
uing one, each day of violation will constitute a separate offense. The amount of any such penalty shall be assessed by the
FHWA's Associate Administrator for the Office of Motor Carriers, by written notice. In determining the amount of such penalty, the Associate Administrator, or his/her authorized dele-
gate shall take into account the nature, circumstances, extent,
the gravity of the violation committed and, with respect to the
person found to have committed such violation, the degree of
culpability, any history of prior offenses, ability to pay, effect

on ability to continue to do business, and such other matters as justice may require.

Subpart B — Motor Carriers of Passengers

§387.25 Purpose and scope.

This subpart prescribes the minimum levels of financial responsibility required to be maintained by for-hire motor carriers of passengers operating motor vehicles in interstate or foreign commerce. The purpose of these regulations is to create additional incentives to carriers to operate their vehicles in a safe manner and to assure that they maintain adequate levels of financial responsibility.

§387.27 Applicability.

(a) This subpart applies to for-hire motor carriers transporting passengers in interstate or foreign commerce.

(b) **Exception.** The rules in this subpart do not apply to—

(1) A motor vehicle transporting only school children and teachers to or from school;

(2) A motor vehicle providing taxicab service and having a seating capacity of less than 7 passengers and not operated on a regular route or between specified points;

(3) A motor vehicle carrying less than 16 individuals in a single daily round trip to commute to and from work; and

(4) A motor vehicle operated by a motor carrier under contract providing transportation of preprimary, primary, and secondary students for extracurricular trips organized, sponsored, and paid by a school district.

§387.29 Definitions.

As used in this subpart—

Accident — includes continuous or repeated exposure to the same conditions resulting in public liability which the insured neither expected nor intended.

Bodily injury — means injury to the body, sickness, or disease including death resulting from any of these.

Endorsement — an amendment to an insurance policy.

Financial responsibility — the financial reserves (e.g., insurance policies or surety bonds) sufficient to satisfy liability amounts set forth in this subpart covering public liability.

For hire carriage means the business of transporting, for compensation, passengers and their property, including any compensated transportation of the goods or property or another.

Insured and principal — the motor carrier named in the policy of insurance, surety bond, endorsement, or notice of cancellation, and also the fiduciary of such motor carrier.

Insurance premium — the monetary sum an insured pays an insurer for acceptance of liability for public liability claims made against the insured.

Motor carrier means a for-hire motor carrier. The term includes, but is not limited to, a motor carrier's agent, officer, or representative; an employee responsible for hiring, supervising, training, assigning, or dispatching a driver; or an employee concerned with the installation, inspection, and maintenance of motor vehicle equipment and/or accessories.

Property damage — means damage to or loss of use of tangible property.

Public liability — liability for bodily injury or property damage.

Seating capacity — any plan view location capable of accommodating a person at least as large as a 5th percentile adult female, if the overall seat configuration and design and vehicle design is such that the position is likely to be used as a seating position while the vehicle is in motion, except for auxiliary seating accommodations such as temporary or folding jump seats. Any bench or split bench seat in a passenger car, truck or multipurpose passenger vehicle with a gross vehicle weight rating less than 10,000 pounds, having greater than 50 inches of hip room (measured in accordance with SEA Standards J1100(a)) shall have not less than three designated seating positions, unless the seat design or vehicle design is such that the center position cannot be used for seating.

§387.31 Financial responsibility required.

(a) No motor carrier shall operate a motor vehicle transporting passengers until the motor carrier has obtained and has in effect the minimum levels of financial responsibility as set forth in §387.33 of this subpart.

(b) Policies of insurance, surety bonds, and endorsements required under this section shall remain in effect continuously until terminated.

(1) Cancellation may be effected by the insurer or the insured motor carrier giving 35 days notice in writing to the other. The 35 days notice shall commence to run from the date the notice is mailed. Proof of mailing shall be sufficient proof of notice.

(2) **Exception.** Policies of insurance and surety bonds may be obtained for a finite period of time to cover any lapse in continuous compliance.

(3) **Exception.** Mexican motor carriers may meet the minimum financial responsibility requirements of this subpart by obtaining insurance coverage, in the required amounts, for periods of 24 hours or longer, from insurers that meet the requirements of §387.35 of this subpart. A Mexican motor carrier so insured must have available for inspection in each of its vehicles copies of the following documents:

(i) The required insurance endorsement (Form MCS-90B); and

(ii) An insurance identification card, binder, or other document issued by an authorized insurer which specifies both the effective date and the expiration date of the temporary insurance coverage authorized by this exception.

Mexican motor carriers insured under this exception are also exempt from the notice of cancellation requirements stated on Form MCS-90B.

(c) Policies of insurance and surety bonds required under this section may be replaced by other policies of insurance or surety bonds. The liability of retiring insurer or surety, as to events after the termination date, shall be considered as having terminated on the effective date of the replacement policy of insurance or surety bond or at the end or the 35 day cancellation period required in paragraph (b) of this section, whichever is sooner.

(d) Proof of the required financial responsibility shall be maintained at the motor carrier's principal place of business. The proof shall consist of—

(1) "Endorsement(s) for Motor Carriers of Passengers Policies of Insurance for Public Liability Under Section 18 of the Bus Regulatory Reform Act of 1982" (Form MCS-90B) issued by an insurer(s); or

(2) A "Motor Carrier of Passengers Surety Bond for Public Liability Under Section 18 of the Bus Regulatory Reform Act of 1982" (Form MCS-82B) issued by a surety.

(e) The proof of minimum levels of financial responsibility required by this section shall be considered public information and be produced for review upon reasonable request by a member of the public.

(f) All passenger carrying vehicles operated within the

United States by motor carriers domiciled in a contiguous foreign country, shall have on board the vehicle a legible copy, in English, of the proof of the required financial responsibility (Forms MCS-90B or MCS-82B) used by the motor carrier to comply with paragraph (d) of this section.

(g) Any motor vehicle in which there is no evidence of financial responsibility required by paragraph (f) of this section shall be denied entry into the United States.

§387.33 Financial responsibility, minimum levels.

The minimum levels of financial responsibility referred to in §387.31 of this subpart are hereby prescribed as follows:

Schedule of Limits
Public Liability

For-hire motor carriers of passengers operating in interstate or foreign commerce.

Vehicle Seating Capacity	Effective Dates	
	Nov. 19, 1983	Nov. 19, 1985
(1) Any vehicle with a seating capacity of 16 passengers or more	$2,500,000	$5,000,000
(2) Any vehicle with a seating capacity of 15 passengers or less[1]	750,000	1,500,000

[1]Except as provided in §387.27(b).

§387.35 State authority and designation of agent.

A policy of insurance or surety bond does not satisfy the financial responsibility requirements of this subpart unless the insurer or surety furnishing the policy or bond is—

(a) Legally authorized to issue such policies or bonds in each State in which the motor carrier operates, or

(b) Legally authorized to issue such policies or bonds in the State in which the motor carrier has its principal place of business or domicile, and is willing to designate a person upon whom process, issued by or under the authority of any court having jurisdiction of the subject matter, may be served in any proceeding at law or equity brought in any State in which the motor carrier operates; or

(c) Legally authorized to issue such policies or bonds in any State of the United States and eligible as an excess or surplus lines insurer in any State in which business is written, and is willing to designate a person upon whom process, issued by or under the authority of any court having jurisdiction of the subject matter, may be served in any proceeding at law or equity brought in any State in which the motor carrier operates.

§387.37 Fiduciaries.

The coverage of fiduciaries shall attach at the moment of succession of such fiduciaries.

§387.39 Forms.

Endorsements for policies of insurance (Illustration I) and surety bonds (Illustration II) must be in the form prescribed by the FHWA and approved by the OMB. Endorsements to policies of insurance and surety bonds shall specify that coverage thereunder will remain in effect continuously until terminated as required in §387.31 of this subpart. The continuous coverage requirement does not apply to Mexican motor carriers insured under §387.31(b)(3) of this subpart. The endorsement and surety bond shall be issued in the exact name of the motor carrier.

U.S. Department
of Transportation
Federal Highway
Administration

Expiration Date
Form Approved
OMB No.

ENDORSEMENT FOR
MOTOR CARRIER POLICIES OF INSURANCE FOR PUBLIC LIABILITY
UNDER SECTION 18 OF THE BUS REGULATORY REFORM ACT OF 1982

Issued to _____ of _____

Dated at _____ this _____ day of _____, 19____

Amending Policy No. _____ Effective Date _____

Name of Insurance Company _____

Countersigned by _____

Authorized Company Representative

The policy to which this endorsement is attached provides primary or excess insurance, as indicated by "[X]", for the limits shown:

[ ] This insurance is primary and the company shall not be liable for amounts in excess of $ _____ for each accident.

[ ] This insurance is excess and the company shall not be liable for amounts in excess of $ ____ for each accident in excess of the underlying limit of $ _____ for each accident.

Whenever required by the Bureau or the ICC, the company agrees to furnish the Bureau or the ICC a duplicate of said policy and all its endorsements. The company also agrees, upon telephone request by an authorized representative of the Bureau or the ICC, to verify that the policy is in force as of a particular date. The telephone number to call is: _____

Cancellation of this endorsement may be effected by the company or the insured by giving (1) thirty-five (35) days notice in writing to the other party (said 35 days notice to commence from the date the notice is mailed, proof of mailing shall be sufficient proof of notice), and (2) if the insured is subject to the ICC's jurisdiction, by providing thirty (30) days notice to the ICC (said 30 days notice to commence from the date the notice is received by the ICC at its office in Washington, D.C.).

ACCIDENT includes continuous or repeated exposure to conditions which results in Public Liability which the insured neither expected nor intended.

BODILY INJURY means injury to the body, sickness, or disease to any person, including death resulting from any of these.

The insurance policy to which this endorsement is attached provides automobile liability insurance and is amended to assure compliance by the insured, within the limits stated herein, as a for-hire motor carrier of passengers with Section 18 of the Bus Regulatory Reform Act of 1982 and the rules and regulations of the Federal Highway Administration's Bureau of Motor Carrier Safety (Bureau) and the Interstate Commerce Commission (ICC).

In consideration of the premium stated in the policy to which this endorsement is attached, the insurer (the company) agrees to pay, within the limits of liability described herein, any final judgment recovered against the insured for public liability resulting from negligence in the operation, maintenance or use of motor vehicles subject to financial responsibility requirements of Section 18 of the Bus Regulatory Reform Act of 1982 regardless of whether or not each motor vehicle is specifically described in the policy and whether or not such negligence occurs on any route or in any territory authorized to be served by the insured or elsewhere. Such insurance as is afforded, for public liability, does not apply to injury to or death of the insured's employees while engaged in the course of their employment, or property transported by the insured, designated as cargo. It is understood and agreed that no condition, provision, stipulation, or limitation contained in the policy, this endorsement, or any other endorse-

MOTOR CARRIER means a for-hire carrier of passengers by motor vehicle.

PROPERTY DAMAGE means damage to or loss of use of tangible property.

PUBLIC LIABILITY means liability for bodily injury or property damage.

ment thereon, or violation thereof, shall relieve the company from liability or from the payment of any final judgment, within the limits of liability herein described, irrespective of the financial condition, insolvency or bankruptcy of the insured. However, all terms, conditions, and limitations in the policy to which the endorsement is attached shall remain in full force and effect as binding between the insured and the company. The insured agrees to reimburse the company for any payment made by the company on account of any accident, claim, or suit involving a breach of the terms of the policy, and for any payment that the company would not have been obligated to make under the provisions of the policy except for the agreement contained in this endorsement.

It is further understood and agreed that, upon failure of the company to pay any final judgment recovered against the insured as provided herein, the judgment creditor may maintain an action in any court of competent jurisdiction against the company to compel such payment.

The limits of the company's liability for the amounts prescribed in this endorsement apply separately to each accident and any payment under the policy because of any one accident shall not operate to reduce the liability of the company for the payment of final judgments resulting from any other accident.

The Bus Regulatory Reform Act of 1982 requires limits of financial responsibility according to vehicle seating capacity. It is the MOTOR CARRIER'S obligation to obtain the required limits of financial responsibility.
THE SCHEDULE OF LIMITS SHOWN ON THE REVERSE SIDE DOES NOT PROVIDE COVERAGE.
The limits shown in the schedule are for information purposes only.

SCHEDULE OF LIMITS
PUBLIC LIABILITY

For-hire motor carriers of passengers operating in interstate or foreign commerce

Vehicle Seating Capacity	Effective Dates	
	Nov. 19, 1983	Nov. 19, 1985
(1) Any vehicle with a seating capacity of 16 passengers or more.	$2,500,000	$5,000,000
(2) Any vehicle with a seating capacity of 15 passengers or less.	$ 750,000	$1,500,000

MOTOR CARRIER PUBLIC LIABILITY SURETY BOND UNDER SECTION 18 OF THE BUS REGULATORY REFORM ACT OF 1982

Form Approved
OMB No.

PARTIES

Surety Company and Principal Place of Business Address

Motor Carrier Principal, I.C.C. Docket No., and Principal Place of Business Address

_____

_____

_____

PURPOSE

This is an agreement between the Surety and the Principal under which the Surety, its successors and assignees, agree to be responsible for the payment of any final judgment or judgments against the Principal for public liability and property damage claims in the sums prescribed herein, subject to the governing provisions and following conditions.

GOVERNING PROVISIONS

(1) Section 18 of the Bus Regulatory Reform Act of 1982

(2) Rules and regulations of the Federal Highway Administration's Bureau of Motor Carrier Safety (Bureau)

(3) Rules and regulations of the Interstate Commerce Commission (ICC)

CONDITIONS

The Principal is or intends to become a motor carrier of passengers subject to the applicable governing provisions relating to financial responsibility for the protection of the public.

This bond assures compliance by the Principal with the applicable governing provisions, and shall inure to the benefit of any person or persons who shall recover a final judgment or judgments against the Principal for public liability or property damage claims (excluding injury to or death of the Principal's employees while engaged in the course of their employment, and loss of or damage to property of the Principal, and the cargo transported by the Principal). If every final judgment shall be paid for such claims resulting from the negligent operation, maintenance, or use of motor vehicles in transportation subject to the applicable governing provisions, then this obligation shall be void, otherwise it will remain in full effect.

Within the limits described herein, the Surety extends to such losses regardless of whether such motor vehicles are specifically described herein and whether occurring on the route or in the territory authorized to be served by the Principal or elsewhere.

The liability of the Surety for each motor vehicle subject to the applicable governing provisions for each accident shall not exceed $ _____, and shall be a continuing one notwithstanding any recovery thereunder.

The surety agrees, upon telephone request by an authorized representative of the Bureau or ICC, to verify that the surety bond is in force as of a particular date. The telephone number to call is:

This bond is effective from _____ (12:01 a.m., standard time, at the address of the Principal as stated herein) and shall continue in force until terminated as described herein. The Principal or the Surety may at any time terminate this bond by giving (1) thirty-five (35) days notice in writing to the other party (said 35 days notice to commence from the date the notice is mailed, proof of mailing shall be sufficient proof of notice), and (2) if the Principal is subject to the ICC's jurisdiction, by providing thirty (30) days notice to the ICC (said 30 days notice to commence from the date notice is received by the ICC at its office in Washington, D.C.). The Surety shall not be liable for the payment of any judgment or judgments against the Principal for public liability or property damage claims resulting from accidents which occur after the termination of this bond as described herein, but such termination shall not affect the liability of the Surety from the payment of any such judgment or judgments resulting from accidents which occur during the time the bond is in effect,

(AFFIX CORPORATE SEAL)

Date _____

Surety _____

City _____ State _____

By _____

ACKNOWLEDGEMENT OF SURETY

STATE OF _____ COUNTY OF _____

On this _____ day of _____, 19____, before me personally came _____, who, being by me duly sworn, did depose and say that he resides in _____ ; that he is the _____ of the _____ corporation described in and which executed the foregoing instrument; that he knows the seal of said corporation; that the seal affixed to said instrument is such corporate seal; that it was so affixed by order of the board of directors of said corporation; that he signed his name thereto by like order, and he duly acknowledged to me that he executed the same for and on behalf of said corporation.

_____

_____
Title of official administering oath

(OFFICIAL SEAL)

Surety Company file No. _____

Form MCS-828
(11-83)

§387.41 Violation and penalty.

Any person (except an employee who acts without knowledge) who knowingly violates the rules of this subpart shall be liable to the United States for civil penalty of no more than $10,000 for each violation, and if any such violation is a continuing one, each day of violation will constitute a separate offense. The amount of any such penalty shall be assessed by the Associate Administrator for Motor Carriers or his/her designee, by written notice. In determining the amount of such penalty, the Associate Administrator or his/her designee shall take into account the nature, circumstances, extent, the gravity of the violation committed and, with respect to the person found to have committed such violation, the degree of culpability, any history of prior offenses, ability to pay, effect on ability to continue to do business, and such other matters as justice may require.

Subpart C — Surety Bonds and Policies of Insurance for Motor Carriers and Property Brokers

§387.301 Surety bond, certificate of insurance, or other securities.

(a) **Public liability.** (1) No common or contract carrier or foreign (Mexican) motor private carrier or foreign motor carrier transporting exempt commodities subject to Subchapter II, Chapter 105, Subtitle IV of Title 49 of the United States Code shall engage in interstate or foreign commerce, and no certificate or permit shall be issued to such a carrier or remain in force unless and until there shall have been filed with and accepted by the Commission surety bonds, and certificates of insurance, proof of qualifications as self-insurer, or other securities or agreements, in the amounts prescribed in §387.303, conditioned to pay any final judgment recovered against such motor carrier for bodily injuries to or the death of any person resulting from the negligent operation, maintenance or use of motor vehicles in transportation subject to Subchapter II, Chapter 105, Subtitle IV of Title 49 of the United States Code, or for loss of or damage to property of others, or, in the case of motor carriers of property operating freight vehicles described in §387.303(b)(2) of this part, for environmental restoration.

(2) Motor Carriers of property which are subject to the conditions set forth in paragraph (a)(1) of this section and transport the commodities described in §387.303(b)(2), are required to obtain security in the minimum limits prescribed in §387.303(b)(2).

(b) **Common carriers—cargo insurance; exempt commodities.** No common carrier by motor vehicle subject to Subchapter II, Chapter 105, Subtitle IV of Title 49 of the United States Code, nor any foreign (Mexican) common carrier of exempt commodities, shall engage in interstate or foreign commerce, nor shall any certificate be issued to such a carrier or remain in force unless and until there shall have been filed with and accepted by the Commission, a surety bond, certificate of insurance, proof of qualifications as a self-insurer, or other securities or agreements in the amounts prescribed in §387.303, conditioned upon such carrier making compensation to shippers or consignees for all property belonging to shippers or consignees and coming into the possession of such carrier in connection with its transportation service: Provided, That the requirements of this paragraph shall not apply in connection with the transportation of the following commodities:

Agricultural ammonium nitrate.

Agricultural nitrate of soda.

Anhydrous ammonia—used as a fertilizer only.

Ashes, wood or coal.

Bituminous concrete (also known as blacktop or amosite), including mixtures of asphalt paving.

Cement, dry, in containers or in bulk.

Cement, building blocks.

Charcoal.

Chemical fertilizer.

Cinder blocks.

Cinders, coal.

Coal.

Coke.

Commercial fertilizer.

Concrete materials and added mixtures

Corn cobs.

Cottonseed hulls.

Crushed stone.

Drilling salt.

Dry fertilizer.

Fish scrap.

Fly ash.

Forest products; viz: Logs, billets, or bolts, native woods, Canadian wood or Mexican pine; pulpwood, fuel wood, wood kindling; and wood sawdust or shavings (shingle tow) other than jewelers' or paraffined.

Foundry and factory sweepings.

Garbage.

Gravel, other than bird gravel.

Hardwood and parquet flooring.

Haydite.

Highway construction materials, when transported in dump trucks and unloaded at destination by dumping.

Ice.

Iron ore.

Lime and limestone.

Liquid fertilizer solutions, in bulk, in tank vehicles.

Lumber.

Manure.

Meat scraps.

Mud drilling salt.

Ores in bulk, including ore concentrates.

Paving materials, unless contain oil hauled in tank vehicles.

Peat moss.

Peeler cores.

Plywood.

Poles and piling, other than totem poles.

Potash, used as commercial fertilizer.

Pumice stone, in bulk in dump vehicles.

Salt, in bulk or in bags.

Sand, other than asbestos, bird, iron, monazite, processed, or tobacco sand.

Sawdust.

Scoria stone.

Scrap iron.

Scrap steel.

Shells, clam, mussel, or oyster.

Slag, other than slag with commercial value for the further extraction of metals.

Slag, derived aggregates—cinders.

Slate, crushed or scrap.

Slurry, as waste material.

Soil, earth or marl, other than infusorial, diatomaceous, tripoli, or inoculated soil or earth.

Stone, unglazed and unmanufactured, including ground agricultural limestone.

Sugar beet pulp.

Sulphate of ammonia, in bulk, used as fertilizer.

Surfactants.

Trap rock.

Treated poles.

Veneer.

Volcanic scoria.

Waste, hazardous and nonhazardous, transported solely for purposes of disposal.

Water, other than mineral or prepared water.

Wood chips, not processed.

Wooden pallets, unassembled.

Wrecked or disabled motor vehicles.

Other materials or commodities of low value, upon specific application to and approval by the Commission.

(c) **Continuing compliance required.** Such security as is accepted by the Commission in accordance with the requirements of Section 10927, Subchapter II, Chapter 109, Subtitle IV of Title 49 of the United States Code shall remain in effect at all times.

§387.303 Security for the protection of the public: Minimum limits.

(a) **Definitions:** (1) "Primary security" means public liability coverage provided by the insurance or surety company responsible for the first dollar of coverage.

(2) "Excess security" means public liability coverage above the primary security, or above any additional underlying security, up to and including the required minimum limits set forth in paragraph (b)(2) of this section.

(b)(1) Motor carriers subject to §387.301(a)(1) are required to have security for the required minimum limits as follows:

(i) Small Freight Vehicles:

Kind of equipment	Transportation provided	Minimum limits
Fleet including only vehicles under 10,000 pounds GVWR.	Commodities not subject to 49 CFR §387.303(b)(2).	$300,000

(ii) Passenger Carriers:

Kind of Equipment		
	Effective dates	
Vehicle seating capacity	Nov. 19, 1983	Nov. 19, 1985
(1) Any vehicle with a seating capacity of 16 passengers or more	$2,500,000	$5,000,000
(2) Any vehicle with a seating capacity of 15 passengers or less	750,000	1,500,000

(2) Motor carriers subject to §387.301(a)(2) are required to have security for the required minimum limits as follows:

Kind of equipment	Commodity transported	July 1, 1983*	January 1, 1985*
(a) Freight Vehicles of 10,000 Pounds or More GVWR.	Property (non-hazardous)	$ 500,000	$ 750,000
(b) Freight Vehicles of 10,000 Pounds or More GVWR.	Hazardous substances, as defined in 49 CFR 171.8, transported in cargo tanks, portable tanks, or hopper-type vehicles with capacities in excess of 3,500 water gallons, or in bulk Class A or B explosives, poison gas (Poison A) liquefied compressed gas or compressed gas, of highway route controlled quantity radioactive materials as defined in 40 CFR 173.455.	1,000,000	5,000,000

Kind of equipment	Commodity transported	July 1, 1983*	January 1, 1985*
(c) Freight Vehicles of 10,000 Pounds or More GVWR.	Oil listed in 49 CFR 172.101; hazardous waste, hazardous materials and hazardous substances defined in 49 CFR 171.8 and listed in 49 CFR 172.101, but not mentioned in (b) above or (d) below.	$ 500,000	$1,000,000
(d) Freight Vehicles Under 10,000 Pounds GVWR.	Any quantity of Class A or B explosives; any quantity of poison gas (Poison A); or highway route controlled quantity radioactive materials as defined in 49 CFR 173.455.	1,000,000	5,000,000

*NOTE: The effective date of the current required minimum limit in 49 CFR 387.303(b)(2) was January 6, 1983, in accordance with the requirements of Pub. L 97-424, 96 Stat. 2097.

(3) Motor carriers subject to the minimum limits governed by this section, which are also subject to Department of Transportation limits requirements, are at no time required to have security for more than the required minimum limits established by the Secretary of Transportation in the applicable provisions of 49 CFR Part 387— Minimum Levels of Financial Responsibility for Motor Carriers.

(4) **Foreign motor carriers and foreign motor private carriers.** Foreign motor carriers and foreign motor private carriers (Mexican), subject to the requirements of 49 U.S.C. 13902(c) and 49 CFR part 368 regarding obtaining certificates of registration from the Commission, must meet our minimum financial responsibility requirements by obtaining insurance coverage, in the required amounts, for periods of 24 hours or longer, from insurance or surety companies, that meet the requirements of 49 CFR 387.315. These carriers must have available for inspection, in each vehicle operating in the United States, copies of the following documents:

(i) The certificate of registration;

(ii) The required insurance endorsement (Form MCS-90); and

(iii) An insurance identification card, binder, or other document issued by an authorized insurer which specifies both the effective date and the expiration date of the insurance coverage.

Notwithstanding the provisions of §387.301(a)(1), the filing of evidence of insurance is not required as a condition to the issuance of a certificate of registration. Further, the reference to continuous coverage at §387.313(a)(6) and the reference to cancellation notice at §387.313(d) are not applicable to these carriers.

(c) **Motor common carriers: Cargo liability**. Security required to compensate shippers or consignees for loss damage to property belonging to shippers or or consignees and coming into the possession of motor carriers in connection with their transportation service, (1) for loss of or damage to property carried on any one motor vehicle — $5,000, (2) for loss of or damage to or aggregate of losses or damages of or to property occurring at any one time and place — $10,000.

§387.305 Combination vehicles.

The following combinations will be regarded as one motor vehicle for purposes of this part, (a) a tractor and trailer or semitrailer when the tractor is engaged solely in drawing the trailer or semitrailer, and (b) a truck and trailer when both together bear a single load.

§387.307 Property broker surety bond or other security.

(a) **Security.** A property broker must have a surety bond or trust fund in effect for $10,000. The Commission will not issue a property broker license until a surety bond or trust fund for the full limits of liability prescribed herein is in effect. The broker license shall remain in effect only as long as a surety bond or trust fund remains in effect and shall ensure the financial responsibility of the broker.

(b) **Evidence of security.** Evidence of a surety bond must be filed using the Commission's prescribed Form BMC-84. Evidence of a trust fund with a financial institution must be filed using the Commission's prescribed Form BMC 85. The surety bond or the trust fund shall ensure the financial responsibility of the broker by providing for payments to shippers or motor carriers if the broker fails to carry out its contracts, agreements, or arrangements for the supplying of transportation by authorized motor carriers.

(c) **Financial Institution** — when used in this section and in forms prescribed under this section, where not otherwise distinctly expressed or manifestly incompatible with the intent thereof, shall mean — Each agent, agency, branch or office within the United States of any person, as defined by the Interstate Commerce Act, doing business in one or more of the capacities listed below:

(1) An insured bank (as defined in section 3(h) of the Federal Deposit Insurance Act (12 U.S.C. 1813(h));

(2) A commercial bank or trust company;

(3) An agency or branch of a foreign bank in the United States;

(4) An insured institution (as defined in section 401(a) of the National Housing Act (12 U.S.C. 1724(a));

(5) A thrift institution (savings bank, building and loan association, credit union, industrial bank or other);

(6) An insurance company;

(7) A loan or finance company; or

(8) A person subject to supervision by any state or federal bank supervisory authority.

(d) **Forms and Procedures —**

(1) **Forms for broker surety bonds and trust agreements.** Form BMC-84 broker surety bond will be filed with the Commission for the full security limits under subsection (a); or Form BMC-85 broker trust fund agreement will be filed with the Commission for the full security limits under paragraph (a) of this section.

(2) **Broker surety bonds and trust fund agreements in effect continuously.** Surety bonds and trust fund agreements shall specify that coverage thereunder will remain in effect continuously until terminated as herein provided.

(i) **Cancellation notice.** The surety bond and the trust fund agreement may be cancelled as only upon 30 days' written notice to the Commission, on prescribed Form BMC 36, by the principal or surety for the surety bond, and on prescribed Form BMC 85, by the trustor/broker or trustee for the trust fund agreement. The notice period commences upon the actual receipt of the ntoice at the Commission's Washington, DC office.

(ii) **Termination by replacement.** Broker surety bonds or trust fund agreements which have been accepted by the Commission under these rules may be replaced by other surety bonds or trust fund agreements, and the liability of the retiring surety or trustee under such surety bond or trust fund agreements shall be considered as having terminated as of the effective date of the replacement surety bond or trust fund agreement. However, such termination shall not affect the liability of the surety or the trustee hereunder for the payment of any damages arising as the result of contracts, agreements or arrangements made by the broker for the supplying of transportation prior to the date such termination becomes effective.

(3) **Filing and copies.** Broker surety bonds and trust fund agreements must be filed with the Commission in duplicate.

§387.309 Qualifications as a self-insurer and other securities or agreements.

(a) **As a self-insurer.** The Commission will consider and will approve, subject to appropriate and reasonable conditions, the application of a motor carrier to qualify as a self-insurer, if the carrier furnishes a true and accurate statement of its financial condition and other evidence that establishes to the satisfaction of the Commission the ability of the motor carrier to satisfy its obligation for bodily injury liability, property damage liability, or cargo liability. Application Guidelines: In addition to filing Form BMC 40, applicants for authority to self-insure against bodily injury and property damage claims should submit evidence that will allow the Commission to determine:

(1) The adequacy of the tangible net worth of the motor carrier in relation to the size of operations and the extent of its request for self-insurance authority. Applicant should demonstrate that it will maintain a net worth that will ensure that it will be able to meet its statutory obligations to the public to indemnify all claimants in the event of loss.

(2) The existence of a sound self-insurance program. Applicant should demonstrate that is has established, and will maintain, an insurance program that will protect the public against all claims to the same extent as the minimum security limits applicable to applicant under §387.303 of this part. Such a program may include, but not be limited to, one or more of the following: irrevocable letters of credit; irrevocable trust funds; reserves; sinking funds; third party financial guarantees, parent company or affiliate sureties; excess insurance coverage; or other similar arrangements.

(3) The existence of an adequate safety program. Applicant must submit evidence of a current "satisfactory" safety rating by the United States Department of Transportation. Non-rated carriers need only certify that they have not been rated. Applications by carriers with a less than satisfactory rating will be summarily denied. Any self-insurance authority granted by the Commission will automatically expire 30 days after a carrier re-

ceives a less than satisfactory rating from DOT.

(4) *Additional information.* Applicant must submit such additional information to support its application as the Commission may require.

(b) **Other securities or agreements.** The ommission also will consider applications for approval of other securities or agreements and will approve any such application if satisfied that the security or agreement offered will afford the security for the protection of the public contemplated by 49 U.S.C. 13906.

§387.311 Bonds and certificates of insurance.

(a) **Public liability.** Each Form BMC 82 surety bond filed with the Commission must be for the full limits of liability required under §387.303(b)(1). Form MCS-82 surety bonds and other forms of similar import prescribed by the Department of Transportation, may be aggregated to comply with the minimum security limits required under §387.303(b)(1) or §387.303(b)(2). Each Form BMC 91 certificate of insurance filed with the Commission will always represent the full security minimum limits required for the particular carrier, while it remains in force, under §§387.303(b)(1) or 387.303(b)(2), whichever is applicable. Any previously executed Form BMC 91 filed before the current revision which is left on file with the Commission after the effective date of this regulation, and not canceled within 30 days of that date will be deemed to certify the same coverage limits as would the filing of a revised Form BMC 91. Each Form BMC 91X certificate of insurance filed with the Commission will represent the full security limits under §§387.303(b)(1) or 387.303(b)(2) or the specific security limits of coverage as indicated on the face of the form. If the filing reflects aggregation, the certificate must show clearly whether the insurance is primary or, if excess coverage, the amount of underlying coverage as well as amount of the maximum limits of coverage. *Each Form BMC 91MX certificate of insurance filed with the Commission will represent the security limits of coverage as indicated on the face of the form. The Form BMC 91MX must show clearly whether the insurance is primary or, if excess coverage, the amount of underlying coverage as well as amount of the maximum limits of coverage.

(b) **Cargo liability.** Each Form BMC 83 surety bond filed with the Commission must be for the full limits of liability required under §387.303(c). Each Form BMC 34 certificate of insurance filed with the Commission will represent the full security limits under §387.303(c) or the specific limits of coverage as indicated on the face of the form. If the filing reflects aggregation, the certificate must show clearly whether the insurance is primary or, if excess coverage, the amount of underlying coverage as well as amount of the maximum limits of coverage.

(c) Each policy of insurance in connection with certificate of insurance which is filed with the Commission, the shall be amended by attachment of the appropriate endorsement prescribed by the Commission or the Department of Transportation and the certificate of insurance filed thereto must accurately reflect that endorsement.

*Note: Aggregation to meet the requirement of §387.303(b)(1) will not be allowed until the completion of our rulemaking in Ex Parte No. MC-5 (Sub-No. 2), *Motor Carrier and Freight Forwarder Insurance Procedures and Minimum Amounts of Liability.*

§387.313 Forms and procedure.

(a) **Forms for endorsements, certificates of insurance, and others.**

(1) **In form prescribed.** Endorsements for policies of insurance and surety bonds, certificates of insurance, applications to qualify as a self-insurer, or for approval of other securities or agreements, and notices of cancellation must be in the form prescribed and approved by the Commission.

(2) **Aggregation of Insurance.** **When insurance is provided by more than one insurer in order to aggregate security limits for carriers operating only freight vehicles under 10,000 pounds Gross Vehicle Weight Rating, as defined in §387.303(b)(1), a separate Form BMC 90, with the specific amounts of underlying and limits of coverage shown thereon or appended thereto, and Form BMC 91X certificate is required of each insurer.

For aggregation of insurance for all other carriers to cover security limits under §387.303(b)(1) or (b)(2), a separate Department of Transportation prescribed form endorsement and *Form BMC 91X* certificate is required of each insurer.

When insurance is provided by more than one insurer to aggregate coverage for security limits under Section 387.303(c) a separate Form BMC 32 endorsement and Form BMC 34 certificate of insurance is required for each insurer.

For aggregation of insurance for foreign motor private carriers of nonhazardous commodities to cover security limits under §387.303(b)(4), a separate Form BMC 90 with the specific amounts of underlying and limits of coverage shown thereon or appended thereto, or Department of Transportation prescribed form endorsement, and Form BMC 91MX certificate is required for each insurer.

**Note: See NOTE for Rule 387.311. Also, it should be noted that DOT is considering prescribing adaptions of the Form MCS 90 endorsement and the Form MCS 82 surety bond for use by passenger carriers and Rules §§387.311 and 387.313 have been written sufficiently broad to provide for this contingency when new forms are prescribed by that Agency.

(3) **Use of Certificates and Endorsements in BMC Series.**—**Form BMC 91** certificates of insurance will be filed with the Commission for the full security limits under §387.303(b)(1) or (b)(2).

Form BMC 91X certificate of insurance will be filed to represent full coverage or any level of aggregation for the security limits under §387.303(b)(1) or (b)(2).

Form BMC 90 endorsement will be used with each filing of Form BMC 91 or Form BMC 91X certificate with the Commission which certifies to coverage not governed by the requirements of the Department of Transportation.

Form BMC 32 endorsement and *Form BMC 34* certificate of insurance and *Form BMC 83* surety bonds are used for the limits of cargo liability under §1043.2(c).

Form BMC 91MX certificate of insurance will be filed to represent any level of aggregation for the security limits under §387.303(b)(4).

(4) **Use of Endorsements in MCS Series**. When Security limits certified under §387.303(b)(1) or (b)(2) involves coverage also required by the Department of Transportation a *Form MCS endorsement prescribed by the Department of Transportation such as,* and including, the *Form MCS 90* endorsement is required.

(5) **Surety bonds.** When surety bonds are used rather than certificates of insurance, *Form BMC 82* is required for the security limits under §1043.2(b)(1) not subject to regulation by the Department of Transportation, and *Form MCS 82*, or any form of similar import prescribed by the Department of Transportation, is used for the security limits subject also to minimum coverage requirements of the Department of Transportation.

(6) **Surety bonds and certificates in effect continuously.**— Surety bonds and certificates of insurance shall specify that coverage thereunder will remain in effect continuously until terminated as herein provided, except (1) when filed express-

ly to fill prior gaps or lapses in coverage or to cover grants of emergency temporary authority of unusually short duration and the filing clearly so indicates, or (2) in special or unusual circumstances, when special permission is obtained for filing certificates of insurance or surety bonds on terms meeting other particular needs of the situation.

(b) **Filing and copies.** Certificates of insurance, surety bonds, and notices of cancellation must be filed with the Commission in triplicate.

(c) **Name of insured.** Certificates of insurance and surety bonds shall be issued in the full and correct name of the individual, partnership, corporation or other person to whom the certificate, permit, or license is, or is to be, issued. In the case of a partnership all partners shall be named.

(d) **Cancellation notice.** Except as provided in paragraph (e) of this section, surety bonds, certificates of insurance and other securities or agreements shall not be cancelled or withdrawn until 30 days after written notice has been submitted to the Commission at its offices in Washington, DC, on the prescribed form (Form BMC-35, Notice of Cancellation Motor Carrier Policies of Insurance under 49 U.S.C. 13906, and BMC-36, Notice of Cancellation Motor Carrier and Broker Surety Bonds, as appropriate) by the insurance company, surety or sureties, motor carrier, broker or other party thereto, as the case may be, which period of thirty (30) days shall commence to run from the date such notice on the prescribed form is actually received by the Commission.

(e) **Termination by replacement.** Certificates of insurance or surety bonds which have been accepted by the Commission under these rules may be replaced by other certificates of insurance, surety bonds or other security, and the liability of the retiring insurer or surety under such certificates of insurance or surety bonds shall be considered as having terminated as of the effective date of the replacement certificate of insurance, surety bond or other security, provided the said replacement certificate, bond or other security is acceptable to the Commission under the rules and regulations in this part.

CROSS REFERENCE: For list of forms prescribed, see §1003.1(b) of this chapter.

§387.315 Insurance and surety companies.

A certificate of insurance or surety bond will not be accepted by the Commission unless issued by an insurance or surety company that is authorized (licensed or admitted) to issue bonds or underlying insurance policies:

(a) In each state in which the motor carrier is authorized by the Commission to operate, or

(b) In the state in which the motor carrier has its principal place of business or domicile, and will designate in writing upon request by the Commission, a person upon whom process, issued by or under the authority of a court of competent jurisdiction, may be served in any proceeding at law or equity brought in any state in which the carrier operates, or

(c) In any state, and is eligible as an excess or surplus lines insurer in any state in which business is written, and will make the designation of process agent described in paragraph (b) of this section.

§387.317 Refusal to accept, or revocation by the FHWA of surety bonds, etc.

The Commission may, at any time, refuse to accept or, may revoke its acceptance of any surety bond, certificate of insurance, qualifications as a self-insurer, or other securities or agreements if, in its judgment such security does not comply with these sections or for any reason fails to provide satisfactory or adequate protection for the public. Revocation of acceptance of any certificate of insurance, surety bond or other security shall not relieve the motor carrier from compliance with §387.301(d).

§387.319 Fiduciaries.

(a) **Definitions.** The terms "insured" and "principal" as used in a certificate of insurance, surety bond, and notice of cancellation, filed by or for a motor carrier, include the motor carrier and its fiduciary as the moment of succession. The term "fiduciary" means any person authorized by law to collect and preserve property of incapacitated, financially disabled, bankrupt, or deceased holders of operating rights, and assignees of such holders.

(b) Insurance coverage in behalf of fiduciaries to apply concurrently. The coverage furnished under the provisions of this section on behalf of fiduciaries shall not apply subsequent to the effective date of other insurance, or other security, filed with and approved by the Commission in behalf of such fiduciaries. After the coverage provided in this section shall have been in effect thirty (30) days, it may be cancelled or withdrawn within the succeeding period of thirty (30) days by the insurer, the insured, the surety, or the principal upon ten (10) days' notice in writing to the Commission at its office in Washington, D.C., which period of ten (10) days shall commence to run from the date such notice is actually received by the Commission. After such coverage has been in effect for a total of sixty (60) days, it may be cancelled or withdrawn only in accordance with §1043.7.

§387.321 Operations in foreign commerce.

No motor carrier may operate in the United States in the course of transportation between places in a foreign country or between a place in one foreign country and a place in another foreign country unless and until there shall have been filed with and accepted by the Commission a certificate of insurance, surety bond, proof of qualifications as a self-insurer, or other securities or agreements in the amount prescribed in §387.303(b), conditioned to pay any final judgment recovered against such motor carrier for bodily injuries to or the death of any person resulting from the negligent operation, maintenance, or use of motor vehicles in transportation between places in a foreign country or between a place in one foreign country and a place in another foreign country, insofar as such transportation takes place in the United States, or for loss of or damage to property of others. The security for the protection of the public required by this section shall be maintained in effect at all times and shall be subject to the provisions of §§387.309 through 387.319. The requirements of §387.315(a) shall be satisfied if the insurance or surety company, in addition to having been approved by this Commission, is legally authorized to issue policies or surety bonds in at least one of the States in the United States, or one of the Provinces in Canada, and has filed with this Commission the name and address of a person upon whom legal process may be served in each State in or through which the motor carrier operates. Such designation may from time to time be changed by like designation similarly filed, but shall be maintained during the effectiveness of any certificate of insurance or surety bond issued by the company, and thereafter with respect to any claims arising during the effectiveness of such certificate or bond. The term "motor carrier" as used in this section shall not include private carriers or carriers operating under the partial exemption from regulation in 49 U.S.C. 13503 and 13506.

§387.323 Electronic filing of surety bonds, trust fund agreements, certificates of insurance and cancellations.

(a) Insurers may, at their option and in accordance with the requirements and procedures set forth in paragraphs (a) through (d) of this section, file forms BMC 34, BMC 35, BMC 36, BMC 82, BMC 83, BMC 84 BMC 85, BMC 91, and BMC 91X electronically, in lieu of using the prescribed printed forms.

(b) Each insurer must obtain authorization to file electronically by registering with the Commission. An individual account number and password for computer access will be issued to each registered insurer.

(c) All files to be transmitted must be in an ASCII fixed format, i.e., all records must have the same number of fields and same length. The record layouts for electronic filing transactions are as described in the following table:

ELECTRONIC INSURANCE FILING TRANSACTIONS

Field name	Number of positions	Description	Required F=filing C=cancel B=both	Start field	End field
Record type	1 Numeric	1 = Filing	B	1	1
		2 = Cancellation			
Insurer number .	8 Text	ICC Assigned Insurer Number (Home Office) With Suffix (Issuing Office). If Different, e.g. 12345-01.	B	2	9
Filing type	1 Numeric	1 = BI & PD	B	10	10
		2 = Cargo			
		3 = Bond			
		4 = Trust Fund			
ICC docket number......	8 Text	ICC Assigned MC or FF Number, e.g., MC000045.	B	11	18

ELECTRONIC INSURANCE FILING TRANSACTIONS, Continued

Field name	Number of positions	Description	Required F=filing C=cancel B=both	Start field	End field
Insured legal name	120 Text ..	Legal Name	B	19	138
Insured d/b/a name ...	60 Text	Doing Business As Name If Different From Legal Name.	B	139	198
Insured address .	35 Text	Either street or mailing address	B	199	233
Insured city	30 Text	....	B	234	263
Insured state	2 Text	....	B	264	265
Insured zip code	9 Numeric	(Do not include dash if using 9 digit code)	B	266	274
Insured country .	2 Text	(Will default to US) ...	B	275	276
Form code	10 Text	BMC-91, BMC-91X, BMC-34, BMC-35, ETC	B	277	286
Full, primary or excess coverage ...	1 Text	If BMC-91X, P or E = indicator of primary or excess policy; 1 = Full under §387.303(b)(1); 2 = Full under §387.303(b)(2).	F	287	287
Limit of liability ..	5 Numeric	$ in Thousands	F	288	292
Underlying limit of liability ..	5 Numeric	$ in Thousands (will default to $000 if Primary).	F	293	297

ELECTRONIC INSURANCE FILING TRANSACTIONS, Continued

Field name	Number of positions	Description	Required F=filing C=cancel B=both	Start field	End field
Effective date	8 Text	MM/DD/YY Format for both Filing or Cancellation.	B	298	305
Policy number .	25 Text	Surety companies may enter bond number.	B	306	330

(d) All registered insurers agree to furnish upon request to the Commission a duplicate original of any policy (or policies) and all endorsements, surety bond, trust fund agreement, or other filing.

Subpart D — Surety Bonds and Policies of Insurance for Freight Forwarders

§387.401 Definitions.

(a) **Freight forwarder** means a person holding itself out to the general public (other than as an express, pipeline, rail. sleeping car, motor, or water carrier) to provide transportation of property for compensation in interstate commerce, and in the ordinary course of its business:

(1) Performs or provides for assembling, consolidating, break-bulk, and distribution of shipments; and

(2) Assumes responsibility for transportation from place of receipt to destination; and

(3) Uses for any part of the transportation a carrier subject to Commission jurisdiction.

(b) **Household goods freight forwarder** (HHGFF) means a freight forwarder of household goods, unaccompanied baggage, or used automobiles.

(c) **Motor vehicle** means any vehicle, machine, tractor, trailer, or semitrailer propelled or drawn by mechanical power and used to transport property, but does not include any vehicle, locomotive, or car operated exclusively on a rail or rails. The following combinations will be regarded as one motor vehicle:

(1) A tractor that draws a trailer or semitrailer; and
(2) A truck and trailer bearing a single load.

§387.403 General requirements.

(a) **Cargo**. A freight forwarder (including a HHGFF) may not operate until it has filed with the Commission an appropriate surety bond, certificate of insurance, qualifications as a self-insurer, or other securities or agreements, in the amounts prescribed at §387.405, for loss of or damage to property.

(b) **Public liability.** A HHGFF may not perform transfer, collection, and delivery service until it has filed with the Commission and appropriate surety bond, certificate of insurance, qualifications as a self-insurer, or other securities or agreements, in the amounts prescribed at §387.405, conditioned to pay any final judgment recovered against such HHGFF for bodily injury to or the death of any person, or loss of or damage to property (except cargo) of others, or, in the case of freight vehicles described at 49 CFR 387.303(b)(2), for environmental restoration, resulting from the negligent operation, maintenance, or use of motor vehicles operated by or under its control in performing such service.

§387.405 Limits of liability.

The minimum amounts for cargo and public liability security are identical to those prescribed for motor carriers at 49 CFR 387.303.

§387.407 Surety bonds and certificates of insurance.

(a) The limits of liability under §387.405 may be provided by aggregation under the procedures at 49 CFR part 387, subpart C.

(b) Each policy of insurance used in connection with a certificate of insurance filed with the Commission shall be amended by attachment of the appropriate endorsement prescribed by the Commission (or the Department of Transportation, where applicable).

§387.409 Insurance and surety companies.

A certificate of insurance or surety bond will not be accepted by the Commission unless issued by an insurance or surety company that is authorized (licensed or admitted) to issue bonds or underlying insurance policies:

(a) In each state in which the freight forwarder is authorized by the Commission to perform service, or

(b) In the state in which the freight forwarder has its principal place of business or domicile, and will designate in writing upon request by the Commission, a person upon whom process, issued by or under the authority of a court of competent jurisdiction, may be served in any proceeding at law or equity brought in any State in which the freight forwarder performs service; or

(c) In any state, and is eligible as an excess or surplus lines insurer in any State in which business is written, and will make the designation of process agent prescribed in paragraph (b) of this section.

§387.411 Qualifications as a self-insurer and other securities or agreements.

(a) **Self-insurer.** The Commission will approve the application of a freight forwarder to qualify as a self-insurer if it is able to meet its obligations for bodily-injury, property-damage, and cargo liability without adversely affecting its business.

(b) **Other securities and agreements.** The Commission will grant applications for approval of other securities and agreements if the public will be protected as contemplated by 49 U.S.C. 13906(c).

§387.413 Forms and procedure.

(a) **Forms.** Endorsements for policies of insurance, surety bonds, certificates of insurance, applications to qualify as a self-insurer or for approval of other securities or agreements and notices of cancellation must be in the form prescribed at 49 CFR part 387, subpart C.

CROSS REFERENCE: For list of forms prescribed, see §1003.3 of this chapter.

(b) **Procedure.** Certificates of insurance, surety bonds and notices of cancellation must be filed with the Commission in triplicate.

(c) **Names.** Certificates of insurance and surety bonds shall be issued in the full name (including any trade name) of the individual, partnership (all partners named), corporation, or other person holding or to be issued the permit.

(d) **Cancellation.** Except as provided in paragraph (e) of this section, certificates of insurance, surety bonds and other securities and agreements shall not be cancelled or withdrawn until 30 days after the Commission receives written notice from the insurance company, surety, freight forwarder, or other party, as the case may be.

(e) **Termination by replacement.** Certificates of insurance or surety bonds may be replaced by other certificates of insurance, surety bonds or other security, and the liability of the retiring insurer or surety shall be considered as having terminated as of the replacement's effective date, if acceptable to the Commission.

§387.415 Acceptance and revocation by the FHWA.

The Commission may at any time refuse to accept or may revoke its acceptance of any surety bond, certificate of insurance, qualifications as a self-insurer, or other security or agreement that does not comply with these rules or fails to provide adequate public protection.

§387.417 Fiduciaries.

(a) **Interpretations.** The terms "insured" and "principal" as used in a certificate of insurance, surety bond, and notice of cancellation, filed by or for a freight forwarder, include the freight forwarder and its fiduciary (as defined at 49 CFR 387.319(a)) as of the moment of succession.

(b) **Span of security coverage.** The coverage furnished for a fiduciary shall not apply after the effective date of other insurance or security, filed with and accepted by the Commission for such fiduciary. After the coverage shall have been in effect 30 days, it may be cancelled or withdrawn within the succeeding 30 days by the insurer, the insured, the surety, or the principal 10 days after the Commission receives written notice. After such coverage has been in effect 60 days, it may be cancelled or withdrawn only in accordance with §387.413(d).

§387.419 Electronic filing of surety bonds, certificates of insurance and cancellations.

Insurers may, at their option and in accordance with the requirements and procedures set forth at 49 CFR 387.323, file certificates of insurance, surety bonds, and other securities and agreements electronically.

PART 390 — GENERAL

Subpart A — General Applicability and Definitions

Subpart B — General Requirements and Information

Subpart C — [Removed and reserved.]

Subpart D — [Removed and reserved.]

AUTHORITY: 49 U.S.C. 13301, 13902, 31132, 31133, 31136, 31502, 31504; sec. 204, Pub. L. 104-88, 109 Stat. 803, 941 (49 U.S.C. 701 note); sec. 217, Pub. L. 105-159, 113 Stat. 1748, 1767; and 49 CFR 1.73.

Subpart A — General Applicability and Definitions

§390.1 Purpose.

This part establishes general applicability, definitions, general requirements and information as they pertain to persons subject to this chapter.

§390.3 General applicability.

(a) The rules in Subchapter B of this chapter are applicable to all employers, employees, and commercial motor vehicles, which transport property or passengers in interstate commerce.

(b) The rules in Part 383, Commercial Driver's License Standards; Requirements and Penalties, are applicable to every person who operates a commercial motor vehicle, as defined in §383.5 of this subchapter, in interstate or intrastate commerce and to all employers of such persons.

(c) The rules in Part 387, Minimum levels of financial responsibility for motor carriers, are applicable to motor carriers as provided in §§387.3 or 387.27 of this subchapter.

(d) **Additional requirements.** Nothing in Subchapter B of this chapter shall be construed to prohibit an employer from requiring and enforcing more stringent requirements relating to safety of operation and employee safety and health.

(e) **Knowledge of and compliance with the regulations.**

(1) Every employer shall be knowledgeable of and comply with all regulations contained in this subchapter which are applicable to that motor carrier's operations.

(2) Every driver and employee shall be instructed regarding, and shall comply with, all applicable regulations contained in this subchapter.

(3) All motor vehicle equipment and accessories required by this subchapter shall be maintained in compliance with all applicable performance and design criteria set forth in this subchapter.

(f) **Exceptions.** Unless otherwise specifically provided, the rules in this subchapter do not apply to—

(1) All school bus operations as defined in §390.5;

(2) Transportation performed by the Federal government, a State, or any political subdivision of a State, or an agency established under a compact between States that has been approved by the Congress of the United States;

(3) The occasional transportation of personal property by individuals not for compensation nor in the furtherance of a commercial enterprise;

(4) The transportation of human corpses or sick and injured persons;

(5) The operation of fire trucks and rescue vehicles while involved in emergency and related operations;

(6) The operation of commercial motor vehicles designed or used to transport between 9 to 15 passengers (including the driver). However, motor carriers operating these vehicles for compensation are required to comply with 49 CFR 385.21, Motor carrier identification report, 49 CFR 390.15, Assistance in investigations and special studies, and 49 CFR 390.21, Marking of commercial motor vehicles (except §390.21(b)(1)).

§390.5 Definitions.

Unless specifically defined elsewhere, in this subchapter:

Accident means—

(1) Except as provided in paragraph (2) of this definition, an occurrence involving a commercial motor vehicle operating on a highway in interstate or intrastate commerce which results in:

(i) A fatality;

(ii) Bodily injury to a person who, as a result of the injury, immediately receives medical treatment away from the scene of the accident; or

(iii) One or more motor vehicles incurring disabling damage as a result of the accident, requiring the motor vehicles to be transported away from the scene by a tow truck or other motor vehicle.

(2) The term *accident* does not include:

(i) An occurrence involving only boarding and alighting from a stationary motor vehicle; or

(ii) An occurrence involving only the loading or unloading of cargo.

Alcohol concentration (AC) means the concentration of alcohol in a person's blood or breath. When expressed as a percentage it means grams of alcohol per 100 milliliters of blood or grams of alcohol per 210 liters of breath.

Bus means any motor vehicle designed, constructed, and or used for the transportation of passengers, including taxicabs.

Business district means the territory contiguous to and including a highway when within any 600 feet along such highway there are buildings in use for business or industrial purposes, including but not limited to hotels, banks, or office buildings which occupy at least 300 feet of frontage on one side or 300 feet collectively on both sides of the highway.

Charter transportation of passengers means transportation, using a bus, of a group of persons who pursuant to a common purpose, under a single contract, at a fixed charge for the motor vehicle, have acquired the exclusive use of the motor vehicle to travel together under an itinerary either specified in advance or modified after having left the place of origin.

Commercial motor vehicle means any self-propelled or towed motor vehicle used on a highway in interstate commerce to transport passengers or property when the vehicle—

(1) Has a gross vehicle weight rating or gross combination weight rating, or gross vehicle weight or gross combination weight, of 4,536 kg (10,001 pounds) or more, whichever is greater; or

(2) Is designed or used to transport more than 8 passengers (including the driver) for compensation; or

(3) Is designed or used to transport more than 15 passengers, including the driver, and is not used to transport passengers for compensation; or

(4) Is used in transporting material found by the Secretary of Transportation to be hazardous under 49 U.S.C. 5103 and transported in a quantity requiring placarding under regulations prescribed by the Secretary under 49 CFR, subtitle B, chapter I, subchapter C.

Conviction means an unvacated adjudication of guilt, or a determination that a person has violated or failed to comply with the law in a court of original jurisdiction or by an authorized administrative tribunal, an unvacated forfeiture of bail or collateral deposited to secure the person's appearance in court, a plea of guilty or nolo contendere accepted by the court, the payment of a fine or court cost, or violation of a condition of release without bail, regardless of whether or not the penalty is rebated, suspended, or probated.

Direct Assistance means transportation and other relief services provided by a motor carrier or its driver(s) incident to the immediate restoration of essential services (such as, electricity, medical care, sewer, water, telecommunications, and telecommunication transmissions) or essential supplies (such as, food and fuel). It does not include transportation related to long-term rehabilitation of damaged physical infrastructure or routine commercial deliveries after the initial threat to life and property has passed.

Disabling damage means damage which precludes departure of a motor vehicle from the scene of the accident in its usual manner in daylight after simple repairs.

(1) *Inclusions.* Damage to motor vehicles that could have been driven, but would have been further damaged if so driven.

(2) *Exclusions.*

(i) Damage which can be remedied temporarily at the scene of the accident without special tools or parts.

(ii) Tire disablement without other damage even if no spare tire is available.

(iii) Headlamp or taillight damage.

(iv) Damage to turn signals, horn, or windshield wipers which makes them inoperative.

Driveaway-towaway operation means any operation in which a motor vehicle constitutes the commodity being transported and one or more set of wheels of the motor vehicle being transported are on the surface of the roadway during transportation.

Driver means any person who operates any commercial motor vehicle.

Driving a commercial motor vehicle while under the influence of alcohol means committing any one or more of the following acts in a CMV: driving a CMV while the person's alcohol concentration is 0.04 percent or more; driving under the influence of alcohol, as prescribed by State law; or refusal to undergo such testing as is required by any State or jurisdiction in the enforcement of §383.51(b)(2)(i)(A) or (B), or §392.5(a)(2).

Emergency means any hurricane, tornado, storm (e.g. thunderstorm, snowstorm, icestorm, blizzard, sandstorm, etc.), high water, wind-driven water, tidal wave, tsunami, earthquake, volcanic eruption, mud slide, drought, forest fire, explosion, blackout or other occurrence, natural or man-made, which interrupts the delivery of essential services (such as, electricity, medical care, sewer, water, telecommunications, and telecommunication transmissions) or essential supplies (such as, food and fuel) or otherwise immediately threatens human life or public welfare, provided such hurricane, tornado or other event results in:

(1) A declaration of an emergency by the President of the United States, the Governor of a State, or their authorized representatives having authority to declare emergencies; by the Regional Director of Motor Carriers for the region in which the occurrence happens; or by other Federal, State or local government officials having authority to declare emergencies; or

(2) A request by a police officer for tow trucks to move wrecked or disabled motor vehicles.

Emergency relief means an operation in which a motor carrier or driver of a commercial motor vehicle is providing direct assistance to supplement State and local efforts and capabilities to save lives or property or to protect public health and safety as a result of an emergency as defined in this section.

Employee means any individual, other than an employer, who is employed by an employer and who in the course of his or her employment directly affects commercial motor vehicle safety. Such term includes a driver of a commercial motor vehicle (including an independent contractor while in the course of operating a commercial motor vehicle), a mechanic, and a freight handler. Such term does not include an employee of the United States, any State, any political subdivision of a State, or any agency established under a compact between States and approved by the Congress of the United States who is acting within the course of such employment.

Employer means any person engaged in a business affecting interstate commerce who owns or leases a commercial motor vehicle in connection with that business, or assigns employees to operate it, but such term does not include the United States, any state, any political subdivision of a State, or an agency established under a compact between States approved by the Congress of the United States.

Exempt intracity zone means the geographic area of a municipality or the commercial zone of that municipality described by the FHWA in 49 CFR part 372, subpart B. The descriptions are printed in Appendix F to Subchapter B of this Chapter. The term "exempt intracity zone" does not include any municipality or commercial zone in the State of Hawaii. For purposes of §391.2(d), a driver may be considered to operate a commercial motor vehicle wholly within an exempt intracity zone notwithstanding any common control, management, or arrangement for a continuous carriage or shipment to or from a point without such zone.

Exempt motor carrier means a person engaged in transportation exempt from economic regulation by the Interstate Commerce Commission (ICC) under 49 U.S.C. 10526, "Exempt motor carriers" are subject to the safety regulations set forth in this subchapter.

Farm vehicle driver means a person who drives only a commercial motor vehicle that is—

(a) Controlled and operated by a farmer as a private motor carrier of property;

(b) Being used to transport either—

(1) Agricultural products, or

(2) Farm machinery, farm supplies, or both, to or from a farm;

(c) Not being used in the operation of a for-hire motor carrier;

(d) Not carrying hazardous materials of a type or quantity that requires the commercial motor vehicle to be placarded in accordance with §177.823 of this subtitle; and

(e) Being used within 150 air-miles of the farmer's farm.

Farmer means any person who operates a farm or is directly involved in the cultivation of land, crops, or livestock which—

(a) Are owned by that person; or

(b) Are under the direct control of that person.

Fatality means any injury which results in the death of a person at the time of the motor vehicle accident or within 30 days of the accident.

Federal Highway Administrator means the chief executive of the Federal Highway Administration, an agency within the Department of Transportation.

For-hire motor carrier means a person engaged in the transportation of goods or passengers for compensation.

Gross combination weight rating (GCWR) means the value specified by the manufacturer as the loaded weight of a combination (articulated) motor vehicle. In the absence of a value specified by the manufacturer, GCWR will be determined by adding the GVWR of the power unit and the total weight of the towed unit and any load thereon.

Gross vehicle weight rating (GVWR) means the value specified by the manufacturer as the loaded weight of a single motor vehicle.

Hazardous material means a substance or material which has been determined by the Secretary of Transportation to be capable of posing an unreasonable risk to health, safety, and property when transported in commerce, and which has been so designated.

Hazardous substance means a material, and its mixtures or solutions, that is identified in the appendix to §172.101, List of Hazardous Substances and Reportable Quantities, of this title when offered for transportation in one package, or in one transport motor vehicle if not packaged, and when the quantity of the material therein equals or exceeds the reportable quantity (RQ). This definition does not apply to petroleum products that are lubricants or fuels, or to mixtures or solutions of hazardous substances if in a concentration less than that shown in the table in §171.8 of this title, based on the reportable quantity (RQ) specified for the materials listed in the Appendix to §172.101.

Hazardous waste means any material that is subject to the hazardous waste manifest requirements of the EPA specified in 40 CFR Part 262 or would be subject to these requirements absent an interim authorization to a State under 40 CFR Part 123, Subpart F.

Highway means any road, street, or way, whether on public or private property, open to public travel, "Open to public travel" means that the road section is available, except during scheduled periods, extreme weather or emergency conditions, passable by four-wheel standard passenger cars, and open to the general public for use without restrictive gates, prohibitive signs, or regulation other than restrictions based on size, weight, or class of registration. Toll plazas of public toll roads are not considered restrictive gates.

Interstate commerce means trade, traffic, or transportation in the United States—

(1) Between a place in a State and a place outside of such State (including a place outside of the United States);

(2) Between two places in a State through another State or a place outside of the United States; or

(3) Between two places in a State as part of trade, traffic, or transportation originating or terminating outside the State or the United States.

Intrastate commerce means any trade, traffic, or transportation in any State which is not described in the term "interstate commerce."

Medical examiner means a person who is licensed, certified, and/or registered, in accordance with applicable State laws and regulations, to perform physical examinations. The term includes, but is not limited to, doctors of medicine, doctors of osteopathy, physician assistants, advanced practice nurses, and doctors of chiropractic.

Motor carrier means a for-hire motor carrier or a private motor carrier. The term includes a motor carrier's agents, officers and representatives as well as employees responsible for hiring, supervising, training, assigning, or dispatching of drivers and employees concerned with the installation, inspection, and maintenance of motor vehicle equipment and/or accessories. For purposes of subchapter B, this definition includes the terms **employer** and **exempt motor carrier**.

Motor vehicle means any vehicle, machine, tractor, trailer, or semitrailer propelled or drawn by mechanical power and used upon the highways in the transportation of passengers or property, or any combination thereof determined by the Federal Highway Administration, but does not include any vehicle, locomotive, or car operated exclusively on a rail or rails, or a trolley bus operated by electric power derived from a fixed overhead wire, furnishing local passenger transportation similar to street-railway service.

Multiple-employer driver means a driver, who in any period of 7 consecutive days, is employed or used as a driver by more than one motor carrier.

Operator — See driver.

Other terms — Any other term used in this subchapter is used in its commonly accepted meaning, except where such other term has been defined elsewhere in this subchapter. In that event, the definition therein given shall apply.

Out-of-service order means a declaration by an authorized enforcement officer of a Federal, State, Canadian, Mexican, or local jurisdiction that a driver, a commercial motor vehicle, or a motor carrier operation, is out-of-service pursuant to §§386.72, 392.5, 395.13, 396.9, or compatible laws, or the North American Uniform Out-of-Service Criteria.

Person means any individual, partnership, association, corporation, business trust, or any other organized group of individuals.

Principal place of business means the single location desıgnated by the motor carrier, normally its headquarters, for purposes of identification under this subchapter. The motor carrier must make records required by parts 382, 387, 390, 391, 395, 396, and 397 of this subchapter available for inspection at this location within 48 hours (Saturdays, Sundays, and Federal holidays excluded) after a request has been made by a special agent or authorized representative of the Federal Highway Administration.

Private motor carrier means a person who provides transportation of property or passengers, by commercial motor vehicle, and is not a for-hire motor carrier.

Private motor carrier of passengers (business) means a private motor carrier engaged in the interstate transportation of passengers which is provided in the furtherance of a commercial enterprise and is not available to the public at large.

Private motor carrier of passengers (nonbusiness) means private motor carrier involved in the interstate transportation of passengers that does not otherwise meet the definition of a private motor carrier of passengers (business).

Radar detector means any device or mechanism to detect the emission of radio microwaves, laser beams or any other future speed measurement technology employed by enforcement personnel to measure the speed of commercial motor vehicles upon public roads and highways for enforcement purposes. Excluded from this definition are radar detection devices that meet both of the following requirements:

(1) Transported outside the driver's compartment of the commercial motor vehicle. For this purpose, the *driver's compartment* of a passenger-carrying CMV shall include all space designed to accommodate both the driver and the passengers; and

(2) Completely inaccessible to, inoperable by, and imperceptible to the driver while operating the commercial motor vehicle.

Regional Director of Motor Carriers means the Director of the Office of Motor Carriers, Federal Highway Administration, for a given geographical region of the United States.

Residential district means the territory adjacent to and including a highway which is not a business district and for a distance of 300 feet or more along the highway is primarily improved with residences.

School bus means a passenger motor vehicle which is designed or used to carry more than 10 passengers in addition to the driver, and which the Secretary determines is likely to be significantly used for the purpose of transporting preprimary, primary, or secondary school students to such schools from home or from such schools to home.

School bus operation means the use of a school bus to transport only school children and/or school personnel from home to school and from school to home.

Secretary means the Secretary of Transportation.

Single-employer driver means a driver who, in any period of 7 consecutive days, is employed or used as a driver solely by a single motor carrier. This term includes a driver who operates a commercial motor vehicle on an intermittent, casual, or occasional basis.

Special agent See Appendix B to Subchapter B — Special agents.

State means a State of the United States and the District of Columbia and includes a political subdivision of a State.

Trailer includes:

(a) **Full trailer** means any motor vehicle other than a pole trailer which is designed to be drawn by another motor vehicle and so constructed that no part of its weight, except for the towing device, rests upon the self-propelled towing motor vehicle. A semitrailer equipped with an auxiliary front axle (converter dolly) shall be considered a full trailer.

(b) **Pole trailer** means any motor vehicle which is designed to be drawn by another motor vehicle and attached to the towing motor vehicle by means of a "reach" or "pole," or by being "boomed" or otherwise secured to the towing motor vehicle, for transporting long or irregularly shaped loads such as poles, pipes, or structural members, which generally are capable of sustaining themselves as beams between the supporting connections.

(c) **Semitrailer** means any motor vehicle, other than a pole trailer, which is designed to be drawn by another motor vehicle and is constructed so that some part of its weight rests upon the self-propelled towing motor vehicle.

Truck means any self-propelled commercial motor vehicle except a truck tractor, designed and/or used for the transportation of property.

Truck tractor means a self-propelled commercial motor vehicle designed and/or used primarily for drawing other vehicles.

United States means the 50 States and the District of Columbia.

§390.7 Rules of construction.

(a) In Part 325 of Subchapter A and in this subchapter, unless the context requires otherwise:

(1) Words imparting the singular include the plural;

(2) Words imparting the plural include the singular;

(3) Words imparting the present tense include the future tense.

(b) In this subchapter the word—

(1) **"Officer"** includes any person authorized by law to perform the duties of the office;

(2) **"Writing"** includes printing and typewriting;

(3) **"Shall"** is used in an imperative sense;

(4) **"Must"** is used in an imperative sense;

(5) **"Should"** is used in a recommendatory sense;

(6) **"May"** is used in a permissive sense; and

(7) **"Includes"** is used as a word of inclusion, not limitation.

Subpart B — General Requirements and Information

§390.9 State and local laws, effect on.

Except as otherwise specifically indicated, Subchapter B of this chapter is not intended to preclude States or subdivisions thereof from establishing or enforcing State or local laws relating to safety, the compliance with which would not prevent full compliance with these regulations by the person subject thereto.

§390.11 Motor carrier to require observance of driver regulations.

Whenever in Part 325 of Subchapter A or in this subchapter a duty is prescribed for a driver or a prohibition is imposed upon the driver, it shall be the duty of the motor carrier to require observance of such duty or prohibition. If the motor carrier is a driver, the driver shall likewise be bound.

§390.13 Aiding or abetting violations.

No person shall aid, abet, encourage, or require a motor carrier or its employees to violate the rules of this chapter.

§390.15 Assistance in investigations and special studies.

(a) A motor carrier shall make all records and information pertaining to an accident available to an authorized representative or special agent of the Federal Highway Administration upon request or as part of any inquiry within such time as the request or inquiry may specify. A motor carrier shall give an authorized representative of the Federal Highway Administration all reasonable assistance in the investigation of any accident including providing a full, true and correct answer to any question of the inquiry.

(b) Motor carriers shall maintain for a period of one year after an accident occurs, an accident register containing at least the following information:

(1) A list of accidents containing for each accident:

(i) Date of accident,

(ii) City or town in which or most near where the accident occurred and the State in which the accident occurred,

(iii) Driver name,

(iv) Number of injuries,

(v) Number of fatalities, and

(vi) Whether hazardous materials, other than fuel spilled from the fuel tanks of motor vehicles involved in the accident, were released.

(2) Copies of all accident reports required by State or other governmental entities or insurers.

(Approved by the Office of Management and Budget under control number 2125-0526)

§390.17 Additional equipment and accessories.

Nothing in this subchapter shall be construed to prohibit the use of additional equipment and accessories, not inconsistent with or prohibited by this subchapter, provided such equipment and accessories do not decrease the safety of operation of the commercial motor vehicles on which they are used.

§390.19 Motor carrier identification report.

(a) Each motor carrier that conducts operations in interstate commerce must file a Motor Carrier Identification Report, form MCS–150 at the following times:

(1) Before it begins operations; and

(2) Every 24 months, according to the following schedule:

USDOT Number ending in:	Must file by last day of:
1	January.
2	February.
3	March.
4	April.
5	May.
6	June.
7	July.
8	August.
9	September.
0	October.

(3) If the next-to-last digit of its USDOT number is odd, the motor carrier shall file its update in every odd-numbered calendar year. If the next-to-last digit of the USDOT number is even, the motor carrier shall file its update in every even-numbered calendar year.

(4) Notwithstanding the schedule set forth in paragraph (a)(2) of this section, a motor carrier that would be required to file the MCS-150 by the end of January or February, 2001 must file the form by the end of March, 2001.

(b) The Motor Carrier Identification Report, Form MCS-150, with complete instructions, is available from all FMCSA Service Centers and Division offices nationwide and from the FMCSA's web site at: *http://www.mcs.dot.gov/factsfigs/formspubs.htm* or by calling 1-800-832-5660.

(c) The completed Motor Carrier Identification Report, Form MCS-150, shall be filed with the FMCSA's Office of Data Analysis and Information Systems, 400 Seventh Street, SW., Washington, DC 20590. A for-hire motor carrier should submit the Form MCS-150 along with its application for operating authority (Form OP-1) to the appropriate address referenced on that form or may submit it separately to the address mentioned in this section.

(d) Only the legal name or a single trade name of the motor carrier may be used on the motor carrier identification report (Form MCS-150).

(e) A motor carrier that fails to file a Motor Carrier Identification Report, Form MCS-150, or furnishes misleading information or makes false statements upon form MCS-150, is subject to the penalties prescribed in 49 U.S.C. 521(b)(2)(B).

(f) Upon receipt and processing of the Motor Carrier Identification Report, form MCS-150, the FMCSA will issue the motor carrier an identification number (USDOT number). The motor carrier must display the number on each self-propelled CMV, as defined in §390.5, along with the additional information required by §390.21.

(g) A motor carrier that registers its vehicles in a State that participates in the Performance and Registration Information Systems Management (PRISM) program (authorized under section 4004 of the Transportation Equity Act for the 21st Century [(Public Law 105-178, 112 Stat. 107)] is exempt from the requirements of this section, provided it files all the required information with the appropriate State office.

[Approved by the Office of Management and Budget under control number 2126-0013]

§390.21 Marking of CMVs.

(a) **General.** Every self-propelled CMV, as defined in §390.5, subject to subchapter B of this chapter must be marked as specified in paragraphs (b), (c), and (d) of this section.

(b) **Nature of marking.** The marking must display the following information:

(1) The legal name or a single trade name of the motor carrier operating the self-propelled CMV, as listed on the motor carrier identification report (Form MCS-150) and submitted in accordance with §390.19.

(2) The motor carrier identification number issued by the FMCSA, preceded by the letters "USDOT".

(3) If the name of any person other than the operating carrier appears on the CMV, the name of the operating carrier must be followed by the information required by paragraphs (b)(1), and (2) of this section, and be preceded by the words "operated by."

(4) Other identifying information may be displayed on the vehicle if it is not inconsistent with the information required by this paragraph.

(5) Each motor carrier shall meet the following requirements pertaining to its operation:

(i) All CMVs that are part of a motor carrier's existing fleet on July 3, 2000, and which are marked with an ICCMC number must come into compliance with paragraph (b)(2) of this section by July 3, 2002.

(ii) All CMVs that are part of a motor carrier's existing fleet on July 3, 2000, and which are not marked with the legal name or a single trade name on both sides of their CMVs, as shown on the Motor Carrier Identification Report, Form MCS–150, must come into compliance with paragraph (b)(1) of this section by July 5, 2005.

(iii) All CMVs added to a motor carrier's fleet on or after July 3, 2000, must meet the requirements of this section before being put into service and operating on public ways.

(c) **Size, shape, location, and color of marking.** The marking must—

(1) Appear on both sides of the self-propelled CMV;

(2) Be in letters that contrast sharply in color with the background on which the letters are placed;

(3) Be readily legible, during daylight hours, from a distance of 50 feet (15.24 meters) while the CMV is stationary; and

(4) Be kept and maintained in a manner that retains the legibility required by paragraph (c)(3) of this section.

(d) **Construction and durability.** The marking may be painted on the CMV or may consist of a removable device, if that device meets the identification and legibility requirements of paragraph (c) of this section, and such marking must be maintained as required by paragraph (c)(4) of this section.

(e) **Rented CMVs.** A motor carrier operating a self-propelled CMV under a rental agreement having a term not in excess of 30 calendar days meets the requirements of this section if:

(1) The CMV is marked in accordance with the provisions of paragraphs (b) through (d) of this section; or

(2) The CMV is marked as set forth in paragraph (e)(2)(i) through (iv) of this section:

(i) The legal name or a single trade name of the lessor is displayed in accordance with paragraphs (c) and (d) of this section.

(ii) The lessor's identification number preceded by the letters "USDOT" is displayed in accordance with paragraphs (c) and (d) of this section; and

(iii) The rental agreement entered into by the lessor and the renting motor carrier conspicuously contains the following information:

(A) The name and complete physical address of the principal place of business of the renting motor carrier.

(B) The identification number issued the renting motor carrier by the FMCSA, preceded by the letters "USDOT," if the motor carrier has been issued such a number. In lieu of the identification number required in this paragraph, the following may be shown in the rental agreement:

(1) Information which indicates whether the motor carrier is engaged in "interstate" or "intrastate" commerce; and

(2) Information which indicates whether the renting motor carrier is transporting hazardous materials in the rented CMV;

(C) The sentence: "This lessor cooperates with all Federal, State, and local law enforcement officials nationwide to provide the identity of customers who operate this rental CMV"; and

(iv) The rental agreement entered into by the lessor and the renting motor carrier is carried on the rental CMV during the full term of the rental agreement. See the leasing regulations at 49 CFR 376 for information that should be included in all leasing documents.

(f) **Driveaway services.** In driveaway services, a removable device may be affixed on both sides or at the rear of a single driven vehicle. In a combination driveaway operation, the device may be affixed on both sides of any one unit or at the rear of the last unit. The removable device must display the legal name or a single trade name of the motor carrier and the motor carrier's USDOT number.

§390.23 Relief from regulations.

(a) Parts 390 through 399 of this chapter shall not apply to any motor carrier or driver operating a commercial motor vehicle to provide emergency relief during an emergency, subject to the following time limits:

(1) **Regional emergencies.**

(i) The exemption provided by paragraph (a)(1) of this section is effective only when:

(A) An emergency has been declared by the President of the United States, the Governor of a State, or their authorized representatives having authority to declare emergencies; or

(B) The Regional Director of Motor Carriers has declared that a regional emergency exists which justifies an exemption from parts 390 through 399 of this chapter.

(ii) Except as provided in §390.25, this exemption shall not exceed the duration of the motor carrier's or driver's direct assistance in providing emergency relief, or 30 days from the date of the initial declaration of the emergency or the exemption from the regulations by the Regional Director of Motor Carriers, whichever is less.

(2) **Local emergencies.**

(i) The exemption provided by paragraph (a)(2) of this section is effective only when:

(A) An emergency has been declared by a Federal, State, or local government official having authority to declare an emergency; or

(B) The Regional Director of Motor Carriers has declared that a local emergency exists which justifies an exemption from parts 390 through 399 of this chapter.

(ii) This exemption shall not exceed the duration of the motor carrier's or driver's direct assistance in providing emergency relief, or 5 days from the date of the initial declaration of the emergency or the exemption from the regulations by the Regional Director of Motor Carriers, whichever is less.

(3) **Tow Trucks responding to emergencies.**

(i) The exemption provided by paragraph (a)(3) of this section is effective only when a request has been made by a Federal, State or local police officer for tow trucks to move wrecked or disabled motor vehicles.

(ii) This exemption shall not exceed the length of the motor carrier's or driver's direct assistance in providing emergency relief, or 24 hours from the time of the initial request for assistance by the Federal, State or local police officer, whichever is less.

(b) Upon termination of direct assistance to the regional or local emergency relief effort, the motor carrier or driver is subject to the requirements of parts 390 through 399 of this chapter, with the following exception: A driver may return empty to the motor carrier's terminal or the driver's normal work reporting location without complying with parts 390 through 399 of this chapter. However, a driver who informs the motor carrier that he or she needs immediate rest shall be permitted at least 8 consecutive hours off duty before the driver is required to return to such terminal or location. Having returned to the terminal or other location, the driver must be relieved of all duty and responsibilities. Direct assistance terminates when a driver or commercial motor vehicle is used in interstate commerce to transport cargo not destined for the emergency relief effort, or when the motor carrier dispatches such driver or commercial motor vehicle to another location to begin operations in commerce.

(c) When the driver has been relieved of all duty and responsibilities upon termination of direct assistance to a regional or local emergency relief effort, no motor carrier shall permit or require any driver used by it to drive nor shall any such driver drive in commerce until:

(1) The driver has met the requirements of §395.3(a) of this chapter; and

(2) The driver has had at least 24 consecutive hours off-duty when:

(A) The driver has been on duty for more than 60 hours in any 7 consecutive days at the time the driver is relieved of all duty if the employing motor carrier does not operate every day in the week, or

(B) The driver has been on duty for more than 70 hours in any 8 consecutive days at the time the driver is relieved of all duty if the employing motor carrier operates every day in the week.

§390.25 Extension of relief from regulations—emergencies.

The Regional Director of Motor Carriers may extend the 30-day time period of the exemption contained in §390.23(a)(1), but not the 5-day time period contained in §390.23(a)(2) or the 24-hour period contained in §390.23(a)(3). Any motor carrier or driver seeking to extend the 30-day limit shall obtain approval from the Regional Director of Motor Carriers in the region in which the motor carrier's principal place of business is located before the expiration of the 30-day period. The motor carrier or driver shall give full details of the additional relief requested. The Regional Director of Motor Carriers shall determine if such relief is necessary taking into account both the severity of the ongoing emergency and the nature of the relief services to be provided by the carrier or driver. If the Regional Director of Motor Carriers approves an extension of the exemption, he or she shall establish a new time limit and place on the motor carrier or driver any other restrictions deemed necessary.

§390.27 Locations of motor carrier safety service centers.

Service center	Territory included	Location of office
Eastern	CT, DC, DE, MA, MD, ME, NH, NY, PA, PR, RI, VA, VT, WV.	City Crescent Building, #10 South Howard Street, Suite 4000, Baltimore, MD 21201-2819.
Midwestern ..	IA, IL, IN, KS, MI, MO, MN, NE, OH, WI	19900 Governors Drive, Suite 210, Olympia Fields, IL 60461-1021.
Southern ...	AL, AR, FL, GA, KY, LA, MS, NC, NM, OK, SC, TN, TX	61 Forsyth Street, SW, Suite 17T75, Atlanta, GA 30303-3104.
Western	American Samoa, AK, AZ, CA, CO, Guam, HI, ID, Mariana Islands, MT, ND, NV, OR, SD, UT, WA, WY.	201 Mission Street, Suite 2100, San Francisco, CA 94105-1838.

§390.29 Location of records or documents.

(a) A motor carrier with multiple offices or terminals may maintain the records and documents required by this subchapter at its principal place of business, a regional office, or driver work-reporting location unless otherwise specified in this subchapter.

(b) All records and documents required by this subchapter which are maintained at a regional office or driver work-reporting location shall be made available for inspection upon request by a special agent or authorized representative of the Federal Highway Administration at the motor carrier's principal place of business or other location specified by the agent or representative within 48 hours after a request is made. Saturdays, Sundays, and Federal holidays are excluded from the computation of the 48-hour period of time.

§390.31 Copies of records or documents.

(a) All records and documents required to be maintained under this subchapter must be preserved in their original form for the periods specified, unless the records and documents are suitably photographed and the microfilm is retained in lieu of the original record for the required retention period.

(b) To be acceptable in lieu of original records, photographic copies of records must meet the following minimum requirements:

(1) Photographic copies shall be no less readily accessible than the original record or document as normally filed or preserved would be and suitable means or facilities shall be available to locate, identify, read, and reproduce such photographic copies.

(2) Any significant characteristic, feature or other attribute of the original record or document, which photgraphy in black and white will not preserve, shall be clearly indicated before the photograph is made.

(3) The reverse side of printed forms need not be copied if nothing has been added to the printed matter common to all such forms, but an identified specimen of each form shall be on the film for reference.

(4) Film used for photographing copies shall be of permanent record-type meeting in all respects the minimum specifications of the National Bureau of Standards, and all processes recommended by the manufacturer shall be observed to protect it from deterioration or accidental destruction.

(5) Each roll of film shall include a microfilm of a certificate or certificates stating that the photographs are direct or facsim-

ile reproductions of the original records. Such certificate(s) shall be executed by a person or persons having personal knowledge of the material covered thereby.

(c) All records and documents required to be maintained under this subchapter may be destroyed after they have been suitably photographed for preservation.

(d) **Exception.** All records except those requiring a signature may be maintained through the use of computer technology provided the motor carrier can produce, upon demand, a computer printout of the required data.

§390.33 Commercial motor vehicles used for purposes other than defined.

Whenever a commercial motor vehicle of one type is used to perform the functions normally performed by a commercial motor vehicle of another type, the requirements of this subchapter and Part 325 of Subchapter A shall apply to the commercial motor vehicle and to its operation in the same manner as though the commercial motor vehicle were actually a commercial motor vehicle of the latter type.

Example: If a commercial motor vehicle other than a bus is used to perform the functions normally performed by a bus, the regulations pertaining to buses and to the transportation of passengers shall apply to that commercial motor vehicle.

§390.35 Certificates, reports, and records: falsification, reproduction, or alteration.

No motor carrier, its agents, officers, representatives, or employees shall make or cause to make—

(a) A fraudulent or intentionally false statement on any application, certificate, report, or record required by Part 325 of subchapter A or this subchapter;

(b) A fraudulent or intentionally false entry on any application, certificate, report, or record required to be used, completed, or retained, to comply with any requirement of this subchapter or Part 325 of Subchapter A; or

(c) A reproduction, for fraudulent purposes, of any application, certificate, report, or record required by this subchapter or Part 325 of Subchapter A.

§390.37 Violation and penalty.

Any person who violates the rules set forth in this subchapter or Part 325 of Subchapter A may be subject to civil or criminal penalties.

Subpart C — [Removed and reserved.]

Subpart D — [Removed and reserved.]

PART 391 — QUALIFICATIONS OF DRIVERS

Subpart A — General

Subpart B — Qualification and Disqualification of Drivers

Subpart C — Background and Character

Subpart D — Examinations and Tests

Subpart E — Physical Qualifications and Examinations

Subpart F — Files and Records

Subpart G — Limited Exemptions

AUTHORITY: 49 U.S.C. 504, 31133, 31136, and 31502; and 49 CFR 1.48.

Subpart A — General

§391.1 Scope of the rules in this part; additional qualifications; duties of carrier-drivers.

(a) The rules in this part establish minimum qualifications for persons who drive commercial motor vehicles as, for, or on behalf of motor carriers. The rules in this part also establish minimum duties of motor carriers with respect to the qualifications of their drivers.

(b) A motor carrier who employs himself/herself as a driver must comply with both the rules in this part that apply to motor carriers and the rules in this part that apply to drivers.

§391.2 General exemptions.

(a) **Farm custom operation.** The rules in this part do not apply to a driver who drives a commercial motor vehicle controlled and operated by a person engaged in custom-harvesting operations, if the commercial motor vehicle is used to—

(1) Transport farm machinery, supplies, or both, to or from a farm for custom-harvesting operations on a farm; or

(2) Transport custom-harvested crops to storage or market.

(b) **Apiarian industries.** The rules in this part do not apply to a driver who is operating a commercial motor vehicle controlled and operated by a beekeeper engaged in the seasonal transportation of bees.

(c) **Certain farm vehicle drivers.** The rules in this part do not apply to a farm vehicle driver except a farm vehicle driver who drives an articulated (combination) commercial motor vehicle as defined in §390.5. (For limited exemptions for farm vehicle drivers of articulated commercial motor vehicles see §391.67.)

Subpart B — Qualification and Disqualification of Drivers

§391.11 General qualifications of drivers.

(a) A person shall not drive a commercial motor vehicle unless he/she is qualified to drive a commercial motor vehicle. Except as provided in §391.63, a motor carrier shall not require or permit a person to drive a commercial motor vehicle unless that person is qualified to drive a commercial motor vehicle.

(b) Except as provided in Subpart G of this part, a person is qualified to drive a motor vehicle if he/she—

(1) Is at least 21 years old;

(2) Can read and speak the English language sufficiently to converse with the general public, to understand highway traffic signs and signals in the English language, to respond to official inquiries, and to make entries on reports and records;

(3) Can, by reason of experience, training, or both, safely operate the type of commercial motor vehicle he/she drives;

(4) Is physically qualified to drive a commercial motor vehicle in accordance with Subpart E — Physical Qualifications and Examinations of this part;

(5) Has a currently valid commercial motor vehicle operator's license issued only by one State or jurisdiction;

(6) Has prepared and furnished the motor carrier that employs him/her with the list of violations or the certificate as required by §391.27;

(7) Is not disqualified to drive a commercial motor vehicle under the rules in §391.15;

(8) Has successfully completed a driver's road test and has been issued a certificate of driver's road test in accordance with §391.31, or has presented an operator's license or a certificate of road test which the motor carrier that employs him/her has accepted as equivalent to a road test in accordance with §391.33.

§391.13 Responsibilities of drivers.

In order to comply with the requirements of §392.9(a) and §393.9 of this subchapter, a motor carrier shall not require or permit a person to drive a commercial motor vehicle unless the person—

(a) Can, by reason of experience, training, or both, determine whether the cargo he/she transports (including baggage in a passenger-carrying commercial motor vehicle) has been properly located, distributed, and secured in or on the commercial motor vehicle he/she drives;

(b) Is familiar with methods and procedures for securing cargo in or on the commercial motor vehicle he/she drives.

§391.15 Disqualification of drivers

(a) **General.** A driver who is disqualified shall not drive a commercial motor vehicle. A motor carrier shall not require or permit a driver who is disqualified to drive a commercial motor vehicle.

(b) **Disqualification for loss of driving privileges.** (1) A driver is disqualified for the duration of the driver's loss of his/

her privilege to operate a commercial motor vehicle on public highways, either temporarily or permanently, by reason of the revocation, suspension, withdrawal, or denial of an operator's license, permit, or privilege, until that operator's license, permit, or privilege is restored by the authority that revoked, suspended, withdrew, or denied it.

(2) A driver who receives a notice that his/her license, permit, or privilege to operate a commercial motor vehicle has been revoked, suspended, or withdrawn shall notify the motor carrier that employs him/her of the contents of the notice before the end of the business day following the day the driver received it.

(c) **Disqualification for criminal and other offenses.**

(1) **General rule.** A driver who is convicted of (or forfeits bond or collateral upon a charge of) a disqualifying offense specified in paragraph (c)(2) of this section is disqualified for the period of time specified in paragraph (c)(3) of this section, if—

(i) The offense was committed during on-duty time as defined in §395.2(a) of this subchapter or as otherwise specified; and

(ii) The driver is employed by a motor carrier or is engaged in activities that are in furtherance of a commercial enterprise in interstate, intrastate, or foreign commerce;

(2) **Disqualifying offenses.** The following offenses are disqualifying offenses:

(i) Driving a commercial motor vehicle while under the influence of alcohol. This shall include:

(A) Driving a commercial motor vehicle while the person's alcohol concentration is 0.04 percent or more;

(B) Driving under the influence of alcohol, as prescribed by State law; or

(C) Refusal to undergo such testing as is required by any State or jurisdiction in the enforcement of §391.15(c)(2)(i)(A) or (B), or §392.5(a)(2).

(ii) Driving a commercial motor vehicle under the influence of a 21 CFR 1308.11 *Schedule I* identified controlled substance, an amphetamine, a narcotic drug, a formulation of an amphetamine, or a derivative of a narcotic drug;

(iii) Transportation, possession, or unlawful use of a 21 CFR 1308.11 *Schedule I* identified controlled substance, amphetamines, narcotic drugs, formulations of an amphetamine, or derivatives of narcotic drugs while the driver is on duty, as the term on-duty time is defined in §395.2 of this subchapter;

(iv) Leaving the scene of an accident while operating a commercial motor vehicle; or

(v) A felony involving the use of a commercial motor vehicle.

(3) **Duration of disqualification—**(i) **First offenders.** A driver is disqualified for 1 year after the date of conviction or forfeiture of bond or collateral if, during the 3 years preceding that date, the driver was not convicted of, or did not forfeit bond or collateral upon a charge of an offense that would disqualify the driver under the rules of this section. **Exemption.** The period of disqualification is 6 months if the conviction or forfeiture of bond or collateral solely concerned the transportation or possession of substances named in paragraph (c)(2)(iii) of this section.

(ii) **Subsequent offenders.** A driver is disqualified for 3 years after the date of his/her conviction or forfeiture of bond or collateral if, during the 3 years preceding that date, he/she was convicted of, or forfeited bond or collateral upon a charge of, an offense that would disqualify him/her under the rules in this section.

(d) **Disqualification for violation of out-of-service orders.**

(1) **General rule.** A driver who is convicted of violating an out-of-service order is disqualified for the period of time specified in paragraph (d)(2) of this section.

(2) **Duration of disqualification for violation of out-of-service orders.**

(i) **First violation.** A driver is disqualified for not less than 90 days nor more than one year if the driver is convicted of a first violation of an out-of-service order.

(ii) **Second violation.** A driver is disqualified for not less than one year nor more than five years if, during any 10-year period, the driver is convicted of two violations of out-of-service orders in separate incidents.

(iii) **Third or subsequent violation.** A driver is disqualified for not less than three years nor more than five years if, during any 10-year period, the driver is convicted of three or more violations of out-of-service orders in separate incidents.

(iv) **Special rule for hazardous materials and passenger offenses.** A driver is disqualified for a period of not less than 180 days nor more than two years if the driver is convicted of a first violation of an out-of-service order while transporting hazardous materials required to be placarded under the Hazardous Materials Transportation Act (49 U.S.C. 5101 *et seq.*), or while operating commercial motor vehicles designed to transport more than 15 passengers, including the driver. A driver is disqualified for a period of not less than three years nor more than five years if, during any 10-year period, the driver is convicted of any subsequent violations of out-of-service orders, in separate incidents, while transporting hazardous materials required to be placarded under the Hazardous Materials Transportation Act, or while operating commercial motor vehicles designed to transport more than 15 passengers, including the driver.

Subpart C — Background and Character

§391.21 Application for employment.

(a) Except as provided in Subpart G of this part, a person shall not drive a commercial motor vehicle unless he/she has completed and furnished the motor carrier that employs him/her with an application for employment that meets the requirements of paragraph (b) of this section.

(b) The application for employment shall be made on a form furnished by the motor carrier. Each application form must be completed by the applicant, must be signed by him, and must contain the following information:

(1) The name and address of the employing motor carrier;

(2) The applicant's name, address, date of birth, and social security number;

(3) The addresses at which the applicant has resided during the 3 years preceding the date on which the application is submitted;

(4) The date on which the application is submitted;

(5) The issuing State, number, and expiration date of each unexpired commercial motor vehicle operator's license or permit that has been issued to the applicant;

(6) The nature and extent of the applicant's experience in the operation of motor vehicles, including the type of equipment (such as buses, trucks, truck tractors, semitrailers, full trailers, and pole trailers) which he/she has operated;

(7) A list of all motor vehicle accidents in which the applicant was involved during the 3 years preceding the date the application is submitted, specifying the date and nature of each accident and any fatalities or personal injuries it caused;

(8) A list of all violations of motor vehicle laws or ordinances (other than violations involving only parking) of which the ap-

plicant was convicted or forfeited bond or collateral during the 3 years preceding the date the application is submitted;

(9) A statement setting forth in detail the facts and circumstances of any denial, revocation, or suspension of any license, permit, or privilege to operate a motor vehicle that has been issued to the applicant, or a statement that no such denial, revocation, or suspension has occurred;

(10) A list of the names and addresses of the applicant's employers during the 3 years preceding the date the application is submitted, together with the dates he/she was employed by, and his/her reason for leaving the employ of, each employer;

(11) For those drivers applying to operate a commercial motor vehicle as defined by Part 383 of this subchapter, a list of the names and addresses of the applicant's employers during the 7-year period preceding the 3 years contained in paragraph (b)(10) of this section for which the applicant was an operator of a commercial motor vehicle, together with the dates of employment and the reasons for leaving such employment.

(12) The following certification and signature line, which must appear at the end of the application form and be signed by the applicant:

This certifies that this application was completed by me, and that all entries on it and information in it are true and complete to the best of my knowledge.

_____

      (Date)   (Applicant's signature)

(c) A motor carrier may require an applicant to provide information in addition to the information required by paragraph (b) of this section on the application form.

(d) Before an application is submitted, the motor carrier shall inform the applicant that the information he provides in accordance with paragraph (b) (10) of this section may be used, and the applicant's prior employers may be contacted, for the purpose of investigating the applicant's background as required by §391.23.

§391.23 Investigation and inquiries.

(a) Except as provided in Subpart G of this part, each motor carrier shall make the following investigations and inquiries with respect to each driver it employs, other than a person who has been a regularly employed driver of the motor carrier for a continuous period which began before January 1, 1971:

(1) An inquiry into the driver's driving record during the preceding 3 years to the appropriate agency of every State in which the driver held a motor vehicle operator's license or permit during those 3 years; and

(2) An investigation of the driver's employment record during the preceding 3 years.

(b) The inquiry to State agencies required by paragraph (a) (1) of this section must be made within 30 days of the date the driver's employment begins and shall be made in the form and manner those agencies prescribe. A copy of the response by each State agency, showing the driver's driving record or certifying that no driving record exists for that driver, shall be retained in the carrier's files as part of the driver's qualification file.

(c) The investigation of the driver's employment record required by paragraph (a) (2) of this section must be made within 30 days of the date his/her employment begins. The investigation may consist of personal interviews, telephone interviews, letters, or any other method of obtaining information that the carrier deems appropriate. Each motor carrier must make a written record with respect to each past employer who was contacted. The record must include the past employer's name and address, the date he/she was contacted, and his/her comments with respect to the driver. The record shall be retained in the motor carrier's files as part of the driver's qualification file.

§391.25 Annual inquiry and review of driving record.

(a) Except as provided in subpart G of this part, each motor carrier shall, at least once every 12 months, make an inquiry into the driving record of each driver it employs, covering at least the preceding 12 months, to the appropriate agency of every State in which the driver held a commercial motor vehicle operator's license or permit during the time period.

(b) Except as provided in subpart G of this part, each motor carrier shall, at least once every 12 months, review the driving record of each driver it employs to determine whether that driver meets minimum requirements for safe driving or is disqualified to drive a commercial motor vehicle pursuant to §391.15.

(1) The motor carrier must consider any evidence that the driver has violated any applicable Federal Motor Carrier Safety Regulations in this subchapter or Hazardous Materials Regulations (49 CFR chapter I, subchapter C).

(2) The motor carrier must consider the driver's accident record and any evidence that the driver has violated laws governing the operation of motor vehicles, and must give great weight to violations, such as speeding, reckless driving, and operating while under the influence of alcohol or drugs, that indicate that the driver has exhibited a disregard for the safety of the public.

(c) Recordkeeping. (1) A copy of the response from each State agency to the inquiry required by paragraph (a) of this section shall be maintained in the driver's qualification file.

(2) A note, including the name of the person who performed the review of the driving record required by paragraph (b) of this section and the date of such review, shall be maintained in the driver's qualification file.

§391.27 Record of violations.

(a) Except as provided in Subpart G of this part, each motor carrier shall, at least once every 12 months, require each driver it employs to prepare and furnish it with a list of all violations of motor vehicle traffic laws and ordinances (other than violations involving only parking) of which the driver has been convicted or on account of which he/she has forfeited bond or collateral during the preceding 12 months.

(b) Each driver shall furnish the list required in accordance with paragraph (a) of this section. If the driver has not been convicted of, or forfeited bond or collateral on account of, any violation which must be listed he/she shall so certify.

(c) The form of the driver's list or certification shall be prescribed by the motor carrier. The following form may be used to comply with this section:

Driver's Certification

I certify that the following is a true and complete list of traffic violations (other than parking violations) for which I have been convicted or forfeited bond or collateral during the past 12 months.

Date of conviction	Offense
_____	_____
_____	_____
_____	_____
_____	_____

Location	Type of motor vehicle operated
_____	_____
_____	_____
_____	_____
_____	_____

If no violations are listed above, I certify that I have not been convicted or forfeited bond or collateral on account of any violation required to be listed during the past 12 months.

_____   _____
(Date of certification)   (Driver's signature)

_____
(Motor carrier's name)

_____
(Motor carrier's address)

_____   _____
(Reviewed by: Signature)   (Title)

(d) The motor carrier shall retain the list or certificate required by this section, or a copy of it, in its files as part of the driver's qualification file.

(e) Drivers who have provided information required by §383.31 of this subchapter need not repeat that information in the annual list of violations required by this section.

Subpart D — Tests

§391.31 Road test.

(a) Except as provided in subpart G, a person shall not drive a commercial motor vehicle unless he/she has first successfully completed a road test and has been issued a certificate of driver's road test in accordance with this section.

(b) The road test shall be given by the motor carrier or a person designated by it. However, a driver who is a motor carrier must be given the test by a person other than himself/herself. The test shall be given by a person who is competent to evaluate and determine whether the person who takes the test has demonstrated that he/she is capable of operating the commercial motor vehicle, and associated equipment, that the motor carrier intends to assign him/her.

(c) The road test must be of sufficient duration to enable the person who gives it to evaluate the skill of the person who takes it at handling the commercial motor vehicle and associated equipment, that the motor carrier intends to assign to him/her. As a minimum, the person who takes the test must be tested, while operating the type of commercial motor vehicle the motor carrier intends to assign him/her, on his/her skill at performing each of the following operations:

(1) The pretrip inspection required by §392.7 of this subchapter;

(2) Coupling and uncoupling of combination units, if the equipment he/she may drive includes combination units;

(3) Placing the commercial motor vehicle in operation;

(4) Use of the commercial motor vehicle's controls and emergency equipment;

(5) Operating the commercial motor vehicle in traffic and while passing other motor vehicles;

(6) Turning the commercial motor vehicle;

(7) Braking, and slowing the commercial motor vehicle by means other than braking; and

(8) Backing and parking the commercial motor vehicle.

(d) The motor carrier shall provide a road test form on which the person who gives the test shall rate the performance of the person who takes it at each operation or activity which is a part of the test. After he/she completes the form, the person who gave the test shall sign it.

(e) If the road test is successfully completed, the person who gave it shall complete a certificate of driver's road test in substantially the form prescribed in paragraph (f) of this section.

(f) The form for the certificate of driver's road test is substantially as follows:

CERTIFICATION OF ROAD TEST

Driver's name_____

Social Security No. _____

Operator's or Chauffeur's License No. _____

State_____

Type of power unit_____

Type of trailer(s)_____

If passenger carrier, type of bus_____

This is to certify that the above-named driver was given a road test under my supervision on _____ 19_____ consisting of approximately _____ miles of driving.

It is my considered opinion that this driver possesses sufficient driving skill to operate safely the type of commercial motor vehicle listed above.

_____
(Signature of examiner)   (Title)

_____
(Organization and address of examiner)

(g) A copy of the certificate required by paragraph (e) of this section shall be given to the person who was examined. The motor carrier shall retain in the driver qualification file of the person who was examined—

(1) The original of the signed road test form required by paragraph (d) of this section; and

(2) The original, or a copy of, the certificate required by paragraph (e) of this section.

§391.33 Equivalent of road test.

(a) In place of, and as equivalent to, the road test required by §391.31, a person who seeks to drive a commercial motor vehicle may present, and a motor carrier may accept—

(1) A valid Commercial Driver's License as defined in §383.5 of this subchapter, but not including double/triple trailer or tank vehicle endorsements, which has been issued to him/her to operate specific categories of commercial motor vehicles and which, under the laws of that State, licenses him/her after successful completion of a road test in a commercial motor vehicle of the type the motor carrier intends to assign to him/her; or

(2) A copy of a valid certificate of driver's road test issued to him/her pursuant to §391.31 within the preceding 3 years.

(b) If a driver presents, and a motor carrier accepts, a license or certificate as equivalent to the road test, the motor carrier shall retain a legible copy of the license or certificate in its files as part of the driver's qualification file.

(c) A motor carrier may require any person who presents a license or certificate as equivalent to the road test to take a road test or any other test of his/her driving skill as a condition to his/her employment as a driver.

§391.35

§391.35 [Removed and reserved.]

§391.37 [Removed and reserved.]

Subpart E — Physical Qualifications and Examinations

§391.41 Physical qualifications for drivers.

(a) A person shall not drive a commercial motor vehicle unless he/she is physically qualified to do so and, except as provided in §391.67, has on his/her person the original, or a photographic copy, of a medical examiner's certificate that he/she is physically qualified to drive a commercial motor vehicle.

(b) A person is physically qualified to drive a commercial motor vehicle if that person—

(1) Has no loss of a foot, a leg, a hand, or an arm, or has been granted a skill performance evaluation certificate pursuant to §391.49;

(2) Has no impairment of:

(i) A hand or finger which interferes with prehension or power grasping; or

(ii) An arm, foot, or leg which interferes with the ability to perform normal tasks associated with operating a commercial motor vehicle; or any other significant limb defect or limitation which interferes with the ability to perform normal tasks associated with operating a commercial motor vehicle; or has been granted a skill performance evaluation certificate pursuant to §391.49.

(3) Has no established medical history or clinical diagnosis of diabetes mellitus currently requiring insulin for control;

(4) Has no current clinical diagnosis of myocardial infarction, angina pectoris, coronary insufficiency, thrombosis, or any other cardiovascular disease of a variety known to be accompanied by syncope, dyspnea, collapse, or congestive cardiac failure;

(5) Has no established medical history or clinical diagnosis of a respiratory dysfunction likely to interfere with his/her ability to control and drive a commercial motor vehicle safely;

(6) Has no current clinical diagnosis of high blood pressure likely to interfere with his/her ability to operate a commercial motor vehicle safely;

(7) Has no established medical history or clinical diagnosis of rheumatic, arthritic, orthopedic, muscular, neuromuscular, or

vascular disease which interferes with his/her ability to control and operate a commercial motor vehicle safely;

(8) Has no established medical history or clinical diagnosis of epilepsy or any other condition which is likely to cause loss of consciousness or any loss of ability to control a commercial motor vehicle;

(9) Has no mental, nervous, organic, or functional disease or psychiatric disorder likely to interfere with his/her ability to drive a commercial motor vehicle safely;

(10) Has distant visual acuity of at least 20/40 (Snellen) in each eye without corrective lenses or visual acuity separately corrected to 20/40 (Snellen) or better with corrective lenses, distant binocular acuity of at least 20/40 (Snellen) in both eyes with or without corrective lenses, field of vision of at least 70° in the horizontal meridian in each eye, and the ability to recognize the colors of traffic signals and devices showing standard red, green, and amber;

(11) First perceives a forced whispered voice in the better ear at not less than 5 feet with or without the use of a hearing aid or, if tested by use of an audiometric device, does not have an average hearing loss in the better ear greater than 40 decibels at 500 Hz, 1,000 Hz, and 2,000 Hz with or without a hearing aid when the audiometric device is calibrated to American National Standard (formerly ASA Standard) Z24.5-1951;

(12)(i) Does not use a controlled substance identified in 21 CFR 1308.11 *Schedule I*, and amphetamine, a narcotic, or any other habit-forming drug.

(ii) *Exception.* A driver may use such a substance or drug, if the substance or drug is prescribed by a licensed medical practtioner who:

(A) Is familiar with the driver's medical history and assigned duties; and

(B) Has advised the driver that the prescribed substance or drug will not adversely affect the driver's ability to safely operate a commercial motor vehicle; and

(13) Has no current clinical diagnosis of alcoholism.

§391.43 Medical examination; certificate of physical examination.

(a) Except as provided in paragraph (b) of this section, the medical examination shall be performed by a licensed medical examiner as defined in §390.5 of this subchapter.

(b) A licensed optometrist may perform so much of the medical examination as pertains to visual acuity, field of vision, and the ability to recognize colors as specified in paragraph (10) of §391.41 (b).

(c) Medical examiners shall:

(1) Be knowledgeable of the specific physical and mental demands associated with operating a commercial motor vehicle and the requirements of this subpart, including the medical advisory criteria prepared by the FHWA as guidelines to aid the medical examiner in making the qualification determination; and

(2) Be proficient in the use of and use the medical protocols necessary to adequately perform the medical examination required by this section.

(d) Any driver authorized to operate a commercial motor vehicle within an exempt intracity zone pursuant to §391.62 shall furnish the examining medical examiner with a copy of the medical findings that led to the issuance of the first certificate of medical examination which allowed the driver to operate a commercial motor vehicle wholly within an exempt intracity zone.

(e) Any driver operating under a limited exemption authorized by §391.64 shall furnish the medical examiner with a copy of the annual medical findings of the endocrinologist, ophthalmologist or optometrist, as required under that section. If the medical examiner finds the driver qualified under the limited exemption in §391.64, such fact shall be noted on the Medical Examiner's Certificate.

(f) The medical examination shall be performed, and its results shall be recorded, substantially in accordance with the following instructions and examination form. Existing forms may be used until current printed supplies are depleted or until November 6, 2001, whichever occurs first.

INSTRUCTIONS FOR PERFORMING AND RECORDING PHYSICAL EXAMINATIONS

The medical examiner must be familiar with 49 CFR 391.41, Physical qualifications for drivers, and should review these instructions before performing the physical examination. Answer each question "yes" or "no" and record numerical readings where indicated on the physical examination form.

The medical examiner must be aware of the rigorous physical, mental, and emotional demands placed on the driver of a commercial motor vehicle. In the interest of public safety, the medical examiner is required to certify that the driver does not have any physical, mental, or organic condition that might affect the driver's ability to operate a commercial motor vehicle safely.

General information. The purpose of this history and physical examination is to detect the presence of physical, mental, or organic conditions of such a character and extent as to affect the driver's ability to operate a commercial motor vehicle safely. The examination should be conducted carefully and should at least include all of the information requested in the following form. History of certain conditions may be cause for rejection. Indicate the need for further testing and/or require evaluation by a specialist. Conditions may be recorded which do not, because of their character or degree, indicate that certification of physical fitness should be denied. However, these conditions should be discussed with the driver and he/she should be advised to take the necessary steps to insure correction, particularly of those conditions which, if neglected, might affect the driver's ability to drive safely.

General appearance and development. Note marked overweight. Note any postural defect, perceptible limp, tremor, or other conditions that might be caused by alcoholism, thyroid intoxication or other illnesses.

Head-eyes. When other than the Snellen chart is used, the results of such test must be expressed in values comparable to the standard Snellen test. If the driver wears corrective lenses for driving, these should be worn while driver's visual acuity is being tested. If contact lenses are worn, there should be sufficient evidence of good tolerance of and adaptation to their use. Indicate the driver's need to wear corrective lenses to meet the vision standard on the Medical Examiner's Certificate by checking the box, "Qualified only when wearing corrective lenses." In recording distance vision use 20 feet as normal. Report all vision as a fraction with 20 as the numerator and the smallest type read at 20 feet as the denominator. Monocular drivers are not qualified to operate commercial motor vehicles in interstate commerce.

Ears. Note evidence of any ear disease, symptoms of aural vertigo, or Meniere's Syndrome. When recording hearing, record distance from patient at which a forced whispered voice can first be heard. For the whispered voice test, the individual should be stationed at least 5 feet from the examiner with the ear being tested turned toward the examiner. The other ear is covered. Using the breath which remains after a normal expiration, the examiner whispers words or random numbers such as 66, 18, 23, etc. The examiner should not use only sibilants (s-sounding test materials). The opposite ear should be tested in the same manner. If the individual fails the whispered voice test, the audiometric test should be administered. For the audiometric test, record decibel loss at 500 Hz, 1,000 Hz, and 2,000 Hz. Average the decibel loss at 500 Hz, 1,000 Hz and 2,000 Hz and record as described on the form. If the individual fails the audiometric test and the whispered voice test has not been administered, the whispered voice test should be performed to determine if the standard applicable to that test can be met.

Throat. Note any irremediable deformities likely to interfere with breathing or swallowing.

Heart. Note murmurs and arrhythmias, and any history of an enlarged heart, congestive heart failure, or cardiovascular disease that is accompanied by syncope, dyspnea, or collapse. Indicate onset date, diagnosis, medication, and any current limitation. An electrocardiogram is required when findings so indicate.

Blood pressure (BP). If a driver has hypertension and/or is being medicated for hypertension, he or she should be recertified more frequently. An individual diagnosed with mild hypertension (initial BP is greater than 160/90 but below 181/105) should be certified for one 3-month period and should be re-certified on an annual basis thereafter if his or her BP is reduced. An individual diagnosed with moderate to severe hypertension (initial BP is greater than 180/104) should not be certified until the BP has been reduced to the mild range (below 181/105). At that time, a 3-month certification can be issued. Once the driver has reduced his or her BP to below 161/91, he or she should be recertified every 6 months thereafter.

Lungs. Note abnormal chest wall expansion, respiratory rate, breath sounds including wheezes or alveolar rales, impaired respiratory function, dyspnea, or cyanosis. Abnormal finds on physical exam may require further testing such as pulmonary tests and/or x-ray of chest.

Abdomen and Viscera. Note enlarged liver, enlarged spleen, abnormal masses, bruits, hernia, and significant abdominal wall muscle weakness and tenderness. If the diagnosis suggests that the condition might interfere with the control and safe operation of a commercial motor vehicle, further testing and evaluation is required.

Genital-urinary and rectal examination. A urinalysis is required. Protein, blood or sugar in the urine may be an indication for further testing to rule out any underlying medical problems. Note hernias. A condition causing discomfort should be evaluated to determine the extent to which the condition might interfere with the control and safe operation of a commercial motor vehicle.

Neurological. Note impaired equilibrium, coordination, or speech pattern; paresthesia; asymmetric deep tendon reflexes; sensory or positional abnormalities; abnormal patellar and Babinski's reflexes; ataxia. Abnormal neurological responses may be an indication for further testing to rule out an underlying medical condition. Any neurological condition should be evaluated for the nature and severity of the condition, the degree of limitation present, the likelihood of progressive limitation, and the potential for sudden incapacitation. In instances where the medical examiner has determined that more frequent monitoring of a condition is appropriate, a certificate for a shorter period should be issued.

Spine, musculoskeletal. Previous surgery, deformities, limitation of motion, and tenderness should be noted. Findings may indicate additional testing and evaluation should be conducted.

Extremities. Carefully examine upper and lower extremities and note any loss or impairment of leg, foot, toe, arm, hand, or finger. Note any deformities, atrophy, paralysis, partial paralysis, clubbing, edema, or hypotonia. If a hand or finger deformity exists, determine whether prehension and power grasp are sufficient to enable the driver to maintain steering wheel grip and to control other vehicle equipment during routine and emergency driving operations. If a foot or leg deformity exists, determine whether sufficient mobility and strength exist to enable the driver to operate pedals properly. In the case of any loss or impairment to an extremity which may interfere with the driver's ability to operate a commercial motor vehicle safely, the medical examiner should state on the medical certificate "medically unqualified unless accompanied by a Skill Performance Evaluation Certificate." The driver must then apply to the Field Service Center of the FMCSA, for the State in which the driver has legal residence, for a Skill Performance Evaluation Certificate under §391.49.

Laboratory and Other Testing. Other test(s) may be indicated based upon the medical history or findings of the physical examination.

Diabetes. If insulin is necessary to control a diabetic driver's condition, the driver is not qualified to operate a commercial motor vehicle in interstate commerce. If mild diabetes is present and it is controlled by use of an oral hypoglycemic drug and/or diet and exercise, it should not be considered disqualifying. However, the driver must remain under adequate medical supervision.

Upon completion of the examination, the medical examiner must date and sign the form, provide his/her full name, office address and telephone number. The completed medical examination form shall be retained on file at the office of the medical examiner.

Medical Examination Report

FOR COMMERCIAL DRIVER FITNESS DETERMINATION

1. DRIVER'S INFORMATION Driver completes this section.

Driver's Name (Last, First, Middle)

Social Security No.   Birthdate M/D/Y   Age   Sex [ ] M [ ] F

Address   City, State, Zip Code

Work Tel. (   )   Home Tel. (   )

New certification [ ]   Recertification [ ]   Follow Up [ ]

Driver License No.

License Class [ ] A [ ] B [ ] C [ ] Other

Date of Exam   State of Issue

2. HEALTH HISTORY Driver completes this section, but medical examiner is encouraged to discuss with driver.

Yes No
- [ ] Any illness or injury in last 5 years?
- [ ] Head/Brain injuries, disorders or illnesses
- [ ] Seizures, epilepsy
    - [ ] medication
- [ ] Eye disorders or impaired vision (except corrective lenses)
- [ ] Ear disorders, loss of hearing or balance
- [ ] Heart disease or heart attack; other cardiovascular condition
    - [ ] medication
- [ ] Heart surgery (valve replacement/bypass, angioplasty, pacemaker)
    - [ ] medication
- [ ] High blood pressure [ ] medication
- [ ] Muscular disease
- [ ] Shortness of breath

Yes No
- [ ] Lung disease, emphysema, asthma, chronic bronchitis
- [ ] Kidney disease, dialysis
- [ ] Liver disease
- [ ] Digestive problems
- [ ] Diabetes or elevated blood sugar controlled by:
    - [ ] diet
    - [ ] pills
    - [ ] insulin
- [ ] Nervous or psychiatric disorders, e.g. severe depression
- [ ] Loss of, or altered consciousness
- [ ] Fainting, dizziness

Yes No
- [ ] Sleep disorders, pauses in breathing while asleep, daytime sleepiness, loud snoring
- [ ] Stroke or paralysis
- [ ] Missing or impaired hand, arm, foot, leg, finger, toe
- [ ] Spinal injury or disease
- [ ] Chronic low back pain
- [ ] Regular, frequent alcohol use
- [ ] Narcotic or habit forming drug use

For any YES answer, indicate onset date, diagnosis, treating physician's name and address, and any current limitation. List all medications (including over-the-counter medications) used regularly or recently.

I certify that the above information is complete and true. I understand that inaccurate, false or missing information may invalidate the examination and my Medical Examiner's Certificate.

Driver's Signature   Date

Medical Examiners Comments on Health History (The medical examiner must review and discuss with the driver any "yes" answers and potential hazards of medications, including over-the-counter medications, while driving.)

TESTING (Medical Examiner completes Section 3 through 7)

3. VISION

Standard: At least 20/40 acuity (Snellen) in each eye with or without correction. At least 70° peripheral in horizontal meridian measured in each eye. The use of corrective lenses should be noted on the Medical Examiner's Certificate.

INSTRUCTIONS: *When either item the Snellen chart is used, zero test results in Snellen-comparable values. In recording distance vision, use 20 feet as normal. Report visual acuity as a ratio with 20 as numerator and the smallest type read at 20 feet as denominator. If the applicant wears corrective lenses, there should be white visual acuity is being tested. If the driver habitually wears contact lenses, or intends to do so while driving, sufficient evidence of good tolerance and adaptation to their use must be obvious. Monocular drivers are not qualified.*

Numerical readings must be provided.

ACUITY	UNCORRECTED	CORRECTED	HORIZONTAL FIELD OF VISION	
Right Eye	20/	20/	Right Eye	°
Left Eye	20/	20/	Left Eye	°
Both Eyes	20/	20/		

Applicant can recognize and distinguish among traffic control signals and devices showing standard red, green, and amber colors?   ☐ Yes   ☐ No

Applicant meets visual acuity requirement only when wearing:
☐ Corrective Lenses

Monocular Vision: ☐ Yes   ☐ No

Complete meet time only if vision testing is done by an ophthalmologist or optometrist

Date of Examination _____   Name of Ophthalmologist or Optometrist (print) _____   Tel No. _____   License No./State of Issue _____   Signature _____

4. HEARING

Standard: a) Most first perceive forced whispered voice ≥ 5 ft., with or without hearing aid, or b) average hearing loss in better ear ≤ 40 dB

INSTRUCTIONS: ☐ Check if hearing aid used to test: ☐ Check if hearing aid required to meet standard.
To convert audiometric test results from ISO to ANSI, -14 dB from ISO for 500 Hz, -10 dB for 1,000 Hz, -8.5 dB for 2,000 Hz. To average, add the readings for 3 frequencies tested and divide by 3.

	Right Ear	Left Ear
	500 Hz	1000 Hz	2000 Hz	500 Hz	1000 Hz	2000 Hz
	Average:	Average:		

Numerical readings must be recorded.

a) Record distance from individual at which forced whispered voice can first be heard.

Right Ear _____ Feet   Left Ear _____ Feet

b) If audiometer is used, record hearing loss in decibels. (sec. to ANSI-224.5-1961)

5. BLOOD PRESSURE / PULSE RATE   Numerical readings must be recorded.

Blood Pressure	Systolic	Diastolic

Driver qualified if ≤ 160/90 on initial exam.

Pulse Rate	☐ Regular	☐ Irregular

GUIDELINES FOR BLOOD PRESSURE EVALUATION

On initial exam

If ≤ 160/90, Qualify 3 mts. only

Within 3 months

If ≤ 160 and/or 90, Qualify for 1 yr. Document Rx & control the 3rd month

If > 160 and/or 104, not qualified until reduced to ≤ 161/105. Then qualify for 3 mts. only.

If > 160 and/or 90, qualify for 6 mos., Document Rx & control the 3rd month

Medical examiner should take at least 2 readings to confirm blood pressure.

6. LABORATORY AND OTHER TEST FINDINGS   Numerical readings must be recorded.

Urinalysis is required. Protein, blood or sugar in the urine may be an indication for further testing to rule out any underlying medical problem.
Other Testing (Describe and record)

URINE SPECIMEN	SP. GR.	PROTEIN	BLOOD	SUGAR

7. PHYSICAL EXAMINATION

Height: _____ (in.)   Weight: _____ (lbs)

The presence of a certain condition may not necessarily disqualify a driver, particularly if the condition is controlled adequately, is not likely to worsen or is readily amenable to treatment. Even if a condition does not disqualify a driver, the medical examiner may consider defining the driver temporarily. Also, the driver should be advised to take the necessary steps to correct the condition as soon as possible particularly if the condition, if neglected, could result in more serious illness that might affect driving.

Check YES if there are any abnormalities. Check NO if the body system is normal. Discuss any YES answers in detail in the space below, and indicate whether it would affect the driver's ability to operate a commercial motor vehicle safely. Enter applicable item number before each comment. If organic disease is present, note that it has been compensated for.

See Instructions To The Medical Examiner for guidance.

BODY SYSTEM	CHECK FOR:	YES?	NO?	BODY SYSTEM	CHECK FOR:	YES?	NO?
1. General Appearance	Marked overweight, tremor, signs of alcoholism, problem drinking, or drug abuse.			7. Abdomen and Viscera	Enlarged liver, enlarged spleen, masses, bruits, hernia, significant abdominal wall muscle weakness.		
2. Eyes	Pupillary equality, reaction to light, accommodation, ocular mobility, ocular muscle imbalance, extraocular movement, nystagmus, exophthalmos, strabismus unconnected by corrective lenses, retinopathy, cataracts, aphakia, glaucoma, macular degeneration.			8. Vascular system	Abnormal pulse and amplitude, carotid or arterial bruits, varicose veins.		
				9. Genito-urinary system.	Hernias.		
3. Ears	Middle ear disease, occlusion of external canal, perforated eardrums.			10. Extremities - Limb impaired. Driver may be subject to SPE certificate if otherwise qualified.	Loss or impairment of leg, foot, toe, arm, hand, finger. Perceptible limp, deformities, atrophy, weakness, paralysis, clubbing, edema, hypotonia. Insufficient grasp and prehension in upper limb to maintain steering wheel grip. Insufficient mobility and strength in lower limb to operate pedals properly.		
4. Mouth and Throat	Irremediable deformities likely to interfere with breathing or swallowing.						
5. Heart	Murmurs, extra sounds, enlarged heart, pacemaker.			11. Spine, other musculoskeletal	Previous surgery, deformities, limitation of motion, tenderness		
6. Lungs and chest, not including breast examination.	Abnormal chest wall expansion, abnormal respiratory rate, abnormal breath sounds including wheezes or alveolar rales, impaired respiratory function, dyspnea, cyanosis. Abnormal findings on physical exam may require further testing such as pulmonary tests and/or x-ray of chest.			12. Neurological	Impaired equilibrium, coordination or speech pattern; paresthesia, asymmetric deep tendon reflexes, sensory or positional abnormalities, abnormal patellar and Babinski's reflexes, ataxia.		

* COMMENTS:

Note certification status here. See Instructions to the Medical Examiner for guidance.

- [ ] Meets standards in 49 CFR 391.41; qualifies for 2 year certificate
- [ ] Does not meet standards
- [ ] Meets standards, but periodic evaluation required.
  - Due to _____
    - [ ] 3 months [ ] 1 year
    - [ ] 6 months [ ] Other
  - driver qualified only for:
- [ ] Temporarily disqualified due to (condition or medication):
- [ ] Return to medical examiner's office for follow up on _____

- [ ] Wearing corrective lenses
- [ ] Wearing hearing aid
- [ ] Accompanied by a _____ waiver/exemption
- [ ] Driving within an exempt intracity zone.
- [ ] Skill Performance Evaluation (SPE) Certificate
- [ ] Qualified by operation of 49 CFR 391.64

Medical Examiner's Signature _____

Medical Examiner's Name (print) _____

Address _____

Telephone Number _____

If meets standards, complete a Medical Examiner's Certificate according to 49 CFR 391.43(h). (Driver must carry certificate when operating a commercial vehicle.)

49 CFR 391.41 Physical Qualifications for Drivers

THE DRIVER'S ROLE

Responsibilities, work schedules, physical and emotional demands, and lifestyles among commercial drivers vary by the type of driving that they do. Some of the main types of drivers include the following: turn around or short relay drivers (who return to their homes each evening); long relay drivers (who drive 9-10 hours and then have an 8-hour off-duty period), straight through haul (commonly drive team); and those drivers who share the driving by alternating their 4-hour driving periods and 4-hour rest periods).

The following factors may be involved in a driver's performance of duties: abrupt schedule changes and rotating work schedules, which may result in irregular sleep patterns and a driver beginning a trip in a fatigued condition; long hours; extended time away from family and friends, which may have an effect on social support; tight pickup and delivery schedules, with irregularity in work, rest, and eating patterns; the handling of heavy cargo and cargo loading/unloading tasks; and environmental conditions such as excessive vibration, noise, and extremes in temperature. Transporting passengers or hazardous materials may add to the demands on the commercial driver.

There are a number of tasks in addition to the driving task for which a driver is responsible and needs to be fit. Some of these responsibilities are: coupling and uncoupling trailer(s) from the tractor, loading and unloading trailer(s) (sometimes a driver may lift a heavy load or unload as much as 50,000 lbs. of freight after sitting for a long period of time without any stretching period); inspecting the operating condition of tractor and trailer(s) before, during, and after delivery of cargo; filling, installing, and removing heavy tire chains; and manually cranking up and down the landing gear. In addition, a driver must have the perceptual skills to monitor a sometimes complex driving situation, the judgment skills to make quick decisions, when necessary, and the manipulative skills to control his/her vehicle quickly. In addition, a driver must have the perceptual skills to monitor a sometimes complex driving situation, the judgment skills to make quick decisions, when necessary, and the manipulative skills to control and operate the vehicle. The above tasks require agility, the ability to bend and stoop, the ability to maintain a crouching position to inspect the underside of the vehicle, frequent entering and exiting of the cab, and climbing ladders on the tractor and/or trailer(s).

§ 391.41 PHYSICAL QUALIFICATIONS FOR DRIVERS

(a) A person shall not drive a commercial motor vehicle unless he is physically qualified to do so and, except as provided in §391.67, has on his person the original, or a photographic copy, of a medical examiner's certificate that he is physically qualified to drive a commercial motor vehicle.

(b) A person is physically qualified to drive a motor vehicle if that person—

(1) Has no loss of a foot, a leg, a hand, or an arm, or has been granted a Skill Performance Evaluation (SPE) Certificate (formerly Limb Waiver Program) pursuant to §391.49;

(2) Has no impairment of: (i) A hand or finger which interferes with prehension or power grasping; or (ii) An arm, foot, or leg which interferes with the ability to perform normal tasks associated with operating a commercial motor vehicle; or any other significant limb defect or limitation which interferes with the ability to perform normal tasks associated with operating a commercial motor vehicle; or has been granted a SPE Certificate pursuant to §391.49.

(3) Has no established medical history or clinical diagnosis of diabetes mellitus currently requiring insulin for control;

(4) Has no current clinical diagnosis of myocardial infarction, angina pectoris, coronary insufficiency, thrombosis, or any other cardiovascular disease of a variety known to be accompanied by syncope, dyspnea, collapse, or congestive cardiac failure.

(5) Has no established medical history or clinical diagnosis of a respiratory dysfunction likely to interfere with his ability to control and drive a commercial motor vehicle safely.

(6) Has no current clinical diagnosis of high blood pressure likely to interfere with his ability to operate a commercial motor vehicle safely.

(7) Has no established medical history or clinical diagnosis of rheumatic, arthritic, orthopedic, muscular, neuromuscular, or vascular disease which interferes with his ability to control and operate a commercial motor vehicle safely.

(8) Has no established medical history or clinical diagnosis of epilepsy or any other condition which is likely to cause loss of consciousness or any loss of ability to control a commercial motor vehicle;

(9) Has no mental, nervous, organic, or functional disease or psychiatric disorder likely to interfere with his ability to drive a commercial motor vehicle safely.

(10) Has distant visual acuity of at least 20/40 (Snellen) in each eye without corrective lenses or visual acuity separately corrected to 20/40 (Snellen) or better with corrective lenses, distant binocular acuity of at least 20/40 (Snellen) in both eyes with or without corrective lenses, field of vision of at least 70 degrees in the horizontal meridian in each eye, and the ability to recognize the colors of traffic signals and devices showing standard red, green and amber;

(11) First perceives a forced whispered voice in the better ear not less than 5 feet with or without the use of a hearing aid, or, if tested by use of an audiometric device, does not have an average hearing loss in the better ear greater than 40 decibels at 500 Hz, 1,000 Hz and 2,000 Hz with or without a hearing aid when the audiometric device is calibrated to American National Standard (formerly ASA Standard) Z24.5-1951.

(12) (i) Does not use a controlled substance identified in 21 CFR 1308.11 Schedule I, an amphetamine, a narcotic, or any other habit-forming drug. (ii) Exception: A driver may use such a substance or drug, if the substance or drug, is prescribed by a licensed medical practitioner who (A) Is familiar with the driver's medical history and assigned duties; and (B) Has advised the driver that the prescribed substance or drug will not adversely affect the driver's ability to safely operate a commercial motor vehicle; and

(13) Has no current clinical diagnosis of alcoholism.

INSTRUCTIONS TO THE MEDICAL EXAMINER

Federal Motor Carrier Safety Regulations - Advisory Criteria

General Information

The purpose of this examination is to determine a driver's physical qualification to operate a commercial motor vehicle (CMV) in interstate commerce according to the requirements in 49 CFR 391.41-49. Therefore, the medical examiner must be knowledgeable of the standards and, if applicable, any guidelines developed by the FMCSA to assist the medical examiner in making the qualification determination. The medical examiner will be familiar with the driver's responsibilities and work environment and is referred to the section on the form The Driver's Role.

In addition to reviewing the Health History section with the driver and conducting the physical examination, the medical examiner should discuss common prescription and over-the-counter medications relative to the side effects and hazards of these medications while driving. Educate driver to read warning labels on all medications. History of certain conditions may be cause for rejection, particularly if associated with inadequate, or may indicate the need for additional laboratory tests or more detailed examination perhaps by a medical specialist. These decisions are individual choices to be made by the examiner in the light of individual circumstances and the driver's job responsibilities, work schedule and potential for disorders to render driver unsafe.

Medical conditions should be recorded even if they are not cause for denial and they should be discussed with the driver to encourage appropriate management. The advisory criteria are not all inclusive and conditions are especially needed when a condition, if neglected, could develop into a serious illness that could affect driving.

If at the time of examination the examiner determines the driver is fit to drive and is also able to perform non-driving responsibilities as may be required, the medical examiner signs the medical certificate indicating the driver meets current regulations. Under current regulations the certificate is valid for two years unless the driver has a medical condition that does not prohibit driving but does require more frequent monitoring. The medical certificate then must be issued for a shorter length of time. The physical examination should be done carefully and at least as extensively as described by section's standards printed in italics and the reference by section is provided under 49 CFR 391.41-49.

Interpretation of Medical Standards

Since the issuance of the regulations for physical qualifications of commercial drivers, the Federal Motor Carrier Safety Administration (FMCSA) has published recommended Advisory Criteria to help medical examiners in determining whether a driver meets the physical qualifications for commercial driving. These recommendations have been incorporated in this document (1)-(13), the medical examiner should use them as a reference to directly relevant to the physical examination and (2) are not already included in the medical examination form. The specific regulation is printed in italics and the reference by section is highlighted.

Diabetes
§ 391.41(b)(3)

A person is physically qualified to drive a commercial motor vehicle if that person:

Has no established medical history or clinical diagnosis of diabetes mellitus currently requiring insulin for control

Diabetes mellitus is a disease, which on occasion, can result in a loss of consciousness or disorientation in time and space. Individuals who require insulin for control have conditions which can get out of control by the use of too much or too little insulin so that a loss of consciousness with or without convulsions is possible. Insulin dependent person may suffer from symptoms of hypoglycemic or hyperglycemic reactions (diabetic coma) depending on their insulin levels. The administration of insulin is, within itself, a complicated process requiring insulin, syringe, needle, alcohol sponge, and a sterile technique. Factors related to long haul commercial motor vehicle operation, such as fatigue, lack of sleep, poor diet, emotional conditions, stress, and concomitant illness, compound the diabetic problem. Thus, because of these inherent dangers, the FMCSA has consistently held that a driver required to use insulin for control does not meet the minimum physical requirements of the FMCSA.

Hypoglycemic drugs taken orally are sometimes prescribed for diabetic individuals to help control the disease by stimulating the natural production of insulin. If the condition can be controlled by the use of oral medication and diet, then an individual may be qualified under the present rule.

(See Cardiovascular Report on Diabetic Disorders and Commercial Drivers and Insulin-Using Commercial Motor Vehicle Drivers at http://www.fmcsa.gov/rulesregs/medreports.htm)

Cardiovascular Condition
§ 391.41(b)(4)

A person is physically qualified to drive a commercial motor vehicle if that person:

Has no current clinical diagnosis of myocardial infarction, angina pectoris, coronary insufficiency, thrombosis or any other cardiovascular disease of a variety known to be accompanied by syncope, dyspnea, collapse or congestive cardiac failure

The term "has no current clinical diagnosis of" is specifically designed to encompass "a clinical diagnosis of (1) a current cardiovascular condition, or (2) a cardiovascular condition which has not fully stabilized regardless of the time limit." The term "known to be accompanied" used to indicate clinical diagnosis of a cardiovascular disease (1) which is accompanied by symptoms.

Loss of Limb:
§ 391.41(b)(1)

A person is physically qualified to drive a commercial motor vehicle if that person:

has no loss of a foot, leg, hand or an arm, or has been granted a Skill Performance Evaluation (SPE) Certificate pursuant to Section 391.49.

Limb Impairment:
§ 391.41(b)(2)

A person is physically qualified to drive a commercial motor vehicle if that person:

Has no impairment of: (1) A hand or finger which interferes with prehension or power grasping; or (2) An arm, foot, or leg which interferes with the ability to perform normal tasks associated with operating a commercial motor vehicle; or (3) any other significant limb defect or limitation which interferes with the ability to perform normal tasks associated with operating a commercial motor vehicle; or (4) has been granted a Skill Performance Evaluation Certificate pursuant to Section 391.49.

A person who suffers loss of a foot, leg, hand or arm or whose limb impairment in any way interferes with the safe performance of normal tasks associated with operating a commercial motor vehicle, is subject to the Skill Performance Evaluation (SPE) Certificate Program pursuant to and set forth in 391.49. (assuming the person is otherwise qualified).

With the advancement of technology, medical aids and equipment modifications have been developed to compensate for certain disabilities. The SPE Certificate Program (formerly the Limb Waiver Program) was designed to allow persons with the loss of a foot or limb or with functional impairment to qualify under the Federal Motor Carrier Safety Regulations (FMCSRs) by use of prosthetic devices or equipment modifications which enable them to safely operate a commercial motor vehicle. Since then we are now in a position to evaluate individual drivers who are not otherwise physically qualified to drive. If the driver is found to be otherwise qualified, the SPE certificate's are necessary to be consistent with safety and public interest.

The SPE certificate is issued to otherwise medically qualified (391.41(b)(3) through (13)), the medical examiner must check on the medical certificate that the driver is qualified only if accompanied by a SPE certificate. The driver and the employing motor carrier are subject to appropriate penalty if the driver operates a motor vehicle without a current SPE certificate for his/her physical disability.

accompanied by symptoms of syncope, dyspnea, collapse or congestive cardiac failure; and/or (2) which is likely to cause syncope, dyspnea, collapse or congestive cardiac failure.

It is the intent of the FMCSRs to render unqualified a driver who has a current cardiovascular disease which is accompanied by and/or likely to cause symptoms of syncope, dyspnea, collapse or congestive cardiac failure. However, the presence of a cardiovascular disease is not in itself unqualifying, especially if the nature and severity of an individual's condition will likely cause symptoms of cardiovascular insufficiency, is not an individual basis and qualification rests with the medical examiner and the motor carrier. In those cases where there is an occurrence of cardiovascular insufficiency (myocardial infarction, thrombosis, etc.), it is suggested before a driver is certified that he or she have a normal resting and stress electrocardiogram (E.C.G.), no residual complications and no physical limitations, and is taking no medication likely to interfere with safe driving.

Certain arteries bypass surgery and pacemaker implantation are remedial procedures and thus, not unqualifying. Coumadin is a medical treatment which can improve the health and safety of the driver and should not, by its use, medically disqualify a commercial driver. The emphasis should be on the underlying medical condition(s) which require treatment and the general health of the driver. The FMCSA should be contacted at (202) 366-1790 for additional recommendations regarding the physical qualification of drivers on coumadin.

(See Conference on Cardiac Disorders and Commercial Drivers at http://www.fmcsa.dot.gov/rulecsrgs/medreports.htm)

Respiratory Dysfunction
§ 391.41(b)(5)

A person is physically qualified to drive a commercial motor vehicle if that person:

Has no established medical history or clinical diagnosis of a respiratory dysfunction likely to interfere with ability to control and drive a commercial motor vehicle safely.

Since a driver must be alert at all times, any change in his or her mental state or in direct contact with the loss of driver's ability adequately to perform his responsibilities while driving. Even the slightest impairment in respiratory function under emergency conditions (when greater oxygen supply is necessary for performance) may be detrimental to safe driving. There are many conditions that interfere with oxygen exchange and may result in incapacitation, including hypoxemia and ... If the medical consumer detects a respiratory dysfunction, that in any way is likely to interfere with the driver's ability to safely control and drive a commercial motor vehicle, the driver must be referred to a specialist for further evaluation and therapy. Anticoagulation for the treatment of pulmonary thromboembolism is not unqualifying once adequate anticoagulation dose is achieved, provided lower extremity venous examinations remain normal and the treating physician gives a favorable recommendation.

(See Conference on Pulmonary/Respiratory Disorders and Commercial Drivers at http://www.fmcsa.dot.gov/rulecsrgs/medreports.htm)

Hypertension
§ 391.41(b)(6)

A person is physically qualified to drive a commercial motor vehicle if that person:

Has no current clinical diagnosis of high blood pressure likely to interfere with ability to operate a commercial motor vehicle safely.

Hypertension alone is unlikely to cause sudden collapse; however, the likelihood increases when target organ damage, particularly cerebral vascular disease, is present. This regulatory criteria is based on FMCSA's Cardiac Conference recommendations, which used the report of the 1994 Joint National Committee on Detection, Evaluation, and Treatment of High Blood Pressure.

A blood pressure of 161-180 and/or 91-104 diastolic is considered mild hypertension, and the driver is not recommended unqualified during evaluation and institution of treatment. The driver is given a 3-month period to reduce his or her blood pressure to less than or equal to 160/90. He/she is only valid for the 3-month period. If the driver is subsequently found qualified with a blood pressure less than or equal to 160/90 during the certifying physical examination, may be certified for a 1-year period, but should confirm blood pressure control in the third month of the 1-year period. The individual should be certified annually thereafter. The expiration date must be considered.

A blood pressure of greater than 180 systolic and/or greater than 104 diastolic, is considered moderate to severe. The driver may not be qualified, even temporarily, until his or her blood pressure has been reduced to less than 181/105. The examining physicians may temporarily certify the individual once the individual's blood pressure is below 181 and/or 105. For blood pressure greater than 180 and/or 104, documentation of continued control should be made every 6 months. The individual should be certified biannually thereafter.

Commercial drivers who present for certification with normal blood pressures but are taking medications for hypertension should be certified for 1 year. For persons with blood pressure in the mild or moderate to severe range. Annual recertification is recommended if the medical examiner can certify on the same basis as individuals. The blood pressure at the time of the medical certificate.

An elevated blood pressure finding should be confirmed by at least two subsequent measurements taken on different days. Note the drivers regarding smoking, cardiovascular disease as relatives, and immoderate use of alcohol. An electrocardiogram (ECG) and blood profile, including glucose, cholesterol, BUN, creatinine and triglycerides should be made. An echocardiogram and chest x-ray are desirable in subjects with moderate or severe hypertension.

Since the presence of target damage increases the risk of sudden collapse; group 3 or 4 hypertensive retinopathy, left ventricular hypertrophy and elevated serum creatinine (echocardiogram), or LCV by Late criteria, evidence of severely reduced left ventricular function, or serum creatinine of greater than 2.5 warrants the driver being found unqualified to receive a commercial motor vehicle. In such cases, commence treatment include nonpharmacologic and pharmacologic modalities as well as counseling to reduce other risk factors. Most antihypertensive medications also have side effects, the importance of which must be judged on an individual basis. Individuals must be alerted to the hazards of these medications while driving. Side effects of somnolence, or syncope are particularly undesirable in commercial drivers.

A commercial driver who has normal blood pressure 3 or more months after a successful reduction for pheochromo-cytoma, primary aldosteronism (unless bilateral adrenalectomy has been performed), renal-arterial disease, or unilateral renal surgical intervention with no evidence of target organ damage, and who shown is no evidence of target organ disease, should be considered and is consistent with birth above. (See Conference on Cardiac Disorders and Commercial Drivers at http://www.fmcsa.dot.gov/rulecsrgs/medreports.htm)

Rheumatic, Arthritic, Orthopedic, Muscular, Neuromuscular or Vascular Disease
§ 391.41(b)(7)

A person is physically qualified to drive a commercial motor vehicle if that person:

Has no established medical history or clinical diagnosis of rheumatic, arthritic, orthopedic, muscular, neuromuscular or vascular disease which interferes with ability to control and operate a commercial motor vehicle safely.

Certain diseases are known to have acute episodes of transient muscle weakness, poor muscular coordination (ataxia), abnormal sensations (paresthesia), decreased muscular tone (hypotonia), visual disturbances and pain which may be suddenly incapacitating. With each recurring episode, these symptoms may become more pronounced and remain for longer periods of time. Other diseases have more insidious onsets and display symptoms of muscle wasting (atrophy), swelling and paresthesis which may not suddenly incapacitate a person but may cause recurring episodes and eventually interfere with the ability to operate a motor vehicle. In many instances these diseases are degenerative in nature or may result in deterioration of the involved area. Once the individual has been diagnosed as having a rheumatic, arthritic, orthopedic, muscular, neuromuscular or...

vascular disease, then he/she has an established history of that disease. The physician, when examining an individual, should consider the following: (1) the nature and severity of the individual's condition (such as sensory loss or loss of strength); (2) the degree of limitation present (such as range of motion); (3) the likelihood of progressive limitation (not always present initially but may manifest itself over time); and (4) the likelihood of sudden incapacitation. If serious enough, symptoms of such conditions can be medically disqualifying. In cases where more frequent monitoring is required, a certificate for a shorter time period may be issued
(See Conference on Neurological Disorders and Commercial Drivers at http://www.fmcsa.dot.gov/rulesregs/medreports.htm)

Epilepsy
§ 391.41(b)(8)

A person is physically qualified to drive a commercial motor vehicle if that person:

Has no established medical history or clinical diagnosis of epilepsy or any other condition which is likely to cause loss of consciousness or any loss of ability to control a motor vehicle

Epilepsy is a chronic functional disease characterized by seizures or loss of consciousness and motor control, resulting in loss of voluntary muscle control which may not require anticonvulsant medication. The decision as to whether that person's condition will likely cause loss of consciousness or loss of ability to control a motor vehicle is made on an individual basis by the medical examiner in consultation with the treating physician. Before certification is considered, it is suggested that a rest of at least seven years, free of the episode. Following the waiting period, it is suggested that the individual have a complete neurological examination. If the results of the examination are negative and anticonvulsant medication is not required, then the driver may be qualified. In those individual cases where a driver has a seizure or an episode of loss of consciousness that resulted from a known medical cause and is unlikely to recur, the driver may be qualified after recovering from the seizure or loss of consciousness. If an individual has had a sudden unexplained episode of loss of consciousness with no known medical cause, or a documented history of any specific disturbance(s), certification should be deferred until the driver has fully recovered from that condition and has no existing residual complication, and has not required anticonvulsant medication for the appropriate time period. In all situations, certification should also be deferred until the driver has been off medication for the appropriate time period and remains free of seizures.
(See Conference on Neurological Disorders and Commercial Drivers at http://www.fmcsa.dot.gov/rulesregs/medreports.htm)

Mental Disorders
§ 391.41(b)(9)

A person is physically qualified to drive a commercial motor vehicle if that person:

Has no mental, nervous, organic or functional disease or psychiatric disorder likely to interfere with ability to drive a motor vehicle safely

Emotional or adjustment problems contribute directly to an individual's level of memory, reasoning, attention and judgment. These problems often underlie physical disorders. A variety of functional disorders can cause drowsiness, dizziness, confusion, weakness or paralysis that may lead to incoordination, inattention, loss of functional control and susceptibility in accidents while driving. Physical fatigue, headache, impaired coordination, recurring physical ailment and chronic "nagging" pain may be present to such a degree that certification for commercial driving is not usable. Somatic and psychosomatic complaints should be thoroughly examined when determining an individual's overall ability to drive. Disorders of a periodically incapacitating nature, even in the early stages of development, may warrant disqualification.

Many bus and truck drivers have documented that "nervous trouble" related to neurotic, personality, emotional or adjustment problems is responsible for a significant fraction of their preventable accidents. The degree to which an individual is unable or unwilling to properly control and operate their motor vehicle can be predictive in assessing an individual's mental alertness and likelihood to cope with the stresses of commercial motor vehicle driving.

When examining the driver, it should be kept in mind that individuals who live under chronic emotional upsets may have deeply ingrained maladaptive or erratic behavior patterns. Excessively antagonistic, suspicious, instinctive, impulsive, aggressive, paranoid or severely depressed behavior greatly interfere with the driver's ability to drive safely. Those individuals who are highly susceptible to frequent states of emotional instability (schizophrenia, affective psychoses, paranoia, anxiety or depressive neuroses) may warrant disqualification. Careful consideration should be given to the side effects and interactions of medications in the overall qualification determination. See Psychiatric Conference Report for specific recommendations on the use of these medications and potential hazards for driving.
(See Conference on Psychiatric Disorders and Commercial Drivers at http://www.fmcsa.dot.gov/rulesregs/medreports.htm)

Vision
§ 391.41(b)(10)

A person is physically qualified to drive a commercial motor vehicle if that person:

Has distant visual acuity of at least 20/40 (Snellen) in each eye with or without corrective lenses or visual acuity separately corrected to 20/40 (Snellen) or better with corrective lenses, distant binocular acuity of at least 20/40 (Snellen) in both eyes with or without corrective lenses, field of vision of at least 70 degrees in the horizontal meridian in each eye, and the ability to recognize the colors of traffic signals and devices showing standard red, green and amber

The term "ability to recognize the colors of" is interpreted to mean if a person can recognize and distinguish among traffic control signals and devices showing standard red, green and amber. So he/she may have some type of color perception deficiency, if he/she can recognize and distinguish among traffic control signals and devices showing standard red, green and amber, he/she meets the minimum standard, s he/she may have some type of color perception deficiency. If certain color perception tests are administered (such as Ishihara, Pseudoisochromatic, Yarn) and if such findings are questionable for using signal red, green and amber they may be employed to determine the driver's ability to recognize those colors.

Contact lenses are permissible if there is sufficient evidence to indicate that the driver has good tolerance and is well adapted to their use. Use of a contact lens in one eye for distance visual acuity and another lens in the other eye for near vision is not acceptable, nor telescopic lenses acceptable for the driving of commercial motor vehicles.

If an individual meets the criteria by the use of glasses or contact lenses, the following statement shall appear on the Medical Examiner's Certificate: "Qualified only if wearing corrective lenses"
(See Visual Disorders and Commercial Drivers at http://www.fmcsa.dot.gov/rulesregs/medreports.htm)

Hearing
§ 391.41(b)(11)

A person is physically qualified to drive a commercial motor vehicle if that person:

First perceives a forced whispered voice in the better ear at not less than 5 feet with or without the use of a hearing aid or, if tested by use of an audiometric device, does not have an average hearing loss in the better ear greater than 40 decibels at 500 Hz, 1,000 Hz and 2,000 Hz with or without a hearing aid when the audiometric device is calibrated to American National Standard (formerly ASA Standard) Z24.5-1951

Since the perceived standard under the FMCSRs is the American Standards Association (ASA), it may be necessary to convert the audiometric results from the ISA standard to the ANSI standard. Instructions are included on the Medical Examination report form.

If an individual meets the criteria by using a hearing aid, the driver must wear that hearing aid and have it in operation at all times while driving. Also, the driver should be in possession of a spare power source for the hearing aid.

For the whispered voice test, the individual should be stationed at least 5 feet from the examiner with the ear being tested turned toward the examiner. The other ear is covered. Using the breath which remains after a normal expiration, the examiner whispers words (a random numbers such as 66, 18, 23, and five) before the child uses any sibilant (the s-sounding test materials). The opposite ear should be tested in the same manner. If the individual fails the whispered voice test, the audiometric test should be administered.

If an individual meets the criteria by the use of a hearing aid, the following statement must appear on the Medical Examiner's Certificate "Qualified only when wearing a hearing aid."

[See Hearing Disorders and Commercial Motor Vehicle Drivers at
http://www.fmcsa.dot.gov/rulesregs/medreports.htm]

Drug Use
§ 391.41(b)(12)
A person is physically qualified to drive a commercial motor vehicle if that person:

Does not use a controlled substance identified in 21 CFR 1308.11 Schedule I, an amphetamine, a narcotic, or any other habit-forming drug. Exception: A driver may use such a substance or drug, if the substance or drug is prescribed by a licensed medical practitioner who is familiar with the driver's medical history and assigned duties; and has informed the driver that the prescribed substance or drug will not adversely affect the driver's ability to safely operate a commercial motor vehicle.

This exception does not apply to methadone. The intent of the medical certification process is so medically examine a driver to ensure that the driver has no medical condition which interferes with the safe performance of driving tasks on a public road. If a driver uses a Schedule I drug or other habit-forming drug, it may be cause for the driver to be found medically unqualified. Motor carriers are encouraged to obtain a practitioner's written statement about the effects on transportation safety of the use of a particular drug.

A test for controlled substances is not required as part of this biennial certification process. The FMCSA or the driver's employer may conduct drug tests directly for information on controlled substances and alcohol testing under Part 382 of the FMCSRs.

The term "uses" is designed to encompass instances of prohibited drug use determined by a physician through established medical means. This may or may not involve body fluid testing. If body fluid testing takes place, positive test results should be confirmed by a second test of greater

specificity. The term "habit-forming" is intended to include any drug or medication generally recognized as capable of becoming habitual, and which may impair the user's ability to operate a commercial motor vehicle safely.

The driver as medically unqualified for the duration of the prohibited drug's use and until a second examination shows the driver is free from the prohibited drug's use.

Recertification may involve a substance abuse evaluation, the successful completion of a drug rehabilitation program, and a negative drug test result. Additionally, given that the certification period is normally two years, the examiner has the option to certify for a period of less than 2 years if the examiner determines more frequent monitoring is required.

[See Conference on Neurological Disorders and Commercial Drivers and Conference on Psychiatric Disorders and Commercial Drivers at
http://www.fmcsa.dot.gov/rulesregs/medreports.htm]

Alcoholism
§ 391.41(b)(13)
A person is physically qualified to drive a commercial motor vehicle if that person:

Has no current clinical diagnosis of alcoholism

The term "current clinical diagnosis of" is specifically designed to encompass a current alcoholic illness or those instances where the individual's physical condition has not fully stabilized, regardless of the time element. If an individual shows signs of having an alcohol-use problem he or she should be referred to a specialist. After continuing medical treatment, he or she may be considered for certification.

(g) If the medical examiner finds that the person he/she examined is physically qualified to drive a commercial motor vehicle in accordance with §391.41(b), the medical examiner shall complete a certificate in the form prescribed in paragraph (h) of this section and furnish one copy to the person who was examined and one copy to the motor carrier that employs him/her.

(h) The medical examiner's certificate shall be substantially in accordance with the following form. Existing forms may be used until current printed supplies are depleted or until November 6, 2001, whichever occurs first.

MEDICAL EXAMINER'S CERTIFICATE

I certify that I have examined _____ in accordance with the Federal Motor Carrier Safety Regulations (49 CFR 391.41-391.49) and with knowledge of the driving duties, I find this person is qualified; and, if applicable, only when:

☐ wearing corrective lenses

☐ wearing hearing aid

driving within an exempt intracity zone (49 CFR 391.62)

accompanied by a Skill Performance Evaluation Certificate (SPE)

☐ accompanied by a _____ waiver/exemption

☐ Qualified by operation of 49 CFR 391.64

The information I have provided regarding this physical examination is true and complete. A complete examination form with any attachment embodies my findings completely and correctly, and is on file in my office.

SIGNATURE OF MEDICAL EXAMINER _____ TELEPHONE _____ DATE _____

MEDICAL EXAMINER'S NAME (PRINT) _____

☐ MD ☐ DO ☐ Chiropractor

☐ Physician Assistant ☐ Advanced Practice Nurse

MEDICAL EXAMINER'S LICENSE OR CERTIFICATE NO. / ISSUING STATE _____

SIGNATURE OF DRIVER _____ DRIVER'S LICENSE NO. _____ STATE _____

ADDRESS OF DRIVER _____

MEDICAL CERTIFICATE EXPIRATION DATE _____

§391.45 Persons who must be medically examined and certified.

Except as provided in §391.67, the following persons must be medically examined and certified in accordance with §391.43 as physically qualified to operate a commercial motor vehicle:

(a) Any person who has not been medically examined and certified as physically qualified to operate a commercial motor vehicle;

(b)(1) Any driver who has not been medically examined and certified as qualified to operate a commercial motor vehicle during the preceding 24 months; or

(2) Any driver authorized to operate a commercial motor vehicle only with an exempt intracity zone pursuant to §391.62, or only by operation of the exemption in §391.64, if such driver has not been medically examined and certified as qualified to drive in such zone during the preceding 12 months; and

(c) Any driver whose ability to perform his/her normal duties has been impaired by a physical or mental injury or disease.

§391.47 Resolution of conflicts of medical evaluation.

(a) **Applications.** Applications for determination of a driver's medical qualifications under standards in this part will only be accepted if they conform to the requirements of this section.

(b) **Content.** Applications will be accepted for consideration only if the following conditions are met.

(1) The application must contain the name and address of the driver, motor carrier, and all physicians involved in the proceeding.

(2) The applicant must submit proof that there is a disagreement between the physician for the driver and the physician for the motor carrier concerning the driver's qualifications.

(3) The applicant must submit a copy of an opinion and report including results of all tests of an impartial medical specialist in the field in which the medical conflict arose. The specialist should be one agreed to by the motor carrier and the driver.

(i) In cases where the driver refuses to agree on a specialist and the applicant is the motor carrier the applicant must submit a statement of his/her agreement to submit the matter to an impartial medical specialist in the field, proof that he/she has requested the driver to submit to the medical specialist, and the response, if any, of the driver to his/her request.

(ii) In cases where the motor carrier refuses to agree on a medical specialist, the driver must submit an opinion and test results of an impartial medical specialist, proof that he/she has requested the motor carrier to agree to submit the matter to the medical specialist and the response, if any, of the motor carrier to his/her request.

(4) The applicant must include a statement explaining in detail why the decision of the medical specialist identified in para-

graph (b)(3) of this section is unacceptable.

(5) The applicant must submit proof that the medical specialist mentioned in paragraph (b)(3) of this section was provided, prior to his/her determination, the medical history of the driver and an agreed-upon statement of the work the driver performs.

(6) The applicant must submit the medical history and statement of work provided to the medical specialist under paragraph (b)(5) of this section.

(7) The applicant must submit all medical records and statements of the physicians who have given opinions on the driver's qualifications.

(8) The applicant must submit a description and a copy of all written and documentary evidence upon which the party making application relies in the form set out in 49 CFR §386.37.

(9) The application must be accompanied by a statement of the driver that he/she intends to drive in interstate commerce not subject to the commercial zone exemption or a statement of the carrier that he/she has used or intends to use the driver for such work.

(10) The applicant must submit three copies of the application and all records.

(c) **Information.** The Director, Office of Motor Carrier Research and Standards may request further information from the applicant if he/she determines that a decision cannot be made on the evidence submitted. If the applicant fails to submit the information requested, the Director, Office of Motor Carrier Research and Standards may refuse to issue a determination.

(d)(1) **Action.** Upon receiving a satisfactory application the Director, Office of Motor Carrier Research and Standards shall notify the parties (the driver, motor carrier, or any other interested party) that the application has been accepted and that a determination will be made. A copy of all evidence received shall be attached to the notice.

(2) **Reply.** Any party may submit a reply to the notification within 15 days after service. Such reply must be accompanied by all evidence the party wants the Director, Office of Motor Carrier Research and Standards to consider in making his/her determination. Evidence submitted should include all medical records and test results upon which the party relies.

(3) **Parties.** A party for the purposes of this section includes the motor carrier and the driver, or anyone else submitting an application.

(e) **Petitions to review, burden of proof.** The driver or motor carrier may petition to review the Director's determination. Such petition must be submitted in accordance with §386.13(a) of this chapter. The burden of proof in such a proceeding is on the petitioner.

(f) **Status of driver.** Once an application is submitted to the Director, Office of Motor Carrier Research and Standards, the driver shall be deemed disqualified until such time as the Director, Office of Motor Carrier Research and Standards makes a determination, or until the Director, Office of Motor Carrier Research and Standards orders otherwise.

§391.49 Alternative physical qualification standards for the loss or impairment of limbs.

(a) A person who is not physically qualified to drive under §391.41(b)(1) or (b)(2) and who is otherwise qualified to drive a commercial motor vehicle, may drive a commercial motor vehicle, if the State Director, FMCSA, has granted a Skill Performance Evaluation (SPE) Certificate to that person.

(b) **SPE certificate.**—(1) **Application.** A letter of application for an SPE certificate may be submitted jointly by the person (driver applicant) who seeks an SPE certificate and by the motor carrier that will employ the driver applicant, if the application is accepted.

(2) **Application address.** The application must be addressed to the applicable field service center, FMCSA, for the State in which the co-applicant motor carrier's principal place of business is located. The address of each, and the States serviced, are listed in §390.27 of this chapter.

(3) **Exception.** A letter of application for an SPE certificate may be submitted unilaterally by a driver applicant. The application must be addressed to the field service center, FMCSA, for the State in which the driver has legal residence. The driver applicant must comply with all the requirements of paragraph (c) of this section except those in (c)(1)(i) and (iii). The driver applicant shall respond to the requirements of paragraphs (c)(2)(i) to (v) of this section, if the information is known.

(c) A letter of application for an SPE certificate shall contain:

(1) Identification of the applicant(s):

(i) Name and complete address of the motor carrier coapplicant;

(ii) Name and complete address of the driver applicant;

(iii) The U.S. DOT Motor Carrier Identification Number, if known; and

(iv) A description of the driver applicant's limb impairment for which SPE certificate is requested.

(2) Description of the type of operation the driver will be employed to perform:

(i) State(s) in which the driver will operate for the motor carrier coapplicant (if more than 10 States, designate general geographic area only);

(ii) Average period of time the driver will be driving and/or on duty, per day;

(iii) Type of commodities or cargo to be transported;

(iv) Type of driver operation (*i.e.*, sleeper team, relay, owner operator, etc.); and

(v) Number of years experience operating the type of commercial motor vehicle(s) requested in the letter of application and total years of experience operating all types of commercial motor vehicles.

(3) Description of the commercial motor vehicle(s) the driver applicant intends to drive:

(i) Truck, truck tractor, or bus make, model, and year (if known);

(ii) Drive train;

(A) Transmission type (automatic or manual—if manual, designate number of forward speeds);

(B) Auxiliary transmission (if any) and number of forward speeds; and

(C) Rear axle (designate single speed, 2 speed, or 3 speed).

(iii) Type of brake system;

(iv) Steering, manual or power assisted;

(v) Description of type of trailer(s) (i.e., van, flatbed, cargo tank, drop frame, lowboy, or pole);

(vi) Number of semitrailers or full trailers to be towed at one time;

(vii) For commercial motor vehicles designed to transport passengers, indicate the seating capacity of commercial motor vehicle; and

(viii) Description of any modification(s) made to the commercial motor vehicle for the driver applicant; attach photograph(s) where applicable.

(4) Otherwise qualified:

(i) The coapplicant motor carrier must certify that the driver applicant is otherwise qualified under the regulations of this part;

(ii) In the case of a unilateral application, the driver applicant must certify that he/she is otherwise qualified under the regulations of this part.

(5) Signature of applicant(s):

(i) Driver applicant's signature and date signed;

(ii) Motor carrier official's signature (if application has a coapplicant), title, and date signed. Depending upon the motor carrier's organizational structure (corporation, partnership, or proprietorship), the signer of the application shall be an officer, partner, or the proprietor.

(d) The letter of application for an SPE certificate shall be accompanied by:

(1) A copy of the results of the medical examination performed pursuant to §391.43;

(2) A copy of the medical certificate completed pursuant to §391.43(h);

(3) A medical evaluation summary completed by either a board qualified or board certified physiatrist (doctor of physical medicine) or orthopedic surgeon. The coapplicant motor carrier or the driver applicant shall provide the physiatrist or orthopedic surgeon with a description of the job-related tasks the driver applicant will be required to perform;

(i) The medical evaluation summary for a driver applicant disqualified under §391.41(b)(1) shall include:

(A) An assessment of the functional capabilities of the driver as they relate to the ability of the driver to perform normal tasks associated with operating a commercial motor vehicle; and

(B) A statement by the examiner that the applicant is capable of demonstrating precision prehension (*e.g.*, manipulating knobs and switches) and power grasp prehension (*e.g.*, holding and maneuvering the steering wheel) with each upper limb separately. This requirement does not apply to an individual who was granted a waiver, absent a prosthetic device, prior to the publication of this amendment.

(ii) The medical evaluation summary for a driver applicant disqualified under §391.41(b)(2) shall include:

(A) An explanation as to how and why the impairment interferes with the ability of the applicant to perform normal tasks associated with operating a commercial motor vehicle;

(B) An assessment and medical opinion of whether the condition will likely remain medically stable over the lifetime of the driver applicant; and

(C) A statement by the examiner that the applicant is capable of demonstrating precision prehension (*e.g.*, manipulating knobs and switches) and power grasp prehension (*e.g.*, holding and maneuvering the steering wheel) with each upper limb separately. This requirement does not apply to an individual who was granted an SPE certificate, absent an orthotic device, prior to the publication of this amendment.

(4) A description of the driver applicant's prosthetic or orthotic device worn, if any;

(5) Road test:

(i) A copy of the driver applicant's road test administered by the motor carrier coapplicant and the certificate issued pursuant to §391.31(b) through (g); or

(ii) A unilateral applicant shall be responsible for having a road test administered by a motor carrier or a person who is competent to administer the test and evaluate its results.

(6) Application for employment:

(i) A copy of the driver applicant's application for employment completed pursuant to §391.21; or

(ii) A unilateral applicant shall be responsible for submitting a copy of the last commercial driving position's employment application he/she held. If not previously employed as a commercial driver, so state.

(7) A copy of the driver applicant's SPE certificate of certain physical defects issued by the individual State(s), where applicable; and

(8) A copy of the driver applicant's State Motor Vehicle Driving Record for the past 3 years from each State in which a motor vehicle driver's license or permit has been obtained.

(e) **Agreement.** A motor carrier that employs a driver with an SPE certificate agrees to:

(1) File promptly (within 30 days of the involved incident) with the Medical Program Specialist, FMCSA service center, such documents and information as may be required about driving activities, accidents, arrests, license suspensions, revocations, or withdrawals, and convictions which involve the driver applicant. This applies whether the driver's SPE certificate is a unilateral one or has a coapplicant motor carrier;

(i) A motor carrier who is a coapplicant must file the required documents with the Medical Program Specialist, FMCSA for the State in which the carrier's principal place of business is located; or

(ii) A motor carrier who employs a driver who has been issued a unilateral SPE certificate must file the required documents with the Medical Program Specialist, FMCSA service center, for the State in which the driver has legal residence.

(2) Evaluate the driver with a road test using the trailer the motor carrier intends the driver to transport or, in lieu of, accept a certificate of a trailer road test from another motor carrier if the trailer type(s) is similar, or accept the trailer road test done during the Skill Performance Evaluation if it is a similar trailer type(s) to that of the prospective motor carrier. Job tasks, as stated in paragraph (e)(3) of this section, are not evaluated in the Skill Performance Evaluation;

(3) Evaluate the driver for those nondriving safety related job tasks associated with whatever type of trailer(s) will be used and any other nondriving safety related or job related tasks unique to the operations of the employing motor carrier; and

(4) Use the driver to operate the type of commercial motor vehicle defined in the SPE certificate only when the driver is in compliance with the conditions and limitations of the SPE certificate.

(f) The driver shall supply each employing motor carrier with a copy of the SPE certificate.

(g) The State Director, FMCSA, may require the driver applicant to demonstrate his or her ability to safely operate the commercial motor vehicle(s) the driver intends to drive to an agent of the State Director, FMCSA. The SPE certificate form will identify the power unit (bus, truck, truck tractor) for which the SPE certificate has been granted. The SPE certificate forms will also identify the trailer type used in the Skill Performance Evaluation; however, the SPE certificate is not limited to that specific trailer type. A driver may use the SPE certificate with other trailer types if a successful trailer road test is completed in accordance with paragraph (e)(2) of this section. Job tasks, as stated in paragraph (e)(3) of this section, are not evaluated during the Skill Performance Evaluation.

(h) The State Director, FMCSA, may deny the application for SPE certificate or may grant it totally or in part and issue the SPE certificate subject to such terms, conditions, and limitations as deemed consistent with the public interest. The SPE certificate is valid for a period not to exceed 2 years from date of issue, and may be renewed 30 days prior to the expiration date.

(i) The SPE certificate renewal application shall be submitted to the Medical Program Specialist, FMCSA service center, for the State in which the driver has legal residence, if the SPE certificate was issued unilaterally. If the SPE certificate has a coapplicant, then the renewal application is submitted to the Medical Program Specialist, FMCSA field service center, for the State in which the coapplicant motor carrier's principal place of business is located. The SPE certificate renewal application shall contain the following:

(1) Name and complete address of motor carrier currently employing the applicant;

(2) Name and complete address of the driver;

(3) Effective date of the current SPE certificate;

(4) Expiration date of the current SPE certificate;

(5) Total miles driven under the current SPE certificate;

(6) Number of accidents incurred while driving under the current SPE certificate, including date of the accident(s), number of fatalities, number of injuries, and the estimated dollar amount of property damage;

(7) A current medical examination report;

(8) A medical evaluation summary pursuant to paragraph (d)(3) of this section, if an unstable medical condition exists. All handicapped conditions classified under §391.41(b)(1) are considered unstable. Refer to paragraph (d)(3)(ii) of this section for the condition under §391.41(b)(2) which may be considered medically stable.

(9) A copy of driver's current State motor vehicle driving record for the period of time the current SPE certificate has been in effect;

(10) Notification of any change in the type of tractor the driver will operate;

(11) Driver's signature and date signed; and

(12) Motor carrier coapplicant's signature and date signed.

(j)(1) Upon granting an SPE certificate, the State Director, FMCSA, will notify the driver applicant and co-applicant motor carrier (if applicable) by letter. The terms, conditions, and limitations of the SPE certificate will be set forth. A motor carrier shall maintain a copy of the SPE certificate in its driver qualification file. A copy of the SPE certificate shall be retained in the motor carrier's file for a period of 3 years after the driver's employment is terminated. The driver applicant shall have the SPE certificate (or a legible copy) in his/her possession whenever on duty.

(2) Upon successful completion of the skill performance evaluation, the State Director, FMCSA, for the State where the driver applicant has legal residence, must notify the driver by letter and enclose an SPE certificate substantially in the following form:

Skill Performance Evaluation Certificate

Name of Issuing Agency:_____
Agency Address: _____
Telephone Number: (   )_____

Issued Under 49 CFR 391.49, subchapter B of the Federal Motor Carrier Safety Regulations

Driver's Name:_____
Effective Date: _____
SSN:_____
DOB:_____
Expiration Date:_____
Address:_____
_____
_____

Driver Disability: _____
Check One:__New__Renewal
Driver's License:_____
       (State)   (Number)

In accordance with 49 CFR 391.49, subchapter B of the Federal Motor Carrier Safety Regulations (FMCSRs), the driver application for a skill performance evaluation (SPE) certificate is hereby granted authorizing the above-named driver to operate in interstate or foreign commerce under the provisions set forth below. This certificate is granted for the period shown above, not to exceed 2 years, subject to periodic review as may be found necessary. This certificate may be renewed upon submission of a renewal application. Continuation of this certificate is dependent upon strict adherence by the above-named driver to the provisions set forth below and compliance with the FMCSRs. Any failure to comply with provisions herein may be cause for cancellation.

CONDITIONS: As a condition of this certificate, reports of all accidents, arrests, suspensions, revocations, withdrawals of driver licenses or permits, and convictions involving the above-named driver shall be reported in writing to the Issuing Agency by the EMPLOYING MOTOR CARRIER within 30 days after occurrence.

LIMITATIONS:

1. Vehicle Type (power unit):*_____

2. Vehicle modification(s): _____

3. Prosthetic or Orthotic device(s) (Required to be Worn While Driving): _____
_____

4. Additional Provision(s): _____
_____

NOTICE: To all MOTOR CARRIERS employing a driver with an SPE certificate. This certificate is granted for the operation of the *power unit only*. It is the responsibility of the employing motor carrier to evaluate the driver with a road test using the trailer type(s) the motor carrier intends the driver to transport, or in lieu of, accept the trailer road test done during the SPE if it is a similar trailer type(s) to that of the prospective motor carrier. Also, it is the responsibility of the employing motor carrier to evaluate the driver for those non-driving safety-related job tasks associated with the type of trailer(s) utilized, as well as, any other non-driving safety-related or job-related tasks unique to the operations of the employing motor carrier.

The SPE of the above named driver was given by a Skill Performance Evaluation Program Specialist. It was successfully completed utilizing the above named power unit and _____(trailer, if applicable)

The tractor or truck had a _____ transmission.

Please read the *NOTICE* paragraph above.

Name: _____
Signature: _____
Title: _____
Date: _____

(k) The State Director, FMCSA, may revoke an SPE certificate after the person to whom it was issued is given notice of the proposed revocation and has been allowed a reasonable opportunity to appeal.

(l) Falsifying information in the letter of application, the renewal application, or falsifying information required by this section by either the applicant or motor carrier is prohibited.

Subpart F — Files and Records

§391.51 General requirements for driver qualification files.

(a) Each motor carrier shall maintain a driver qualification file for each driver it employs. A driver's qualification file may be combined with his/her personnel file.

(b) The qualification file for a driver must include:

(1) The driver's application for employment completed in accordance with §391.21;

(2) A written record with respect to each past employer who was contacted and a copy of the response by each State agency, pursuant to §391.23 involving investigation and inquiries;

(3) The certificate of driver's road test issued to the driver pursuant to §391.31(e), or a copy of the license or certificate which the motor carrier accepted as equivalent to the driver's road test pursuant to §391.33;

(4) The response of each State agency to the annual driver record inquiry required by §391.25(a);

(5) A note relating to the annual review of the driver's driving record as required by §391.25(c)(2);

(6) A list or certificate relating to violations of motor vehicle laws and ordinances required by §391.27;

(7) The medical examiner's certificate of his/her physical qualification to drive a commercial motor vehicle as required by §391.43(f) or a legible photographic copy of the certificate; and

(8) A letter from the Regional Director of Motor Carriers granting a waiver of a physical disqualification, if a waiver was issued under §391.49.

(c) Except as provided in paragraph (d) of this section, each driver's qualification file shall be retained for as long as a driver is employed by that motor carrier and for three years thereafter.

(d) The following records may be removed from a driver's qualification file three years after the date of execution:

(1) The response of each State agency to the annual driver record inquiry required by §391.25(a);

(2) The note relating to the annual review of the driver's driving record as required by §391.25(c)(2);

(3) The list or certificate relating to violations of motor vehicle laws and ordinances required by §391.27;

(4) The medical examiner's certificate of the driver's physical qualification to drive a commercial motor vehicle or the photographic copy of the certificate as required by §391.43(f); and

(5) The letter issued under §391.49 granting a waiver of a physical disqualification.

(Approved by the Office of management and Budget under control number 2125-0065)

Subpart G — Limited Exemptions

§391.61 Drivers who were regularly employed before January 1, 1971.

The provisions of §391.21 (relating to applications for employment), §391.23 (relating to investigations and inquiries), and §391.31 (relating to road tests) do not apply to a driver who has been a single-employer driver (as defined in §390.5 of this subchapter) of a motor carrier for a continuous period which began before January 1, 1971, as long as he/she continues to be a single-employer driver of that motor carrier.

§391.62 Limited exemptions for intra-city zone drivers.

The provisions of §§391.11(b)(1) and 391.41(b)(1) through (b)(11) do not apply to a person who:

(a) Was otherwise qualified to operate and operated a commercial motor vehicle in a municipality or exempt intracity zone thereof throughout the one-year period ending November 18, 1988;

(b) Meets all the other requirements of this section;

(c) Operates wholly within the exempt intracity zone (as defined in 49 CFR 390.5);

(d) Does not operate a vehicle used in the transportation of hazardous materials in a quantity requiring placarding under regulations issued by the Secretary under 49 U.S.C. chapter 51; and

(e) Has a medical or physical condition which:

(1) Would have prevented such person from operating a commercial motor vehicle under the Federal Motor Carrier Safety Regulations contained in this subchapter;

(2) Existed on July 1, 1988, or at the time of the first required physical examination after that date; and

(3) The examining physician has determined this condition has not substantially worsened since July 1, 1988, or at the time of the first required physical examination after that date.

§391.63 Multiple-employer drivers.

(a) If a motor carrier employs a person as a multiple-employer driver (as defined in §390.5 of this subchapter) the motor carrier shall comply with all requirements of this part, except that the motor carrier need not —

(1) Require the person to furnish an application for employment in accordance with §391.21;

(2) Make the investigations and inquiries specified in §391.23 with respect to that person;

(3) Perform the annual driving record inquiry required by §391.25(a);

(4) Perform the annual review of the person's driving record required by §391.25(b); or

(5) Require the person to furnish a record of violations or a certificate in accordance with §391.27.

(b) Before a motor carrier permits a multiple-employer driver to drive a commercial motor vehicle, the motor carrier must obtain his/her name, his/her social security number, and the identification number, type and issuing State of his/her commercial motor vehicle operator's license. The motor carrier must maintain this information for 3 years after employment of the multiple-employer driver ceases.

(Approved by the Office of Management and Budget under control number 2125-0081)

§391.64 Grandfathering for certain drivers participating in vision and diabetes waiver study programs.

(a) The provisions of §391.41(b)(3) do not apply to a driver who was a participant in good standing on March 31, 1996, in a waiver study program concerning the operation of commercial motor vehicles by insulin-controlled diabetic drivers; provided:

(1) The driver is physically examined every year, including an examination by a board-certified/eligible endocrinologist attesting to the fact that the driver is:

(i) Otherwise qualified under §391.41;

(ii) Free of insulin reactions (an individual is free of insulin reactions if that individual does not have severe hypoglycemia or hypoglycemia unawareness, and has less than one documented, symptomatic hypoglycemic reaction per month);

(iii) Able to and has demonstrated willingness to properly monitor and manage his/her diabetes; and

(iv) Not likely to suffer any diminution in driving ability due to his/her diabetic condition.

(2) The driver agrees to and complies with the following conditions:

(i) A source of rapidly absorbable glucose shall be carried at all times while driving;

(ii) Blood glucose levels shall be self-monitored one hour prior to driving and at least once every four hours while driving or on duty prior to driving using a portable glucose monitoring device equipped with a computerized memory;

(iii) Submit blood glucose logs to the endocrinologist or medical examiner at the annual examination or when otherwise directed by an authorized agent of the FHWA;

(iv) Provide a copy of the endocrinologist's report to the medical examiner at the time of the annual medical examination; and

(v) Provide a copy of the annual medical certification to the employer for retention in the driver's qualification file and retain a copy of the certification on his/her person while driving for presentation to a duly authorized Federal, State or local enforcement official.

(b) The provisions of §391.41(b)(10) do not apply to a driver who was a participant in good standing on March 31, 1996, in a waiver study program concerning the operation of commercial motor vehicles by drivers with visual impairment in one eye; provided:

(1) The driver is physically examined every year, including an examination by an ophthalmologist or optometrist attesting to the fact that the driver:

(i) Is otherwise qualified under §391.41; and

(ii) Continues to measure at least 20/40 (Snellen) in the better eye.

(2) The driver provides a copy of the ophthalmologist or optometrist report to the medical examiner at the time of the annual medical examination.

(3) The driver provides a copy of the annual medical certification to the employer for retention in the driver's qualification file and retains a copy of the certification on his/her person while driving for presentation to a duly authorized federal, state or local enforcement official.

§391.65 Drivers furnished by other motor carriers.

(a) A motor carrier may employ a driver who is not a regularly employed driver of that motor carrier without complying with the generally applicable driver qualification file requirements in this part, if —

(1) The driver is regularly employed by another motor carrier; and

(2) The motor carrier which regularly employs the driver certifies that the driver is fully qualified to drive a commercial motor vehicle in a written statement which—

(i) Is signed and dated by an officer or authorized employee of the regularly employing carrier;

(ii) Contains the driver's name and signature;

(iii) Certifies that the driver has been regularly employed as defined in §390.5;

(iv) Certifies that the driver is fully qualified to drive a commercial motor vehicle under the rules in Part 391 of the Federal Motor Carrier Safety Regulations;

(v) States the expiration date of the driver's medical examiner's certificate;

(vi) Specifies an expiration date for the certificate, which shall be not longer that 2 years or, if earlier, the expiration date of the driver's current medical examiner's certificate; and

(vii) After April 1, 1977, is substantially in accordance with the following form:

(Name of driver)   (SS No.)

(Signature of driver)

I certify that the above named driver, as defined in §390.5 is regularly driving a commercial motor vehicle operated by the below named carrier and is fully qualified under Part 391, Federal Motor Carrier Safety Regulations. His current medical examiner's certificate expires on _____

(Date)

This certificate expires: _____

(Date not later than expiration date of medical certificate)

Issued on _____

(Date)

Issued by _____

(Name of carrier)

(Address)

(Signature)(Title)

(b) A motor carrier that obtains a certificate in accordance with paragraph (a)(2) of this section shall:

(1) Contact the motor carrier which certified the driver's qualifications under this section to verify the validity of the certificate. This contact may be made in person, by telephone, or by letter.

(2) Retain a copy of that certificate in its files for three years.

(c) A motor carrier which certifies a driver's qualifications under this section shall be responsible for the accuracy of the certificate. The certificate is no longer valid if the driver leaves the employment of the motor carrier which issued the certificate or is no longer qualified under the rules in this part.

§391.67 Farm vehicle drivers of articulated commercial motor vehicles.

The following rules in this part do not apply to a farm vehicle driver (as defined in §390.5 of this subchapter) who is 18 years of age or older and who drives an articulated commercial motor vehicle:

(a) Section 391.11(b)(1), (b)(6), and (b)(8) (relating to general qualifications of drivers);

(b) Subpart C (relating to disclosure of, investigation into, and inquiries about the background, character, and driving record of drivers);

(c) Subpart D (relating to road tests); and

(d) Subpart F (relating to maintenance of files and records).

§391.68 Private motor carrier of passengers (nonbusiness).

The following rules in this part do not apply to a private motor carrier of passengers (nonbusiness) and its drivers:

(a) Section 391.11(b)(1), (b)(6), and (b)(8), (relating to general qualifications of drivers);

(b) Subpart C (relating to disclosure of, investigation into, and inquiries about the background, character, and driving record of, drivers);

(c) So much of §§391.41 and 391.45 as require a driver to be medically examined and to have a medical examiner's certificate on his/her person; and

(d) Subpart F (relating to maintenance of files and records).

§391.69 Private motor carrier of passengers (business).

The provisions of §391.21 (relating to applications for employment), §391.23 (relating to investigations and inquiries), and §391.31 (relating to road tests) do not apply to a driver who was a single-employer driver (as defined in §390.5 of this subchapter) of a private motor carrier of passengers (business) as of July 1, 1994, so long as the driver continues to be a single-employer driver of that motor carrier.

§391.71 [Removed and reserved]

PART 392 — DRIVING OF COMMERCIAL MOTOR VEHICLES

Subpart A — General

Subpart E — License Revocation; Duties of Driver

392.40 [Removed and reserved.]
392.41 [Removed and reserved.]
392.42 [Removed.]

Subpart F — Fueling Precautions

392.50 Ignition of fuel; prevention.
392.51 Reserve fuel; materials of trade.
392.52 [Removed and reserved.]

Subpart G — Prohibited Practices

392.60 Unauthorized persons not to be transported.
392.61 [Removed and reserved.]
392.62 Safe operation, buses.
392.63 Towing or pushing loaded buses.
392.64 Riding within closed commercial motor vehicles without proper exits.
392.65 [Removed and reserved.]
392.66 Carbon monoxide; use of commercial motor vehicle when detected.
392.67 Heater, flame-producing; on commercial motor vehicle in motion.
392.68 [Removed and reserved.]
392.69 [Removed and reserved.]
392.71 Radar detectors; use and/or possession.

AUTHORITY: 49 U.S.C. 31136 and 31502; and 49 CFR 1.48.

Subpart A — General

§392.1 Scope of the rules in this part.

Every motor carrier, its officers, agents, representatives, and employees responsible for the management, maintenance, operation, or driving of commercial motor vehicles, or the hiring, supervising, training, assigning, or dispatching of drivers, shall be instructed in and comply with the rules in this part.

§392.2 Applicable operating rules.

Every commercial motor vehicle must be operated in accordance with the laws, ordinances, and regulations of the jurisdiction in which it is being operated. However, if a regulation of the

Federal Highway Administration imposes a higher standard of care than that law, ordinance or regulation, the Federal Highway Administration regulation must be complied with.

§392.3 Ill or fatigued operator.

No driver shall operate a commercial motor vehicle, and a motor carrier shall not require or permit a driver to operate a commercial motor vehicle, while the driver's ability or alertness is so impaired, or so likely to become impaired, through fatigue, illness, or any other cause, as to make it unsafe for him/her to begin or continue to operate the commercial motor vehicle. However, in a case of grave emergency where the hazard to occupants of the commercial motor vehicle or other users of the highway would be increased by compliance with this section, the driver may continue to operate the commercial motor vehicle to the nearest place at which that hazard is removed.

§392.4 Drugs and other substances.

(a) No driver shall be on duty and possess, be under the influence of, or use, any of the following drugs or other substances:

(1) Any 21 CFR 1308.11 *Schedule I* substance;

(2) An amphetamine or any formulation thereof (including, but not limited, to "pep pills," and "bennies");

(3) A narcotic drug or any derivative thereof; or

(4) Any other substance, to a degree which renders the driver incapable of safely operating a motor vehicle.

(b) No motor carrier shall require or permit a driver to violate paragraph (a) of this section.

(c) Paragraphs (a) (2), (3), and (4) do not apply to the possession or use of a substance administered to a driver by or under the instructions of a licensed medical practitioner, as defined in §382.107 of this subchapter, who has advised the driver that the substance will not affect the driver's ability to safely operate a motor vehicle.

(d) As used in this section, "possession" does not include possession of a substance which is manifested and transported as part of a shipment.

§392.5 Alcohol prohibition.

(a) No driver shall—

(1) Use alcohol, as defined in §382.107 of this subchapter, or be under the influence of alcohol, within 4 hours before going on duty or operating, or having physical control of, a commercial

motor vehicle; or

(2) Use alcohol, be under the influence of alcohol, or have any measured alcohol concentration or detected presence of alcohol, while on duty, or operating, or in physical control of a commercial motor vehicle; or

(3) Be on duty or operate a commercial motor vehicle while the driver possesses wine of not less than one-half of one per centum of alcohol by volume, beer *as defined in 26 U.S.C. 5052(a), of the Internal Revenue Code of 1954,* and distilled spirits *as defined in section 5002(a)(8), of such Code.* However, this does not apply to possession of wine, beer, or distilled spirits which are:

(i) Manifested and transported as part of a shipment; or

(ii) Possessed or used by bus passengers.

(b) No motor carrier shall require or permit a driver to—

(1) Violate any provision of paragraph (a) of this section; or

(2) Be on duty or operate a commercial motor vehicle if, by the driver's general appearance or conduct or by other substantiating evidence, the driver appears to have used alcohol within the preceding 4 hours.

(c) Any driver who is found to be in violation of the provisions of paragraph (a) or (b) of this section shall be placed out-of-service immediately for a period of 24 hours.

(1) The 24-hour out-of-service period will commence upon issuance of an out-of-service order.

(2) No driver shall violate the terms of an out-of-service order issued under this section.

(d) Any driver who is issued an out-of-service order under this section shall:

(1) Report such issuance to his/her employer within 24 hours; and

(2) Report such issuance to a State official, designated by the State which issued his/her driver's license, within 30 days unless the driver chooses to request a review of the order. In this case, the driver shall report the order to the State official within 30 days of an affirmation of the order by either the Regional Director of Motor Carriers for the Region or the Associate Administrator.

(e) Any driver who is subject to an out-of-service order under this section may petition for review of that order by submitting a petition for review in writing within 10 days of the issuance of the order to the Regional Director of Motor Carriers for the Region in which the order was issued. The Regional Director of

Motor Carriers may affirm or reverse the order. Any driver adversely affected by such order of the Regional Director of Motor Carriers may petition the Associate Administrator for review in accordance with 49 CFR 386.13.

§392.6 Schedules to conform with speed limits.

No motor carrier shall schedule a run nor permit nor require the operation of any commercial motor vehicle between points in such period of time as would necessitate the commercial vehicle being operated at speeds greater than those prescribed by the jurisdictions in or through which the commercial motor vehicle is being operated.

§392.7 Equipment, inspection and use.

No commercial motor vehicle shall be driven unless the driver thereof shall have satisfied himself/herself that the following parts and accessories are in good working order, nor shall any driver fail to use or make use of such parts and accessories when and as needed:

Service brakes, including trailer brake connections.
Parking (hand) brake.
Steering mechanism.
Lighting devices and reflectors.
Tires.
Horn.
Windshield wiper or wipers.
Rear-vision mirror or mirrors.
Coupling devices.

§392.8 Emergency equipment, inspection, and use.

No commercial motor vehicle shall be driven unless the driver thereof is satisfied that the emergency equipment required by §393.95 of this subchapter is in place and ready for use; nor shall any driver fail to use or make use of such equipment when and as needed.

§392.9 Safe loading.

(a) **General.** No person shall drive a commercial motor vehicle and a motor carrier shall not require or permit a person to drive a commercial motor vehicle unless—

(1) The commercial motor vehicle's cargo is properly distributed and adequately secured as specified in §§393.100-393.106 of this subchapter.

(2) The commercial motor vehicle's tailgate, tailboard, doors, tarpaulins, its spare tire and other equipment used in its operation, and the means of fastening the commercial motor vehicle's cargo are secured; and

(3) The commercial motor vehicle's cargo or any other object does not obscure the driver's view ahead or to the right or left sides, interfere with the free movement of his/her arms or legs, prevent his/her free and ready access to accessories required for emergencies, or prevent the free and ready exit of any person from the commercial motor vehicle's cab or driver's compartment.

(b) **Drivers of trucks and truck tractors.** Except as provided in paragraph (b)(4) of this section, the driver of a truck or truck tractor must—

(1) Assure himself/herself that the provisions of paragraph (a) of this section have been complied with before he/she drives that commercial motor vehicle;

(2) Examine the commercial motor vehicle's cargo and its load-securing devices within the first 25 miles after beginning a trip and cause any adjustments to be made to the cargo or load-securing devices (other than steel strapping) as may be necessary to maintain the security of the commercial motor vehicle's load; and

(3) Reexamine the commercial motor vehicle's cargo and its load-securing devices periodically during the course of transportation and cause any adjustments to be made to the cargo or load-securing devices (other than steel strapping) as may be necessary to maintain the security of the commercial motor vehicle's load. A periodic reexamination and any necessary adjustments must be made—

(i) When the driver makes a change of his/her duty status; or

(ii) After the commercial motor vehicle has been driven for 3 hours; or

(iii) After the commercial motor vehicle has been driven for 150 miles, whichever occurs first.

(4) The rules in this paragraph do not apply to the driver of a sealed commercial motor vehicle who has been ordered not to open it to inspect its cargo or to the driver of a commercial motor vehicle that has been loaded in a manner that makes inspection of its cargo impracticable.

§392.9a [Removed and reserved.]

§392.9b [Removed and reserved.]

Subpart B — Driving of Vehicles

§392.10 Railroad grade crossings; stopping required.

(a) Except as provided in paragraph (b) of this section, the driver of a commercial motor vehicle specified in paragraphs (1) through (6) of this section shall not cross a railroad track or tracks at grade unless he/she first: Stops the commercial motor vehicle within 50 feet of, and not closer than 15 feet to, the tracks; thereafter listens and looks in each direction along the tracks for an approaching train; and ascertains that no train is approaching. When it is safe to do so, the driver may drive the commercial motor vehicle across the tracks in a gear that permits the commercial motor vehicle to complete the crossing without a change of gears. The driver must not shift gears while crossing the tracks.

(1) Every bus transporting passengers,

(2) Every commercial motor vehicle transporting any quantity of a Division 2.3 chlorine.

(3) Every commercial motor vehicle which, in accordance with the regulations of the Department of Transportation, is required to be marked or placarded with one of the following classifications:

(i) Division 1.1

(ii) Division 1.2, or Division 1.3

(iii) Division 2.3 Poison gas

(iv) Division 4.3

(v) Class 7

(vi) Class 3 Flammable

(vii) Division 5.1

(viii) Division 2.2

(ix) Division 2.3 Chlorine

(x) Division 6.1 Poison

(xi) Division 2.2 Oxygen

(xii) Division 2.1

(xiii) Class 3 Combustible liquid

(xiv) Division 4.1

(xv) Division 5.1

(xvi) Division 5.2

(xvii) Class 8

(xviii) Division 1.4

(4) Every cargo tank motor vehicle, whether loaded or empty, used for the transportation of any hazardous material as de-

fined in the Hazardous Materials Regulations of the Department of Transportation, Parts 107 through 180 of this title.

(5) Every cargo tank motor vehicle transporting a commodity which at the time of loading has a temperature above its flashpoint as determined by Sec. 173.120 of this title.

(6) Every cargo tank motor vehicle, whether loaded or empty, transporting any commodity under exemption in accordance with the provisions of Subpart B of Part 107 of this title.

(b) A stop need not be made at:

(1) A streetcar crossing, or railroad tracks used exclusively for industrial switching purposes, within a business district, as defined in §390.5 of this chapter,

(2) A railroad grade crossing when a police officer or crossing flagman directs traffic to proceed,

(3) A railroad grade crossing controlled by a functioning highway traffic signal transmitting a green indication which, under local law, permits the commercial motor vehicle to proceed across the railroad tracks without slowing or stopping,

(4) An abandoned railroad grade crossing which is marked with a sign indicating that the rail line is abandoned,

(5) An industrial or spur line railroad grade crossing marked with a sign reading "Exempt." Such "Exempt" signs shall be erected only by or with the consent of the appropriate State or local authority.

§392.11 Railroad grade crossings; slowing down required.

Every commercial motor vehicle other than those listed in §392.10 shall, upon approaching a railroad grade crossing, be driven at a rate of speed which will permit said commercial motor vehicle to be stopped before reaching the nearest rail of such crossing and shall not be driven upon or over such crossing until due caution has been taken to ascertain that the course is clear.

§392.12 [Removed and reserved.]

§392.13 [Removed and reserved.]

§392.14 Hazardous conditions; extreme caution.

Extreme caution in the operation of a commercial motor vehicle shall be exercised when hazardous conditions, such as those caused by snow, ice, sleet, fog, mist, rain, dust, or smoke, adversely affect visibility or traction. Speed shall be reduced when such conditions exist. If conditions become sufficiently dangerous, the operation of the commercial motor vehicle shall be discontinued and shall not be resumed until the commercial motor vehicle can be safely operated. Whenever compliance with the foregoing provisions of this rule increases hazard to passengers, the commercial motor vehicle may be operated to the nearest point at which the safety of passengers is assured.

§392.15 [Removed and reserved.]

§392.16 Use of seat belts.

A commercial motor vehicle which has a seat belt assembly installed at the driver's seat shall not be driven unless the driver has properly restrained himself/herself with the seat belt assembly.

§392.18 [Removed and reserved.]

Subpart C — Stopped Vehicles

§392.20 [Removed and reserved.]

§392.21 [Removed and reserved.]

§392.22 Emergency signals; stopped commercial motor vehicles.

(a) **Hazard warning signal flashers.** Whenever a commercial motor vehicle is stopped upon the traveled portion of a highway or the shoulder of a highway for any cause other than necessary traffic stops, the driver of the stopped commercial motor vehicle shall immediately activate the vehicular hazard warning signal flashers and continue the flashing until the driver places the warning devices required by paragraph (b) of this section. The flashing signals shall be used during the time the warning devices are picked up for storage before movement of the commercial motor vehicle. The flashing lights may be used at other times while a commercial motor vehicle is stopped in addition to, but not in lieu of, the warning devices required by paragraph (b) of this section.

(b) **Placement of warning devices—**

(1) **General rule.** Except as provided in paragraph (b)(2) of this section, whenever a commercial motor vehicle is stopped upon the traveled portion or the shoulder of a highway for any cause other than necessary traffic stops, the driver shall, as

soon as possible, but in any event within 10 minutes, place the warning devices required by §393.95 of this subchapter, in the following manner:

(i) One on the traffic side of and 4 paces (approximately 3 meters or 10 feet) from the stopped commercial motor vehicle in the direction of approaching traffic;

(ii) One at 40 paces (approximately 30 meters or 100 feet) from the stopped commercial motor vehicle in the center of the traffic lane or shoulder occupied by the commercial motor vehicle and in the direction of approaching traffic; and

(iii) One at 40 paces (approximately 30 meters or 100 feet) from the stopped commercial motor vehicle in the center of the traffic lane or shoulder occupied by the commercial motor vehicle and in the direction away from approaching traffic.

(2) **Special rules**—(i) **Fusees (and liquid-burning flares.** The driver of a commercial motor vehicle equipped with only fusees or liquid-burning flares shall place a lighted fusee or liquid-burning flare at each of the locations specified in paragraph (b)(1) of this section. There shall be at least one lighted fusee or liquid-burning flare at each of the prescribed locations, as long as the commercial motor vehicle is stopped. Before the stopped commercial motor vehicle is moved, the driver shall extinguish and remove each fusee or liquid-burning flare.

(ii) **Daylight hours.** Except as provided in paragraph (b)(2)(iii) of this section, during the period lighted lamps are not required, three bidirectional reflective triangles, or three lighted fusees or liquid-burning flares shall be placed as specified in paragraph (b)(1) of this section within a time of 10 minutes. In the event the driver elects to use only fusees or liquid-burning flares in lieu of bidirectional reflective triangles or red flags, the driver must ensure that at least one fusee or liquid-burning flare remains lighted at each of the prescribed locations as long as the commercial motor vehicle is stopped or parked.

(iii) **Business or residential districts.** The placement of warning devices is not required within the business or residential district of a municipality, except during the time lighted lamps are required and when street or highway lighting is insufficient to make a commercial motor vehicle clearly discernable at a distance of 500 feet to persons on the highway.

(iv) **Hills, curves, and obstructions.** If a commercial motor vehicle is stopped within 500 feet of a curve, crest of a hill, or other obstruction to view, the driver shall place the warning signal required by paragraph (b)(1) of this section in the direction of the obstruction to view a distance of 100 feet to 500 feet from the stopped commercial motor vehicle so as to afford ample warning to other users of the highway.

(v) **Divided or one-way roads.** If a commercial motor vehicle is stopped upon the traveled portion or the shoulder of a divided or one-way highway, the driver shall place the warning devices required by paragraph (b)(1) of this section, one warning device at a distance of 200 feet and one warning device at a distance of 100 feet in a direction toward approaching traffic in the center of the lane or shoulder occupied by the commercial motor vehicle. He/she shall place one warning device at the traffic side of the commercial motor vehicle within 10 feet of the rear of the commercial motor vehicle.

(vi) **Leaking, flammable material.** If gasoline or any other flammable liquid, or combustible liquid or gas seeps or leaks from a fuel container or a commercial motor vehicle stopped upon a highway, no emergency warning signal producing a flame shall be lighted or placed except at such a distance from any such liquid or gas as will assure the prevention of a fire or explosion.

§392.24 Emergency signals; flame-producing.

No driver shall attach or permit any person to attach a lighted fusee or other flame-producing emergency signal to any part of a commercial motor vehicle.

§392.25 Flame producing devices.

No driver shall use or permit the use of any flame-producing emergency signal for protecting any commercial motor vehicle transporting Division 1.1, Division 1.2, or Division 1.3 explosives; any cargo tank motor vehicle used for the transportation of any Class 3 or Division 2.1, whether loaded or empty; or any commercial motor vehicle using compressed gas as a motor fuel. In lieu thereof, emergency reflective triangles, red electric lanterns, or red emergency reflectors shall be used, the placement of which shall be in the same manner as prescribed in §392.22(b).

Subpart D — Use of Lighted Lamps and Reflectors

§392.30 [Removed and reserved.]

§392.31 [Removed and reserved.]

§392.32 [Removed and reserved.]

§392.33 Obscured lamps or reflectors.

No commercial motor vehicle shall be driven when any of the required lamps or reflectors are obscured by the tailboard, by any part of the load, by dirt, or otherwise.

Subpart E — License Revocation: Duties of Driver

§392.40 [Removed and reserved.]

§392.41 [Removed and reserved.]

§392.42 [Removed.]

Subpart F — Fueling Precautions

§392.50 Ignition of fuel; prevention.

No driver or any employee of a motor carrier shall:

(a) Fuel a commercial motor vehicle with the engine running, except when it is necessary to run the engine to fuel the commercial motor vehicle;

(b) Smoke or expose any open flame in the vicinity of a commercial motor vehicle being fueled;

(c) Fuel a commercial motor vehicle unless the nozzle of the fuel hose is continuously in contact with the intake pipe of the fuel tank;

(d) Permit, insofar as practicable, any other person to engage in such activities as would be likely to result in fire or explosion.

§392.51 Reserve fuel; materials of trade.

Small amounts of fuel for the operation or maintenance of a commercial motor vehicle (including its auxiliary equipment) may be designated as materials of trade (see 49 CFR 171.8).

(a) The aggregate gross weight of all materials of trade on a motor vehicle may not exceed 200 kg (440 pounds).

(b) Packaging for gasoline must be made of metal or plastic and conform to requirements of 49 CFR Parts 171, 172, 173, and 178 or requirements of the Occupational Safety and Health Administration contained in 29 CFR 1910.106.

(c) For Packing Group II (including gasoline), Packing Group III (including aviation fuel and fuel oil), or ORM–D, the material is limited to 30 kg (66 pounds) or 30 L (8 gallons).

(d) For diesel fuel, the capacity of the package is limited to 450 L (119 gallons).

(e) A Division 2.1 material in a cylinder is limited to a gross weight of 100 kg (220 pounds). (A Division 2.1 material is a flammable gas, including liquefied petroleum gas, butane, propane, liquefied natural gas, and methane).

§392.52 [Removed and reserved.]

Subpart G — Prohibited Practices

§392.60 Unauthorized persons not to be transported.

(a) Unless specifically authorized in writing to do so by the motor carrier under whose authority the commercial motor vehicle is being operated, no driver shall transport any person or permit any person to be transported on any commercial motor vehicle other than a bus. When such authorization is issued, it shall state the name of the person to be transported, the points where the transportation is to begin and end, and the date upon which such authority expires. No written authorization, however, shall be necessary for the transportation of:

(1) Employees or other persons assigned to a commercial motor vehicle by a motor carrier;

(2) Any person transported when aid is being rendered in case of an accident or other emergency;

(3) An attendant delegated to care for livestock.

(b) This section shall not apply to the operation of commercial motor vehicles controlled and operated by any farmer and used in the transportation of agricultural commodities or products thereof from his/her farm or in the transportation of supplies to his/her farm.

§392.61 [Removed and reserved.]

§392.62 Safe operation, buses.

No person shall drive a bus and a motor carrier shall not require or permit a person to drive a bus unless—

(a) All standees on the bus are rearward of the standee line or other means prescribed in §393.90 of this subchapter;

(b) All aisle seats in the bus conform to the requirements of §393.91 of this subchapter; and

(c) Baggage or freight on the bus is stowed and secured in a manner which assures—

(1) Unrestricted freedom of movement to the driver and his proper operation of the bus;

(2) Unobstructed access to all exits by any occupant of the bus; and

(3) Protection of occupants of the bus against injury resulting from the falling or displacement of articles transported in the bus.

§392.63 Towing or pushing loaded buses.

No disabled bus with passengers aboard shall be towed or pushed; nor shall any person use or permit to be used a bus with passengers aboard for the purpose of towing or pushing any disabled motor vehicle, except in such circumstances where the hazard to passengers would be increased by observance of the foregoing provisions of this section, and then only in traveling to the nearest point where the safety of the passengers is assured.

§392.64 Riding within closed commercial motor vehicles without proper exits.

No person shall ride within the closed body of any commercial motor vehicle unless there are means on the inside thereof of obtaining exit. Said means shall be in such condition as to permit ready operation by the occupant.

§392.65 [Removed and reserved.]

§392.66 Carbon monoxide; use of commercial motor vehicle when detected.

(a) No person shall dispatch or drive any commercial motor vehicle or permit any passengers thereon, when the following conditions are known to exist, until such conditions have been remedied or repaired:

(1) Where an occupant has been affected by carbon monoxide;

(2) Where carbon monoxide has been detected in the interior of the commercial motor vehicle;

(3) When a mechanical condition of the commercial motor vehicle is discovered which would be likely to produce a hazard to the occupants by reason of carbon monoxide.

(b) [Reserved]

§392.67 Heater, flame-producing; on commercial motor vehicle in motion.

No open flame heater used in the loading or unloading of the commodity transported shall be in operation while the commercial motor vehicle is in motion.

§392.68 [Removed and reserved.]

§392.69 [Removed and reserved.]

§392.71 Radar detectors; use and/or possession.

(a) No driver shall use a radar detector in a commercial motor vehicle, or operate a commercial motor vehicle that is equipped with or contains any radar detector.

(b) No motor carrier shall require or permit a driver to violate paragraph (a) of this section.

PART 393 — PARTS AND ACCESSORIES NECESSARY FOR SAFE OPERATION

Subpart A — General

AUTHORITY: Section 1041(b) of Pub. L. 102-240, 105 Stat. 1914, 1993 (1991); 49 U.S.C. 3102; 49 U.S.C. app. 2505; 49 CFR 1.48.

Subpart A — General

§393.1 Scope of the rules in this part.

Every employer and employee shall comply and be conversant with the requirements and specifications of this part. No employer shall operate a commercial motor vehicle, or cause or permit it to be operated, unless it is equipped in accordance with the requirements and specifications of this part.

§393.3 Additional equipment and accessories.

Nothing contained in this subchapter shall be construed to prohibit the use of additional equipment and accessories, not inconsistent with or prohibited by this subchapter, provided such equipment and accessories do not decrease the safety of operation of the motor vehicles on which they are used.

§393.5 Definitions.

As used in this part, the following words and terms are construed to mean:

Agricultural Commodity Trailer. A trailer that is designed to transport bulk agricultural commodities in off-road harvesting sites and to a processing plant or storage location, as evidenced by skeletal construction that accommodates harvest containers, a maximum length of 28 feet, and an arrangement of air control lines and reservoirs that minimizes damage in field operations.

Antilock Brake System or ABS means a portion of a service brake system that automatically controls the degree of rotational wheel slip during braking by:

(1) Sensing the rate of angular rotation of the wheels;

(2) Transmitting signals regarding the rate of wheel angular rotation to one or more controlling devices which interpret those signals and generate responsive controlling output signals; and

(3) Transmitting those controlling signals to one or more modulators which adjust brake actuating forces in response to those signals.

Brake. An energy conversion mechanism used to stop, or hold a vehicle stationary.

Brake tubing/hose. Metallic brake tubing, nonmetallic brake tubing and brake hose are conduits or lines used in a brake system to transmit or contain the medium (fluid or vacuum) used to apply the motor vehicle's brakes.

Bus. A vehicle designed to carry more than 15 passengers, including the driver.

Chassis. The load-supporting frame in a truck or trailer, exclusive of any appurtenances which might be added to accommodate cargo.

Clearance Lamp. A lamp used on the front and the rear of a motor vehicle to indicate its overall width and height.

Container Chassis. A semitrailer of skeleton construction limited to a bottom frame, one or more axles, specially built and fitted with locking devices for the transport of cargo containers, so that when the chassis and container are assembled, the units serve the same function as an over the road trailer.

Converter dolly. A motor vehicle consisting of a chassis equipped with one or more axles, a fifth wheel and/or equivalent mechanism, and drawbar, the attachment of which converts a semitrailer to a full trailer.

Curb Weight. The weight of a motor vehicle with standard equipment, maximum capacity of fuel, oil, and coolant; and, if so equipped, air conditioning and additional weight of optional engine. Curb weight does not include the driver.

Emergency Brake System. A mechanism designed to stop a vehicle after a single failure occurs in the service brake system of a part designed to contain compressed air or brake fluid or vacuum (except failure of a common valve, manifold brake fluid housing or brake chamber housing).

Fifth Wheel. A device mounted on a truck tractor or similar towing vehicle (e.g., converter dolly) which interfaces with and couples to the upper coupler assembly of a semitrailer.

Fuel Tank Fitting. Any removable device affixed to an opening in the fuel tank with the exception of the filler cap.

Grommet. A device that serves as a support and protection to that which passes through it.

Hazard Warning Signal. Lamps that flash simultaneously to the front and rear, on both the right and left sides of a commercial motor vehicle, to indicate to an approaching driver the presence of a vehicular hazard.

Head Lamps. Lamps used to provide general illumination ahead of a motor vehicle.

Heater. Any device or assembly of devices or appliances used to heat the interior of any motor vehicle. This includes a catalytic heater which must meet the requirements of §177.834(1) of this title when flammable liquid or gas is transported.

Heavy Hauler Trailer. A trailer with one or more of the following characteristics:

(1) Its brake lines are designed to adapt to separation or extension of the vehicle frame; or

(2) Its body consists only of a platform whose primary cargo-carrying surface is not more than 40 inches above the ground in an unloaded condition, except that it may include sides that are designed to be easily removable and a permanent "front-end structure" as that term is used in Section 393.106 of this title.

Identification Lamps. Lamps used to identify certain types of commercial motor vehicles.

Lamp. A device used to produce artificial light.

Length of a manufactured home. The largest exterior length in the traveling mode, including any projections which contain interior space. Length does not include bay windows, roof projections, overhangs, or eaves under which there is no interior space, nor does it include drawbars, couplings or hitches.

License Plate Lamp. A lamp used to illuminate the license plate on the rear of a motor vehicle.

Low chassis vehicle. (1) A trailer or semitrailer manufactured on or after January 26, 1998, having a chassis which extends behind the rearmost point of the rearmost tires and which has a lower rear surface that meets the guard width, height, and rear surface requirements of §571.224 in effect on the date of manufacture, or a subsequent edition.

(2) A motor vehicle, not described by paragraph (1) of this definition, having a chassis which extends behind the rearmost point of the rearmost tires and which has a lower rear surface that meets the guard configuration requirements of §393.86(b)(1).

Manufactured home means a structure, transportable in one or more sections, which in the traveling mode, is eight body feet or more in width or forty body feet or more in length, or, when erected on site, is three hundred twenty or more square feet, and which is built on a permanent chassis and designed to be used as a dwelling with or without a permanent foundation when connected to the required utilities, and includes the plumbing, heating, air-conditioning, and electrical systems contained therein. Calculations used to determine the number of square feet in a structure will be based on the structure's exterior dimensions measured at the largest horizontal projections when erected on site. These dimensions will include all expandable rooms, cabinets, and other projections containing interior space, but do not include bay windows. This term includes all structures which meet the *above* requirements except the size requirements and with respect to which the manufacturer voluntarily files a certification pursuant to 24 CFR 3282.13 and complies with the standards set forth in 24 CFR part 3280.

Parking Brake System. A brake system used to hold a vehicle stationary.

Play. Any free movement of components.

Pulpwood Trailer. A trailer or semitrailer that is designed exclusively for harvesting logs or pulpwood and constructed with a skeletal frame with no means for attachment of a solid bed, body, or container.

Rear Extremity. The rearmost point on a motor vehicle that falls above a horizontal plane located 560 mm (22 inches) above the ground and below a horizontal plane located 1,900 mm (75 inches) above the ground when the motor vehicle is stopped on level ground; unloaded; its fuel tanks are full; the tires (and air suspension, if so equipped) are inflated in accordance with the manufacturer's recommendations; and the motor vehicle's cargo doors, tailgate, or other permanent structures are positioned as they normally are when the vehicle is in motion. Nonstructural protrusions such as taillamps, rubber bumpers, hinges and latches are excluded from the determination of the rearmost point.

Reflective Material. A material conforming to Federal Specification L-S-300, "Sheeting and Tape, Reflective; Non-exposed Lens, Adhesive Backing," (September 7, 1965) meeting the performance standard in either Table 1 or Table 1A of SAE Standard J594f, "Reflex Reflectors" (January, 1977).

Reflex Reflector. A device which is used on a vehicle to give an indication to an approaching driver by reflected light from the lamps on the approaching vehicle.

Saddle-mount. A device, designed and constructed as to be readily demountable, used in driveaway-towaway operations to perform the functions of a conventional fifth wheel:

(1) Upper-half. "Upper-half" of a "saddle-mount" means that part of the device which is securely attached to the towed vehicle and maintains a fixed position relative thereto, but does not include the "king-pin;"

(2) Lower-half. "Lower-half" of a "saddle-mount" means that part of the device which is securely attached to the towing vehicle and maintains a fixed position relative thereto but does not include the "king-pin;" and

(3) King-pin. "King-pin" means that device which is used to connect the "upper-half" to the "lower-half" in such manner as to permit relative movement in a horizontal plane between the towed and towing vehicles.

Service Brake System. A primary brake system used for slowing and stopping a vehicle.

Side Extremity. The outermost point on a side of the motor vehicle that is above a horizontal plane located 560 mm (22 inches) above the ground, below a horizontal plane located 1,900 mm (75 inches) above the ground, and between a transverse vertical plane tangent to the rear extremity of the vehicle and a transverse vertical plane located 305 mm (12 inches) forward of that plane when the vehicle is unloaded; its fuel tanks are full; and the tires (and air suspension, if so equipped) are inflated in accordance with the manufacturer's recommendations. Non-structural protrusions such as taillights, hinges and latches are excluded from the determination of the outermost point.

Side Marker Lamp (Intermediate). A lamp shown to the side of a trailer to indicate the approximate middle of a trailer 30 feet or more in length.

Side Marker Lamps. Lamps used on each side of a trailer to indicate its overall length.

Special Purpose Vehicle. (1) A trailer or semitrailer manufactured on or after January 26, 1998, having work-performing equipment that, while the motor vehicle is in transit, resides in or moves through the area that could be occupied by the horizontal member of the rear impact guard, as defined by the guard width, height and rear surface requirements of §571.224 (paragraphs S5.1.1 through S5.1.3), in effect on the date of manufacture, or a subsequent edition.

(2) A motor vehicle, not described by paragraph (1) of this definition, having work-performing equipment that, while the motor vehicle is in transit, resides in or moves through the area that could be occupied by the horizontal member of the rear impact guard, as defined by the guard width, height and rear surface requirements of §393.86(b)(1).

Steering Wheel Lash. The condition in which the steering wheel may be turned through some part of a revolution without associated movement of the front wheels.

Stop Lamps. Lamps shown to the rear of a motor vehicle to indicate that the service brake system is engaged.

Tail Lamps. Lamps used to designate the rear of a motor vehicle.

Turn Signals. Lamps used to indicate a change in direction by emitting a flashing light on the side of a motor vehicle towards which a turn will be made.

Upper Coupler Assembly. A structure consisting of an upper coupler plate, king-pin and supporting framework which interfaces with and couples to a fifth wheel.

Upper Coupler Plate. A plate structure through which the king-pin neck and collar extend. The bottom surface of the plate contacts the fifth wheel when coupled.

Wheels Back Vehicle. (1) A trailer or semitrailer manufactured on or after January 26, 1998, whose rearmost axle is permanently fixed and is located such that the rearmost surface of the tires (of the size recommended by the vehicle manufacturer for the rear axle) is not more than 305 mm (12 inches) forward of the transverse vertical plane tangent to the rear extremity of the vehicle.

(2) A motor vehicle, not described by paragraph (1) of this definition, whose rearmost axle is permanently fixed and is located such that the rearmost surface of the tires (of the size recommended by the vehicle manufacturer for the rear axle) is not more than 610 mm (24 inches) forward of the transverse vertical plane tangent to the rear extremity of the vehicle.

Width of a manufactured home. The largest exterior width in the traveling mode, including any projections which contain interior space. Width does not include bay windows, roof projections, overhangs, or eaves under which there is no interior space.

§393.7 Matter incorporated by reference.

(a) **Incorporation by reference.** Part 393 includes references to certain matter or materials. The text of the materials is not included in the regulations contained in part 393. The materials are hereby made a part of the regulations in part 393. The Director of the *Federal Register* has approved the materials incorporated by reference in accordance with 5 U.S.C. 552(a) and 1 CFR part 51. For materials subject to change, only the specific version approved by the Director of the *Federal Register* and specified in the regulation are incorporated. Material is incorporated as it exists on the date of the approval and a notice of any change in these materials will be published in the *Federal Register*.

(b) **Availability.** The materials incorporated by reference are available as follows:

(1) Standards of the Underwriters Laboratories, Inc. Information and copies may be obtained by writing to: Underwriters Laboratories, Inc., 333 Pfingsten Road, Northbrook, Illinois 60062.

(2) Specifications of the American Society for Testing and Materials. Information and copies may be obtained by writing to: American Society for Testing and Materials, 1916 Race

Street, Philadelphia, Pennsylvania 19103.

(3) Specifications of the National Association of Chain Manufacturers. Information and copies may be obtained by writing to: National Association of Chain Manufacturers, P.O. Box 3143, York, Pennsylvania 17402-0143.

(4) Specifications of the Web Sling and Tiedown Association. Information and copies may be obtained by writing to: Web Sling and Tiedown Association, Inc., 710 East Ogden Avenue, Suite 113, Naperville, Illinois 60563.

(5) Manuals of the Wire Rope Technical Board. Information and copies may be obtained by writing to: Wire Rope Technical Committee, P.O. Box 849, Stevensville, Maryland 21666.

(6) Standards of the Cordage Institute. Information and copies may be obtained by writing to: Cordage Institute, 350 Lincoln Street, # 115, Hingham, Massachusetts 02043.

(7)-(9) [Reserved].

(10) All of the materials incorporated by reference are available for inspection at:

(i) The Department of Transportation Library, 400 Seventh Street, SW., Washington, DC 20590 in Room 2200. These documents are also available for inspection and copying as provided in 49 CFR part 7, appendix D; and

(ii) The Office of the Federal Register, 800 North Capitol Street, NW, Suite 700, Washington, DC.

Subpart B — Lighting Devices, Reflectors, and Electrical Equipment

§393.9 Lamps operable.

All lamps required by this subpart shall be capable of being operated at all times.

§393.11 Lighting devices and reflectors.

The following Table 1 sets forth the required color, position, and required lighting devices by type of commercial motor vehicle. Diagrams illustrating the locations of lighting devices and reflectors, by type and size of commercial motor vehicle, are shown immediately following Table 1. All lighting devices on motor vehicles placed in operation after March 7, 1989, must meet the requirements of 49 CFR 571.108 in effect at the time of manufacture of the vehicle. Motor vehicles placed in operation on or before March 7, 1989 must meet either the requirements of this Subchapter or Part 571 of this title in effect at the time of manufacture.

TABLE 1—REQUIRED COMMERCIAL VEHICLE LIGHTING EQUIPMENT

Item on the vehicle	Quantity	Color	Location	Position	Height above road surface in inches measured from the center of the lamp at curb weight	Required lighting devices/vehicles
Headlamps	2 At Least	White	Front	On the front of the same height, on equal number at each side of the vertical centerline as far apart as practicable.	Not less than 22 nor more than 54.	A,B,C
Turn Signal (Front) See Footnotes #2 & 12	2	Amber	At or Near Front	On each side of the vertical centerline at the same height and as far apart as practicable.	Not Less Than 15 nor more than 83.	A,B,C,
Identification Lamp (Front) Footnote #1	3	Amber	Front	Mounted on the vertical centerline of the vehicle or the vertical centerline of the cab where different from the centerline of the vehicle.	All three on same level as close as practicable to the top of the vehicle with lamp centers spaced not less than 6 inches or more than 12 inches apart.	B,C
Tail Lamp See Footnotes #5 & 11	2	Red	Rear	One lamp each side of the vertical centerline at the same height and as far apart as practicable.	Both on the same level between 15 and 72.	A,B,C,D, E,F,G,H
Stop Lamp See Footnotes #5 & 13	2	Red	Rear	One lamp each side of the vertical centerline at the same height and as far apart as practicable.	Both on the same level between 15 and 72.	A,B,C,D, E,F,G
Clearance Lamps See Footnotes #9, 10 & 15	2	Amber	One on each side of front.	One on each side of the vertical centerline to indicate width.	Both on same level as high as practicable	B,C,D,G, H
	2	Red	One on each side of rear.	One on each side of the vertical centerline to indicate overall width.	Both on same level as high as practicable.	B,D,G,H
Side Marker Lamp Intermediate	2	Amber	One on each side	At or near midpoint between front and rear side marker lamps. If over 30' in length.	Not less than 15	A,B,D,F, G
Reflex Reflector Intermediate (Side).	2	Amber	One on each side	At or near midpoint between front and rear side reflections if over 30' in length.	Between 15 and 60.	A,B,D,F, G
Reflex Reflector (Rear) See Footnotes #5, 6 & 8 ...	2	Red	Rear	One on each side of vertical centerline as far apart as practicable	Both on same level, between 15 and 60.	A,B,C,D, E,F,G
Reflex Reflector (Rear Side) Footnote #4	2	Red	One on each side (rear)	As far to the rear as practicable	Both on same level, between 15 and 60	A,B,D,F, G

TABLE 1—REQUIRED COMMERCIAL VEHICLE LIGHTING EQUIPMENT, Continued

Item on the vehicle	Quantity	Color	Location	Position	Height above road surface in inches measured from the center of the lamp at curb weight	Required lighting devices/ vehicles
Reflex Reflector (Front Side)	2	Amber	One on each side (front).	As far to the front as practicable	Between 15 and 60.	A,B,C,D, F,G
License Plate lamp rear See Footnote #11	1	White	At rear license plate	To illuminate the license plate from the top or sides.	No requirements.	A,B,C,D, F,G
Side Marker Lamp (Front)	2	Amber	One on each side	As far to the front as practicable.	Not less than 15.	A,B,C,D, F
Side Marker Lamp (Rear) See Footnotes #4 & 8 ...	2	Red	One on each side	As far to the rear as practicable	Not less than 15 and on the rear of trailer, not more than 60.	A,B,D,F, G
Turn Signal (Rear) See Footnotes #5 & 12	2	Amber or Red	Rear	One lamp on each side of the vertical centerline as far apart as practicable.	Both on the same level, between 15 and 83.	A,B,C,D, E,F,G
Identification Lamp (Rear) See Footnotes #3, 7 & 15.	3	Red	Rear	One as close as practicable to vertical centerline. One on each side with lamp centers spaced not less than 6" or more than 12" apart.	All three on same level as close as practicable to the top of the vehicle.	B,D,G
Vehicular Hazard Warning Flashing Lamps See Footnote #12	2	Amber	Front	One lamp on each side of vertical centerline as far apart as practicable.	Both on some level, between 15 and 83.	A,B,C,D, E,F,G
	2	Amber or Red	Rear	....	....	
Backup Lamp See Footnote #14	1	White	Rear	Rear	No requirement	A,B,C
Parking Lamp	2	Amber or white	Front	One lamp on each side of vertical centerline as far as practicable.	Both on some level, between 15 and 72.	A

*Lighting Required per Type of Commercial Vehicle as Shown Last Column of Table.
A. Small buses and trucks less than 80 inches in overall width.
B. Buses and trucks 80 inches or more in overall width.
C. Truck tractors.
D. Large semitrailers and full trailers 80 inches or more in overall width except converter dollies.
E. Converter dolly.
F. Small semitrailers and full trailers less than 80 inches in overall width.
G. Pole Trailers.
H. Projecting loads.
Lamps and reflectors may be combined as permitted by Paragraphs 393.22 and S4.4 of 49 CFR 571.108. Equipment combinations.

Footnote—1

Identification lamps may be mounted on the vertical centerline of the cab where different from the centerline of the vehicle, except where the cab is not more than 42 inches wide at the front roofline, then a single lamp at the center of the cab shall be deemed to comply with the requirements for identification lamps. No part of the identification lamps or their mountings may extend below the top of the vehicle windshield.

Footnote—2

Unless the turn signals on the front are so constructed (double-faced) and located as to be visible to passing drivers, two turn signals are required on the rear of the truck tractor, one at each side as far apart as practicable.

Footnote—3

The identification lamps need not be visible or lighted if obscured by a vehicle in the same combination.

Footnote—4

Any semitrailer or full trailer vehicles manufactured on and after March 1, 1979, shall be equipped with rear side-marker lamps at a height of not less than 15 inches (381 mm) nor more than 60 inches (1524 mm) above the road surface, as measured from the center of the lamp on the vehicle at curb weight. The rear side marker lamps shall be visible in the vehicle's rearview mirrors when the trailer is tracking straight.

Footnote—5

For purposes of these regulations, each converter dolly shall be equipped with one stop lamp, one tail lamp, and two reflectors on the rear at each side when towed singly by another vehicle. Each converter dolly shall be equipped with turn signals at the rear if the converter dolly obscures the turn signals at the rear of the towing vehicle when towed singly by another vehicle.

Footnote—6

Pole trailers will have two reflectors, one on each side, placed to indicate extreme width of the trailer.

Footnote—7

Pole trailers may have three identification lamps mounted on the vertical centerline of the rear of the cab of the truck tractor drawing the pole trailer, and higher than the load being transported, in lieu of the three identification lamps mounted on the rear vertical centerline of the trailer.

Footnote—8

Pole trailers shall have on the rearmost support for the load, one combination marker lamp or two single lamps showing amber to the front and red to the rear and side, mounted on each side to indicate maximum width of the pole trailer, and one red reflector on each side of the rearmost support for the load.

Footnote—9

Any motor vehicle transporting a load which extends more than 4 inches beyond the width of the motor vehicle, or having projections beyond the rear of such vehicles, shall be equipped with the following lamps in addition to other required lamps, have the loads marked

Loads projecting more than 4 inches beyond sides of motor vehicles:

(1) The foremost edge of the projecting load at its outermost extremity shall be marked with an amber lamp visible from the front and both sides.

(2) The rearmost edge of the projecting load at its outermost extremity shall be marked with a red lamp visible from the rear and side.

(3) If any portion of the projecting load extends beyond both the foremost and rearmost edge, it shall be marked with an amber lamp visible from the front, both sides, and rear.

(4) If the projecting load does not measure more than 3 feet from front to rear, it shall be marked with an amber lamp visible from the front, both sides, and rear, except that if the projection is located at or near the rear it shall be marked by a red lamp visible from front, side, and rear.

Footnote—10

Projections beyond rear of motor vehicles. Motor vehicles transporting loads which extend more than 4 feet beyond the rear of the motor vehicle, or which have these tailboards or tailgates extending more than 4 feet beyond the body, shall have projections marked as follows:

(1) On each side of the projecting load, one red lamp, visible from the side, located so as to indicate maximum overhang.

(2) On the rear of the projecting load, two red lamps, visible from the rear, one at each side; and two red reflectors visible from the rear, one at each side, located so as to indicate maximum width.

Footnote—11

To be illuminated when tractor headlamps are illuminated.

Footnote—12

Every bus, truck, and truck tractor shall be equipped with a signaling system that, in addition to signaling turning movements, shall have a switch or combination of switches that will cause the two front turn signals and the two rear signals to flash simultaneously as a vehicular traffic signal warning, required by §392.22(a). The system shall be capable of flashing simultaneously with the ignition of the vehicle on or off.

Footnote—13

To be actuated upon application of service brakes.

Footnote—14

Backup lamp required to operate when bus, truck, or truck tractor is in reverse.

Footnote—15

When the rear identification lamps are mounted at the extreme height of a vehicle, rear clearance lamps need not meet the requirement that they be located as close as practicable to the top of the vehicle.

Truck Tractor Rear View

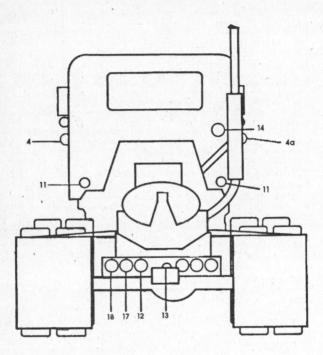

Truck Tractor Front & Side View

Large Trailers

REAR

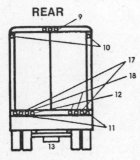

FRONT

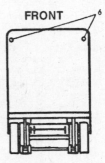

EACH SIDE

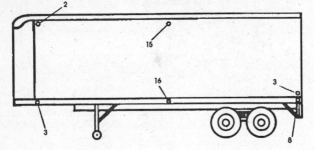

Over 80 Inches

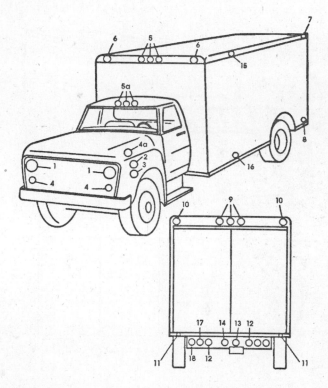

Under 80 Inches

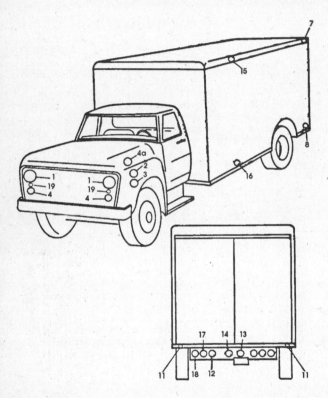

Under 80 Inches

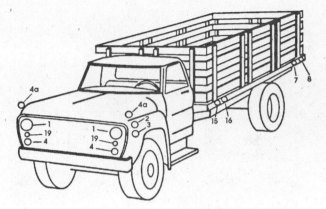

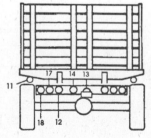

Large Bus

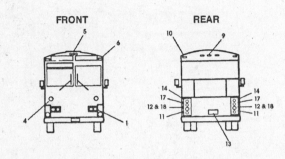

FRONT

REAR

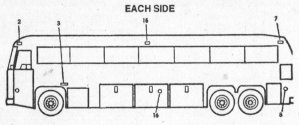

EACH SIDE

Pole Trailers All Vehicle Widths

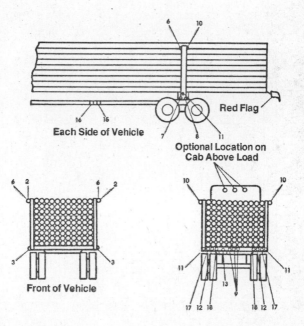

Red Flag

Each Side of Vehicle

Optional Location on
Cab Above Load

Front of Vehicle

Container Chassis

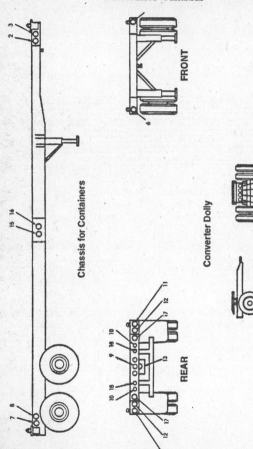

Chassis for Containers

FRONT

REAR

Converter Dolly

Legend (Used in illustrations)

1. Headlamps (2)-White (4 optional)
2. Side-marker lamps. Front (2)-Amber
3. Side-reflectors. Front (2)-Amber
4. Turn-signal lamps. Front (2)-Amber
4a. Turn-signal lamps. Front (2)-Amber (Optional location)
5. Identification lamps. Front (3)-Amber
5a. Identification lamps. Front (3)-Amber (Optional location)
6. Clearance lamps. Front (2)-Amber
7. Side-marker lamps. Rear (2)-Red
8. Side-reflectors. Rear (2)-Red
9. Identification lamps. Rear (3)-Red
10. Clearance lamps. Rear (2)-Red
11. Reflectors Rear (2)-Red
12. Stop lamps. Rear (2)-Red
13. License plate lamp. Rear (1)-White
14. Backup lamp. Rear (1)-White (location optional provided optional requirements are met)
15. Side-marker Lamps. Intermediate (2)-Amber (if vehicle is 30′ or more overall length)
16. Side reflectors. Intermediate (2)-Amber (if vehicle is 30′ or more overall length)
17. Turn signal lamps. Rear (2)-Amber or Red
18. Tail lamps. Rear (2)-Red
19. Parking lamps. Front (2)-Amber or White

§393.13 Retroreflective sheeting and reflex reflectors, requirements for semitrailers and trailers manufactured before December 1, 1993.

(a) **Applicability.** All trailers and semitrailers manufactured prior to December 1, 1993, which have an overall width of 2,032 mm (80 inches) or more and a gross vehicle weight rating of 4,536 kg (10,001 pounds) or more, except trailers that are manufactured exclusively for use as offices or dwellings, pole trailers (as defined in Sec. 390.5), and trailers transported in a driveaway-towaway operation, must be equipped with retroreflective sheeting or an array of reflex reflectors that meet the requirements of this section. Motor carriers have until June 1, 2001 to comply with the requirements of this section.

(b) **Retroreflective sheeting and reflex reflectors.** Motor carriers are encouraged to retrofit their trailers with a conspicuity system that meets all of the requirements applicable to trailers manufactured on or after December 1, 1993, including the use of retroreflective sheeting or reflex reflectors in a red and white pattern (see Federal Motor Vehicle Safety Standard No. 108 (49 CFR 571.108), S5.7, Conspicuity systems). Motor carriers which do not retrofit their trailers to meet the requirements of FMVSS No. 108, for example by using an alternative color pattern, must comply with the remainder of this paragraph and with paragraph (c) or (d) of this section. Retroreflective sheeting or reflex reflectors in colors or color combinations other than red and white may be used on the sides or lower rear area of the semitrailer or trailer until June 1, 2009. The alternate color or color combination must be uniform along the sides and lower rear area of the trailer. The retroreflective sheeting or reflex reflectors on the upper rear area of the trailer must be white and conform to the requirements of FMVSS No. 108 (S5.7). Red retroreflective sheeting or reflex reflectors shall not be used along the sides of the trailer unless it is used as part of a red and white pattern. Retroreflective sheeting shall have a width of at least 50 mm (2 inches).

(c) **Locations for retroreflective sheeting.**

(1) **Sides.** Retroreflective sheeting shall be applied to each side of the trailer or semitrailer. Each strip of retroreflective sheeting shall be positioned as horizontally as practicable, beginning and ending as close to the front and rear as practicable. The strip need not be continuous but the sum of the length of all of the segments shall be at least half of the length of the trailer and the spaces between the segments of the strip shall be distributed as evenly as practicable. The centerline for each strip of retroreflective sheeting shall be between 375 mm (15 inches) and 1,525 mm (60 inches) above the road surface when measured with the trailer empty or unladen, or as close as practicable to this area. If necessary to clear rivet heads or other similar obstructions, 50 mm (2 inches) wide retroreflective sheeting may be separated into two 25 mm (1 inch) wide strips of the same length and color, separated by a space of not more than 25 mm (1 inch).

(2) **Lower rear area.** The rear of each trailer and semitrailer must be equipped with retroreflective sheeting. Each strip of retroreflective sheeting shall be positioned as horizontally as

practicable, extending across the full width of the trailer, beginning and ending as close to the extreme edges as practicable. The centerline for each of the strips of retroreflective sheeting shall be between 375 mm (15 inches) and 1,525 mm (60 inches) above the road surface when measured with the trailer empty or unladen, or as close as practicable to this area.

(3) **Upper rear area.** Two pairs of white strips of retroreflective sheeting, each pair consisting of strips 300 mm (12 inches) long, must be positioned horizontally and vertically on the right and left upper corners of the rear of the body of each trailer and semitrailer, as close as practicable to the top of the trailer and as far apart as practicable. If the perimeter of the body, as viewed from the rear, is not square or rectangular, the strips may be applied along the perimeter, as close as practicable to the uppermost and outermost areas of the rear of the body on the left and right sides.

(d) **Locations for reflex reflectors.**

(1) **Sides.** Reflex reflectors shall be applied to each side of the trailer or semitrailer. Each array of reflex reflectors shall be positioned as horizontally as practicable, beginning and ending as close to the front and rear as practicable. The array need not be continuous but the sum of the length of all of the array segments shall be at least half of the length of the trailer and the spaces between the segments of the strip shall be distributed as evenly as practicable. The centerline for each array of reflex reflectors shall be between 375 mm (15 inches) and 1,525 mm (60 inches) above the road surface when measured with the trailer empty or unladen, or as close as practicable to this area. The center of each reflector shall not be more than 100 mm (4 inches) from the center of each adjacent reflector in the segment of the array. If reflex reflectors are arranged in an alternating color pattern, the length of reflectors of the first color shall be as close as practicable to the length of the reflectors of the second color.

(2) **Lower rear area.** The rear of each trailer and semitrailer must be equipped with reflex reflectors. Each array of reflex reflectors shall be positioned as horizontally as practicable, extending across the full width of the trailer, beginning and ending as close to the extreme edges as practicable. The centerline for each array of reflex reflectors shall be between 375 mm (15 inches) and 1,525 mm (60 inches) above the road surface when measured with the trailer empty or unladen, or as close as prac-

ticable to this area. The center of each reflector shall not be more than 100 mm (4 inches) from the center of each adjacent reflector in the segment of the array.

(3) **Upper rear area.** Two pairs of white reflex reflector arrays, each pair at least 300 mm (12 inches) long, must be positioned horizontally and vertically on the right and left upper corners of the rear of the body of each trailer and semitrailer, as close as practicable to the top of the trailer and as far apart as practicable. If the perimeter of the body, as viewed from the rear, is not square or rectangular, the arrays may be applied along the perimeter, as close as practicable to the uppermost and outermost areas of the rear of the body on the left and right sides. The center of each reflector shall not be more than 100 mm (4 inches) from the center of each adjacent reflector in the segment of the array.

§393.17 Lamps and reflectors - combinations in driveaway-towaway operation.

A combination of motor vehicles engaged in driveaway-towaway operation must be equipped with operative lamps and reflectors conforming to the rules in this section.

(a) The towing vehicle must be equipped as follows:

(1) On the front, there must be at least two headlamps, an equal number at each side, two turn signals, one at each side, and two clearance lamps, one at each side.

(2) On each side, there must be at least one side-marker lamp, located near the front of the vehicle.

(3) On the rear, there must be at least two tail lamps, one at each side, and two stop lamps, one at each side.

(b) Except as provided in paragraph (c) of this section, the rearmost towed vehicle of the combination (including the towed vehicle or a tow-bar combination, the towed vehicle of a single saddle-mount combination, and the rearmost towed vehicle of a double or triple saddle-mount combination) or, in the case of a vehicle full-mounted on a saddle-mount vehicle, either the full-mounted vehicle or the rearmost saddle-mounted vehicle must be equipped as follows:

(1) On each side, there must be at least one side-marker lamp, located near the rear of the vehicle.

(2) On the rear, there must be at least two tail lamps, two stop lamps, two turn signals, two clearance lamps, and two reflectors, one of each type at each side. In addition, if any vehicle

in the combination is 80 inches or more in overall width, there must be three identification lamps on the rear.

(c) If the towed vehicle in a combination is a mobile structure trailer, it must be equipped in accordance with the following lighting devices. For the purposes of this part, "mobile structure trailer" means a trailer that has a roof and walls, is at least 10 feet wide, and can be used off road for dwelling or commercial purposes.

(1) When the vehicle is operated in accordance with the terms of a special permit prohibiting operation during the times when lighted lamps are required under §392.30, it must have on the rear—

(i) Two stop lamps, one on each side of the vertical centerline, at the same height, and as far apart as practicable;

(ii) Two tail lamps, one on each side of the vertical centerline, at the same height, and as far apart as practicable;

(iii) Two red reflex reflectors, one on each side of the vertical centerline, at the same height, and as far apart as practicable; and

(iv) Two turn signal lamps, one on each side of the vertical centerline, at the same height, and as far apart as practicable.

(2) At all other times, the vehicle must be equipped as specified in paragraph (b) of this section.

(d) An intermediate towed vehicle in a combination consisting of more than two vehicles (including the first saddle-mounted vehicle of a double saddle-mount combination and the first and second saddle-mount vehicles of a triple saddle-mount combination) must have one side-marker lamp on each side, located near the rear of the vehicle.

(Tow-bar diagram to illustrate §393.17.)

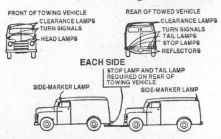

FRONT OF TOWING VEHICLE
CLEARANCE LAMPS
TURN SIGNALS
HEAD LAMPS

REAR OF TOWED VEHICLE
CLEARANCE LAMPS
TURN SIGNALS
TAIL LAMPS
STOP LAMPS
REFLECTORS

EACH SIDE

STOP LAMP AND TAIL LAMP REQUIRED ON REAR OF TOWING VEHICLE

SIDE-MARKER LAMP

SIDE-MARKER LAMP

Lamps may be combined as permitted by §393.22(e). Color of exterior lighting devices shall conform to requirements of §393.25(e). Color of reflectors shall conform to requirements of §393.26(d).

(Double-saddle-mount diagram to illustrate §393.17.)

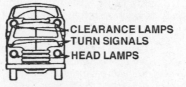

FRONT OF TOWING VEHICLE

—CLEARANCE LAMPS
—TURN SIGNALS
—HEAD LAMPS

REAR OF REARMOST TOWED VEHICLE
CLEARANCE LAMPS

IDENT LAMPS
STOP LAMPS
TAIL LAMPS
TURN SIGNALS
REFLECTORS

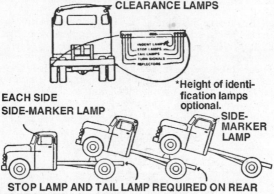

*Height of identi-
fication lamps
optional.

**EACH SIDE
SIDE-MARKER LAMP**

**SIDE-
MARKER
LAMP**

**STOP LAMP AND TAIL LAMP REQUIRED ON REAR
OF TOWING VEHICLE**

Lamps may be combined as permitted by §393.22. Color of extnerior lighting devices shall conform to requirements of §393.25(e). Color of reflectors shall conform to requirements of §393.26(d).

(Single-saddle-mount diagram to illustrate §393.17.)

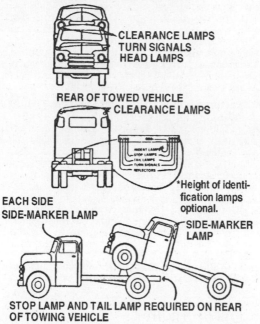

FRONT OF TOWING VEHICLE

CLEARANCE LAMPS
TURN SIGNALS
HEAD LAMPS

REAR OF TOWED VEHICLE
CLEARANCE LAMPS

IDENT LAMPS
STOP LAMPS
TAIL LAMPS
TURN SIGNALS
REFLECTORS

*Height of identi-
fication lamps
optional.

EACH SIDE
SIDE-MARKER LAMP

SIDE-MARKER
LAMP

STOP LAMP AND TAIL LAMP REQUIRED ON REAR
OF TOWING VEHICLE

Lamps may be combined as permitted by §393.22. Color of exterior lighting devices shall conform to requirements of §393.25(e). Color of reflectors shall conform to requirements of §393.26(d).

§393.19 Requirements for turn signaling systems.

(a) Every bus, truck, or truck tractor shall be equipped with a signaling system that in addition to signaling turning movements shall have a switch or combination of switches that will cause the two front turn signals and the two rear turn signals to flash simultaneously as a vehicular traffic hazard warning as required by §392.22 with the ignition on or off.

(b) Every semitrailer and full trailer shall be equipped so as to have the two rear turn signals to flash simultaneously with the two front turn signals of the towing vehicle as a vehicular traffic hazard warning as required by §392.22(a).

§393.20 Clearance lamps to indicate extreme width and height.

Clearance lamps shall be mounted so as to indicate the extreme width of the motor vehicle (not including mirrors) and as near the top thereof as practicable: Provided, That when rear identification lamps are mounted at the extreme height of the vehicle, rear clearance lamps may be mounted at optional height: And provided further, That when mounting of front clearance lamps at the highest point of a trailer results in such lamps failing to mark the extreme width of the trailer, such lamps may be mounted at optional height but must indicate the extreme width of the trailer. Clearance lamps on truck tractors shall be so located as to indicate the extreme width of the truck tractor cab.

(Diagram to illustrate §393.20 for mounting of front clearance lamps on truck tractors with sleeper cabs.)

FRONT

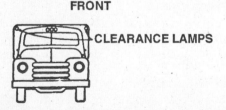

CLEARANCE LAMPS

(Diagram to illustrate §393.20 for mounting of lamps on vehicles without permanent top or sides.)

FRONT

CLEARANCE
LAMPS

REAR

CLEARANCE
LAMPS

EACH SIDE

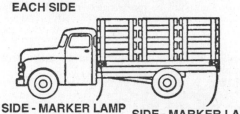

SIDE - MARKER LAMP   SIDE - MARKER LAMP

Lamps may be combined as permitted by §393.22. Color of exterior lighting devices shall conform to requirements of §393.25(e). Color of reflectors shall conform to requirements of §393.26(d).

§393.22 Combination of lighting devices and reflectors.

(a) **Permitted combinations.** Except as provided in paragraph (b) of this section, two or more lighting devices and reflectors (whether or not required by the rules in this part) may be combined optically if —

(1) Each required lighting device and reflector conforms to the applicable rules in this Part; and

(2) Neither the mounting nor the use of a nonrequired lighting device or reflector impairs the effectiveness of a required lighting device or reflector or causes that device or reflector to be inconsistent with the applicable rules in this Part.

(b) **Prohibited combinations.** (1) A turn signal lamp must not be combined optically with either a head lamp or other lighting device or combination of lighting devices that produces a greater intensity of light than the turn signal lamp;

(2) A turn signal lamp must not be combined optically with a stop lamp unless the stop lamp function is always deactivated when the turn signal function is activated;

(3) A clearance lamp must not be combined optically with a tail lamp or identification lamp.

§393.23 Lighting devices to be electric.

Lighting devices shall be electric, except that red liquid-burning lanterns may be used on the end of loads in the nature of poles, pipes, and ladders projecting to the rear of the motor vehicle.

§393.24 Requirements for head lamps and auxiliary road lighting lamps.

(a) **Mounting.** Head lamps and auxiliary road lighting lamps shall be mounted so that the beams are readily adjustable, both vertically and horizontally, and the mounting shall be such that the aim is not readily disturbed by ordinary conditions or service.

(b) **Head lamps required.** Every bus, truck, and truck tractor shall be equipped with a headlighting system composed of at least two head lamps, not including fog or other auxiliary lamps, with an equal number on each side of the vehicle. The headlighting system shall provide an upper and lower distribution of light, selectable at the driver's will.

(c) **Fog, adverse-weather, and auxiliary road-lighting lamps.** For the purposes of this section, fog, adverse - weather, auxiliary road lighting lamps, when installed, are considered to be a part of the headlighting system. Such lamps may be used in lieu of head lamps under conditions making their use advisable if there be at least one such lamp conforming to the appropriate SAE Standard[1] for such lamps on each side of the vehicle.

(d) **Aiming and intensity.** Head lamps shall be constructed and installed so as to provide adequate and reliable illumination and shall conform to the appropriate specification set forth in the SAE Standards[1] for "Electric Head Lamps for Motor Vehicles" or "Sealed-Beam Head Lamp Units for Motor Vehicles."

§393.25 Requirements for lamps other than head lamps.

(a) **Mounting.** All lamps shall be permanently and securely mounted in workmanlike manner on a permanent part of the motor vehicle, except that temporary lamps on motor vehicles being transported in driveaway-towaway operations and temporary electric lamps on projecting loads need not be permanently mounted nor mounted on a permanent part of the vehicle. The requirement for three identification lamps on the centerline of a vehicle will be met as to location by one lamp on the centerline, with the other two at right and left. All temporary lamps must be firmly attached.

(b) **Visibility.** All required exterior lamps shall be so mounted as to be capable of being seen at all distances between 500 feet and 50 feet under clear atmospheric conditions during the time lamps are required to be lighted. The light from front clearance and front identification lamps shall be visible to the front, that from sidemarker lamps to the side, that from rear

---

[1] Wherever reference is made in these regulations to SAE Standards or SAE Recommended Practices, they shall be:

(a) As found in the 1985 edition of the SAE Handbook with respect to parts and accessories other than lighting devices and reflectors.

(b) When reference is made in these regulations to SAE Standards or SAE Recommended Practices, they shall be as found in the 1985 edition of the SAE Handbook:

(1) With respect to parts and accessories other than lighting devices and reflectors:

(2) Lighting devices and reflectors on motor vehicles manufactured on and after March 7, 1990, shall conform to FMVSS 571.108 (49 CFR 571.108) in effect at the time of manufacture of the vehicle. Should a conflict arise between FMVSS 571.108 and a SAE Standard, FMVSS 571.108 will prevail.

The "SAE Handbook" and Pamphlet No. TR-34 are published by the SAE, Inc., 400 Commonwealth Drive, Warrendale, Pennsylvania 15096.

clearance, rear identification, and tail lamps to the rear, and that from projecting loadmarker lamps from those directions required by §393.11. This shall not be construed to apply to lamps on one unit which are obscured by another unit of a combination of vehicles.

(c) **Specifications.** All required lamps except those already installed on vehicles tendered for transportation in driveaway and towaway operations shall conform to appropriate requirements of the SAE Standards and/or Recommended Practices[1] as indicated below, except that the minimum required marking of lamps conforming to the 1985 requirements shall be as specified in paragraph (d) of this section. Projecting load marker lamps shall conform to the requirements for clearance, side-marker, and identification lamps. Turn signals shall conform to the requirements for Class A, Type I turn signals, provided:

(1) Lamps on vehicles made before July 1, 1961, excepting replacement lamps as specified in paragraph (c)(2) of this section, shall conform to the 1952 requirements.

(2) Lamps on vehicles made on and after July 1, 1961, and replacement lamps installed on and after December 31, 1961, shall conform to the 1985 requirements.

(3) Lamps temporarily attached to vehicles transported in driveaway and towaway operations on and after December 31, 1961, shall conform to the 1985 requirements.

(d) **Certification and markings.** All lamps required to conform to the requirements of the SAE Standards shall be certified by the manufacturer or supplier that they do so conform, by markings indicated below. The markings in each case shall be visible when the lamp is in place on the vehicle:

(1) Stop lamps shall be marked with the manufacturer's or supplier's name or trade name and shall be marked "SAE-S".

(2) Turn signals units shall be marked with the manufacturer's or supplier's name or trade name and shall be marked "SAE-AI" or "SAE-I".

(3) Tail lamps shall be marked with the manufacturer's or supplier's name or trade name and shall be marked "SAE-T".

(4) Clearance, side marker, identification, and projecting load-marker lamps, except combination lamps, shall be marked with the manufacturer's or supplier's name or trade name and shall be marked "SAE" or "SAE-P".

---

[1]See footnote 1 to Sec. 393.24(c)

(5) Combination lamps shall be marked with the manufacturer's or supplier's name or trade name and shall be marked "SAE" followed by the appropriate letters indicating the individual lamps combined. The letter "A", as specified in §393.26 (c), may be included to certify that a reflector in the combination conforms to the requirements appropriate to such marking. If the letter "I" follows a letter "A" immediately, the two letters shall be deemed to refer to a turn signal unit, as specified in paragraph (d)(2) of this section. Combination clearance and side marker lamps may be marked "SAE-PC".

(e) **Lighting devices to be steady-burning.** All exterior lighting devices shall be of the steady-burning type except turn signals on any vehicle, stop lamps when used as turn signals, warning lamps on school buses when operating as such, and warning lamps on emergency and service vehicles authorized by State or local authorities, and except that lamps combined into the same shell or housing with any turn signal may be turned off by the same switch that turns the signal on for flashing and turned on again when the turn signal as such is turned off. This paragraph shall not be construed to prohibit the use of vehicular hazard warning signal flashers as required by §392.22 or permitted by §392.18.

(f) **Stop lamp operation.** All stop lamps on each motor vehicle or combination of motor vehicles shall be actuated upon application of any of the service brakes, except that such actuation is not required upon activation of the emergency feature of trailer brakes by means of either manual or automatic control on the towing vehicle, and except that stop lamps on a towing vehicle need not be actuated when service brakes are applied to the towed vehicles or vehicles only, and except that no stop lamp need be actuated as such when it is in use as a turn signal or when it is turned off by the turn signal switch as provided in paragraph (e) of this section.

§393.26 Requirements for reflectors.

(a) **Mounting.** All required reflectors shall be mounted upon the motor vehicle at a height not less than 15 inches nor more than 60 inches above the ground on which the motor vehicle stands, except that reflectors shall be mounted as high as practicable on motor vehicles which are so constructed as to make compliance with the 15-inch requirement impractical. They shall be so installed as to perform their function adequately and reliably, and except for temporary reflectors required for vehicles in driveaway-towaway operations, or on projecting loads, all reflectors shall be permanently and securely mounted in workmanlike manner so as to provide the maximum of stability and the minimum likelihood of damage. Required reflectors otherwise properly mounted may be securely installed on flexible strapping or belting provided that under conditions of normal operation they reflect light in the required directions. Required temporary reflectors mounted on motor vehicles during the time they are in transit in any driveaway-towaway operation must be firmly attached.

(b) **Specifications**. All required reflectors except those installed on vehicles tendered for transportation in driveaway and towaway operations shall comply with FMVSS 571.108 (49 CFR 571.108) in effect at the time the vehicle was manufactured or the current FMVSS 571.108 requirements.

(c) **Certification and markings**. All reflectors required to conform to the specifications in paragraph (b) shall be certifed by the manufacturer or supplier that they do so conform, by marking with the manufacturer's or supplier's name or trade name and the letters "SAE-A". The marking in each case shall be visible when the reflector is in place on the vehicle.

(d) **Retroreflective surfaces.** Retroreflective surfaces other than required reflectors may be used, provided:

(1) Designs do not resemble traffic control signs, lights, or devices, except that straight edge striping resembling a barricade pattern may be used.

(2) Designs do not tend to distort the length and/or width of the motor vehicle.

(3) Such surfaces shall be at least 3 inches from any required lamp or reflector unless of the same color as such lamp or reflector.

(4) No red color shall be used on the front of any motor vehicle, except for display of markings or placards required by §177.823 of this title.

(5) Retroreflective license plates required by State or local authorities may be used.

§393.27 Wiring specifications.

(a) Wiring for both low voltage (tension) and high voltage (tension) circuits shall be constructed and installed so as to meet design requirements. Wiring shall meet or exceed, both mechanically and electrically, the following SAE Standards as found in the 1985 edition of the SAE Handbook:

(1) Commercial vehicle engine ignition systems-SAE J557-High Tension Ignition Cable.

(2) Commercial vehicle battery cable-SAE J1127-Jan 80-Battery Cable.

(3) Other commercial vehicle wiring-SAE J1128-Low Tension Primary Cable.

(b) The source of power and the electrical wiring shall be of such size and characteristics as to provide the necessary voltage as the design requires to comply with FMVSS 571.108.

(c) Lamps shall be properly grounded.

Note: This shall not prohibit the use of the frame or other metal parts of a motor vehicle as a return ground system provided truck-tractor semitrailer/full trailer combinations are electrically connected.

§393.28 Wiring to be protected.

(a) The wiring shall—

(1) Be so installed that connections are protected from weather, abrasion, road splash, grease, oil, fuel and chafing;

(2) Be grouped together, when possible, and protected by nonconductive tape, braid, or other covering capable of withstanding severe abrasion or shall be protected by being enclosed in a sheath or tube;

(3) Be properly supported in a manner to prevent chafing;

(4) Not be so located as to be likely to be charred, overheated, or enmeshed in moving parts;

(5) Not have terminals or splices located above the fuel tank except for the fuel sender wiring and terminal; and

(6) Be protected when passing through holes in metal by a grommet, or other means, or the wiring shall be encased in a protective covering.

(b) The complete wiring system including lamps, junction boxes, receptacle boxes, conduit and fittings must be weather resistant.

(c) Harness connections shall be accomplished by a mechanical means.

§393.29 Grounds.

The battery ground and trailer return ground connections on a grounded system shall be readily accessible. The contact surfaces of electrical connections shall be clean and free of oxide, paint, or other nonconductive coating.

§393.30 Battery installation.

Every storage battery on every vehicle, unless located in the engine compartment, shall be covered by a fixed part of the motor vehicle or protected by a removable cover or enclosure. Removable covers, or enclosures shall be substantial and shall be securely latched or fastened. The storage battery compartment and adjacent metal parts which might corrode by reason of battery leakage shall be painted or coated with an acidresisting paint or coating and shall have openings to provide ample battery ventilation and drainage. Whenever the cable to the starting motor passes through a metal compartment, the cable shall be protected against grounding by an acid and waterproof insulating bushing. Wherever a battery and a fuel tank are both placed under the driver's seat, they shall be partitioned from each other, and each compartment shall be provided with an independent cover, ventilation, and drainage.

§393.31 Overload protective devices.

(a) The current to all low tension circuits shall pass through overload protective devices except that this requirement shall not be applicable to battery-to-starting motor or battery-to-generator circuits, ignition and engine control circuits, horn circuits, electrically-operated fuel pump circuits, or electric brake circuits.

(b) Trucks, truck-tractors, and buses meeting the definition of a commercial motor vehicle and manufactured after June 30, 1953 shall have protective devices for electrical circuits arranged so that:

(1) The headlamp circuit or circuits shall not be affected by a short circuit in any other lighting circuits on the motor vehicle; or

(2) The protective device shall be an automatic reset overload circuit breaker if the headlight circuit is protected in common with other circuits.

§393.32 Detachable electrical connections.

Electrical wiring between towing and towed vehicles shall be contained in a cable or cables or entirely within another substantially constructed protective device. All such electrical wiring shall be mechanically and electrically adequate and free of short or open circuits. Suitable provision shall be rmade in every such detachable connection to afford reasonable assurance against connection in an incorrect manner or accidental disconnection. Detachable connections made by twisting together wires from the towed and towing units are prohibited. Precaution shall be taken to provide sufficient slack in the connecting wire or cable to accommodate without damage all normal motions of the parts to which they are attached.

§393.33 Wiring, installation.

Electrical wiring shall be systematically arranged and installed in a workmanlike manner. All detachable wiring, except temporary wiring connections for driveaway-towaway operations, shall be attached to posts or terminals by means of suitable cable terminals which conform to the SAE Standard[1] for "Cable Terminals" or by cable terminals which are mechanically and electrically at least equal to such terminals. The number of wires attached to any post shall be limited to the number which such post was designed to accommodate. The presence of bare, loose, dangling, chafing, or poorly connected wires is prohibited.

Subpart C — Brakes

§393.40 Required brake systems.

(a) **General.** A bus, truck, truck tractor, or a combination of motor vehicles must have brakes adequate to control the movement of, and to stop and hold, the vehicle or combination of vehicles.

(b) **Specific systems required.** (1) A bus, truck, truck tractor, or combination of motor vehicles must have —

(i) A service brake system that conforms to the requirements of §393.52; and

(ii) A parking brake system that conforms to the requirements of §393.41.

(2) A bus, truck, truck tractor, or a combination of motor vehicles manufactured on or after July 1, 1973, must have an emergency brake system that conforms to the requirements of §393.52(b) and consists of either—

(i) Emergency features of the service brake system; or

(ii) A system separate from the service brake system.

---

[1]See footnote 1 to 393.24(c).

A control by which the driver applies the emergency brake system must be located so that the driver can readily operate it when he/she is properly restrained by any seat belt assembly provided for his/her use. The control for applying the emergency brake system may be combined with either the control for applying the service brake system or the control for applying the parking brake system. However, all three controls may not be combined.

(c) **Interconnected systems.** (1) If the brake systems specified in paragraph (b) of this section are interconnected in any way, they must be designed, constructed, and maintained so that, upon the failure of any part of the operating mechanism of one or more of the systems (except the service brake actuation pedal or valve)—

(i) The vehicle will have operative brakes; and

(ii) In the case of a vehicle manufactured on or after July 1, 1973, the vehicle will have operative brakes capable of performing as specified in §393.52(b).

(2) A motor vehicle to which the emergency brake system requirements of Federal Motor Vehicle Safety Standard No. 105 (§571.105 of this title) applied at the time of its manufacture conforms to the requirements of paragraph (c)(1) of this section if—

(i) It is maintained in conformity with the emergency brake requirements of Standard No. 105 in effect on the date of its manufacture; and

(ii) It is capable of performing as specified in §393.52(b), except upon structural failure of its brake master cylinder body or effectiveness indicator body.

(3) A bus conforms to the requirements of paragraph (c)(1) of this section if it meets the requirements of §393.44 and is capable of performing as specified in §393.52(b).

§393.41 Parking brake system.

(a) Every commercial motor vehicle manufactured on and after one year after March 7, 1989, except an agricultural commodity trailer, converter dolly, heavy hauler or pulpwood trailer, shall at all times be equipped with a parking brake system adequate to hold the vehicle or combination under any condition of loading as required by FMVSS 571.121. An agricultural commodity trailer, heavy hauler or pulpwood trailer shall carry sufficient chocking blocks to prevent movement when parked.

(b) The parking brake system shall at all times be capable of being applied in conformance with the requirements of paragraph (a) of this section by either the driver's muscular effort, or by spring action, or by other energy, provided, that if such other energy is depended on for application of the parking brake, then an accumulation of such energy shall be isolated from any common source and used exclusively for the operation of the parking brake.

(c) The parking brake system shall be held in the applied position by energy other than fluid pressure, air pressure, or electric energy. The parking brake system shall be such that it cannot be released unless adequate energy is available upon release of the parking brake to make immediate further application with the required effectiveness.

§393.42 Brakes required on all wheels.

(a) Every commercial motor vehicle shall be equipped with brakes acting on all wheels.

(b) **Exception.** (1) Trucks or truck tractors having three or more axles—

(i) Need not have brakes on the front wheels if the vehicle was manufactured before July 25, 1980; or

(ii) Manufactured between July 24, 1980, and October 27, 1986, must be retrofitted to meet the requirements of this section within one year from February 26, 1987, if the brake components have been removed.

(2) Any motor vehicle being towed in a driveaway-towaway operation must have operative brakes as may be necessary to ensure compliance with the performance requirements of §393.52. This paragraph is not applicable to any motor vehicle towed by means of a towbar when any other vehicle is full-mounted on such towed motor vehicle or any combination of motor vehicles utilizing three or more saddle-mounts. (See §393.71(a)(3).)

(3) Any full trailer, any semitrailer, or any pole trailer having a GVWR of 3,000 pounds or less must be equipped with brakes if the weight of the towed vehicle resting on the towing vehicle exceeds 40 percent of the GVWR of the towing vehicle.

(Diagrams to illustrate §393.42 for brake requirements for light trailers.)

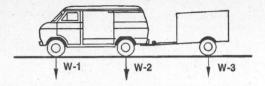

(Semitrailer or 2-wheel pole trailer of 3,000 pounds gross weight or less must be equipped with brakes if W-3 is greater than 40 percent of the sum of W-1 and W-2.)

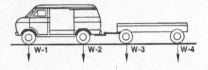

(Full trailer or 4-wheel pole trailer of 3,000 pounds gross weight or less must be equipped with brakes if the sum of W-3 and W-4 is greater than 40 percent of the sum of W-1 and W-2.)

§393.43 Breakaway and emergency braking.

(a) Every motor vehicle, if used to tow a trailer equipped with brakes, shall be equipped with means for providing that in case of breakaway of such trailer the service brakes on the towing vehicle will be sufficiently operative to stop the towing vehicle.

(b) Every truck or truck tractor equipped with air brakes, when used for towing other vehicles equipped with air brakes, shall be equipped with two means of activating the emergency features of the trailer brakes. One of these means shall operate automatically in the event of reduction of the towing vehicle air supply to a fixed pressure which shall not be lower than 20 pounds per square inch nor higher than 45 pounds per square inch. The other means shall be a manually controlled device readily operable by a person seated in the driving seat. Its emergency position or method of operation shall be clearly indicated. In no instance may the manual means be so arranged as to permit its use to prevent operation of the automatic means. The automatic and manual means required by this section may be, but are not required to be, separate.

(c) Every truck tractor and truck when used for towing other vehicles equipped with vacuum brakes, shall have, in addition to the single control required by §393.49 to operate all brakes of the combination, a second manual control device which can be used to operate the brakes on the towed vehicles in emergencies. Such second control shall be independent of brake air, hydraulic, and other pressure, and independent of other controls, unless the braking system be so arranged that failure of the pressure on which the second control depends will cause the towed vehicle brakes to be applied automatically. The second control is not required by this rule to provide modulated or graduated braking.

(d) Every trailer required to be equipped with brakes shall be equipped with brakes of such character as to be applied automatically and promptly upon breakaway from the towing vehicle, and means shall be provided to maintain application of the brakes on the trailer in such case for at least 15 minutes.

(e) Air brake systems installed on towed vehicles shall be so designed, by the use of "no-bleed-back" relay emergency valves or equivalent devices, that the supply reservoir used to provide air for brakes shall be safeguarded against backflow of air to the towing vehicle upon reduction of the towing vehicle air pressure.

(f) The requirements of paragraphs (b), (c), and (d) of this section shall not be applicable to motor vehicles in driveaway-towaway operations.

§393.44 Front brake lines, protection.

On every bus, if equipped with air brakes, the braking system shall be so constructed that in the event any brake line to any of the front wheels is broken, the driver can apply the brakes on the rear wheels despite such breakage. The means used to apply the brakes may be located forward of the driver's seat as long as it can be operated manually by the driver when the driver is properly restrained by any seat belt assembly provided for use. Every bus shall meet this requirement or comply with the regulations in effect at the time of its manufacture.

§393.45 Brake tubing and hose, adequacy.

(a) **General requirements.** Brake tubing and brake hose must—

(1) Be designed and constructed in a manner that insures

proper, adequate, and continued functioning of the tubing or hose;

(2) Be installed in a manner that insures proper continued functioning of the tubing or hose;

(3) Be long and flexible enough to accommodate without damage all normal motions of the parts to which it is attached;

(4) Be suitably secured against chafing, kinking, or other mechanical damage;

(5) Be installed in a manner that prevents it from contacting the vehicle's exhaust system or any other source of high temperatures; and

(6) Conform to the applicable requirements of paragraph (b) or (c) of this section. In addition, all hose installed on and after January 1, 1981, must conform to those applicable subsections of FMVSS 106 (49 CFR 571.106).

(b) **Special requirements for metallic brake tubing, nonmetallic brake tubing, coiled nonmetallic brake tubing and brake hose.**

(1) Metallic brake tubing, nonmetallic brake tubing, coiled nonmetallic brake tubing, and brake hose installed on a commercial motor vehicle on and after March 7, 1989, must meet or exceed one of the following specifications set forth in the SAE Handbook 1985 edition:

(i) Metallic Air Brake Tubing—SAE Recommended Practice J1149—Metallic Air Brake System Tubing and Pipe—July 76.

(ii) Nonmetallic Air Brake Tubing—SAE Recommended Practice J844—Nonmetallic Air Brake System Type B—OCT 80.

(iii) Air Brake Hose—SAE Recommended Practice J1402-Automotive Air Brake Hose and Hose Assemblies—JUN 85.

(iv) Hydraulic Brake Hose—SAE Recommended Practice J1401 Road Vehicle-Hydraulic Brake Hose Assemblies for Use with Non-Petroleum Base Hydraulic Fluid JUN 85.

(v) Vacuum Brake Hose—SAE Recommended Practice J1403 Vacuum Brake Hose JUN 85.

(2) Except as provided in paragraph (c) of this section, brake hose and brake tubing installed on a motor vehicle before March 7, 1989, must conform to 49 CFR 393.45 effective October 31, 1983.

(c) **Nonmetallic brake tubing**. Coiled nonmetallic brake tubing may be used for connections between towed and towing vehicles or between the frame of a towed vehicle and the unsprung subframe of an adjustable axle of that vehicle if—

(1) The coiled tubing has a straight segment (pigtail) at each end that is at least 2 inches in length and is encased in a spring guard or similar device which prevents the tubing from kinking at the fitting at which it is attached to the vehicle; and

(2) The spring guard or similar device has at least 2 inches of closed coils or similar surface at its interface with the fitting and extends at least $1\ ^1\!/_2$ inches into the coiled segment of the tubing from its straight segment.

(d) **Brake tubing and brake hose, uses**. Metallic and non-metallic brake tubing is intended for use in areas of the brake system where relative movement in the line is not anticipated. Brake hose and coiled nonmetallic brake tubing is intended for use in the brake system where substantial relative movement in the line is anticipated or the hose/coiled nonmetallic brake tubing is exposed to potential tension or impact such as between the frame and axle in a conventional type suspension system (axle attached to frame by suspension system). Nonmetallic brake tubing may be used through an articulation point provided movement is less than 4.5 degrees in a vertical plane, and 7.4 degrees in a transverse horizontal plane.

§393.46 Brake tubing and hose connections.

All connections for air, vacuum, or hydraulic braking systems shall:

(a) Be adequate in material and construction to insure proper continued functioning;

(b) Be designed, constructed, and installed so as to insure, when properly connected, an attachment free of leaks, constrictions, or other defects;

(c) Have suitable provision in every detachable connection to afford reasonable assurance against accidental disconnection;

(d) Have the vacuum brake engine manifold connection at least $^3\!/_8$ inch in diameter.

(e) If installed on a vehicle on or after January 1, 1981, meet requirements under applicable subsections of FMVSS 106 (49 CFR 571.106).

(f) Splices in tubing if installed on a vehicle after March 7, 1989, must use fittings that meet the requirements of SAE Standard J512-OCT 80 Automotive Tube Fittings or for air brake systems SAE J246—March 81 Spherical and Flanged Sleeve (Compression) Tube Fittings as found in the SAE Handbook 1985 edition.

§393.47 Brake lining.

The brake lining on every motor vehicle shall be so constructed and installed as not to be subject to excessive fading and grabbing and shall be adequate in thickness, means of attachment, and physical characteristics to provide for safe and reliable stopping of the motor vehicle.

§393.48 Brakes to be operative.

(a) **General rule.** Except as provided in paragraphs (b) and (c) of this section, all brakes with which a motor vehicle is equipped must at all times be capable of operating.

(b) **Devices to reduce or remove front-wheel braking effort.** A motor vehicle may be equipped with a device to reduce the braking effort upon its front wheels or, in the case of a three-axle truck or truck tractor manufactured before March 1, 1975, to remove the braking effort upon its front wheels, if that device conforms to, and is used in compliance with, the rules in paragraph (b)(1) or (2) of this section.

(1) **Manually operated devices.** A manually operated device to reduce or remove the front-wheel braking effort must not be—

(i) Installed in a motor vehicle other than a bus, truck, or truck tractor; or

(ii) Installed in a bus, truck, or truck tractor manufactured after February 28, 1975; or

(iii) Used in the reduced mode except when the vehicle is operating under adverse conditions such as wet, snowy, or icy roads.

(2) **Automatic Devices.** An automatic device to reduce the front-wheel braking effort by up to 50 percent of the normal braking force, regardless of whether or not antilock system failure has occurred on any axle, must not—

(i) Be operable by the driver except upon application of the control that activates the braking system; and

(ii) Be operable when the pressure that transmits brake control application force exceeds—

(A) 85 psig on air-mechanical braking systems; or

(B) 85 percent of the maximum system pressure in the case of vehicles utilizing other than compressed air.

(c) **Towed vehicle.** Paragraph (a) of this section does not apply to—

(1) A disabled vehicle being towed; or

(2) A vehicle being towed in a driveaway-towaway operation which is exempt from the general rule of §393.42 under paragraph (b) of that section.

§393.49 Single valve to operate all brakes.

Every motor vehicle, the date of manufacture of which is subsequent to June 30, 1953, which is equipped with power brakes, shall have the braking system so arranged that one application valve shall when applied operate all the service brakes on the motor vehicle or combination of motor vehicles. This requirement shall not be construed to prohibit motor vehicles from being equipped with an additional valve to be used to operate the brakes on a trailer or trailers or as provided in §393.44. This section shall not be applicable to driveaway-towaway operations unless the brakes on such operations are designed to be operated by a single valve.

§393.50 Reservoirs required.

(a) **General.** Every commercial motor vehicle using air or vacuum for braking shall be equipped with reserve capacity or a reservoir sufficient to ensure a full service brake application with the engine stopped without depleting the air pressure or vacuum below 70 percent of that pressure or degree of vacuum indicated by the gauge immediately before the brake application is made. For purposes of this section, a full service brake application is considered to be made when the service brake pedal is pushed to the limit of its travel.

(b) **Safeguarding of air and vacuum.** (1) Every bus, truck, and truck tractor, when equipped with air or vacuum reservoirs and regardless of date of manufacture, shall have such reservoirs so safeguarded by a check valve or equivalent device that in the event of failure or leakage in its connection to the source of compressed air or vacuum the air or vacuum supply in the reservoir shall not be depleted by the leak or failure.

(2) Means shall be provided to establish the check valve to be in working order. On and after May 1, 1966, means other than loosening or disconnection of any connection between the source of compressed air or vacuum and the check valve, and necessary tools for operation of such means, shall be provided to prove that the check valve is in working order. The means shall be readily accessible either from the front, side, or rear of the vehicle, or from the driver's compartment.

(i) In air brake systems with one reservoir, the means shall be a cock, valve, plug, or equivalent device arranged to vent a cavity having free communication with the connection between the check valve and the source of compressed air or vacuum.

(ii) Where air is delivered by a compressor into one tank or compartment (wet tank), and air for braking is taken directly from another tank or compartment (dry tank) only, with the required check valve between the tanks or compartments, a manually operated drain cock on the first (wet) tank or compartment will serve as a means herein required if it conforms to the requirements herein.

(iii) In vacuum systems stopping the engine will serve as the required means, the system remaining evacuated as indicated by the vacuum gauge.

§393.51 Warning devices and gauges.

(a) **General.** In the manner and to the extent specified in paragraphs (b), (c), (d), and (e) of this section, a bus, truck, or truck tractor must be equipped with a signal that provides a warning to the driver when a failure occurs in the vehicle's service brake system.

(b) **Hydraulic brakes.** A vehicle manufactured on or after July 1, 1973, and having service brakes activated by hydraulic fluid must be equipped with a warning signal that performs as follows:

(1) If Federal Motor Vehicle Safety Standard No. 105 (§571.105 of this title) was applicable to the vehicle at the time it was manufactured, the warning signal must conform to the requirements of that standard.

(2) If Federal Motor Vehicle Safety Standard No. 105 (§571.105) was not applicable to the vehicle at the time it was manufactured, the warning signal must become operative, before or upon application of the brakes in the event of a hydraulic-type complete failure of a partial system. The signal must be readily audible or visible to the driver.

(c) **Air brakes.** A vehicle (regardless of the date it was manufactured) having service brakes activated by compressed air (air-mechanical brakes) or a vehicle towing a vehicle having service brakes activated by compressed air (air-mechanical brakes) must be equipped, and perform, as follows:

(1) The vehicle must have a low air pressure warning device that conforms to the requirements of either paragraph (c)(1)(i)

or (ii) of this section.

(i) If Federal Motor Vehicle Safety Standard No. 121 (§571.121 of this title) was applicable to the vehicle at the time it was manufactured, the warning device must conform to the requirements of that standard.

(ii) If Federal Motor Vehicle Safety Standard No. 121 (§571.121) was not applicable to the vehicle at the time it was manufactured, the vehicle must have a device that provides a readily audible or visible continuous warning to the driver whenever the pressure of the compressed air in the braking system is below a specified pressure, which must be at least one-half of the compressor governor cutout pressure.

(2) The vehicle must have a pressure gauge which indicates to the driver the pressure in pounds per square inch available for braking.

(d) **Vacuum brakes.** A vehicle (regardless of the date it was manufactured) having service brakes activated by vacuum or a vehicle towing a vehicle having service brakes activated by vacuum must be equipped with—

(1) A device that provides a readily audible or visible continuous warning to the driver whenever the vacuum in the vehicle's supply reservoir is less than 8 inches of mercury; and

(2) A vacuum gauge which indicates to the driver the vacuum in inches of mercury available for braking.

(e) **Hydraulic brakes applied or assisted by air or vacuum.** A vehicle having a braking system in which hydraulically activated service brakes are applied or assisted by compressed air or vacuum must be equipped with both a warning signal that conforms to the requirements of paragraph (b) of this section and a warning device that conforms to the requirements of either paragraph (c) or paragraph (d) of this section.

(f) **Maintenance.** The warning signals, devices, and gauges required by this section must be maintained in operative condition.

§393.52 Brake performance.

(a) Upon application of its service brakes, a motor vehicle or combination of motor vehicles must under any condition of loading in which it is found on a public highway, be capable of—

(1) Developing a braking force at least equal to the percentage of its gross weight specified in the table in paragraph (d) of this section;

(2) Decelerating to a stop from 20 miles per hour at not less than the rate specified in the table in paragraph (d) of this section; and

(3) Stopping from 20 miles per hour in a distance, measured from the point at which movement of the service brake pedal or control begins, that is not greater than the distance specified in the table in paragraph (d) of this section.

(b) Upon application of its emergency brake system and with no other brake system applied, a motor vehicle or combination of motor vehicles must, under any condition of loading in which it is found on a public highway, be capable of stopping from 20 miles per hour in a distance, measured from the point at which movement of the emergency brake control begins, that is not greater than the distance specified in the table in paragraph (d) of this section.

(c) Conformity to the stopping-distance requirements of paragraphs (a) and (b) of this section shall be determined under the following conditions:

(1) Any test must be made with the vehicle on a hard surface that is substantially level, dry, smooth, and free of loose material.

(2) The vehicle must be in the center of a 12-foot-wide lane when the test begins and must not deviate from that lane during the test.

(d) Vehicle brake performance table:

Type of motor vehicle	Service brake systems			Emergency brake systems
	Braking fore as a percentage of gross vehicle or combination weight	Deceleration in feet per second per second	Application and braking distance in feet from initial speed of 20 m.p.h.	Application and braking distance in feet from initial speed of 20 m.p.h.
A. *Passenger-carrying vehicles.*				
(1) Vehicles with a seating capacity of 10 persons or less, including driver, and built on a passenger car chassis	65.2	21	20	54
(2) Vehicles with a seating capacity of more than 10 persons, including driver, and built on a passenger car chassis; vehicles built on a truck or bus chassis and having a manufacturer's GVWR of 10,000 pounds or less	52.8	17	25	66
(3) All other passenger-carrying vehicles	43.5	14	35	85
B. *Property-carrying vehicles.*				
(1) Single unit vehicles having a manufacturer's GVWR of 10,000 pounds or less	52.8	17	25	66
(2) Single unit vehicles having a manufacturer's GVWR of more than 10,000 pounds, except truck tractors. Combinations of a 2-axle towing vehicle and trailer having a GVWR of 3,000 pounds or less. All combinations of 2 or less vehicles in driveway or towaway operation	43.4	14	35	85
(3) All other property-carrying vehicles and combinations of property-carrying vehicles	43.5	14	40	90

(see note on following page)

Note: (a) There is a definite mathematical relationship between the figures in columns 2 and 3, if the decelerations set forth in column 3 are divided by 32.2 feet per second per second, the figures in column 2 will be obtained. (For example, 21 divided by 32.2 equals 65.2 percent.) Column 2 is included in the tabulation because certain brake-testing devices utilize this factor.

(b) The decelerations specified in column 3 are an indication of the effectiveness of the basic brakes, and as measured in practical brake testing are the maximum decelerations attained at some time during the stop.

These decelerations as measured in brake tests cannot be used to compute the values in column 4 because the deceleration is not sustained at the same rate over the entire period of the stop. The deceleration increases from zero to a maximum during a period of brake-system application and brake-force buildup. Also, other factors may cause the deceleration to decrease after reaching a maximum. The added distance which results because maximum deceleration is not sustained is included in the figures in column 4 but is not indicated by the usual brake-testing devices for checking deceleration.

(c) The distances in column 4 and the decelerations in column 3 are not directly related. "Brake-system application and braking distance in feet" (column 4) is a definite measure of the overall effectiveness of the braking system, being the distance traveled between the point at which the driver starts to move the braking controls and the point at which the vehicle comes to rest. It includes distance traveled while the brakes are being applied and distance traveled while the brakes are retarding the vehicle.

(d) The distance traveled during the period of brake-system application and brake-force buildup varies with vehicle type, being negligible for many passenger cars and greatest for combinations of commercial vehicles. This fact accounts for the variation from 20 to 40 feet in the values in column 4 for the various classes of vehicles.

(e) The terms "GVWR" and "GVW" refer to the manufacturer's gross vehicle rating and the actual gross vehicle weight, respectively.

§393.53 Automatic brake adjusters and brake adjustment indicators.

(a) **Automatic brake adjusters (hydraulic brake systems)**. Each commercial motor vehicle manufactured on or after October 20, 1993, and equipped with a hydraulic brake system, shall meet the automatic brake adjustment system requirements of Federal Motor Vehicle Safety Standard No. 105 (49 CFR 571.105, S5.1) applicable to the vehicle at the time it was manufactured.

(b) **Automatic brake adjusters (air brake systems).** Each commercial motor vehicle manufactured on or after October 20, 1994, and equipped with an air brake system, shall meet the automatic brake adjustment system requirements of Federal Motor Vehicle Safety Standard No. 121 (49 CFR 571.121, S5.1.8) applicable to the vehicle at the time it was manufactured.

(c) **Brake adjustment indicator (air brake systems).** On each commercial motor vehicle manufactured on or after October 20, 1994, and equipped with an air brake system which contains an external automatic adjustment mechanism and an exposed pushrod, the condition of service brake under-adjustment shall be displayed by a brake adjustment indicator conforming to the requirements of Federal Motor Vehicle Safety Standard No. 121 (49 CFR 571.121, S5.1.8) applicable to the vehicle at the time it was manufactured.

§393.55 Antilock brake systems.

(a) **Hydraulic brake systems.** Each truck and bus manufactured on or after March 1, 1999 (except trucks and buses engaged in driveaway-towaway operations), and equipped with a hydraulic brake system, shall be equipped with an antilock brake system that meets the requirements of Federal Motor Vehicle Safety Standard (FMVSS) No. 105 (49 CFR 571.105, S5.5).

(b) **ABS malfunction indicators for hydraulic braked vehicles.** Each hydraulic braked vehicle subject to the requirements of paragraph (a) of this section shall be equipped with an ABS malfunction indicator system that meets the requirements of FMVSS No. 105 (49 CFR 571.105, S5.3).

(c) **Air brake systems.** (1) Each truck tractor manufactured on or after March 1, 1997 (except truck tractors engaged in driveaway-towaway operations), shall be equipped with an antilock brake system that meets the requirements of FMVSS No. 121 (49 CFR 571.121, S5.1.6.1(b)).

(2) Each air braked commercial motor vehicle other than a truck tractor, manufactured on or after March 1, 1998 (except commercial motor vehicles engaged in driveaway-towaway operations), shall be equipped with an antilock brake system that meets the requirements of FMVSS No. 121 (49 CFR 571.121, S5.1.6.1(a) for trucks and buses, S5.2.3 for semitrailers, converter dollies and full trailers).

(d) **ABS malfunction circuits and signals for air braked vehicles.**

(1) Each truck tractor manufactured on or after March 1, 1997, and each single-unit air braked vehicle manufactured on or after March 1, 1998, subject to the requirements of paragraph (c) of this section, shall be equipped with an electrical circuit that is capable of signaling a malfunction that affects the generation or transmission of response or control signals to the

vehicle's antilock brake system (49 CFR 571.121, S5.1.6.2(a)).

(2) Each truck tractor manufactured on or after March 1, 2001, and each single-unit vehicle that is equipped to tow another air-braked vehicle, subject to the requirements of paragraph (c) of this section, shall be equipped with an electrical circuit that is capable of transmitting a malfunction signal from the antilock brake system(s) on the towed vehicle(s) to the trailer ABS malfunction lamp in the cab of the towing vehicle, and shall have the means for connection of the electrical circuit to the towed vehicle. The ABS malfunction circuit and signal shall meet the requirements of FMVSS No. 121 (49 CFR 571.121, S5.1.6.2(b)).

(3) Each semitrailer, trailer converter dolly, and full trailer manufactured on or after March 1, 2001, and subject to the requirements of paragraph (c)(2) of this section, shall be equipped with an electrical circuit that is capable of signaling a malfunction in the trailer's antilock brake system, and shall have the means for connection of this ABS malfunction circuit to the towing vehicle. In addition, each trailer manufactured on or after March 1, 2001, subject to the requirements of paragraph (c)(2) of this section, that is designed to tow another air-brake equipped trailer shall be capable of transmitting a malfunction signal from the antilock brake system(s) of the trailer(s) it tows to the vehicle in front of the trailer. The ABS malfunction circuit and signal shall meet the requirements of FMVSS No. 121 (49 CFR 571.121, S5.2.3.2).

(e) **Exterior ABS malfunction indicator lamps for trailers.** Each trailer (including a trailer converter dolly) manufactured on or after March 1, 1998 and before March 1, 2009, and subject to the requirements of paragraph (c)(2) of this section, shall be equipped with an ABS malfunction indicator lamp which meets the requirements of FMVSS No. 121 (49 CFR 571.121, S5.2.3.3).

Subpart D —
Glazing and Window Construction

§393.60 Glazing in specified openings.

(a) **Glazing material.** Glazing material used in windshields, windows, and doors on a motor vehicle manufactured on or after December 25, 1968, shall at a minimum meet the requirements of Federal Motor Vehicle Safety Standard (FMVSS) No. 205 in effect on the date of manufacture of the motor vehicle. The glazing material shall be marked in accordance with FMVSS No. 205 (49 CFR 571.205, S6).

(b) **Windshields required.** Each bus, truck and truck-tractor shall be equipped with a windshield. Each windshield or portion of a multi-piece windshield shall be mounted using the full periphery of the glazing material.

(c) **Windshield condition.** With the exception of the conditions listed in paragraphs (c)(1), (c)(2), and (c)(3) of this section, each windshield shall be free of discoloration or damage in the area extending upward from the height of the top of the steering wheel (excluding a 51 mm (2 inch) border at the top of the windshield) and extending from a 25 mm (1 inch) border at each side of the windshield or windshield panel. **Exceptions:**

(1) Coloring or tinting which meets the requirements of paragraph (d) of this section;

(2) Any crack that is not intersected by any other cracks;

(3) Any damaged area which can be covered by a disc 19 mm (¾ inch) in diameter if not closer than 76 mm (3 inches) to any other similarly damaged area.

(d) **Coloring or tinting of windshields and windows.** Coloring or tinting of windshields and the windows to the immediate right and left of the driver is allowed, provided the parallel luminous transmittance through the colored or tinted glazing is not less than 70 percent of the light at normal incidence in those portions of the windshield or windows which are marked as having a parallel luminous transmittance of not less than 70 percent. The transmittance restriction does not apply to other windows on the commercial motor vehicle.

(e) **Prohibition on obstructions to the driver's field of view**—(1) **Devices mounted at the top of the windshield.** Antennas, transponders, and similar devices must not be mounted more than 152 mm (6 inches) below the upper edge of the windshield. These devices must be located outside the area swept by the windshield wipers, and outside the driver's sight lines to the road and highway signs and signals.

(2) **Decals and stickers mounted on the windshield.** Commercial Vehicle Safety Alliance (CVSA) inspection decals, and stickers and/or decals required under Federal or State laws may be placed at the bottom or sides of the windshield provided such decals or stickers do not extend more than 115 mm (4½ inches) from the bottom of the windshield and are located outside the area swept by the windshield wipers, and outside the

driver's sight lines to the road and highway signs or signals.

§393.61 Window construction.

(a) **Windows in trucks and truck tractors.** Every truck and truck tractor, except vehicles engaged in armored car service, shall have, in addition to the area provided by the windshield, at least one window on each side of the driver's compartment, which window shall have sufficient area to contain either an ellipse having a major axis of 18 inches and a minor axis of 13 inches or an opening containing 200 square inches formed by a rectangle 13 inches by $17\text{-}^3/_4$ inches with corner arcs of 6-inch maximum radius. The major axis of the ellipse and the long axis of the rectangle shall not make an angle of more than 45 degrees with the surface on which the unladen vehicle stands; however, if the cab is designed with a folding door or doors or with clear openings where doors or windows are customarily located, then no windows shall be required in such locations.

(b) **Bus windows.** (1) Except as provided in paragraph (b)(3) of this section a bus manufactured before September 1, 1973, having a seating capacity of more than eight persons shall have, in addition to the area provided by the windshield, adequate means of escape for passengers through windows. The adequacy of such means shall be determined in accordance with the following standards: For each seated passenger space provided, inclusive of the driver there shall be at least 67 square inches of glazing if such glazing is not contained in a push-out window; or at least 67 square inches of free opening resulting from opening of a push-out type window. No area shall be included in this minimum prescribed area unless it will provide an unobstructed opening sufficient to contain an ellipse having a major axis of 18 inches and a minor axis of 13 inches or an opening containing 200 square inches formed by a rectangle 13 inches by $17\text{-}^3/_4$ inches with corner arcs of 6-inch maximum radius. The major axis of the ellipse and the long axis of the rectangle shall make an angle of not more than 45° with the surface on which the unladen vehicle stands. The area shall be measured either by removal of the glazing if not of the pushout type or of the movable sash if of the push-out type, and it shall be either glazed with laminated safety glass or comply with paragraph (c) of this section. No less than 40 percent of such prescribed glazing or opening shall be on one side of any bus.

(2) A bus, including a school bus, manufactured on and after

September 1, 1973, having a seating capacity of more than 10 persons shall have emergency exits in conformity with Federal Motor Vehicle Safety Standard No. 217, Part 571 of this title.

(3) A bus manufactured before September 1, 1973, may conform to Federal Motor Vehicle Safety Standard No. 217, Part 571 of this title, in lieu of conforming to paragraph (b)(1) of this section.

(c) **Push-out window requirements.** (1) Except as provided in paragraph (c)(3) of this section, every glazed opening in a bus manufactured before September 1, 1973, and having a seating capacity of more than eight persons, used to satisfy the requirements of paragraph (b)(1) of this section, if not glazed with laminated safety glass, shall have a frame or sash so designed, constructed, and maintained that it will yield outwardly to provide the required free opening when subjected to the drop test specified in Test 25 of the American Standard Safety Code referred to in §393.60. The height of drop required to open such push-out windows shall not exceed the height of drop required to break the glass in the same window when glazed with the type of laminated glass specified in Test 25 of the Code. The sash for such windows shall be constructed of such material and be of such design and construction as to be continuously capable of complying with the above requirement.

(2) On a bus manufactured on and after September 1, 1973, having a seating capacity of more than 10 persons, each push-out window shall conform to Federal Motor Vehicle Safety Standard No. 217, (§571.217) of this title.

(3) A bus manufactured before September 1, 1973, may conform to Federal Motor Vehicle Safety Standard No. 217, (§571.217) of this title, in lieu of conforming to paragraph (c)(1) of this section.

§393.62 Window obstructions.

Windows, if otherwise capable of complying with §393.61 (a) and (b), shall not be obstructed by bars or other such means located either inside or outside such windows such as would hinder the escape of occupants unless such bars or other such means are so constructed as to provide a clear opening, at least equal to the opening provided by the window to which it is adjacent when subjected to the same test specified in §393.61(c). The point of application of such test force shall be such as will be most likely to result in the removal of the obstruction.

§393.63 Windows, markings.

(a) On a bus manufactured before September 1, 1973, each bus push-out window and any other bus escape window glazed with laminated safety glass required in §393.61 shall be identified as such by clearly legible and visible signs, lettering, or decalcomania. Such marking shall include appropriate wording to indicate that it is an escape window and also the method to be used for obtaining emergency exit.

(b) On a bus manufactured on and after September 1, 1973, emergency exits required in §393.61 shall be marked to conform to Federal Motor Vehicle Safety Standard No. 217, (§571.217) of this title.

(c) A bus manufactured before September 1, 1973, may mark emergency exits to conform to Federal Motor Vehicle Safety Standard No. 217, (§571.217) of this title in lieu of conforming to paragraph (a) of this section.

Subpart E — Fuel Systems

§393.65 All fuel systems.

(a) **Application of the rules in this section.** The rules in this section apply to systems for containing and supplying fuel for the operation of motor vehicles or for the operation of auxiliary equipment installed on, or used in connection with, motor vehicles.

(b) **Location.** Each fuel system must be located on the motor vehicle so that—

(1) No part of the system extends beyond the widest part of the vehicle;

(2) No part of a fuel tank is forward of the front axle of a power unit;

(3) Fuel spilled vertically from a fuel tank while it is being filled will not contact any part of the exhaust or electrical systems of the vehicle, except the fuel level indicator assembly;

(4) Fill pipe openings are located outside the vehicle's passenger compartment and its cargo compartment;

(5) A fuel line does not extend between a towed vehicle and the vehicle that is towing it while the combination of vehicles is in motion; and

(6) No part of the fuel system of a bus manufactured on or after January 1, 1973, is located within or above the passenger

compartment.

(c) **Fuel tank installation.** Each fuel tank must be securely attached to the motor vehicle in a workmanlike manner.

(d) **Gravity or syphon feed prohibited.** A fuel system must not supply fuel by gravity or syphon feed directly to the carburetor or injector.

(e) **Selection control valve location.** If a fuel system includes a selection control valve which is operable by the driver to regulate the flow of fuel from two or more fuel tanks, the valve must be installed so that either—

(1) The driver may operate it while watching the roadway and without leaving his/her driving position; or

(2) The driver must stop the vehicle and leave his/her seat in order to operate the valve.

(f) **Fuel lines.** A fuel line which is not completely enclosed in a protective housing must not extend more than 2 inches below the fuel tank or its sump. Diesel fuel crossover, return, and withdrawal lines which extend below the bottom of the tank or sump must be protected against damage from impact. Every fuel line must be—

(1) Long enough and flexible enough to accommodate normal movements of the parts to which it is attached without incurring damage; and

(2) Secured against chafing, kinking, or other causes of mechanical damage.

(g) **Excess flow valve.** When pressure devices are used to force fuel from a fuel tank, a device which prevents the flow of fuel from the fuel tank if the fuel feed line is broken must be installed in the fuel system.

§393.67 Liquid fuel tanks.

(a) **Application of the rules in this section.** (1) A liquid fuel tank manufactured on or after January 1, 1973, and a side-mounted gasoline tank must conform to all the rules in this section.

(2) A diesel fuel tank manufactured before January 1, 1973, and mounted on a bus must conform to the rules in paragraphs (c)(7)(iii) and (d)(2) of this section.

(3) A diesel fuel tank manufactured before January 1, 1973, and mounted on a vehicle other than bus must conform to the rules in paragraph (c)(7)(iii) of this section.

(4) A gasoline tank, other than a side-mounted gasoline tank, manufactured before January 1, 1973, and mounted on a bus must conform to the rules in paragraphs (c)(1) through (10) and (d)(2) of this section.

(5) A gasoline tank, other than a side-mounted gasoline tank, manufactured before January 1, 1973, and mounted on a vehicle other than a bus must conform to the rules in paragraphs (c)(1) through (10), inclusive, of this section.

(6) **Private motor carrier of passengers.** Motor carriers engaged in the private transportation of passengers may continue to operate a commercial motor vehicle which was not subject to this section or 49 CFR 571.301 at the time of its manufacture, provided the fuel tank of such vehicle is maintained to the original manufacturer's standards.

(b) **Definitions.** As used in this section—

(1) The term "liquid fuel tank" means a fuel tank designed to contain a fuel that is liquid at normal atmospheric pressures and temperatures.

(2) A "side-mounted" fuel tank is a liquid fuel tank which—

(i) If mounted on a truck tractor, extends outboard of the vehicle frame and outside of the plan view outline of the cab; or

(ii) If mounted on a truck, extends outboard of a line parallel to the longitudinal centerline of the truck and tangent to the outboard side of a front tire in a straight ahead position. In determining whether a fuel tank on a truck or truck tractor is side-mounted, the fill pipe is not considered a part of the tank.

(c) **Construction of liquid fuel tanks—**

(1) **Joints.** Joints of a fuel tank body must be closed by arc-, gas-, seam-, or spot-welding, by brazing, by silver soldering, or by techniques which provide heat resistance and mechanical securement at least equal to those specifically named. Joints must not be closed solely by crimping or by soldering with a lead-based or other soft solder.

(2) **Fittings.** The fuel tank body must have flanges or spuds suitable for the installation of all fittings.

(3) **Threads.** The threads of all fittings must be Dryseal American Standard Taper Pipe Thread or Dryseal SAE Short Taper Pipe Thread, specified in Society of Automotive Engineers Standard J476, as contained in the 1971 edition of the "SAE Handbook", except that straight (non-tapered) threads may be used on fittings having integral flanges and using gaskets for sealing. At least four full threads must be in engagement in each fitting.

(4) **Drains and bottom fittings.**

(i) Drains or other bottom fittings must not extend more than $3/4$ of an inch below the lowest part of the fuel tank or sump.

(ii) Drains or other bottom fittings must be protected against damage from impact.

(iii) If a fuel tank has drains the drain fittings must permit substantially complete drainage of the tank.

(iv) Drains or other bottom fittings must be installed in a flange or spud designed to accommodate it.

(5) **Fuel withdrawal fittings.** Except for diesel fuel tanks, the fittings through which fuel is withdrawn from a fuel tank must be located above the normal level of fuel in the tank when the tank is full.

(6) [Reserved]

(7) **Fill pipe.**

(i) Each fill pipe must be designed and constructed to minimize the risk of fuel spillage during fueling operations and when the vehicle is involved in a crash.

(ii) The fill pipe and vents of a fuel tank having a capacity of more than 25 gallons of fuel must permit filling the tank with fuel at a rate of at least 20 gallons per minute without fuel spillage.

(iii) Each fill pipe must be fitted with a cap that can be fastened securely over the opening in the fill pipe. Screw threads or a bayonet-type joint are methods of conforming to the requirements of this subdivision.

(8) **Safety venting system.** A liquid fuel tank with a capacity of more than 25 gallons of fuel must have a venting system which, in the event the tank is subjected to fire, will prevent internal tank pressure from rupturing the tank's body, seams, or bottom opening (if any).

(9) **Pressure resistance.** The body and fittings of a liquid fuel tank with a capacity of more than 25 gallons of fuel must be capable of withstanding an internal hydrostatic pressure equal to 150 percent of the maximum internal pressure reached in the tank during the safety venting systems test specified in paragraph (d)(1) of this section.

(10) **Air vent.** Each fuel tank must be equipped with a nonspill air vent (such as a ball check). The air vent may be combined with the fill-pipe cap or safety vent, or it may be a separate unit installed on the fuel tank.

(11) **Markings.** If the body of the fuel tank is readily visible when the tank is installed on the vehicle, the tank must be plainly marked with its liquid capacity. The tank must also be plainly marked with a warning against filling it to more than 95 percent of its liquid capacity.

(12) **Overfill restriction.** A liquid fuel tank manufactured on or after January 1, 1973, must be designed and constructed so that—

(i) The tank cannot be filled, in a normal filling operation, with a quantity of fuel that exceeds 95 percent of the tank's liquid capacity; and

(ii) When the tank is filled, normal expansion of the fuel will not cause fuel spillage.

(d) **Liquid fuel tank tests.** Each liquid fuel tank must be capable of passing the tests specified in paragraphs (d)(1) and (2) of this section.[1]

(1) **Safety venting system test—**

(i) **Procedure.** Fill the tank three-fourths full with fuel, seal the fuel feed outlet, and invert the tank. When the fuel temperature is between 50°F. and 80°F., apply an enveloping flame to the tank so that the temperature of the fuel rises at a rate of not less than 6°F. and not more than 8°F. per minute.

(ii) **Required performance.** The safety venting system required by paragraph (c)(8) of this section must activate before the internal pressure in the tank exceeds 50 pounds per square inch, gauge, and the internal pressure must not thereafter exceed the pressure at which the system activated by more than five pounds per square inch despite any further increase in the temperature of the fuel.

(2) **Leakage test—**

(i) **Procedure.** Fill the tank to capacity with fuel having a temperature between 50 °F. and 80 °F. With the fill-pipe cap installed, turn the tank through an angle of 150° in any direction about any axis from its normal position.

(ii) **Required performance.** Neither the tank nor any fitting may leak more than a total of one ounce by weight of fuel per minute in any position the tank assumes during the test.

(e) **Side-mounted liquid fuel tank tests.** Each side-

---

[1]The specified tests are a measure of performance only. Manufacturers and carriers may use any alternative procedures which assure that their equipment meets the required performance criteria.

mounted liquid fuel tank must be capable of passing the tests specified in paragraphs (e)(1) and (2) of this section and the tests specified in paragraphs (d)(1) and (2) of this section·

(1) **Drop test**—

(i) **Procedure.** Fill the tank with a quantity of water having a weight equal to the weight of the maximum fuel load of the tank and drop the tank 30 feet onto an unyielding surface so that it lands squarely on one corner.

(ii) **Required performance.** Neither the tank nor any fitting may leak more than a total of 1 ounce by weight of water per minute.

(2) **Fill-pipe test**—

(i) **Procedure.** Fill the tank with a quantity of water having a weight equal to the weight of the maximum fuel load of the tank and drop the tank 10 feet onto an unyielding surface so that it lands squarely on its fill-pipe.

(ii) **Required performance.** Neither the tank nor any fitting may leak more than a total of 1 ounce by weight of water per minute.

(f) **Certification and markings**. Each liquid fuel tank shall be legibly and permanently marked by the manufacturer with the following minimum information:

(1) The month and year of manufacture.

(2) The manufacturer's name on tanks manufactured on and after July 1, 1988, and means of identifying the facility at which the tank was manfactured, and

(3) A certificate that it conforms to the rules in this section applicable to the tank. The certificate must be in the form set forth in either of the following:

(i) If a tank conforms to all rules in this section pertaining to side-mounted fuel tanks: "Meets all FHWA sidemounted tank requirements."

(ii) If a tank conforms to all rules in this section pertaining to tanks which are not side-mounted fuel tanks: "Meets all FHWA requirements for non-side-mounted fuel tanks."

(iii) The form of certificate specified in paragraph (f)(3) (i) or (ii) of this section may be used on a liquid fuel tank manufactured before July 11, 1973, but it is not mandatory for liquid fuel tanks manufactured before March 7, 1989. The form of certification manufactured on or before March 7, 1989, must meet the requirements in effect at the time of manufacture.

§393.69 Liquefied petroleum gas systems.

(a) A fuel system that uses liquefied petroleum gas as a fuel for the operation of a motor vehicle or for the operation of auxiliary equipment installed on, or used in connection with, a motor vehicle must conform to the "Standards for the Storage and Handling of Liquefied Petroleum Gases" of the National Fire Protection Association, Battery March Park, Quincy, MA 02269, as follows:

(1) A fuel system installed before December 31, 1962, must conform to the 1951 edition of the Standards.

(2) A fuel system installed on or after December 31, 1962, and before January 1, 1973, must conform to Division IV of the June 1959 edition of the Standards.

(3) A fuel system installed on or after January 1, 1973, and providing fuel for propulsion of the motor vehicle must conform to Division IV of the 1969 edition of the Standards.

(4) A fuel system installed on or after January 1, 1973, and providing fuel for the operation of auxiliary equipment must conform to Division VII of the 1969 edition of the Standards.

(b) When the rules in this section require a fuel system to conform to a specific edition of the Standards, the fuel system may conform to the applicable provisions in a later edition of the Standards specified in this section.

(c) The tank of a fuel system must be marked to indicate that the system conforms to the Standards.

Subpart F — Coupling Devices and Towing Methods

§393.70 Coupling devices and towing methods, except for driveaway-towaway operations.

(a) **Tracking.** When two or more vehicles are operated in combination, the coupling devices connecting the vehicles shall be designed, constructed, and installed, and the vehicles shall be designed and constructed, so that when the combination is operated in a straight line on a level, smooth, paved surface, the path of the towed vehicle will not deviate more than 3 inches to either side of the path of the vehicle that tows it.

(b) **Fifth wheel assemblies** — (1) **Mounting** — (i) **Lower half.** The lower half of a fifth wheel mounted on a truck tractor or converter dolly must be secured to the frame of that vehicle with properly designed brackets, mounting plates or angles and properly tightened bolts of adequate size and grade, or devices that provide equivalent security. The installation shall not cause cracking, warping, or deformation of the frame. The installation must include a device for positively preventing the lower half of the fifth wheel from shifting on the frame to which it is attached.

(ii) **Upper half.** The upper half of a fifth wheel must be fastened to the motor vehicle with at least the same security required for the installation of the lower half on a truck tractor or converter dolly.

(2) **Locking.** Every fifth wheel assembly must have a locking mechanism. The locking mechanism, and any adapter used in conjunction with it, must prevent separation of the upper and lower halves of the fifth wheel assembly unless a positive manual release is activated. The release may be located so that the driver can operate it from the cab. If a motor vehicle has a fifth wheel designed and constructed to be readily separable, the fifth wheel locking devices shall apply automatically on coupling.

(3) **Location.** The lower half of a fifth wheel shall be located so that, regardless of the condition of loading, the relationship between the kingpin and the rear axle or axles of the towing motor vehicle will properly distribute the gross weight of both the towed and towing vehicles on the axles of those vehicles, will not unduly interfere with the steering, braking, and other maneuvering of the towing vehicle, and will not otherwise contribute to unsafe operation of the vehicles comprising the combination. The upper half of a fifth wheel shall be located so that the weight of the vehicles is properly distributed on their axles and the combination of vehicles will operate safely during normal operation.

(c) **Towing of full trailers.** A full trailer must be equipped with a tow-bar and a means of attaching the tow-bar to the towing and towed vehicles. The tow-bar and the means of attaching it must—

(1) Be structurally adequate for the weight being drawn;

(2) Be properly and securely mounted;

(3) Provide for adequate articulation at the connection without excessive slack at that location; and

(4) Be provided with a locking device that prevents accidental separation of the towed and towing vehicles. The mounting of the trailer hitch (pintle hook or equivalent mechanism) on the towing vehicle must include reinforcement or bracing of the

frame sufficient to produce strength and rigidity of the frame to prevent its undue distortion.

(d) **Safety devices in case of tow-bar failure or disconnection.** Every full trailer and every converter dolly used to convert a semitrailer to a full trailer must be coupled to the frame, or an extension of the frame, of the motor vehicle which tows it with one or more safety devices to prevent the towed vehicle from breaking loose in the event the tow-bar fails or becomes disconnected. The safety device must meet the following requirements:

(1) The safety device must not be attached to the pintle hook or any other device on the towing vehicle to which the tow-bar is attached. However, if the pintle hook or other device was manufactured prior to July 1, 1973, the safety device may be attached to the towing vehicle at a place on a pintle hook forging or casting if that place is independent of the pintle hook.

(2) The safety device must have no more slack than is necessary to permit the vehicles to be turned properly.

(3) The safety device, and the means of attaching it to the vehicles, must have an ultimate strength of not less than the gross weight of the vehicle or vehicles being towed.

(4) The safety device must be connected to the towed and towing vehicles and to the tow-bar in a manner which prevents the tow-bar from dropping to the ground in the event it fails or becomes disconnected.

(5) Except as provided in paragraph (d) (6) of this section, if the safety device consists of safety chains or cables, the towed vehicle must be equipped with either two safety chains or cables or with a bridle arrangement of a single chain or cable attached to its frame or axle at two points as far apart as the configuration of the frame or axle permits. The safety chains or cables shall be either two separate pieces, each equipped with a hook or other means for attachment to the towing vehicle, or a single piece leading along each side of the tow-bar from the two points of attachment on the towed vehicle and arranged into a bridle with a single means of attachment to be connected to the towing vehicle. When a single length of cable is used, a thimble and twin-base cable clamps shall be used to form the forward bridle eye. The hook or other means of attachment to the towing vehicle shall be secured to the chains or cables in a fixed position.

(6) If the towed vehicle is a converter dolly with a solid tongue and without a hinged tow-bar or other swivel between

the fifth wheel mounting and the attachment point of the tongue eye or other hitch device—

(i) Safety chains or cables, when used as the safety device for that vehicle, may consist of either two chains or cables or a single chain or cable used alone;

(ii) A single safety device, including a single chain or cable used alone as the safety device, must be in line with the centerline of the trailer tongue; and

(iii) The device may be attached to the converter dolly at any point to the rear of the attachment point of the tongue eye or other hitch device.

(7) Safety devices other than safety chains or cables must provide strength, security of attachment, and directional stability equal to, or greater than, safety chains or cables installed in accordance with paragraphs (d)(5) and (6) of this section.

(8) When two safety devices, including two safety chains or cables, are used and are attached to the towing vehicle at separate points, the points of attachment on the towing vehicle shall be located equally distant from, and on opposite sides of, the centerline of the towing vehicle. Where two chains or cables are attached to the same point on the towing vehicle, and where a bridle or a single chain or cable is used, the point of attachment must be on the longitudinal centerline of the towing vehicle. A single safety device, other than a chain or a cable, must also be attached to the towing vehicle at a point on its longitudinal centerline.

§393.71 Coupling devices and towing methods, driveaway-towaway operations.

(a) **Number in combination.** (1) No more than three saddle-mounts may be used in any combination.

(2) No more than one tow-bar may be used in any combination.

(3) When motor vehicles are towed by means of triple saddle-mounts, the towed vehicles shall have brakes acting on all wheels which are in contact with the roadway.

(b) **Carrying vehicles on towing vehicle.** (1) When adequately and securely attached by means equivalent in security to that provided in paragraph (j)(2) of this section, a motor vehicle or motor vehicles may be full-mounted on the structure of a towing vehicle engaged in any driveaway-towaway operation.

(2) No motor vehicle or motor vehicles may be full-mounted on a towing vehicle unless the relationship of such full-mounted

vehicles to the rear axle or axles results in proper distribution of the total gross weight of the vehicles and does not unduly interfere with the steering, braking, or maneuvering of the towing vehicle, or otherwise contribute to the unsafe operation of the vehicles comprising the combination.

(c) **Carrying vehicles on towed vehicles.** (1) When adequately and securely attached by means equivalent in security to that provided in paragraph (j)(2) of this section, a motor vehicle or motor vehicles may be full-mounted on the structure of towed vehicles engaged in any driveaway-towaway operation.

(2) No motor vehicle shall be full-mounted on a motor vehicle towed by means of a tow-bar unless the towed vehicle is equipped with brakes and is provided with means for effective application of brakes acting on all wheels and is towed on its own wheels.

(3) No motor vehicle or motor vehicles shall be full-mounted on a motor vehicle towed by means of a saddle-mount unless the centerline of the kingpin or equivalent means of attachment of such towed vehicle shall be so located on the towing vehicle that the relationship to the rear axle or axles results in proper distribution of the total gross weight of the vehicles and does not unduly interfere with the steering, braking, or maneuvering of the towing vehicle or otherwise contribute to the unsafe operation of vehicles comprising the combination; and unless a perpendicular to the ground from the center of gravity of the full-mounted vehicles lies forward of the centerline of the rear axle of the saddle-mounted vehicle.

(4) If a motor vehicle towed by means of a double saddle-mount has any vehicle full-mounted on it, such saddle-mounted vehicle shall at all times while so loaded have effective brakes acting on those wheels which are in contact with the roadway.

(d) **Bumper tow-bars on heavy vehicles prohibited.** Tow-bars of the type which depend upon the bumpers as a means of transmitting forces between the vehicles shall not be used to tow a motor vehicle weighing more than 5,000 pounds.

(e) **Front wheels of saddle-mounted vehicles restrained.** A motor vehicle towed by means of a saddle-mount shall have the motion of the front wheels restrained if under any condition of turning of such wheels they will project beyond the widest part of either the towed or towing vehicle.

(f) **Vehicles to be towed in forward position.** Unless the steering mechanism is adequately locked in a straight forward position, all motor vehicles towed by means of a saddle-mount shall be towed with the front end mounted on the towing vehicle.

(g) **Means required for towing.** (1) No motor vehicle or motor vehicles shall be towed in driveaway-towaway operations by means other than tow-bar or saddle-mount connections which shall meet the requirements of this section.

(2) For the purpose of the regulations of this part:

(i) Coupling devices such as those used for towing house trailers and employing ball and socket connections shall be considered as tow-bars;

(ii) Motor vehicles or parts of motor vehicles adequately, securely, and rigidly attached by devices meeting the requirements of paragraph (n) of this section shall be considered as one vehicle in any position in any combination.

(h) **Requirements for tow-bars.** Tow-bars shall comply with the following requirements:

(1) **Tow-bars, structural adequacy and mounting.** Every tow-bar shall be structurally adequate and properly installed and maintained. To insure that it is structurally adequate, it must, at least, meet the requirements of the following table:

| Gross weight of towed vehicle (pounds)[1] | Longitudinal strength in tension and compression[2] | | Strength as a beam (in any direction concentrated load at center)[2,3] |
	All towbars	New towbars acquired and used by a motor carrier after Sept. 30, 1948	
	Pounds	Pounds	Pounds
Less than 5,000	3,000	6,500	3,000
5,000 and over			
Less than 10,000	6,000	(¹)	(¹)
10,000 and over			
Less than 15,000	9,000	(¹)	(¹)

[1]The required strength of tow-bars for towed vehicles of 15,000 pounds and over gross weight and of new tow-bars acquired and used after Sept. 30, 1948, for towed vehicles of 5,000 pounds and over gross weight shall be computed by means of the following formulae: Longitudinal strength = gross weight of towed vehicle x 1.3. Strength as a beam = gross weight of towed vehicle x 0.6.

[2]In testing, the whole unit shall be tested with all clamps, joints, and pins so mounted and fastened as to approximate conditions of actual operation.

[3]This test shall be applicable only to tow-bars which are, in normal operation, subjected to a bending movement such as tow-bars for house trailers.

(2) **Tow-bars, jointed.** The tow-bar shall be so constructed as to freely permit motion in both horizontal and vertical planes between the towed and towing vehicles. The means used to provide the motion shall be such as to prohibit the transmission of stresses under normal operation between the towed and towing vehicles, except along the longitudinal axis of the tongue or tongues.

(3) **Tow-bar fastenings.** The means used to transmit the stresses to the chassis or frames of the towed and towing vehicles may be either temporary structures or bumpers or other integral parts of the vehicles: Provided, however, that the means used shall be so constructed, installed, and maintained that, when tested as an assembly, failure in such members shall not occur when the weakest new tow-bar which is permissible under paragraph (h)(1) of this section is subjected to the tests given therein.

(4) **Means of adjusting length.** On tow-bars, adjustable as to length, the means used to make such adjustment shall fit tightly and not result in any slackness or permit the tow-bar to bend. With the tow-bar supported rigidly at both ends and with a load of 50 pounds at the center, the sag, measured at the center, in any direction shall not exceed 0.25 inch under any condition of adjustment as to length.

(5) **Method of clamping.** Adequate means shall be provided for securely fastening the tow-bar to the towed and towing vehicles.

(6) **Tow-bar connection to steering mechanism.** The tow-bar shall be provided with suitable means of attachment to and actuation of the steering mechanism, if any, of the towed vehicle. The attachment shall provide for sufficient angularity of movement of the front wheels of the towed vehicle so that it may follow substantially in the path of the towing vehicle without cramping the tow-bar. The tow-bar shall be provided with suitable joints to permit such movement.

(7) **Tracking**. The tow-bar shall be so designed, constructed, maintained, and mounted as to cause the towed vehicle to follow substantially in the path of the towing vehicle. Tow-bars of such design or in such condition as to permit the towed vehicle to deviate more than 3 inches to either side of the path of a tow-

ing vehicle moving in a straight line as measured from the center of the towing vehicle are prohibited.

(8) **Passenger car-trailer type couplings.** Trailer couplings used for driveaway-towaway operations of passenger car trailers shall conform to Society of Automotive Engineers Standard No. J684c, "Trailer Couplings and Hitches — Automotive Type," July 1970.[1]

(9) **Marking tow-bars.** Every tow-bar acquired and used in driveaway-towaway operations by a motor carrier shall be plainly marked with the following certification of the manufacturer thereof (or words of equivalent meaning):

This tow-bar complies with the requirements of the Federal Highway Administration for (maximum gross weight for which tow-bar is manufactured) vehicles.

Allowable Maximum Gross Weight_____

Manufactured_____
(Month and year)

by_____
(Name of manufacturer)

Tow-bar certification manufactured before March 7, 1989 must meet requirements in effect at the time of manufacture.

(10) **Safety devices in case of tow-bar failure or disconnection.** (i) The towed vehicle shall be connected to the towing vehicle by a safety device to prevent the towed vehicle from breaking loose in the event the tow-bar fails or becomes disconnected. When safety chains or cables are used as the safety device for that vehicle, at least two safety chains or cables meeting the requirements of paragraph (h)(10)(ii) of this section shall be used. The tensile strength of the safety device and the means of attachment to the vehicles shall be at least equivalent to the corresponding longitudinal strength for tow-bars required in the table of paragraph (h)(1) of this section. If safety chains or cables are used as the safety device, the required strength shall be the combined strength of the combination of chains and cables.

(ii) If chains or cables are used as the safety device, they shall be crossed and attached to the vehicles near the points of bumper attachments to the chassis of the vehicles. The length of chain used shall be no more than necessary to permit free turning of the vehicles. The chains shall be attached to the tow-bar at the point of crossing or as close to that point as is practicable.

---

[1] See footnote 1 to Sec. 393.24(c).

(iii) A safety device other than safety chains or cables must provide strength, security of attachment, and directional stability equal to, or greater than, that provided by safety chains or cables installed in accordance with paragraph (h)(10)(ii) of this section. A safety device other than safety chains or cables must be designed, constructed, and installed so that, if the tow-bar fails or becomes disconnected, the tow-bar will not drop to the ground.

(i) [Reserved]

(j) **Requirements for upper-half of saddle-mounts.** The upper-half of any saddle-mount shall comply with the following requirements:

(1) **Upper-half connection to towed vehicle.** The upper-half shall be securely attached to the frame or axle of the towed vehicle by means of U-bolts or other means providing at least equivalent security.

(2) **U-bolts or other attachments.** U-bolts used to attach the upper-half to the towed vehicles shall be made of steel rod, free of defects, so shaped as to avoid at any point a radius of less than 1 inch; Provided, however, that a lesser radius may be utilized if the U-bolt is so fabricated as not to cause more than 5 percent reduction in cross-sectional area at points of curvature, in which latter event the minimum radius shall be one-sixteenth inch. U-bolts shall have a diameter not less than required by the following table:

DIAMETER OF U-BOLTS IN INCHES

Weights in pounds of heaviest towed vehicle	Double or triple saddle-mount			Single saddle-mount[1]
	Front mount	Middle or front mount	Rear mount	
Up to 5,000	0.625	0.5625	0.0500	0.500
5,000 and over	0.6875	0.625	0.5625	0.5625

[1] The total weight of all the vehicles being towed shall govern. If other devices are used to accomplish the same purposes as U-bolts they shall have at least equivalent strength of U-bolts made of mild steel. Cast iron shall not be used for clamps or any other holding devices.

(3) **U-bolts and points of support, location.** The distance between the most widely separated U-bolts shall not be less than 9 inches. The distance between the widely separated points where the upper-half supports the towed vehicle shall

not be less than 9 inches, except that saddle-mounts employing ball and socket joints shall employ a device which clamps the axle of the towed vehicle throughout a length of not less than 5 inches.

(4) **Cradle-type upper-halves, specifications.** Upper-halves of the cradle-type using vertical members to restrain the towed vehicle from relative movement in the direction of motion of the vehicles shall be substantially constructed and adequate for the purpose. Such cradle-mounts shall be equipped with at least one bolt or equivalent means to provide against relative vertical movement between the upper-half and the towed vehicle. Bolts, if used, shall be at least one-half inch in diameter. Devices using equivalent means shall have at least equivalent strength. The means used to provide against relative vertical motion between the upper-half and the towed vehicle shall be such as not to permit a relative motion of over one-half inch. The distance between the most widely separated points of support between the upper-half and the towed vehicle shall be at least 9 inches.

(5) **Lateral movement of towed vehicle.** (i) Towed vehicles having a straight axle or an axle having a drop of less than 3 inches, unless the saddle-mount is constructed in accordance with paragraph (m)(2) of this section, shall be securely fastened by means of chains or cables to the upper-half so as to insure against relative lateral motion between the towed vehicle and the upper-half. The chains or cables shall be at least $^3/_{16}$-inch diameter and secured by bolts of at least equal diameter.

(ii) Towed vehicles with an axle with a drop of 3 inches or more, or connected by a saddle-mount constructed in accordance with paragraph (m)(2) of this section, need not be restrained by chains or cables provided that the upper-half is so designed as to provide against such relative motion.

(iii) Chains or cables shall not be required if the upper-half is so designed as positively to provide against lateral movement of the axle.

(k) **Requirements for lower half of saddle-mounts.** The lower half of any saddle-mount shall comply with the following requirements:

(1) **U-bolts or other attachments.** U-bolts used to attach the lower half to the towing vehicle shall be made of steel rod, free of defects, so shaped as to avoid at any point a radius of less

than 1 inch: Provided, however, That a lesser radius may be utilized if the U-bolt is so fabricated as not to cause more than 5 percent reduction in cross-sectional area at points of curvature, in which latter event the minimum radius shall be one-sixteenth inch. U-bolts shall have a total cross-sectional area not less than as required by the following table:

TOTAL CROSS-SECTIONAL AREA OF U-BOLTS IN SQUARE INCHES

Weights in pounds of heaviest towed vehicle	Double or triple saddle-mount			Single saddle-mount[1]
	Front mount	Middle or front mount	Rear mount	
Up to 5,000	1.2	1.0	0.8	0.8
5,000 and over	1.4	1.2	1.0	1.0

[1]The total weight of all the vehicles being towed shall govern. If other devices are used to accomplish the same purposes as U-bolts they shall have at least equivalent strength of U-bolts made of mild steel. Cast iron shall not be used for clamps or any other holding devices.

(2) **Shifting.** Adequate provision shall be made by design and installation to provide against relative movement between the lower-half and the towing vehicle especially during periods of rapid acceleration and deceleration. To insure against shifting, designs of the tripod type shall be equipped with adequate and securely fastened hold-back chains or similar devices.

(3) **Swaying.** (i) Adequate provision shall be made by design and installation to provide against swaying or lateral movement of the towed vehicle relative to the towing vehicle. To insure against swaying, lower-halves designed with cross-members attached to but separable from vertical members shall have such cross-members fastened to the vertical members by at least two bolts on each side. Such bolts shall be of at least equivalent cross-sectional area as those required for U-bolts for the corresponding saddle-mount as given in the table in paragraph (k)(1) of this section. The minimum distance between the most widely separated points of support of the cross-member by the vertical member shall be three inches as measured in a direction parallel to the longitudinal axis of the towing vehicle.

(ii) The lower-half shall have a bearing surface on the frame of the towing vehicle of such dimensions that the pressure exerted by the lower-half upon the frame of the towing vehicle shall not exceed 200 pounds per square inch under any conditions of static loading. Hardwood blocks or blocks of other suitable material, such as hard rubber, aluminum or brakelining, if used between the lower-half and the frame of the towing vehicle shall be at least $\frac{1}{2}$ inch thick, 3 inches wide, and a combined length of 6 inches.

(iii) Under no condition shall the highest point of support of the towed vehicle by the upper-half be more than 24 inches, measured vertically, above the top of the frame of the towing vehicle, measured at the point where the lower-half rests on the towing vehicle.

(4) **Wood blocks.** (i) Hardwood blocks of good quality may be used to build up the height of the front end of the towed vehicle, provided that the total height of such wood blocks shall not exceed 8 inches and not over two separate pieces are placed upon each other to obtain such height; however, hardwood blocks, not over 4 in number, to a total height not to exceed 14 inches, may be used if the total cross-sectional area of the U-bolts used to attach the lower-half of the towing vehicle is at least 50 percent greater than that required by the table contained in paragraph (k)(1) of this section, or, if other devices are used in lieu of U-bolts, they shall provide for as great a resistance to bending as is provided by the larger U-bolts above prescribed.

(ii) Hardwood blocks must be at least 4 inches in width and the surfaces between blocks or block and lower-half or block and upper-half shall be planed and so installed and maintained as to minimize any tendency of the towed vehicle to sway or rock.

(5) **Cross-member, general requirements.** The cross-member, which is that part of the lower-half used to distribute the weight of the towed vehicle equally to each member of the frame of the towing vehicle, if used, shall be structurally adequate and properly installed and maintained adequately to perform this function.

(6) **Cross-member, use of wood.** No materials, other than suitable metals, shall be used as the cross-member, and wood may not be used structurally in any manner that will result in its being subject to tensile stresses. Wood may be used in cross-members if supported throughout its length by suitable metal cross-members.

(7) **Lower-half strength.** The lower-half shall be capable of supporting the loads given in the following table. For the purpose of test, the saddle-mount shall be mounted as normally op-

erated and the load applied through the upper-half:

MINIMUM TEST LOAD IN POUNDS

Weights in pounds of heaviest towed vehicle	Double or triple saddle-mount			Single saddle-mount[1]
	Front mount	Middle or front mount	Rear mount	
Up to 5,000	15,000	10,000	5,000	5,000
5,000 and over	30,000	20,000	10,000	10,000

[1]The total weight of all the vehicles being towed shall govern.

(l) **Requirements for kingpins of saddle-mounts.** The kingpin of any saddle-mount shall comply with the following requirements:

(1) **Kingpin size.** (i) Kingpins shall be constructed of steel suitable for the purpose, free of defects, and having a diameter not less than required by the following table:

DIAMETER OF SOLID KINGPIN IN INCHES

Weight in pounds of heaviest towed vehicle	Double or triple saddle-mount						Single saddle-mount[1]	
	Front mount		Middle or front mount		Rear mount			
	Mild steel	H.T.S. [2]	Mild steel	H.T.S. [2]	Mild steel	H.T.S. [2]	Mild steel	H.T.S. [2]
Up to 5,000	1.125	1.000	1.000	0.875	0.875	0.750	0.875	0.750
5,000 & over	1.500	1.125	1.250	1.000	1.000	0.875	1.000	0.875

[1]The total weight of all the vehicles being towed shall govern.

[2]High tensile steel is steel having a minimum ultimate strength of 65,000 pounds per square inch.

(ii) If a ball and socket joint is used in place of a kingpin, the diameter of the neck of the ball shall be at least equal to the diameter of the corresponding solid kingpin given in the above table. If hollow kingpins are used, the metallic cross-sectional area shall be at least equal to the cross-sectional area of the corresponding solid kingpin.

(2) **Kingpin fit.** If a kingpin bushing is not used, the kingpin shall fit snugly into the upper and lower-halves but shall not bind. Those portions of the upper or lower-halves in moving contact with the kingpin shall be smoothly machined with no rough or sharp edges. The bearing surface thus provided shall not be

less in depth than the radius of the kingpin.

(3) **Kingpin bushing on saddle-mounts.** The kingpin of all new saddle-mounts acquired and used shall be snugly enclosed in a bushing at least along such length of the kingpin as may be in moving contact with either the upper or lower-halves. The bearing surface thus provided shall not be less in depth than the radius of the kingpin.

(4) **Kingpin to restrain vertical motion.** The kingpin shall be so designed and installed as to restrain the upper-half from moving in a vertical direction relative to the lower-half.

(m) **Additional requirements for saddle-mounts.** Saddle-mounts shall comply with the following requirements:

(1) **Bearing surface between upper and lower-halves.** The upper and lower-halves shall be so constructed and connected that the bearing surface between the two halves shall not be less than 16 square inches under any conditions of angularity between the towing and towed vehicles: Provided, however, That saddle-mounts using a ball and socket joint shall have a ball of such dimension that the static bearing load shall not exceed 800 pounds per square inch, based on the projected cross-sectional area of the ball: And further provided, That saddle-mounts having the upper-half supported by ball, taper, or roller-bearings shall not have such bearings loaded beyond the limits prescribed for such bearings by the manufacturer thereof. The upper-half shall rest evenly and smoothly upon the lower-half and the contact surfaces shall be lubricated and maintained so that there shall be a minimum of frictional resistance between the parts.

(2) **Saddle-mounts, angularity.** All saddle-mounts acquired and used shall provide for angularity between the towing and towed vehicles due to vertical curvatures of the highway. Such means shall not depend upon either the looseness or deformation of the parts of either the saddle-mount or the vehicles to provide for such angularity.

(3) **Tracking.** The saddle-mount shall be so designed, constructed, maintained, and installed that the towed vehicle or vehicles will follow substantially in the path of the towing vehicle without swerving. Towed vehicles shall not deviate more than 3 inches to either side of the path of the towing vehicle when moving in a straight line.

(4) **Prevention of frame bending.** Where necessary, provision shall be made to prevent the bending of the frame of the

towing vehicle by insertion of suitable blocks inside the frame channel to prevent kinking. The saddle-mount shall not be so located as to cause deformation of the frame by reason of cantilever action.

(5) **Extension of frame.** No saddle-mount shall be located at a point to the rear of the frame of a towing vehicle.

(6) **Nuts, secured.** All nuts used on bolts, U-bolts, kingpins, or in any other part of the saddle-mount shall be secured against accidental disconnection by means of cotter-keys, lockwashers, double nuts, safety nuts, or equivalent means. Parts shall be so designed and installed that nuts shall be fully engaged.

(7) **Inspection of all parts.** The saddle-mount shall be so designed that it may be disassembled and each separate part inspected for worn, bent, cracked, broken, or missing parts.

(8) **Saddle-mounts, marking.** Every new saddle-mount acquired and used in driveaway-towaway operations by a motor carrier shall have the upper-half and the lower-half separately marked with the following certification of the manufacturer thereof (or words of equivalent meaning).

This saddle-mount complies with the requirements of the Federal Highway Administration for vehicles up to 5,000 pounds (or over 5,000 pounds):

Manufactured _____
(Month and year)

by _____
(Name of manufacturer)

(n) Requirements for devices used to connect motor vehicles or parts of motor vehicles together to form one vehicle—

(1) **Front axle attachment.** The front axle of one motor vehicle intended to be coupled with another vehicle as defined in paragraph (g)(2)(ii) of this section shall be attached with U-bolts meeting the requirements of paragraph (j)(2) of this section.

(2) **Rear axle attachment.** The rear axle of one vehicle shall be coupled to the frame of the other vehicle by means of a connecting device which when in place forms a rectangle. The device shall be composed of two pieces, top and bottom. The device shall be made of 4-inch by $^1/_2$-inch steel bar bent to shape and shall have the corners reinforced with a plate at least 3 inches by $^1/_2$ inch by 8 inches long. The device shall be bolted together with $^3/_4$-inch bolts and at least three shall be used on each side. Wood may be used as spacers to keep the frames apart and it shall be at least 4 inches square.

Subpart G —
Miscellaneous Parts and Accessories

§393.75 Tires.

(a) No motor vehicle shall be operated on any tire that (1) has body ply or belt material exposed through the tread or sidewall, (2) has any tread or sidewall separation, (3) is flat or has an audible leak, or (4) has a cut to the extent that the ply or belt material is exposed.

(b) Any tire on the front wheels of a bus, truck, or truck tractor shall have a tread groove pattern depth of at least $4/32$ of an inch when measured at any point on a major tread groove. The measurements shall not be made where tie bars, humps, or fillets are located.

(c) Except as provided in paragraph (b) of this section, tires shall have a tread groove pattern depth of at least $2/32$ of an inch when measured in a major tread groove. The measurement shall not be made where tie bars, humps or fillets are located.

(d) No bus shall be operated with regrooved, recapped or retreaded tires on the front wheels.

(e) No truck or truck tractor shall be operated with regrooved tires on the front wheels which have a load carrying capacity equal to or greater than that of 8.25-20 8 ply-rating tires.

(f) **Tire loading restrictions.** With the exception of manufactured homes, no motor vehicle shall be operated with tires that carry a weight greater than that marked on the sidewall of the tire or, in the absence of such a marking, a weight greater than that specified for the tires in any of the publications of any of the organizations listed in Federal Motor Vehicle Safety Standard No. 119 (49 CFR 571.119, S5.1(b)) unless:

(1) The vehicle is being operated under the terms of a special permit issued by the State; and

(2) The vehicle is being operated at a reduced speed to compensate for the tire loading in excess of the manufacturer's rated capacity for the tire. In no case shall the speed exceed 80 km/hr (50 mph).

(g) **Tire loading restrictions for manufactured homes.** Tires used for the transportation of manufactured homes (i.e., tires marked or labeled 7-14.5MH and 8-14.5MH) may be loaded up to 18 percent over the load rating marked on the sidewall of the tire or, in the absence of such a marking, 18 percent over the

§393.76

load rating specified in any of the publications of any of the organizations listed in FMVSS No. 119 (49 CFR 571.119, S5.1(b)). Manufactured homes which are labeled (24 CFR 3282.7(r)) on or after November 16, 1998, must comply with this requirement. Manufactured homes transported on tires overloaded by 9 percent or more must not be operated at speeds exceeding 80 km/hr (50 mph). This provision will expire on December 31, 2001, unless extended by mutual consent of the Federal Motor Carrier Safety Administration and the Department of Housing and Urban Development after review of appropriate tests or other data submitted by the industry or other interested parties.

(h) **Tire inflation pressure**. (1) No motor vehicle shall be operated on a tire which has a cold inflation pressure less than that specified for the load being carried.

(2) If the inflation pressure of the tire has been increased by heat because of the recent operation of the vehicle, the cold inflation pressure shall be estimated by subtracting the inflation buildup factor shown in Table 1 from the measured inflation pressure.

TABLE 1 — INFLATION PRESSURE MEASUREMENT CORRECTION FOR HEAT

Average speed of vehicle in the previous hour	Minimum inflation pressure buildup	
	Tires with 1,814 kg (4,000 lbs.) maximum load rating or less	Tires with over 1,814 kg (4,000 lbs.) load rating
66-88.5 km/hr (41-55 mph)	34.5 kPa (5 psi)	103.4 kPa (15 psi).

§393.76 Sleeper berths.

(a) **Dimensions** — (1) **Size.** A sleeper berth must be at least the following size:

Date of installation on motor vehicle	Length measured on centerline of longitudinal axis (inches)	Width measured on centerline of transverse axis (inches)	Height measured from highest point of top of mattress (inches)[1]
Before January 1, 1953	72	18	18
After December 31, 1952 ...... and before October 1, 1975 .	75	21	21
After September 30, 1975	75	24	24

[1] In the case of a sleeper berth which utilizes an adjustable mechanical suspension system, the required clearance can be measured when the suspension system is adjusted to the height to which it would settle when occupied by a driver.

(2) **Shape.** A sleeper berth installed on a motor vehicle on or after January 1, 1953 must be of generally rectangular shape, except that the horizontal corners and the roof corners may be rounded to radii not exceeding 10-$\frac{1}{2}$ inches.

(3) **Access.** A sleeper berth must be constructed so that an occupant's ready entrance to, and exit from, the sleeper berth is not unduly hindered.

(b) **Location.** (1) A sleeper berth must not be installed in or on a semitrailer or a full trailer other than a house trailer.

(2) A sleeper berth located within the cargo space of a motor vehicle must be securely compartmentalized from the remainder of the cargo space. A sleeper berth installed on or after January 1, 1953 must be located in the cab or immediately adjacent to the cab and must be securely fixed with relation to the cab.

(c) **Exit from the berth.** (1) Except as provided in paragraph (c)(2) of this section, there must be a direct and ready means of exit from a sleeper berth into the driver's seat or compartment. If the sleeper berth was installed on or after January 1, 1963, the exit must be a doorway or opening at least 18 inches high and 36 inches wide. If the sleeper berth was installed before January 1, 1963, the exit must have sufficient area to contain an ellipse having a major axis of 24 inches and a minor axis of 16 inches.

(2) A sleeper berth installed before January 1, 1953 must either:

(i) Conform to the requirements of paragraph (c)(1) of this section; or

(ii) Have at least two exits, each of which is at least 18 inches high and 21 inches wide, located at opposite ends of the vehicle and useable by the occupant without the assistance of any other person.

(d) **Communication with the driver.** A sleeper berth which is not located within the driver's compartment and has no direct entrance into the driver's compartment must be equipped with a means of communication between the occupant and the driver. The means of communication may consist of a telephone, speaker tube, buzzer, pull cord, or other mechanical or electrical device.

§393.77

(e) **Equipment.** A sleeper berth must be properly equipped for sleeping. Its equipment must include:

(1) Adequate bedclothing and blankets; and

(2) Either:

(i) Springs and a mattress; or

(ii) An innerspring mattress; or

(iii) A cellular rubber or flexible foam mattress at least four inches thick; or

(iv) A mattress filled with a fluid and of sufficient thickness when filled to prevent "bottoming-out" when occupied while the vehicle is in motion.

(f) **Ventilation.** A sleeper berth must have louvers or other means of providing adequate ventilation. A sleeper berth must be reasonably tight against dust and rain.

(g) **Protection against exhaust and fuel leaks and exhaust heat.** A sleeper berth must be located so that leaks in the vehicle's exhaust system or fuel system do not permit fuel, fuel system gases, or exhaust gases to enter the sleeper berth. A sleeper berth must be located so that it will not be overheated or damaged by reason of its proximity to the vehicle's exhaust system.

(h) **Occupant restraint.** A motor vehicle manufactured on or after July 1, 1971, and equipped with a sleeper berth must be equipped with a means of preventing ejection of the occupant of the sleeper berth during deceleration of the vehicle. The restraint system must be designed, installed, and maintained to withstand a minimum total force of 6,000 pounds applied toward the front of the vehicle and parallel to the longitudinal axis of the vehicle.

§393.77 Heaters.

On every motor vehicle, every heater shall comply with the following requirements:

(a) **Prohibited types of heaters.** The installation or use of the following types of heaters is prohibited:

(1) **Exhaust heaters.** Any type of exhaust heater in which the engine exhaust gases are conducted into or through any space occupied by persons or any heater which conducts engine compartment air into any such space.

(2) **Unenclosed flame heaters.** Any type of heater employing a flame which is not fully enclosed, except that such heaters are not prohibited when used for heating the cargo of

-314-

tank motor vehicles.

(3) **Heaters permitting fuel leakage.** Any type of heater from the burner of which there could be spillage or leakage of fuel upon the tilting or overturning of the vehicle in which it is mounted.

(4) **Heaters permitting air contamination.** Any heater taking air, heated or to be heated, from the engine compartment or from direct contact with any portion of the exhaust system; or any heater taking air in ducts from the outside atmosphere to be conveyed through the engine compartment, unless said ducts are so constructed and installed as to prevent contamination of the air so conveyed by exhaust or engine compartment gases.

(5) **Solid fuel heaters except wood charcoal.** Any stove or other heater employing solid fuel except wood charcoal.

(6) **Portable heaters.** Portable heaters shall not be used in any space occupied by persons except the cargo space of motor vehicles which are being loaded or unloaded.

(b) **Heater specifications.** All heaters shall comply with the following specifications:

(1) **Heating elements, protection.** Every heater shall be so located or protected as to prevent contact therewith by occupants, unless the surface temperature of the protecting grilles or of any exposed portions of the heaters, inclusive of exhaust stacks, pipes, or conduits shall be lower than would cause contact burns. Adequate protection shall be afforded against igniting parts of the vehicle or burning occupants by direct radiation. Wood charcoal heaters shall be enclosed within a metal barrel, drum, or similar protective enclosure which enclosure shall be provided with a securely fastened cover.

(2) **Moving parts, guards.** Effective guards shall be provided for the protection of passengers or occupants against injury by fans, belts, or any other moving parts.

(3) **Heaters, secured.** Every heater and every heater enclosure shall be securely fastened to the vehicle in a substantial manner so as to provide against relative motion within the vehicle during normal usage or in the event the vehicle overturns. Every heater shall be so designed, constructed, and mounted as to minimize the likelihood of disassembly of any of its parts, including exhaust stacks, pipes, or conduits, upon overturn of the vehicle in or on which it is mounted. Wood charcoal heaters shall be secured against relative motion within the enclosure

required by paragraph (c)(1) of this section, and the enclosure shall be securely fastened to the motor vehicle.

(4) **Relative motion between fuel tank and heater.** When either in normal operation or in the event of overturn, there is or is likely to be relative motion between the fuel tank for a heater and the heater, or between either of such units and the fuel lines between them, a suitable means shall be provided at the point of greatest relative motion so as to allow this motion without causing failure of the fuel lines.

(5) **Operating controls to be protected.** On every bus designed to transport more than 15 passengers, including the driver, means shall be provided to prevent unauthorized persons from tampering with the operating controls. Such means may include remote control by the driver; installation of controls at inaccessible places; control of adjustments by key or keys; enclosure of controls in a locked space, locking of controls, or other means of accomplishing this purpose.

(6) **Heater, hoses.** Hoses for all hot water and steam heater systems shall be specifically designed and constructed for that purpose.

(7) **Electrical apparatus.** Every heater employing any electrical apparatus shall be equipped with electrical conductors, switches, connectors, and other electrical parts of ample current-carrying capacity to provide against overheating; any electric motor employed in any heater shall be of adequate size and so located that it will not be overheated; electrical circuits shall be provided with fuses and/or circuit breakers to provide against electrical overloading; and all electrical conductors employed in or leading to any heater shall be secured against dangling, chafing, and rubbing and shall have suitable protection against any other condition likely to produce short or open circuits.

Note: Electrical parts certified as proper for use by Underwriters' Laboratories, Inc., shall be deemed to comply with the foregoing requirements.

(8) **Storage battery caps.** If a separate storage battery is located within the personnel or cargo space, such battery shall be securely mounted and equipped with nonspill filler caps.

(9) **Combustion heater exhaust construction.** Every heater employing the combustion of oil, gas, liquefied petroleum gas, or any other combustible material shall be provided with substantial means of conducting the products of combus-

tion to the outside of the vehicle: Provided, however, That this requirement shall not apply to heaters used solely to heat the cargo space of motor vehicles where such motor vehicles or heaters are equipped with means specifically designed and maintained so that the carbon monoxide concentration will never exceed 0.2 percent in the cargo space. The exhaust pipe, stack, or conduit if required shall be sufficiently substantial and so secured as to provide reasonable assurance against leakage or discharge of products of combustion within the vehicle and, if necessary, shall be so insulated as to make unlikely the burning or charring of parts of the vehicle by radiation or by direct contact. The place of discharge of the products of combustion to the atmosphere and the means of discharge of such products shall be such as to minimize the likelihood of their reentry into the vehicle under all operating conditions.

(10) **Combustion chamber construction.** The design and construction of any combustion-type heater except cargo space heaters permitted by the proviso of paragraph (c)(9) of this section and unenclosed flame heaters used for heating cargo of tank motor vehicles shall be such as to provide against the leakage of products of combustion into air to be heated and circulated. The material employed in combustion chambers shall be such as to provide against leakage because of corrosion, oxidation or other deterioration. Joints between combustion chambers and the air chambers with which they are in thermal and mechanical contact shall be so designed and constructed as to prevent leakage between the chambers and the materials employed in such joints shall have melting points substantially higher than the maximum temperatures likely to be attained at the points of jointure.

(11) **Heater fuel tank location.** Every bus designed to transport more than 15 passengers, including the driver, with heaters of the combustion type shall have fuel tanks therefor located outside of and lower than the passenger space. When necessary, suitable protection shall be afforded by shielding or other means against the puncturing of any such tank or its connections by flying stones or other objects.

(12) **Heater, automatic fuel control.** Gravity or siphon feed shall not be permitted for heaters using liquid fuels. Heaters using liquid fuels shall be equipped with automatic means for shutting off the fuel or for reducing such flow of fuel to the smallest practicable magnitude, in the event of overturn of the

vehicle. Heaters using liquefied petroleum gas as fuel shall have the fuel line equipped with automatic means at the source of supply for shutting off the fuel in the event of separation, breakage, or disconnection of any of the fuel lines between the supply source and the heater.

(13) **"Tell-tale" indicators.** Heaters subject to paragraph (c)(14) of this section and not provided with automatic controls shall be provided with "tell-tale" means to indicate to the driver that the heater is properly functioning. The requirement shall not apply to heaters used solely for the cargo space in semitrailers or full trailers.

(14) **Shut-off control.** Automatic means, or manual means if the control is readily accessible to the driver without moving from the driver's seat, shall be provided to shut off the fuel and electrical supply in case of failure of the heater to function for any reason, or in case the heater should function improperly or overheat. This requirement shall not apply to wood charcoal heaters or to heaters used solely to heat the contents of cargo tank motor vehicles, but wood charcoal heaters must be provided with a controlled method of regulating the flow of combustion air.

(15) **Certification required.** Every combustion-type heater, except wood charcoal heaters, the date of manufacture of which is subsequent to December 31, 1952, and every wood charcoal heater, the date of manufacture of which is subsequent to September 1, 1953, shall be marked plainly to indicate the type of service for which such heater is designed and with a certification by the manufacturer that the heater meets the applicable requirements for such use. For example, "Meets I.C.C. Bus Heater Requirements," "Meets I.C.C. Flue-Vented Cargo Space Heater Requirements," and after December 31, 1967, such certification shall read "Meets FHWA Bus Heater Requirements," "Meets FHWA Flue-Vented Cargo Space Heater Requirements," etc.

(i) **Exception.** The certification for a catalytic heater which is used in transporting flammable liquid or gas shall be as prescribed under §177.834(l) of this title.

§393.78 Windshield wipers.

(a) Every bus, truck, and truck tractor, having a windshield, shall be equipped with at least two automatically-operating windshield wiper blades, one on each side of the centerline of the windshield, for cleaning rain, snow, or other moisture from the windshield and which shall be in such condition as to provide clear vision for the driver, unless one such blade be so arranged as to clean an area of the windshield extending to within 1 inch of the limit of vision through the windshield at each side: Provided, however, That in driveaway-towaway operations this section shall apply only to the driven vehicle: And provided further, That one windshield wiper blade will suffice under this section when such driven vehicle in driveaway-towaway operation constitutes part or all of the property being transported and has no provision for two such blades.

(b) Every bus, truck, and truck tractor, the date of manufacture of which is subsequent to June 30, 1953, which depends upon vacuum to operate the windshield wipers, shall be so constructed that the operation of the wipers will not be materially impaired by change in the intake manifold pressure.

§393.79 Defrosting device.

Every bus, truck, and truck tractor having a windshield, when operating under conditions such that ice, snow, or frost would be likely to collect on the outside of the windshield or condensation on the inside of the windshield, shall be equipped with a device or other means, not manually operated, for preventing or removing such obstructions to the driver's view: Provided, however, That this section shall not apply in driveaway-towaway operations when the driven vehicle is a part of the shipment being delivered.

§393.80 Rear-vision mirrors.

(a) Every bus, truck, and truck tractor shall be equipped with two rear-vision mirrors, one at each side, firmly attached to the outside of the motor vehicle, and so located as to reflect to the driver a view of the highway to the rear, along both sides of the vehicle. All such regulated rear-vision mirrors and their replacements shall meet, as a minimum, the requirements of FMVSS No. 111 (49 CFR 571.111) in force at the time the vehicle was manufactured.

(b) **Exceptions.** (1) Mirrors installed on a vehicle manufactured prior to January 1, 1981, may be continued in service, provided that if the mirrors are replaced they shall be replaced with mirrors meeting, as a minimum, the requirements of FMVSS No. 111 (49 CFR 571.111) in force at the time the vehicle was manufactured.

(2) Only one outside mirror shall be required, which shall be on the driver's side, on trucks which are so constructed that the driver has a view to the rear by means of an interior mirror.

(3) In driveaway-towaway operations, the driven vehicle shall have at least one mirror furnishing a clear view to the rear. (49 U.S.C. 3102; 49 CFR 1.48)

§393.81 Horn.

Every bus, truck, truck tractor, and every driven motor vehicle in driveaway-towaway operations shall be equipped with a horn and actuating elements which shall be in such condition as to give an adequate and reliable warning signal.

§393.82 Speedometer.

Every bus, truck, and truck tractor shall be equipped with a speedometer indicating vehicle speed in miles per hour, which shall be operative with reasonable accuracy; however, this requirement shall not apply to any driven vehicle which is part of a shipment being delivered in a driveaway-towaway operation if such driven vehicle is equipped with an effective means of limiting its maximum speed to 45 miles per hour, nor to any towed vehicle.

§393.83 Exhaust systems.

(a) Every motor vehicle having a device (other than as part of its cargo) capable of expelling harmful combustion fumes shall have a system to direct the discharge of such fumes. No part shall be located where its location would likely result in burning, charring, or damaging the electrical wiring, the fuel supply, or any combustible part of the motor vehicle.

(b) No exhaust system shall discharge to the atmosphere at a location immediately below the fuel tank or the fuel tank filler pipe.

(c) The exhaust system of a bus powered by a gasoline engine shall discharge to the atmosphere at or within 6 inches forward of the rearmost part of the bus.

(d) The exhaust system of a bus using fuels other than gasoline shall discharge to the atmosphere either:

(1) At or within 15 inches forward of the rearmost part of the vehicle; or

(2) To the rear of all doors or windows designed to be open, except windows designed to be opened solely as emergency exits.

(e) The exhaust system of every truck and truck tractor shall discharge to the atmosphere at a location to the rear of the cab or, if the exhaust projects above the cab, at a location near the rear of the cab.

(f) No part of the exhaust system shall be temporarily repaired with wrap or patches.

(g) No part of the exhaust system shall leak or discharge at a point forward of or directly below the driver/sleeper compartment. The exhaust outlet may discharge above the cab/sleeper roofline.

(h) The exhaust system must be securely fastened to the vehicle.

(i) Exhaust systems may use hangers which permit required movement due to expansion and contraction caused by heat of the exhaust and relative motion between engine and chassis of a vehicle.

§393.84 Floors.

The flooring in all motor vehicles shall be substantially constructed, free of unnecessary holes and openings, and shall be maintained so as to minimize the entrance of fumes, exhaust gases, or fire. Floors shall not be permeated with oil or other substances likely to cause injury to persons using the floor as a traction surface.

§393.85 (Reserved)

§393.86 Rear impact guards and rear end protection.

(a)(1) **General requirements for trailers and semitrailers manufactured on or after January 26, 1998.** Each trailer and semitrailer with a gross vehicle weight rating of 4,536 kg (10,000 pounds) or more, and manufactured on or after January 26, 1998, must be equipped with a rear impact guard that meets the requirements of Federal Motor Vehicle Safety Standard No. 223 (49 CFR 571.223) in effect at the time the vehicle was manufactured. When the rear impact guard is installed on the trailer or semitrailer, the vehicle must, at a minimum, meet the requirements of FMVSS No. 224 (49 CFR 571.224) in effect at the time the vehicle was manufactured. The requirements of paragraph (a) of this section do not apply to pole trailers (as defined in §390.5 of this chapter); pulpwood trailers, low chassis vehicles, special purpose vehicles, wheels back vehicles (as defined in §393.5); and trailers towed in driveaway-towaway operations (as defined in §390.5).

(2) **Impact Guard Width.** The outermost surfaces of the horizontal member of the guard must extend to within 100 mm (4 inches) of the side extremities of the vehicle. The outermost surface of the horizontal member shall not extend beyond the side extremity of the vehicle.

(3) **Guard Height.** The vertical distance between the bottom edge of the horizontal member of the guard and the ground shall not exceed 560 mm (22 inches) at any point across the full width of the member. Guards with rounded corners may curve upward within 255 mm (10 inches) of the longitudinal vertical planes that are tangent to the side extremities of the vehicle.

(4) **Guard Rear Surface.** At any height 560 mm (22 inches) or more above the ground, the rearmost surface of the horizontal member of the guard must be within 305 mm (12 inches) of the rear extremity of the vehicle. This paragraph shall not be construed to prohibit the rear surface of the guard from extending beyond the rear extremity of the vehicle. Guards with rounded corners may curve forward within 255 mm (10 inches) of the side extremity.

(5) **Cross-Sectional Vertical Height.** The horizontal member of each guard must have a cross sectional vertical height of at least 100 mm (3.94 inches) at any point across the guard width.

(6) **Certification and labeling requirements for rear impact protection guards.** Each rear impact guard used to satisfy the requirements of paragraph (a)(1) of this section must be permanently marked or labeled as required by FMVSS No. 223 (49 CFR 571.223, S5.3). The label must be on the forward-facing surface of the horizontal member of the guard, 305 mm (12 inches) inboard of the right end of the guard. The certification label must contain the following information:

(i) The impact guard manufacturer's name and address;

(ii) The statement "Manufactured in _____" (inserting the month and a year that the guard was manufactured); and,

(iii) The letters "DOT", constituting a certification by the guard manufacturer that the guard conforms to all requirements of FMVSS No. 223.

(b)(1) **Requirements for motor vehicles manufactured after December 31, 1952 (except trailers or semitrailers manufactured on or after January 26, 1998).** Each motor vehicle manufactured after December 31, 1952, (except truck tractors, pole trailers, pulpwood trailers, or vehicles in drive-away-towaway operations) in which the vertical distance between the rear bottom edge of the body (or the chassis assembly if the chassis is the rearmost part of the vehicle) and the ground is greater than 76.2 cm (30 inches) when the motor vehicle is empty, shall be equipped with a rear impact guard(s). The rear impact guard(s) must be installed and maintained in such a manner that:

(i) The vertical distance between the bottom of the guard(s) and the ground does not exceed 76.2 cm (30 inches) when the motor vehicle is empty;

(ii) The maximum lateral distance between the closest points between guards, if more than one is used, does not exceed 61 cm (24 inches);

(iii) The outermost surfaces of the horizontal member of the guard are no more than 45.7 cm (18 inches) from each side extremity of the motor vehicle;

(iv) The impact guard(s) are no more than 61 cm (24 inches) forward of the rear extremity of the motor vehicle.

(2) **Construction and Attachment.** The rear impact guard(s) must be substantially constructed and attached by means of bolts, welding, or other comparable means.

(3) **Vehicle Components and Structures that may be used to satisfy the requirements of paragraph (g) of this section.** Low chassis vehicles, special purpose vehicles, or wheels back vehicles constructed and maintained so that the body, chassis, or other parts of the vehicle provide the rear end protection comparable to impact guard(s) conforming to the requirements of paragraph (b)(1) of this section shall be considered to be in compliance with those requirements.

§393.87 Flags on projecting loads.

Any motor vehicle having a load or vehicle component which extends beyond the sides more than 4 inches or more than 4 feet beyond the rear shall have the extremities of the load marked with a red flag, not less than 12 inches square, at each point where a lamp is required by Table 1, §393.11.

§393.88 Television receivers.

Any motor vehicle equipped with a television viewer, screen or other means of visually receiving a television broadcast shall have the viewer or screen located in the motor vehicle at a point to the rear of the back of the driver's seat if such viewer or screen is in the same compartment as the driver and the viewer or screen shall be so located as not to be visible to the driver, while he/she is driving the motor vehicle. The operating controls for the television receiver shall be so located that the driver cannot operate them without leaving the driver's seat.

§393.89 Buses, driveshaft protection.

Any driveshaft extending lengthways under the floor of the passenger compartment of a bus, shall be protected by means of at least one guard or bracket at that end of the shaft which is provided with a sliding connection (spline or other such device) to prevent the whipping of the shaft in the event of failure thereof or of any of its component parts. A shaft contained within a torque tube shall not require any such device.

§393.90 Buses, standee line or bar.

Except as provided below, every bus which is designed and constructed so as to allow standees, shall be plainly marked with a line of contrasting color at least 2 inches wide or equipped with some other means so as to indicate to any person that he/she is prohibited from occupying a space forward of a perpendicular plane drawn through the rear of the driver's seat and perpendicular to the longitudinal axis of the bus. Every bus shall have clearly posted at or near the front, a sign with letters at least one-half inch high stating that it is a violation of the Federal Highway Administration's regulations for a bus to be operated with persons occupying the prohibited area. The requirements of this section shall not apply to any bus being transported in driveaway-towaway operation or to any level of the bus other than that level in which the driver is located nor shall they be construed to prohibit any seated person from occupying permanent seats located in the prohibited area provided such seats are so located that persons sitting therein will not interfere with the driver's safe operation of the bus.

§393.91 Buses, aisle seats prohibited.

No bus shall be equipped with aisle seats unless such seats are so designed and installed as to automatically fold and leave a clear aisle when they are unoccupied. No bus shall be operated if any seat therein is not securely fastened to the vehicle.

§393.92 Buses, marking emergency doors.

Any bus equipped with an emergency door shall have such door clearly marked in letters at least 1 inch in height with the words "Emergency Door" or "Emergency Exit." Emergency doors shall also be identified by a red electric lamp readily visible to passengers which lamp shall be lighted at all times when lamps are required to be lighted by §392.30.

§393.93 Seats, seat belt assemblies, and seat belt assembly anchorages.

(a) **Buses—(1) Buses manufactured on or after January 1, 1965, and before July 1, 1971.** After June 30, 1972, every bus manufactured on or after January 1, 1965, and before July 1, 1971, must be equipped with a Type 1 or Type 2 seat belt assembly that conforms to Federal Motor Vehicle Safety Standard No. 209[1] (§571.209) installed at the driver's seat and seat belt assembly anchorages that conform to the location and geometric requirements of Federal Motor Vehicle Safety Standard No. 210[1] (§571.210) for that seat belt assembly.

(2) **Buses manufactured on or after July 1, 1971.** Every bus manufactured on or after July 1, 1971, must conform to the requirements of Federal Motor Vehicle Safety Standard No. 208[1] (§571.208) (relating to installation of seat belt assemblies) and Federal Motor Vehicle Safety Standard No. 210[1] (§571.210) (relating to installation of seat belt assembly anchorages).

(3) **Buses manufactured on or after January 1, 1972.** Every bus manufactured on or after January 1, 1972, must conform to the requirements of Federal Motor Vehicle Safety Standard No. 207[1] (§571.207) (relating to seating systems).

(b) **Trucks and truck tractors.** (1) **Trucks and truck tractors manufactured on and after January 1, 1965, and before July 1, 1971.** Except as provided in paragraph (d) of this section, after June 30, 1972, every truck and truck tractor manufactured on or after January 1, 1965, and before July 1, 1971, must be equipped with a Type 1 or Type 2 seat belt assembly that conforms to Federal Motor Vehicle Safety Standard No. 209 (§571.209) installed at the driver's seat and at the right front outboard seat, if the vehicle has one, and seat belt assembly anchorages that conform to the location and geometric requirements of Federal Motor Vehicle Safety Standard No. 210 (§571.210) for each seat belt assembly that is required by this subparagraph.

---

[1] Individual copies of Federal Motor Vehicle Safety Standards may be obtained from the National Highway Traffic Safety Administration, Nassif Building, 400 Seventh Street SW, Washington, D.C. 20590.

(2) **Trucks and truck tractors manufactured on or after July 1, 1971.** Every truck and truck tractor manufactured on or after July 1, 1971, except a truck or truck tractor being transported in driveaway-towaway operation and having an incomplete vehicle seating and cab configuration, must conform to the requirements of Federal Motor Vehicle Safety Standard No. 208[1] (§571.208) (relating to installation of seat belt assemblies) and Federal Motor Vehicle Safety Standard No. 210[1] (§571.210) (relating to installation of seat belt assembly anchorages).

(3) **Trucks and truck tractors manufactured on or after January 1, 1972.** Every truck and truck tractor manufactured on or after January 1, 1972, except a truck or truck tractor being transported in driveaway-towaway operation and having an incomplete vehicle seating and cab configuration, must conform to the requirements of Federal Motor Vehicle Safety Standard No. 207 (§571.207) (relating to seating systems).

(c) **Effective date of standards.** Whenever paragraph (a) or (b) of this section requires conformity to a Federal Motor Vehicle Safety Standard, the vehicle or equipment must conform to the version of the Standard that is in effect on the date the vehicle is manufactured or on the date the vehicle is modified to conform to the requirements of paragraph (a) or (b) of this section, whichever is later.

(d) Trucks and truck tractors manufactured on or after January 1, 1965, and before July 1, 1971, and operated in the State of Hawaii, must comply with the provisions of paragraph (b) of this section on and after January 1, 1976.

§393.94 Vehicle interior noise levels.

(a) **Application of the rule in this section.** Except as provided in paragraph (d) of this section, this section applies to all motor vehicles manufactured on and after October 1, 1974. On and after April 1, 1975, this section applies to all motor vehicles manufactured before October 1, 1974.

(b) **General rule.** The interior sound level at the driver's seating position of a motor vehicle must not exceed 90 dB(A) when measured in accordance with paragraph (c) of this section.

---

[1]Standards of the American National Standards Institute are published by the American National Standards Institute. Information and copies may be obtained by writing to the Institute at 1430 Broadway, New York, N.Y.10018.

(c) **Test procedure.**[1] (1) Park the vehicle at a location so that no large reflecting surfaces, such as other vehicles, signboards, buildings, or hills, are within 50 feet of the driver's seating position.

(2) Close all vehicle doors, windows, and vents. Turn off all power-operated accessories.

(3) Place the driver in his/her normal seated position at the vehicle's controls. Evacuate all occupants except the driver and the person conducting the test.

(4) Use a sound level meter which meets the requirements of the American National Standards Institute Standard ANSI S1.4-1971 Specification for Sound Level Meters, for Type 2 Meters. Set the meter to the A-weighting network, "fast" meter response.

(5) Locate the microphone, oriented vertically upward, 6 inches to the right of, in the same plane as, and directly in line with, the driver's right ear.

(6) With the vehicle's transmission in neutral gear, accelerate its engine to either its maximum governed engine speed, if it is equipped with an engine governor, or its speed at its maximum rated horsepower, if it is not equipped with an engine governor. Stabilize the engine at that speed.

(7) Observe the A-weighted sound level reading on the meter for the stabilized engine speed condition. Record that reading, if the reading has not been influenced by extraneous noise sources such as motor vehicles operating on adjacent roadways.

(8) Return the vehicle's engine speed to idle and repeat the procedure specified in paragraphs (c)(6) and (7) of this section until two maximum sound levels within 2 dB of each other are recorded. Numerically average those two maximum sound level readings.

(9) The average obtained in accordance with paragraph (c)(8) of this section is the vehicle's interior sound level at the driver's seating position for the purpose of determining whether the vehicle conforms to the rule in paragraph (b) of this section. However, a 2 dB tolerance over the sound level limitation specified in that paragraph is permitted to allow for variations in test conditions and variations in the capabilities of meters.

(10) If the motor vehicle's engine radiator fan drive is equipped with a clutch or similar device that automatically either reduces the rotational speed of the fan or completely disen-

[1]Standards of the American National Standards Institute are published by the American National Standards Institute. Information and copies may be obtained by writing to the Institute at 1430 Broadway, New York, N.Y.10018.

gages the fan from its power source in response to reduced engine cooling loads the vehicle may be parked before testing with its engine running at high idle or any other speed the operator may choose, for sufficient time but not more than 10 minutes, to permit the engine radiator fan to automatically disengage.

(d) Vehicles manufactured before October 1, 1974, and operated wholly within the State of Hawaii, need not comply with this section until April 1, 1976.

Subpart H — Emergency Equipment

§393.95 Emergency equipment on all power units.

Except for a lightweight vehicle, every bus, truck, truck-tractor, and every driven vehicle in driveaway-towaway operation must be equipped as follows:

(a) **Fire extinguisher.** (1) Except as provided in paragraph (a)(4) of this section, every power unit must be equipped with a fire extinguisher that is properly filled and located so that it is readily accessible for use. The fire extinguisher must be securely mounted on the vehicle. The fire extinguisher must be designed, constructed, and maintained to permit visual determination of whether it is fully charged. The fire extinguisher must have an extinguishing agent that does not need protection from freezing. The fire extinguisher must not use a vaporizing liquid that gives off vapors more toxic than those produced by the substances shown as having a toxicity rating of 5 or 6 in the Underwriters' Laboratories "Classification of Comparative Life Hazard of Gases and Vapors."[1]

(2)(i) Before July 1, 1971, a power unit that is used to transport hazardous materials must be equipped with a fire extinguisher having an Underwriters Laboratories rating[2] of 4 B:C or more. On and after July 1, 1971, a power unit that is used to transport hazardous materials must be equipped with a fire extinguisher having an Underwriters' Laboratories rating[2] of 10 B:C or more.

(ii) Before January 1, 1973, a power unit that is not used to

---

[1] Copies of the Classification can be obtained by writing to Underwriters' Laboratories, Inc., 205 East Ohio Street, Chicago, Ill. 60611.
[2] Underwriters' Laboratories ratings are given to fire extinguishers under the standards of Underwriters' Laboratories, Inc., 205 East Ohio Street, Chicago, Ill. 60611. Extinguishers must conform to the standards in effect on the date of manufacture or on Jan. 1, 1969, whichever is earlier.

transport hazardous materials must be equipped with a fire extinguisher having an Underwriters' Laboratories rating[1] of 4 B:C or more. On and after January 1, 1973, a power unit that is not used to transport hazardous materials must be equipped with either—

(A) A fire extinguisher having an Underwriters' Laboratories rating[1] of 5 B:C or more; or

(B) Two fire extinguishers, each of which has an Underwriters' Laboratories rating[1] of 4 B:C or more.

(iii) Each fire extinguisher required by this subparagraph must be labeled or marked with its Underwriters' Laboratories rating[1] and must meet the requirements of paragraph (a)(1) of this section.

(3) For purposes of this paragraph a power unit is used to transport hazardous materials only if the power unit or a motor vehicle towed by the power unit must be marked or placarded in accordance with §177.823 of this title.

(4) This paragraph does not apply to the driven unit in a driveaway-towaway operation.

(b) [Reserved]

(c) **Spare fuses.** At least one spare fuse or other overload protective device, if the devices used are not of a reset type for each kind and size used. In driveaway-towaway operations, spares located on any one of the vehicles will be deemed adequate.

(d) [Reserved]

(e) [Reserved]

(f) **Warning devices for stopped vehicles.** Except as provided in paragraph (g) of this section, one of the following combinations of warning devices:

(1) **Vehicles equipped with warning devices before January 1, 1974.** Warning devices specified below may be used until replacements are necessary:

(i) Three liquid-burning emergency flares which satisfy the requirements of SAE Standard J597, "Liquid Burning Emergency Flares," and three fusees and two red flags; or

(ii) Three electric emergency lanterns which satisfy the requirements of SAE Standard J596, "Electric Emergency Lan-

---

[1]Underwriters' Laboratories ratings are given to fire extinguishers under the standards of Underwriters' Laboratories, Inc., 205 East Ohio Street, Chicago, Ill. 60611. Extinguishers must conform to the standards in effect on the date of manufacture or on Jan. 1, 1969, whichever is earlier.

terns," and two red flags; or

(iii) Three red emergency reflectors which satisfy the requirements of paragraph (i) of this section, and two red flags; or

(iv) Three red emergency reflective triangles which satisfy the requirements of paragraph (h) of this section; or

(v) Three bidirectional emergency reflective triangles that conform to the requirements of Federal Motor Vehicle Safety Standard No. 125, §571.125 of this title.

(2) **Vehicles equipped with warning devices on and after January 1, 1974.**

(i) Three bidirectional emergency reflective triangles that conform to the requirements of Federal Motor Vehicle Safety Standard No. 125, §571.125 of this title; or

(ii) At least 6 fusees or 3 liquid-burning flares. The vehicle must have as many additional fusees or liquid-burning flares as are necessary to satisfy the requirements of §392.22.

(3) **Supplemental warning devices.** Other warning devices may be used in addition to, but not in lieu of, the required warning devices, provided those warning devices do not decrease the effectiveness of the required warning devices.

(g) **Restrictions on the use of flame-producing devices.** Liquid-burning flares, fusees, oil lanterns, or any signal produced by a flame shall not be carried on any commercial motor vehicle transporting Division 1.1, 1.2, 1.3 (explosives) hazardous materials; any cargo tank motor vehicle used for the transportation of Division 2.1 (flammable gas) or Class 3 (flammable liquid) hazardous materials whether loaded or empty; or any commercial motor vehicle using compressed gas as a motor fuel.

(h) **Requirements for emergency reflective triangles manufactured before January 1, 1974.** (1) Each reflector shall be a collapsible equilateral triangle, with legs not less than 17 inches long and not less than 2 inches wide. The front and back of the exposed leg surfaces shall be covered with red reflective material not less than one half inch in width. The reflective surface, front and back, shall be approximately parallel. When placed in position, one point of the triangle shall be upward. The area within the sides of the triangle shall be open.

(2) **Reflective material:** The reflecting material covering the leg of the equilateral triangle shall comply either with:

(i) The requirements for reflex-reflector elements made of red methyl-methacrylate plastic material, meeting the color, sealing, minimum candlepower, wind test, vibration test, and corrosion resistance test of section 3 and 4 of Federal Specification RR-R-1185, dated November 17, 1966, or

(ii) The requirements for red reflective sheeting of Federal Specification L-S-300, dated September 7, 1965, except that the aggregate candlepower of the assembled triangle, in one direction, shall be not less than eight when measured at 0.2° divergence angle and -4° incidence angle, and not less than 80 percent of the candlepower specified for 1 square foot of material at all other angles shown in Table II, reflective Intensity Values, of L-S-300.

(3) **Reflective surfaces alignment:** Every reflective triangle shall be so constructed that, when the triangle is properly placed, the reflective surfaces shall be in a plane perpendicular to the plane of the roadway surface with a permissible tolerance of ± 10°. Reflective triangles which are collapsible shall be provided with means for holding the reflective surfaces within the required tolerance. Such holding means shall be readily capable of adjustment without the use of tools or special equipment.

(4) **Reflectors mechanical adequacy:** Every reflective triangle shall be of such weight and dimensions as to remain stationary when subjected to a 40 mile per hour wind when properly placed on any clean, dry paved road surface. The reflective triangle shall be so constructed as to withstand reasonable shocks without breakage.

(5) **Reflectors, incorporation in holding device:** Each set of reflective triangles shall be adequately protected by enclosure in a box, rack, or other adequate container specially designed and constructed so that the reflectors may be readily extracted for use.

(6) **Certification:** Every red emergency reflective triangle designed and constructed to comply with these requirements shall be plainly marked with the certification of the manufacturer that it complies therewith.

(i) **Requirements for red emergency reflectors.** Each red emergency reflector shall conform in all respects to the following requirements:

(1) **Reflecting elements required.** Each reflector shall be composed of at least two reflecting elements or surfaces on each side, front and back. The reflecting elements, front and back, shall be approximately parallel.

(2) **Reflecting elements to be Class A.** Each reflecting element or surface shall meet the requirement for a red Class A

reflector contained in the SAE Recommended Practice[1] "Reflex Reflectors." The aggregate candlepower output of all the reflecting elements or surface in one direction shall not be less than 12 when tested in a perpendicular position with observation at one-third degree as specified in the Photometric Test contained in the abovementioned Recommended Practice.

(3) **Reflecting surfaces, protection.** If the reflector or the reflecting elements are so designed or constructed that the reflecting surfaces would be adversely affected by dust, soot, or other foreign matter or contacts with other parts of the reflector or its container, then such reflecting surfaces shall be adequately sealed within the body of the reflector.

(4) **Reflecting surfaces to be perpendicular.** Every reflector shall be so constructed that, when the reflector is properly placed, every reflecting element or surface is in a plane perpendicular to the plane of the roadway surface. Reflectors which are collapsible shall be provided with means for locking the reflector elements or surfaces in the required position; such locking means shall be readily capable of adjustment without the use of tools or special equipment.

(5) **Reflectors, mechanical adequacy.** Every reflector shall be of such weight and dimensions as to remain stationary when subjected to a 40 mile per hour wind when properly placed on any clean, dry, paved road surface. The reflector shall be so constructed as to withstand reasonable shocks without breakage.

(6) **Reflectors, incorporation on holding device.** Each set of reflectors and the reflecting elements or surfaces incorporated therein shall be adequately protected by enclosure in a box, rack, or other adequate container specially designed and constructed so that the reflectors may be readily extracted for use.

(7) **Certification.** Every red emergency reflector designed and constructed to comply with these requirements shall be plainly marked with the certification of the manufacturer that it complies therewith.

(j) **Requirements for fusees and liquid-burning flares.** Each fusee shall be capable of burning for 30 minutes, and each liquid-burning flare shall contain enough fuel to burn continuously for at least 60 minutes. Fusees and liquid-burning flares

---

[1] See footnote 1 to §393.24(c).

shall conform to the requirements of Underwriters Laboratories, Inc., UL No. 912, Highway Emergency Signals, Fourth Edition, July 30, 1979, (with an amendment dated November 9, 1981). (See §393.7(b) for information on the incorporation by reference and availability of this document.) Each fusee and liquid-burning flare shall be marked with the UL symbol in accordance with the requirements of UL 912.

(k) **Requirements for red flags.** Red flags shall be not less than 12 inches square, with standards adequate to maintain the flags in an upright position.

Subpart I – Protection Against Shifting or Falling Cargo

§393.100 General rules for protection against shifting or falling cargo.

(a) **Application and scope of the rules in this section.** This section applies to trucks, truck tractors, semitrailers, full trailers, and pole trailers. Each of those motor vehicles must, when transporting cargo, be loaded and equipped to prevent the shifting or falling of cargo in the manner prescribed by the rules in paragraph (b) of this section. In addition, each cargo carrying motor vehicle must conform to the applicable rules in §393.102, 393.104, and 393.106.

(b) **Basic protection component.** — Each cargo-carrying motor vehicle must be equipped with devices providing protection against shifting or falling cargo that meet the requirements of either paragraph (b)(1), (2), (3), or (4) of this section.

(1) **Option A.** The vehicle must have sides, side-boards, or stakes, and a rear endgate, endboard, or stakes. Those devices must be strong enough and high enough to assure that cargo will not shift upon, or fall from the vehicle. Those devices must have no aperture large enough to permit cargo in contact with one or more of the devices to pass through it.

(2) **Option B.** The vehicle must have at least one tiedown assembly that meets the requirements of §393.102 for each 10 linear feet of lading or fraction thereof (However, a pole trailer or an expandable trailer transporting metal articles under the special rules in paragraph (c) of this section is required only to have two or more of those tiedown assemblies at each end of the trailer). In addition, the vehicle must have as many additional tiedown assemblies meeting the requirements of §393.102 as

are necessary to secure all cargo being transported either by direct contact between the cargo and the tiedown assemblies or by dunnage which is in contact with the cargo and is secured by tiedown assemblies.[1]

(3) **Option C (for vehicles transporting metal articles only).** A vehicle transporting cargo which consists of metal articles must conform to either the rules in paragraph (b)(1), (2), or (4) of this section, or the special rules for transportation of metal articles set forth in paragraph (c) of this section.

(4) **Option D.** The vehicle must have other means of protecting against shifting or falling cargo which are similar to, and at least as effective as, those specified in paragraph (b)(1), (2), or (3) of this section.

(c) **Special rules for metal articles — (1) Scope of the rules in this paragraph.** The rules in this paragraph apply to a motor vehicle transporting cargo consisting of metal articles if that vehicle does not conform to the rules in paragraph (b)(1), (2), or (4) of this section.

(2) **Application of other sections.** A motor vehicle transporting property consisting of metal articles must, regardless of whether the rules in this paragraph apply to it, conform to the rules in §393.102 (relating to securement systems), §393.104 (relating to blocking and bracing of cargo), and §393.106 (relating to front-end structure requirements).

(3) **Coils.** Whenever a motor carrier transports one or more coils of metal which, individually or as a combination banded together, weigh 5,000 pounds or more, the coils shall be secured in the following manner:

(i) Coils with eyes vertical: one or more coils which are grouped and loaded side by side in a transverse or longitudinal row must be secured by—

(a) A tiedown assembly against the front of the coil or row of coils, restraining against forward motion;

(b) A tiedown assembly against the rear of the coil or row of coils, restraining against rearward motion; and

(c) A tiedown assembly over the top of each coil or transverse row of coils, restraining against vertical motion. The same tiedown assembly shall not be used to comply with more than one of the requirements of paragraph (c)(3)(i)(a), (b), or (c) of this section.

---

[1]Tiedown assemblies or dunnage in contact with sufficient exterior (including topmost) pieces of the cargo and securely holding each interior or lower piece comply with this requirement.

COILS— EYE VERTICAL

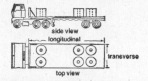

(ii) Coils with eyes crosswise: Each coil or transverse row of coils loaded side by side and having approximately the same outside diameters must be secured by—

(a) A tiedown assembly through the eye of each coil, restricting against forward motion and making an angle of less than 45° with the horizontal when viewed from the side of the vehicle;

(b) A tiedown assembly through the eye of each coil, restricting against rearward motion and making an angle of less than 45° with the horizontal when viewed from the side of the vehicle; and

(c) Timbers, having a nominal cross section of 4 x 4 inches or more and a length which is at least 75 percent of the width of the coil or row of coils, tightly placed against both the front and rear sides of the coil or row of coils and restrained to prevent movement of the coil or coils in the forward and rearward directions.

(d) If coils are loaded to contact each other in the longitudinal direction and relative motion between coils, and between coils and the vehicle, is prevented by tiedown assemblies and timbers—

(1) Only the foremost and rearmost coils must be secured with timbers; and

(2) A single tiedown assembly, restricting against forward motion, may be used to secure any coil except the rearmost one, which must be restrained against rearward motion.

COILS — EYE CROSSWISE

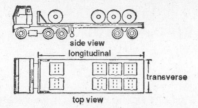

(iii) Coils with eyes lengthwise: A coil or transverse row of coils having approximately equal outside diameters and loaded side by side or a longitudinal row of coils having approximately equal outside diameters and loaded end to end must be secured as follows:

(a) The coil or coils must be restrained against side-by-side and fore-and-aft movement by—

(1) One or more tiedown assemblies over the top of each coil or transverse row; or

(2) Two or more tiedown assemblies through the eye of each coil or longitudinal row; or

(3) One or more tiedown assemblies, crossing from one side of the vehicle to the other, through the eye of each coil or longitudinal row of coils in a transverse row.

(b) Timbers having nominal cross section of 4 x 4 inches or more must be tightly placed against the sides of each coil or against the outboard sides of each transverse row of coils which are loaded side by side so that the timbers restrain against side-to-side movement.

(c) If, in accordance with paragraph (c)(3)(iii)(a)(1) of this section only one tiedown assembly over the top of each coil or transverse row of coils is used to restrain against side-to-side movement and fore-and-aft movement, timbers having a nominal cross section of 2 x 4 inches or more and which are firmly secured to longitudinal blocking must be tightly placed against the front and back of each coil, each longitudinal row of coils and each transverse row of coils in a manner which restricts forward and rearward movement.

COILS—EYE LENGTHWISE

side view

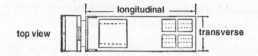

top view longitudinal transverse

(iv) Timber which is used for blocking must be sound lumber which is free of defects (such as knots or cracks) that materially reduce its strength.

(v) Timbers need not be used on vehicles which have depressions in the floor or are equipped with other restraining devices which perform the functions specified for timbers by the rules in this section.

(vi) As used in this section, the term "nominal", when used to describe timber, means commercially dressed sizes generally designated by the dimensions indicated.

(4) **Miscellaneous metal articles.** Except as provided in paragraph (c)(4)(iv) of this section, whenever a motor carrier transports metal articles consisting of cut-to-length bars, plates, rods, sheet and tin mill products, billets, blooms, ingots, slabs, structural shapes, or pipe, and other tubular products and those articles, either individually or as a combination of articles banded or boxed together and handled as a single unit, weigh more than 2,000 pounds, the article shall be secured in the following manner.

(i) A single article, a group of articles, or a combination of articles loaded side by side across the width of the vehicle must be secured by at least one tiedown assembly over its top for at least every 8 feet of its length and at least two tiedown assemblies securing each individual article or combination of articles banded or otherwise secured together and handled as a single unit. However, articles which individually have a length of 8 feet or less and which are securely butted against each other in the fore-and-after direction may be secured by metal angles secured by tiedown assemblies, or they may be secured by a timber having a nominal cross section of 4 x 4 inches or more placed longitudinally over the articles and secured by tiedown assemblies. Tiedown assemblies may not be located beyond the ends of the article which they secure.

(ii) If articles are tiered and each tiered article rests securely on the one beneath it, the tier may be secured in the same manner as a single level of those articles is secured in accordance with the rules in this section.

(iii) Pole trailers must either comply with the requirements of paragraph (c)(4)(i) and (ii) of this section or have at least two tiedown assemblies securing the load to the forward bolster and at least two tiedown assemblies securing the load to the rear bolster.

(iv) The rules in this paragraph do not apply to special loads consisting of machinery or fabricated structural items, such as beams, girders and trusses, which are fastened by special methods. However, those loads must be securely and adequately fastened to the vehicle.

(d) **Special rule for special-purpose vehicles.** The rules in this section do not apply to a vehicle transporting one or more articles which, because of their size, shape, or weight, must be carried on special-purpose vehicles or must be fastened by special methods. However, any article carried on that vehicle must be securely and adequately fastened to the vehicle.

(e) **Special rule for intermodal cargo containers.** Containers designed for the transportation of containerized, intermodal cargo and having integral securement devices must be fastened to the chassis of the motor vehicle with securement devices that prevent them from being unintentionally unfastened. The securement devices must restrain the container from moving more than one-half inch forward, more than one-half inch aft, more than one-half inch to the right, more than one-half inch to the left, or more than one inch vertically when the container is subjected to the following accelerations relative to the vehicle:

Direction of force relative to longitudinal axis of vehicle:	Acceleration in G's
Downward	1.70
Upward	0.50
Lateral	0.30
Longitudinal	1.80

(f) **Effective date.** This section is effective on October 1, 1973.

§393.102 Securement systems.

(a) **Application and scope of the rules in this section.** The rules in this section apply to tiedown assemblies (including chains, cables, steel straps, and fiber webbing), other securement devices, and attachment or fastening devices used in conjunction therewith, which are used to secure cargo to motor vehicles in transit. All devices which are used to secure cargo to a motor vehicle in transit under the rules in this Subpart must conform to the requirements of this section.

(b) **Tiedown assemblies.** Except for integral securement devices of containers designed for the transportation of containerized, intermodal cargo which conform to the rules in §393.100(e), the aggregate working load limit of the tiedown assemblies used to secure an article against movement in any direction must be at least $1/2$ times the weight of the article. With the exception of marking identification, tiedowns used must meet applicable manufacturing standards listed in this paragraph (b).

(1) **Steel strapping.** Steel strapping used as a component of a tiedown assembly must conform to the requirements of the 1991 edition of the American Society for Testing and Materials' Standard Specification for Strapping, Flat Steel and Seals, ASTM D3953-91. Steel strapping which is not marked by the manufacturer with a working load limit, shall be considered to have a working load limit equal to $1/4$ of the breaking strength listed in ASTM D3953-91. (See §393.7(b) for information on the incorporation by reference and availability of this document.) Steel strapping that is one inch wide or wider must have at least two pairs of crimps in each seal and when an end-over-end lap joint is formed, it must be sealed with at least two seals.

(2) **Chain.** Chain used as a component of a tiedown assembly must conform to the requirements of the June 15, 1990, edition of the National Association of Chain Manufacturers' Welded Steel Chain Specifications applicable to all types of chain. (See §393.7(b) for information on the incorporation by reference and availability of this document.)

(3) **Webbing.** Webbing used as a component of a tiedown assembly must conform to the requirements of the 1991 edition of the Web Sling and Tiedown Association's Recommended Stan-

dard Specification for Synthetic Webbing Tiedowns. (See §393.7(b) for information on the incorporation by reference and availability of this document.)

(4) **Wire rope.** Wire rope used as a component of a tiedown assembly must conform to the requirements of the November 1985 second edition of the Wire Rope Technical Board's Wire Rope Users Manual. Wire rope which is not marked by the manufacturer with a working load limit, shall be considered to have a working load limit equal to $1/4$ of the nominal strength listed in the Wire Rope Users Manual. (See §393.7(b) for information on the incorporation by reference and availability of this document.)

(5) **Cordage.** Cordage used as a component of a tiedown assembly, must conform to the applicable Cordage Institute rope standards listed below: PETRS-2, Polyester Fiber Rope, 3-Strand and 8-Strand Constructions, January, 1993; PPRS-2, Polypropylene Fiber Rope, 3-Strand and 8-Strand Constructions, August, 1992; CRS-1, Polyester/Polypropylene Composite Rope Specifications, Three- and Eight-Strand Standard Construction, May 1979; NRS-1, Nylon Rope Specifications, Three- and Eight-Strand Standard Construction, May 1979; C1, Double Braided Nylon Rope Specifications, DBN-January 1984. (See §393.7(b) for information on the incorporation by reference and availability of these documents.)

(6) **Tables of working load limits.** The working load limits listed in the tables in this paragraph are to be used when the tiedown material is not marked by the manufacturer with the working load limit. Tiedown materials which are marked by the manufacturer with working load limits which differ from the table, shall be considered to have a working load limit equal to the value for which they are marked. Synthetic cordage (e.g., nylon, polypropylene, polyester) which is not marked or labeled to enable identification of its composition or working load limit shall be considered to have a working load limit equal to that for polypropylene fiber rope.

Tables to §393.102(b)(6) — Working Load Limits (WLL)

[Chain WLL in pounds (kg)]

Size inch (mm)	Grade 3 proof coil	Grade 4 high test	Grade 7 transport	Grade 8 alloy
$1/4$ (7)	1300 (590)	2600 (1180)	3150 (1430)	3500 (1590)
$5/16$ (8)	1900 (860)	3900 (1770)	4700 (2130)	5100 (2310)
$3/8$ (10)	2650 (1200)	5400 (2450)	6600 (2990)	7100 (3220)

[Chain WLL in pounds (kg)], Continued

Size inch (mm)	Grade 3 proof coil	Grade 4 high test	Grade 7 transport	Grade 8 alloy
$7/16$ (11)	3500 (1590)	5800 (2630)	8750 (3970)	....
$1/2$ (13)	4500 (2040)	9200 (4170)	11300 (5130)	12000 (5440)
$5/8$ (16)	6900 (3130)	11500 (5220)	15800 (7170)	18100 (8210)
Chain Mark	PC	HT	....	T
Examples ..	3	4	7	8
	30	40	70	80

Synthetic Webbing WLL

Width inch (mm)	WLL pounds (kg)
$1-3/4$ (45)	1750 (790)
2 (50)	2000 (910)
3 (75)	3000 (1360)
4 (100)	4000 (1810)

Wire Rope (6 X 37, Fiber Core) WLL

Diameter inch (mm)	WLL pounds (kg)
$1/4$ (7)	1400 (640)
$5/16$ (8)	2100 (950)
$3/8$ (10)	3000 (1360)
$7/16$ (11)	4100 (1860)
$1/2$ (13)	5300 (2400)
$5/8$ (16)	8300 (3770)
$3/4$ (20)	10900 (4940)
$7/8$ (22)	16100 (7300)
1 (25)	20900 (9480)

Manila Rope WLL

Diameter inch (mm)	WLL pounds (kg)
$3/8$ (10)	205 (90)
$7/16$ (11)	265 (120)
$1/2$ (13)	315 (150)
$5/8$ (16)	465 (210)
$3/4$ (20)	640 (290)
1 (25)	1050 (480)

Polypropylene Fiber Rope WLL (3-Strand and 8-Strand Constructions)

Diameter inch (mm)	WLL pounds (kg)
$3/8$ (10)	400 (180)
$7/16$ (11)	525 (240)
$1/2$ (13)	625 (280)
$5/8$ (16)	925 (420)

Polypropylene Fiber Rope WLL (3-Strand and 8-Strand Constructions), Continued	
Diameter inch (mm)	WLL pounds (kg)
3/4 (20)	1275 (580)
1 (25)	2100 (950)

Polyester Fiber Rope WLL (3-Strand and 8-Strand Constructions)	
Diameter inch (mm)	WLL pounds (kg)
3/8 (10)	555 (250)
7/16 (11)	750 (340)
1/2 (13)	960 (440)
5/8 (16)	1500 (680)
3/4 (20)	1880 (850)
1 (25)	3300 (1500)

Nylon Rope WLL	
Diameter inch (mm)	WLL pounds (kg)
3/8 (10)	278 (130)
7/16 (11)	410 (190)
1/2 (13)	525 (240)
5/8 (16)	935 (420)
3/4 (20)	1420 (640)
1 (25)	2520 (1140)

Double Braided Nylon Rope WLL	
Diameter inch (mm)	WLL pounds (kg)
3/8 (10)	336 (150)
7/16 (11)	502 (230)
1/2 (13)	655 (300)
5/8 (16)	1130 (510)
3/4 (20)	1840 (830)
1 (25)	3250 (1470)

Steel Strapping WLL	
Width-thickness inch	WLL pounds (kg)
1-1/4 x 0.029	1190 (540)
1-1/4 x 0.031	1190 (540)
1-1/4 x 0.035	1190 (540)
1-1/4 x 0.044	1690 (770)
1-1/4 x 0.050	1690 (770)
1-1/4 x 0.057	1925 (870)
2 x 0.044	2650 (1200)
2 x 0.050	2650 (1200)

(c) **Load binders and hardware.** The strength of load binders and hardware that are part of, or used in conjunction with, a tiedown assembly must be equal to, or greater than the minimum strength specified for that tiedown assembly in paragraph (b) of this section.

(d) **Attachment to the vehicle.** The hook, bolt, weld, or other connector by which a tiedown assembly is attached to a vehicle, and the mounting place and means of mounting the connector, must be at least as strong as the tiedown assembly when that connector is loaded in any direction in which the tiedown assembly may load it.

(e) **Winches or other fastenings.** The anchorages of a winch or other fastening device mounted on a vehicle and used in conjunction with a tiedown assembly must have a combined tensile strength equal to, or greater than, the strength of the tiedown assembly.

(f) **Adjustability.** A tiedown assembly and its associated connectors and attachment devices must be designed, constructed, and maintained so that the driver of an in-transit vehicle can tighten them. However, the rules in this paragraph do not apply to a securement system in which the tiedown assembly consists of steel strapping or to a tiedown assembly which is not required by the rules in this section.

§393.104 Blocking and bracing.

(a) **Protection against longitudinal movement.** When a motor vehicle carries cargo that is not firmly braced against a front-end structure that conforms to the requirements of §393.106, the cargo must be secured so that, when the vehicle decelerates at a rate of 20 feet per second, per second, the cargo will remain on the vehicle and will not penetrate the vehicle's front-end structure.

(b) **Protection against lateral movement.** When a vehicle carries cargo that may shift sideways in transit, the cargo must either be securely blocked or braced against the sides, sideboards, or stakes of the vehicle or be secured by devices that conform to the requirements of paragraph (b)(2), (b)(3), or (b)(4) of §393.100.

(c) **Effective date.** This section is effective on October 1, 1973.

§393.106 Front-end structure.

(a) **General rule.** (1) Except as provided in paragraph (g) of this section, every cargo-carrying motor vehicle must be equipped with a headerboard or similar device of sufficient strength to prevent load shifting and penetration or crushing of the driver's compartment.

(2) On and after the effective dates specified in paragraph (h) of this section, every cargo-carrying motor vehicle must have a front-end structure that conforms to the rules in this section.

(b) **Location.** The front-end structure must be located between the vehicle's cargo and the vehicle's driver.

(c) **Height and width.** The front-end structure must extend either to a height of 4 feet above the floor of the vehicle or to a height at which it blocks forward movement of any item of cargo being carried on the vehicle, whichever is lower. The front-end structure must have a width which is at least equal to the width of the vehicle or which blocks forward movement of any item of cargo being transported on the vehicle, whichever is narrower.

(d) **Strength.** The front-end structure must be capable of withstanding the horizontal forward static load specified in either paragraph (d)(1) or (2) of this section.

(1) For a front-end structure less than 6 feet in height, a horizontal forward static load equal to one half ($\frac{1}{2}$) of the weight of the cargo being transported on the vehicle uniformly distributed over the entire portion of the front-end structure that is within 4 feet above the vehicle's floor or that is at or below a height above the vehicle's floor at which it blocks forward movement of any item of the vehicle's cargo, whichever is less.

(2) For a front-end structure 6 feet in height or higher, a horizontal forward static load equal to four-tenths (0.4) of the weight of the cargo being transported on the vehicle uniformly distributed over the entire front-end structure.

(e) **Penetration resistance.** The front-end structure must be designed, constructed, and maintained so that it is capable of resisting penetration by any item of cargo that contacts it when the vehicle decelerates at a rate of 20 feet per second, per second. The front-end structure must have no aperture large enough to permit any item of cargo in contact with the structure to pass through it.

(f) **Substitute devices.** The requirements of this section may be met by the use of devices performing the same functions as a front-end structure, if the devices are at least as strong as, and provide protection against shifting cargo at least equal to, a front-end structure which conforms to those requirements.

(g) **Exemptions.** The following motor vehicles are exempt from the rules in this section:

(1) A vehicle which is designed and used exclusively to trans-

port other vehicles, if each vehicle it transports is securely tied down by devices that conform to the requirements of §393.102.

(2) A pole trailer or semitrailer being towed by a truck tractor that is equipped with a front-end structure that conforms to the rules in this section.

(3) A full trailer being towed by a vehicle that is equipped with a front-end structure that conforms to the requirements of this section for a front-end structure.

(4) A full trailer being towed by a vehicle that is loaded in such a manner that the cargo on the towing vehicle conforms to the requirements of this section for a front-end structure.

(5) The rules in paragraphs (d) and (e) of this section do not apply to a motor vehicle manufactured before January 1, 1974.

(h) **Effective dates.** Cargo-carrying motor vehicles which are not exempted by paragraph (g) of this section must conform to the rules in this section as follows:

If the vehicle was manufactured—	It must conform to the rules in paragraph—	On and after—
Before January 1, 1974	(a), (b), and (f)	October 1, 1973 or the date it was manufactured, whichever is later.
Before January 1, 1974	(c)	January 1, 1975
On or after January 1, 1974	(a) through (f) inclusive.	The date it was manufactured.

Paragraphs (d) and (e) of this section do not apply to a motor vehicle that was manufactured before January 1, 1974.

Subpart J — Frames, Cab and Body Components, Wheels, Steering, and Suspension Systems

§393.201 Frames.

(a) The frame of every bus, truck, and truck tractor shall not be cracked, loose, sagging or broken.

(b) Bolts or brackets securing the cab or the body of the vehicle to the frame must not be loose, broken, or missing.

(c) The frame rail flanges between the axles shall not be bent, cut or notched, except as specified by the manufacturer.

(d) All accessories mounted to the truck tractor frame must be bolted or riveted.

(e) No holes shall be drilled in the top or bottom rail flanges, except as specified by the manufacturer.

(f) Field repairs are allowed.

§393.203 Cab and body components.

(a) The cab compartment doors or door parts used as an entrance or exit shall not be missing or broken. Doors shall not sag so that they cannot be properly opened or closed. No door shall be wired shut or otherwise secured in the closed position so that it cannot be readily opened. Exception: When the vehicle is loaded with pipe or bar stock that blocks the door and the cab has a roof exit.

(b) Bolts or brackets securing the cab or the body of the vehicle to the frame shall not be loose, broken, or missing.

(c) The hood must be securely fastened.

(d) All seats must be securely mounted.

(e) The front bumper must not be missing, loosely attached, or protruding beyond the confines of the vehicle so as to create a hazard.

§393.205 Wheels.

(a) Wheels and rims shall not be cracked or broken.

(b) Stud or bolt holes on the wheels shall not be elongated (out of round).

(c) Nuts or bolts shall not be missing or loose.

§393.207 Suspension systems.

(a) **Axles.** No axle positioning part shall be cracked, broken, loose or missing. All axles must be in proper alignment.

(b) **Adjustable axles.** Adjustable axle assemblies shall not have locking pins missing or disengaged.

(c) **Leaf springs**. No leaf spring shall be cracked, broken, or missing nor shifted out of position.

(d) **Coil springs**. No coil spring shall be cracked or broken.

(e) **Torsion bar.** No torsion bar or torsion bar suspension shall be cracked or broken.

(f) **Air Suspensions.** The air pressure regulator valve shall not allow air into the suspension system until at least 55 psi is in the braking system. The vehicle shall be level (not tilting to the left or right). Air leakage shall not be greater than 3 psi in a 5-minute time period when the vehicle's air pressure gauge shows normal operating pressure.

§393.209 Steering wheel systems.

(a) The steering wheel shall be secured and must not have any spokes cracked through or missing.

(b) The steering wheel lash shall not exceed the following parameters:

Steering wheel diameter	Manual steering system	Power steering system
16″ or less	2″+	4 1/2″+
18″	2 1/4″+	4 3/4″+
20″	2 1/2″+	5 1/4″+
22″	2 3/4″+	5 3/4″+

(c) **Steering column.** The steering column must be securely fastened.

(d) **Steering system.** Universal joints shall not be worn, faulty or repaired by welding. The steering gear box shall not have loose or missing mounting bolts or cracks in the gear box or mounting brackets. The pitman arm on the steering gear output shaft shall not be loose. Steering wheels shall turn freely through the limit of travel in both directions.

(e) **Power steering systems.** All components of the power system must be in operating condition. No parts shall be loose or broken. Belts shall not be frayed, cracked or slipping. The system shall not leak. The power steering system shall have sufficient fluid in the reservoir.

PART 394

[REMOVED AND RESERVED]

Editor's Note: Effective March 4, 1993, the Accident Reporting Requirements were deleted. An accident register is now required to be maintained in accordance with Sec. 390.15(b). DOT's definition of an "Accident" is contained in Sec. 390.5.

PART 395 — HOURS OF SERVICE OF DRIVERS

AUTHORITY: 49 U.S.C. 31133, 31136, and 31502; sec, 345, Pub.L. 104-59, 109 Stat. 568, 613; and 49 CFR 1.48

§395.1 Scope of rules in this part.

(a) **General.** (1) The rules in this part apply to all motor carriers and drivers, except as provided in paragraphs (b) through (n) of this section.

(2) The exceptions from Federal requirements contained in paragraphs (l) through (n) do not preempt State laws and regulations governing the safe operation of commercial motor vehicles.

(b) **Adverse driving conditions.** (1) Except as provided in paragraph (i)(2) of this section, a driver who encounters adverse driving conditions, as defined in §395.2, and cannot, because of those conditions, safely complete the run within the 10-hour maximum driving time permitted by §395.3(a) may drive and be permitted or required to drive a commercial motor vehicle for not more than 2 additional hours in order to complete that run or to reach a place offering safety for the occupants of the commercial motor vehicle and security for the commercial motor vehicle and its cargo. However, that driver may not drive or be permitted to drive—

(i) For more than 12 hours in the aggregate following 8 consecutive hours off duty; or

(ii) After he/she has been on duty 15 hours following 8 consecutive hours off duty.

(2) **Emergency conditions.** In case of any emergency, a driver may complete his/her run without being in violation of

the provisions of the regulations in this part, if such run reasonably could have been completed absent the emergency.

(c) **Driver-salesperson.** The provisions of §395.3(b) shall not apply to any driver-salesperson whose total driving time does not exceed 40 hours in any period of 7 consecutive days.

(d) **Oilfield operations.** (1) In the instance of drivers of commercial motor vehicles used exclusively in the transportation of oilfield equipment, including the stringing and picking up of pipe used in pipelines, and servicing of the field operations of the natural gas and oil industry, any period of 8 consecutive days may end with the beginning of any off-duty period of 24 or more successive hours.

(2) In the case of specially trained drivers of commercial motor vehicles which are specially constructed to service oil wells, on-duty time shall not include waiting time at a natural gas or oil well site; **provided,** that all such time shall be fully and accurately accounted for in records to be maintained by the motor carrier. Such records shall be made available upon request of the Federal Highway Administration.

(e) **100 air-mile radius driver.** A driver is exempt from the requirements of Section 395.8 if:

(1) The driver operates within a 100 air-mile radius of the normal work reporting location;

(2) The driver, except a driver salesperson, returns to the work reporting location and is released from work within 12 consecutive hours;

(3) At least 8 consecutive hours off duty separate each 12 hours on duty;

(4) The driver does not exceed 10 hours maximum driving time following 8 consecutive hours off duty; and

(5) The motor carrier that employs the driver maintains and retains for a period of 6 months accurate and true time records showing:

(i) The time the driver reports for duty each day;

(ii) The total number of hours the driver is on duty each day;

(iii) The time the driver is released from duty each day; and

(iv) The total time for the preceding 7 days in accordance with §395.8(j)(2) for drivers used for the first time or intermittently.

(f) **Retail store deliveries.** The provisions of §395.3 (a) and (b) shall not apply with respect to drivers of commercial motor vehicles engaged solely in making local deliveries from retail stores and/or retail catalog businesses to the ultimate consumer, when driving solely within a 100-air mile radius of the driver's work-reporting location, during the period from December 10 to December 25, both inclusive, of each year.

(g) **Sleeper berths.** Drivers using sleeper berth equipment as defined in §395.2 or who are off duty at a natural gas or oil well location, may cumulate the required 8 consecutive hours off duty, as required by §395.3, resting in a sleeper berth in two separate periods totaling 8 hours, neither period to be less than 2 hours, or resting while off duty in other sleeping accommodations at a natural gas or oil well location.

(h) **State of Alaska.** (1) The provisions of §395.3 shall not apply to any driver who is driving a commercial motor vehicle in the State of Alaska. A driver who is driving a commercial motor vehicle in the State of Alaska must not drive or be required or permitted to drive—

(i) More than 15 hours following 8 consecutive hours off duty;

(ii) After being on duty for 20 hours or more following 8 consecutive hours off duty;

(iii) After having been on duty for 70 hours in any period of 7 consecutive days, if the motor carrier for which the driver drives does not operate every day in the week; or

(iv) After having been on duty for 80 hours in any period of 8 consecutive days, if the motor carrier for which the driver drives operates every day in the week.

(2) A driver who is driving a commercial motor vehicle in the State of Alaska and who encounters adverse driving conditions (as defined in §395.2) may drive and be permitted or required to drive a commercial motor vehicle for the period of time needed to complete the run. After he/she completes the run, that driver must be off duty for 8 consecutive hours before he/she drives again.

(i) **State of Hawaii.** The rules in §395.8 do not apply to a driver who drives a commercial motor vehicle in the State of Hawaii, if the motor carrier who employs the driver maintains and retains for a period of 6 months accurate and true records showing—

(1) The total number of hours the driver is on duty each day; and

(2) The time at which the driver reports for, and is released from, duty each day.

(j) **Travel time.** When a driver at the direction of the motor carrier is traveling, but not driving or assuming any other responsibility to the carrier, such time shall be counted as on-duty time unless the driver is afforded at least 8 consecutive hours off duty when arriving at destination, in which case he/she shall be considered off duty for the entire period.

(k) **Agricultural operations.** The provisions of §395.3 shall not apply to drivers transporting agricultural commodities or farm supplies for agricultural purposes in a State if such transportation:

(1) Is limited to an area within a 100 air mile radius from the source of the commodities or the distribution point for the farm supplies, and

(2) Is conducted during the planting and harvesting seasons within such State, as determined by the State.

(l) **Ground water well drilling operations.** In the instance of a driver of a commercial motor vehicle who is used primarily in the transportation and operations of a ground water well drilling rig, any period of 7 or 8 consecutive days may end with the beginning of any off-duty period of 24 or more successive hours.

(m) **Construction materials and equipment.** In the instance of a driver of a commercial motor vehicle who is used primarily in the transportation of construction materials and equipment, any period of 7 or 8 consecutive days may end with the beginning of any off-duty period of 24 or more successive hours.

(n) **Utility service vehicles.** In the instance of a driver of a utility service vehicle, any period of 7 or 8 consecutive days may end with the beginning of any off-duty period of 24 or more successive hours.

§395.2 Definitions.

As used in this part, the following words and terms are construed to mean:

Adverse driving conditions means snow, sleet, fog, other adverse weather conditions, a highway covered with snow or ice, or unusual road and traffic conditions, none of which were apparent on the basis of information known to the person dispatching the run at the time it was begun.

Automatic on-board recording device means an electric, electronic, electromechanical, or mechanical device capable of recording driver's duty status information accurately and automatically as required by §395.15. The device must be integrally synchronized with specific operations of the commercial motor vehicle in which it is installed. At a minimum, the device must record engine use, road speed, miles driven, the date, and time of day.

Driver-salesperson means any employee who is employed solely as such by a private carrier of property by commercial motor vehicle, who is engaged both in selling goods, services, or the use of goods, and in delivering by commercial motor vehicle the goods sold or provided or upon which the services are performed, who does so entirely within a radius of 100 miles of the point at which he/she reports for duty, who devotes not more than 50 percent of his/her hours on duty to driving time. The term **selling goods** for purposes of this section shall include in all cases solicitation or obtaining of reorders or new accounts, and may also include other selling or merchandising activities designed to retain the customer or to increase the sale of goods or services, in addition to solicitation or obtaining of reorders or new accounts.

Driving time means all time spent at the driving controls of a commercial motor vehicle in operation.

Eight consecutive days means the period of 8 consecutive days beginning on any day at the time designated by the motor carrier for a 24-hour period.

Ground water well drilling rig means any vehicle, machine, tractor, trailer, semi-trailer, or specialized mobile equipment propelled or drawn by mechanical power and used on highways to transport water well field operating equipment, including water well drilling and pump service rigs equipped to access ground water.

Multiple stops means all stops made in any one village, town, or city may be computed as one.

On duty time means all time from the time a driver begins to work or is required to be in readiness to work until the time the driver is relieved from work and all responsibility for performing work. **On duty time** shall include:

(1) All time at a plant, terminal, facility, or other property, of a motor carrier or shipper or on any public property, waiting to be dispatched, unless the driver has been relieved from duty by the motor carrier;

(2) All time inspecting, servicing, or conditioning any commercial motor vehicle at any time;

(3) All driving time as defined in the term **driving time;**

(4) All time, other than driving time, in or upon any commercial motor vehicle except time spent resting in a sleeper berth;

(5) All time loading or unloading a commercial motor vehicle, supervising, or assisting in the loading or unloading, attending a commercial motor vehicle being loaded or unloaded, remaining in readiness to operate the commercial motor vehicle, or in giving or receiving receipts for shipments loaded or unloaded;

(6) All time repairing, obtaining assistance, or remaining in attendance upon a disabled commercial motor vehicle;

(7) All time spent providing a breath sample or urine specimen, including travel time to and from the collection site, in order to comply with the random, reasonable suspicion, post-accident, or follow-up testing required by part 382, of this subchapter, when directed by a motor carrier.

(8) Performing any other work in the capacity, employ, or service of a motor carrier; and

(9) Performing any compensated work for a person who is not a motor carrier.

Seven consecutive days means the period of 7 consecutive days beginning on any day at the time designated by the motor carrier for a 24-hour period.

Sleeper berth means a berth conforming to the requirements of §393.76 of this chapter.

Transportation of construction materials and equipment means the transportation of construction and pavement materials, construction equipment, and construction maintenance vehicles, by a driver to or from an active construction site (a construction site between mobilization of equipment and materials to the site to the final completion of the construction project) within a 50 air mile radius of the normal work reporting location of the driver. This paragraph does not apply to the transportation of material found by the Secretary to be hazardous under 49 U.S.C. 5103 in a quantity requiring placarding under regulations issued to carry out such section.

Twenty-four-hour period means any 24-consecutive-hour period beginning at the time designated by the motor carrier for the terminal from which the driver is normally dispatched.

Utility service vehicle means any commercial motor vehicle:

(1) Used in the furtherance of repairing, maintaining, or operating any structures or any other physical facilities necessary for the delivery of public utility services, including the furnishing of electric, gas, water, sanitary sewer, telephone, and television cable or community antenna service;

(2) While engaged in any activity necessarily related to the

ultimate delivery of such public utility services to consumers, including travel or movement to, from, upon, or between activity sites (including occasional travel or movement outside the service area necessitated by any utility emergency as determined by the utility provider); and

(3) Except for any occasional emergency use, operated primarily within the service area of a utility's subscribers or consumers, without regard to whether the vehicle is owned, leased, or rented by the utility.

§395.3 Maximum driving time.

(a) Except as provided in §§395.1(b)(1), 395.1(f), and 395.1(i), no motor carrier shall permit or require any driver used by it to drive nor shall any such driver drive:

(1) More than 10 hours following 8 consecutive hours off duty; or

(2) For any period after having been on duty 15 hours following 8 consecutive hours off duty.

(b) No motor carrier shall permit or require a driver of a commercial motor vehicle to drive, nor shall any driver drive, regardless of the number of motor carriers using the driver's services, for any period after—

(1) Having been on duty 60 hours in any 7 consecutive days if the employing motor carrier does not operate commercial motor vehicles every day of the week; or

(2) Having been on duty 70 hours in any period of 8 consecutive days if the employing motor carrier operates commercial motor vehicles every day of the week.

§395.7 [Removed and reserved.]

§395.8 Driver's record of duty status.

(a) Except for a private motor carrier of passengers (nonbusiness), every motor carrier shall require every driver used by the motor carrier to record his/her duty status for each 24 hour period using the methods prescribed in either paragraphs (a)(1) or (2) of this section.

(1) Every driver who operates a commercial motor vehicle shall record his/her duty status, in duplicate, for each 24-hour period. The duty status time shall be recorded on a specified grid, as shown in paragraph (g) of this section. The grid and the requirements of paragraph (d) of this section may be combined with any company forms. The previously approved format of the Daily Log,

Form MCS-59 or the Multi-day Log, MCS-139 and 139A, which meets the requirements of this section, may continue to be used.

(2) Every driver who operates a commercial motor vehicle shall record his/her duty status by using an automatic on-board recording device that meets the requirements of §395.15 of this part. The requirements of §395.8 shall not apply, except paragraphs (e) and (k)(1) and (2) of this section.

(b) The duty status shall be recorded as follows:

(1) "Off duty" or "OFF."

(2) "Sleeper berth" or "SB" (only if a sleeper berth used).

(3) "Driving" or "D."

(4) "On-duty not driving" or "ON."

(c) For each change of duty status (e.g., the place of reporting for work, starting to drive, on-duty not driving and where released from work), the name of the city, town or village, with State abbreviation, shall be recorded.

Note: If a change of duty status occurs at a location other than a city, town, or village, show one of the following: (1) the highway number and nearest milepost followed by the name of the nearest city, town, or village and State abbreviation, (2) the highway number and the name of the service plaza followed by the name of the nearest city, town, or village and State abbreviation, or (3) the highway numbers of the nearest two intersecting roadways followed by the name of the nearest city, town, or village and State abbreviation.

(d) The following information must be included on the form in addition to the grid:

(1) Date;

(2) Total miles driving today;

(3) Truck or tractor and trailer number;

(4) Name of carrier;

(5) Driver's signature/certification;

(6) 24-hour period starting time (e.g., midnight, 9:00 a.m., noon, 3:00 p.m.);

(7) Main office address;

(8) Remarks;

(9) Name of co-driver;

(10) Total hours (far right edge of grid); and

(11) Shipping document number(s), or name of shipper and commodity.

(e) Failure to complete the record of duty activities of this section or §395.15, failure to preserve a record of such duty activities, or making of false reports in connection with such duty activities shall make the driver and/or the carrier liable to prosecution.

(f) The driver's activities shall be recorded in accordance with the following provisions:

(1) **Entries to be current.** Drivers shall keep their record of duty status current to the time shown for the last change of duty status.

(2) **Entries made by driver only.** All entries relating to driver's duty status must be legible and in the driver's own handwriting.

(3) **Date.** The month, day and year for the beginning of each 24-hour period shall be shown on the form containing the driver's duty status record.

(4) **Total miles driving today.** Total mileage driven during the 24-hour period shall be recorded on the form containing the driver's duty status record.

(5) **Commercial motor vehicle identification.** The driver shall show the number assigned by the motor carrier, or the license number and licensing state of each commercial motor vehicle operated during each 24-hour period on his/her record of duty status. The driver of an articulated (combination) commercial motor vehicle shall show the number assigned by the motor carrier, or the license number and licensing state of each motor vehicle used in each commercial motor vehicle combination operated during that 24-hour period on his/her record of duty status.

(6) **Name of motor carrier.** The name(s) of the motor carrier(s) for which work is performed shall be shown on the form containing the driver's record of duty status. When work is performed for more than one motor carrier during the same 24-hour period, the beginning and finishing time, showing a.m. or p.m., worked for each motor carrier shall be shown after each motor carrier's name. Drivers of leased commercial motor vehicles shall show the name of the motor carrier performing the transportation.

(7) **Signature/certification.** The driver shall certify to the correctness of all entries by signing the form containing the driver's duty status record with his/her legal name or name of record. The driver's signature certifies that all entries required by this section made by the driver are true and correct.

(8) **Time base to be used.**

(i) The driver's duty status record shall be prepared, maintained, and submitted using the time standard in effect at the driver's home terminal, for a 24-hour period beginning with the time specified by the motor carrier for that driver's home terminal.

(ii) The term "7 or 8 consecutive days" means the 7 or 8 consecutive 24-hour periods as designated by the carrier for the driver's home terminal.

(iii) The 24-hour period starting time must be identified on the driver's duty status record. One-hour increments must appear on the graph, be identified, and preprinted. The words "Midnight" and "Noon" must appear above or beside the appropriate one-hour increment.

(9) **Main office address.** The motor carrier's main office address shall be shown on the form containing the driver's duty status record.

(10) **Recording days off duty.** Two or more consecutive 24-hour periods off duty may be recorded on one duty status record.

(11) **Total hours.** The total hours in each duty status: off duty other than in a sleeper berth; off duty in a sleeper berth; driving, and on duty not driving, shall be entered to the right of the grid, the total of such entries shall equal 24 hours.

(12) Shipping document number(s), or name of shipper and commodity shall be shown on the driver's record of duty status.

(g) **Graph grid.** The following graph grid must be incorporated into a motor carrier recordkeeping system which must also contain the information required in paragraph (d) of this section.

§395.8

Graph Grid—Vertically

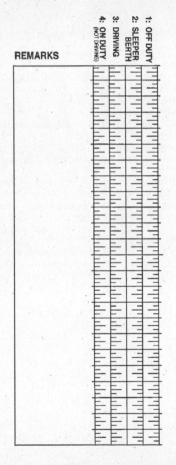

REMARKS

4: ON DUTY (NOT DRIVING)
3: DRIVING
2: SLEEPER BERTH
1: OFF DUTY

Graph Grid—Horizontally

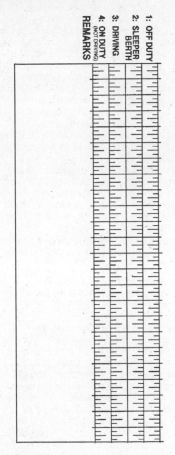

(h) **Graph Grid Preparation.** The graph grid may be used horizontally or vertically and shall be completed as follows:

(1) **Off-duty.** Except for time spent resting in a sleeper berth, a continuous line shall be drawn between the appropriate time markers to record the period(s) of time when the driver is not on duty, is not required to be in readiness to work, or is not under any responsibility for performing work.

(2) **Sleeper berth.** A continuous line shall be drawn between the appropriate time markers to record the period(s) of time off duty resting in a sleeper berth, as defined in §395.2. (If a non-sleeper berth operation, sleeper berth need not be shown on the grid.)

(3) **Driving.** A continuous line shall be drawn between the appropriate time markers to record the period(s) of driving time as defined in §395.2.

(4) **On duty not driving.** A continuous line shall be drawn between the appropriate time markers to record the period(s) of time on duty not driving specified in §395.2.

(5) **Location - Remarks.** The name of the city, town, or village, with State abbreviation where each change of duty status occurs shall be recorded.

Note: If a change of duty status occurs at a location other than a city, town, or village, show one of the following: (1) the highway number and nearest milepost followed by the name of the nearest city, town, or village and State abbreviation, (2) the highway number and the name of the service plaza followed by the name of the nearest city, town, or village and State abbreviation, or (3) the highway numbers of the nearest two intersecting roadways followed by the name of the nearest city, town, or village and State abbreviation.

(i) **Filing driver's record of duty status.** The driver shall submit or forward by mail the original driver's record of duty status to the regular employing motor carrier within 13 days following the completion of the form.

(j) **Drivers used by more than one motor carrier.** (1) When the services of a driver are used by more than one motor carrier during any 24-hour period in effect at the driver's home terminal, the driver shall submit a copy of the record of duty status to each motor carrier. The record shall include:

(i) All duty time for the entire 24-hour period;

(ii) The name of each motor carrier served by the driver during that period; and

(iii) The beginning and finishing time, including a.m. or p.m., worked for each carrier.

(2) Motor carriers, when using a driver for the first time or intermittently, shall obtain from the driver a signed statement giving the total time on duty during the immediately preceding 7 days and the time at which the driver was last relieved from duty prior to beginning work for the motor carriers.

(k) **Retention of driver's record of duty status.** (1) Each motor carrier shall maintain records of duty status and all supporting documents for each driver it employs for a period of six months from the date of receipt.

(2) The driver shall retain a copy of each record of duty status for the previous 7 consecutive days which shall be in his/her possession and available for inspection while on duty.

Note: Driver's record of duty status. The graph grid, when incorpo‑ rated as part of any form used by a motor carrier, must be of sufficient size to be legible.

The following executed specimen grid illustrates how a driv‑ er's duty status should be recorded for a trip from Richmond, Virginia, to Newark, New Jersey. The grid reflects the midnight to midnight 24 hour period.

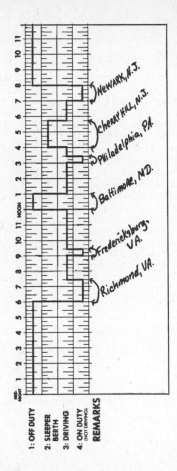

Graph Grid (midnight to midnight operation).

The driver in this instance reported for duty at the motor carrier's terminal. The driver reported for work at 6 a.m., helped load, checked with dispatch, made a pretrip inspection, and performed other duties until 7:30 a.m. when the driver began driving. At 9 a.m. the driver had a minor accident in Fredericksburg, Virginia, and spent one half hour handling details with the local police. The driver arrived at the company's Baltimore, Maryland, terminal at noon and went to lunch while minor repairs were made to the tractor. At 1 p.m. the driver resumed the trip and made a delivery in Philadelphia, Pennsylvania, between 3 p.m. and 3:30 p.m. at which time the driver started driving again. Upon arrival at Cherry Hill, New Jersey, at 4 p.m., the driver entered the sleeper berth for a rest break until 5:45 p.m. at which time the driver resumed driving again. At 7 p.m. the driver arrived at the company's terminal in Newark, New Jersey. Between 7 p.m. and 8 p.m. the driver prepared the required paperwork including completing the driver's record of duty status, driver vehicle inspection report, insurance report for the Fredericksburg, Virginia accident, checked for the next day's dispatch, etc. At 8 p.m., the driver went off duty.

§395.10 [Removed and reserved.]

§395.11 [Removed and reserved.]

§395.12 [Removed and reserved.]

§395.13 Drivers declared out of service.

(a) **Authority to declare drivers Out of Service.** Every special agent of the Federal Highway Administration (as defined in Appendix B to this subchapter) is authorized to declare a driver out of service and to notify the motor carrier of that declaration, upon finding at the time and place of examination that the driver has violated the out of service criteria as set forth in paragraph (b) of this section.

(b) **Out of Service criteria.** (1) No driver shall drive after being on duty in excess of the maximum periods permitted by this part.

(2) No driver required to maintain a record of duty status under §395.8 or §395.15 of this part shall fail to have a record of duty status current on the day of examination and for the prior 7 consecutive days.

(3) **Exception.** A driver failing only to have possession of a record of duty status current on the day of examination and the prior day, but has completed records of duty status up to that time (previous 6 days), will be given the opportunity to make the duty status record current.

(c) **Responsibilities of motor carriers.** (1) No motor carrier shall:

(i) Require or permit a driver who has been declared out of service to operate a commercial motor vehicle until that driver may lawfully do so under the rules in this part.

(ii) Require a driver who has been declared out of service for failure to prepare a record of duty status to operate a commercial motor vehicle until that driver has been off duty for 8 consecutive hours and is in compliance with this section. The consecutive 8 hour off-duty period may include sleeper berth time.

(2) A motor carrier shall complete the "Motor Carrier Certification of Action Taken" portion of the form MCS-63 (Driver-Vehicle Examination Report) and deliver the copy of the form either personally or by mail to the Regional Director of Motor Carriers, Federal Highway Administration, at the address specified upon the form within 15 days following the date of examination. If the motor carrier mails the form, delivery is made on the date it is postmarked.

(d) **Responsibilities of the driver.** (1) No driver who has been declared out of service shall operate a commercial motor vehicle until that driver may lawfully do so under the rules of this Part.

(2) No driver who has been declared out of service, for failing to prepare a record of duty status, shall operate a commercial motor vehicle until the driver has been off duty for 8 consecutive hours and is in compliance with this section.

(3) A driver to whom a form has been tendered declaring the driver out of service shall within 24 hours thereafter deliver or mail the copy to a person or place designated by motor carrier to receive it.

(4) §395.13 does not alter the hazardous materials requirements prescribed in §397.5 pertaining to attendance and surveillance of commercial motor vehicles.

§395.15 Automatic on-board recording devices.

(a) **Authority to use automatic on-board recording device.**

(1) A motor carrier may require a driver to use an automatic on-board recording device to record the driver's hours of service in lieu of complying with the requirements of §395.8 of this part.

(2) Every driver required by a motor carrier to use an automatic on-board recording device shall use such device to record the driver's hours of service.

(b) **Information requirements.**

(1) Automatic on-board recording devices shall produce, upon demand, a driver's hours of service chart, electronic display, or printout showing the time and sequence of duty status changes including the drivers' starting time at the beginning of each day.

(2) The device shall provide a means whereby authorized Federal, State, or local officials can immediately check the status of a driver's hours of service. This information may be used in conjunction with handwritten or printed records of duty status, for the previous 7 days.

(3) Support systems used in conjunction with on-board recorders at a driver's home terminal or the motor carrier's principal place of business must be capable of providing authorized Federal, State or local officials with summaries of an individual driver's hours of service records, including the information specified in §395.8(d) of this part. The support systems must also provide information concerning on-board system sensor failures and identification of edited data. Such support systems should meet the information interchange requirements of the American National Standard Code for Information Interchange (ANS-CII) (EIARS-232/CCITT V.24 port (National Bureau of Standards "Code for Information Interchange," FIPS PUB 1-1)).

(4) The driver shall have in his/her possession records of duty status for the previous 7 consecutive days available for inspection while on duty. These records shall consist of information stored in and retrievable from the automatic on-board recording device, handwritten records, computer generated records, or any combination thereof.

(5) All hard copies of the driver's record of duty status must be signed by the driver. The driver's signature certifies that the information contained thereon is true and correct.

(c) **The duty status and additional information shall be recorded as follows:**

(1) "Off duty" or "OFF", or by an identifiable code or character;

(2) "Sleeper berth" or "SB" or by an identifiable code or character (only if the sleeper berth is used);

(3) "Driving" or "D", or by an identifiable code or character; and

(4) "On-duty not driving" or "ON", or by an identifiable code or character.

(5) Date;

(6) Total miles driving today;

(7) Truck or tractor and trailer number;

(8) Name of carrier;

(9) Main office address;

(10) 24-hour period starting time (e.g., midnight, 9:00 a.m., noon, 3:00 p.m.);

(11) Name of co-driver;

(12) Total hours; and

(13) Shipping document number(s), or name of shipper and commodity.

(d) **Location of duty status change.**

(1) For each change of duty status (e.g., the place and time of reporting for work, starting to drive, on-duty not driving and where released from work), the name of the city, town, or village, with State abbreviation, shall be recorded.

(2) Motor carriers are permitted to use location codes in lieu of the requirements of paragraph (d)(1) of this section. A list of such codes showing all possible location identifiers shall be carried in the cab of the commercial motor vehicle and available at the motor carrier's principal place of business. Such lists shall be made available to an enforcement official on request.

(e) **Entries made by driver only.** If a driver is required to make written entries relating to the driver's duty status, such entries must be legible and in the driver's own handwriting.

(f) **Reconstruction of records of duty status.** Drivers are required to note any failure of automatic on-board recording devices, and to reconstruct the driver's record of duty status for the current day, and the past 7 days, less any days for which the drivers have records, and to continue to prepare a handwritten record of all subsequent duty status until the device is again operational.

(g) **On-board information.** Each commercial motor vehicle must have on-board the commercial motor vehicle an information packet containing the following items:

(1) An instruction sheet describing in detail how data may be stored and retrieved from an automatic on-board recording system; and

(2) A supply of blank driver's records of duty status graph-grids sufficient to record the driver's duty status and other related information for the duration of the current trip.

(h) **Submission of driver's record of duty status.**

(1) The driver shall submit, electronically or by mail, to the employing motor carrier, each record of the driver's duty status within 13 days following the completion of each record;

(2) The driver shall review and verify that all entries are accurate prior to submission to the employing motor carrier; and

(3) The submission of the record of duty status certifies that all entries made by the driver are true and correct.

(i) **Performance of recorders.** Motor carriers that use automatic on-board recording devices for recording their drivers' records of duty status in lieu of the handwritten record shall ensure that:

(1) A certificate is obtained from the manufacturer certifying that the design of the automatic on-board recorder has been sufficiently tested to meet the requirements of this section and under the conditions it will be used;

(2) The automatic on-board recording device permits duty status to be updated only when the commercial motor vehicle is at rest, except when registering the time a commercial motor vehicle crosses a State boundary;

(3) The automatic on-board recording device and associated support systems are, to the maximum extent practicable, tamperproof and do not permit altering of the information collected concerning the driver's hours of service;

(4) The automatic on-board recording device warns the driver visually and/or audibly that the device has ceased to function. Devices installed and operational as of October 31, 1988 and authorized to be used in lieu of the handwritten record of duty status by the FHWA are exempted from this requirement.

(5) Automatic on-board recording devices with electronic displays shall have the capability of displaying the following:

(i) Driver's total hours of driving today;

(ii) The total hours on duty today;

(iii) Total miles driving today;

(iv) Total hours on duty for the 7 consecutive day period, including today;

(v) Total hours on duty for the prior 8 consecutive day period, including the present day; and

(vi) The sequential changes in duty status and the times the changes occurred for each driver using the device.

(6) The on-board recorder is capable of recording separately each driver's duty status when there is a multiple-driver operation;

(7) The on-board recording device/system identifies sensor failures and edited data when reproduced in printed form. Devices installed and operational as of October 31, 1988 and authorized to be used in lieu of the handwritten record of duty status by the FHWA are exempted from this requirement.

(8) The on-board recording device is maintained and recalibrated in accordance with the manufacturer's specifications;

(9) The motor carrier's drivers are adequately trained regarding the proper operation of the device; and

(10) The motor carrier must maintain a second copy (back-up copy) of the electronic hours-of-service files, by month, in a different physical location than where the original data is stored.

(j) **Rescission of authority.**

(1) The FHWA may, after notice and opportunity to reply, order any motor carrier or driver to comply with the requirements of §395.8 of this part.

(2) The FHWA may issue such an order if the FHWA has determined that—

(i) The motor carrier has been issued conditional or unsatisfactory safety rating by the FHWA;

(ii) The motor carrier has required or permitted a driver to establish, or the driver has established, a pattern of exceeding the hours of service limitations of §395.3 of this part;

(iii) The motor carrier has required or permitted a driver to fail, or the driver has failed, to accurately and completely record the driver's hours of service as required in this section; or

(iv) The motor carrier or driver has tampered with or otherwise abused the automatic on-board recording device on any commercial motor vehicle.

PART 396 — INSPECTION, REPAIR, AND MAINTENANCE

AUTHORITY: 49 U.S.C. 31133, 31136, and 31502; 49 CFR 1.48.

§396.1 Scope.

General — Every motor carrier, its officers, drivers, agents, representatives, and employees directly concerned with the inspection or maintenance of motor vehicles shall comply and be conversant with the rules of this part.

§396.3 Inspection, repair and maintenance.

(a) **General** — Every motor carrier shall systematically inspect, repair, and maintain, or cause to be systematically inspected, repaired, and maintained, all motor vehicles subject to its control.

(1) Parts and accessories shall be in safe and proper operating condition at all times. These include those specified in Part 393 of this subchapter and any additional parts and accessories which may affect safety of operation, including but not limited to, frame and frame assemblies, suspension systems, axles and attaching parts, wheels and rims, and steering systems.

(2) Pushout windows, emergency doors, and emergency door marking lights in buses shall be inspected at least every 90 days.

(b) **Required records** — For vehicles controlled for 30 consecutive days or more, except for a private motor carrier of passengers (nonbusiness), the motor carriers shall maintain, or cause to be maintained, the following record for each vehicle:

(1) An identification of the vehicle including company number, if so marked, make, serial number, year, and tire size. In addition, if the motor vehicle is not owned by the motor carrier, the record shall identify the name of the person furnishing the vehicle;

(2) A means to indicate the nature and due date of the various inspection and maintenance operations to be performed;

(3) A record of inspection, repairs and maintenance indicating their date and nature; and

(4) A record of tests conducted on pushout windows, emergency doors, and emergency door marking lights on buses.

(c) **Record retention** — The records required by this section shall be retained where the vehicle is either housed or maintained for a period of 1 year and for 6 months after the motor vehicle leaves the motor carrier's control.

§396.5 Lubrication.

Every motor carrier shall ensure that each motor vehicle subject to its control is—

(a) properly lubricated; and

(b) free of oil and grease leaks.

§396.7 Unsafe operations forbidden.

(a) **General** — A motor vehicle shall not be operated in such a condition as to likely cause an accident or a breakdown of the vehicle.

(b) **Exemption** — Any motor vehicle discovered to be in an unsafe condition while being operated on the highway may be continued in operation only to the nearest place where repairs can safely be effected. Such operation shall be conducted only if it is less hazardous to the public than to permit the vehicle to remain on the highway.

§396.9 Inspection of motor vehicles in operation.

(a) **Personnel authorized to perform inspections** — Every special agent of the FHWA (as defined in Appendix B to this subchapter) is authorized to enter upon and perform inspections of motor carrier's vehicles in operation.

(b) **Prescribed inspection report** — The Driver-Equipment Compliance Check shall be used to record results of motor vehicle inspections conducted by authorized FHWA personnel.

(c) **Motor vehicles declared "out of service".**

(1) Authorized personnel shall declare and mark "out of service" any motor vehicle which by reason of its mechanical condition or loading would likely cause an accident or a breakdown. An "Out of Service Vehicle" sticker shall be used to mark vehicles "out of service".

(2) No motor carrier shall require or permit any person to operate nor shall any person operate any motor vehicle declared and marked "out of service" until all repairs required by the "out of service notice" have been satisfactorily completed. The term "operate" as used in this section shall include towing the vehicle, except that vehicles marked "out of service" may be towed away by means of a vehicle using a crane or hoist. A vehicle combination consisting of an emergency towing vehicle and an "out of service" vehicle shall not be operated unless such combination meets the performance requirements of this subchapter except for those conditions noted on the Driver Equipment Compliance Check.

(3) No person shall remove the "Out of Service Vehicle" sticker from any motor vehicle prior to completion of all repairs, required by the "out of service notice".

(d) **Motor carrier disposition.**

(1) The driver of any motor vehicle receiving an inspection report shall deliver it to the motor carrier operating the vehicle upon his/her arrival at the next terminal or facility. If the driver is not scheduled to arrive at a terminal or facility of the motor carrier operating the vehicle within 24 hours, the driver shall immediately mail the report to the motor carrier.

(2) Motor carriers shall examine the report. Violations or defects noted thereon shall be corrected.

(3) Within 15 days following the date of the inspection, the motor carrier shall —

(i) Certify that all violations noted have been corrected by completing the "Signature of Carrier Official, Title, and Date Signed" portions of the form; and

(ii) Return the completed roadside inspection form to the issuing agency at the address indicated on the form and retain a copy at the motor carrier's principal place of business or where the vehicle is housed for 12 months from the date of the inspection.

§396.11 Driver vehicle inspection report(s).

(a) **Report required.** Every motor carrier shall require its drivers to report, and every driver shall prepare a report in writing at the completion of each day's work on each vehicle operated and the report shall cover at least the following parts and accessories:

-Service brakes including trailer brake connections
-Parking (hand) brake
-Steering mechanism
-Lighting devices and reflectors
-Tires
-Horn
-Windshield wipers
-Rear vision mirrors
-Coupling devices
-Wheels and rims
-Emergency equipment

(b) **Report content.** The report shall identify the vehicle and list any defect or deficiency discovered by or reported to the driver which would affect the safety of operation of the vehicle or result in its mechanical breakdown. If no defect or deficiency is discovered by or reported to the driver, the report shall so indicate. In all instances, the driver shall sign the report. On two-driver operations, only one driver needs to sign the driver vehicle inspection report, provided both drivers agree as to the defects or deficiencies identified. If a driver operates more than one vehicle during the day, a report shall be prepared for each vehicle operated.

(c) **Corrective action.** Prior to requiring or permitting a driver to operate a vehicle, every motor carrier or its agent shall repair any defect or deficiency listed on the driver vehicle inspection report which would be likely to affect the safety of operation of the vehicle.

(1) Every motor carrier or its agent shall certify on the original driver vehicle inspection report which lists any defect or deficiency that the defect or deficiency has been repaired or that repair is unnecessary before the vehicle is operated again.

(2) Every motor carrier shall maintain the original driver vehicle inspection report, the certification of repairs, and the certification of the driver's review for three months from the date the written report was prepared.

(d) **Exceptions.** The rules in this section shall not apply to a private motor carrier of passengers (nonbusiness), a driveaway-towaway operation, or any motor carrier operating only one commercial motor vehicle.

§396.13 Driver inspection.

Before driving a motor vehicle, the driver shall:

(a) Be satisfied that the motor vehicle is in safe operating condition;

(b) Review the last driver vehicle inspection report; and

(c) Sign the report, only if defects or deficiencies were noted by the driver who prepared the report, to acknowledge that the driver has reviewed it and that there is a certification that the required repairs have been performed. The signature requirement does not apply to listed defects on a towed unit which is no longer part of the vehicle combination.

§396.15 Driveaway-towaway operations and inspections.

(a) **General.** Effective December 7, 1989, every motor carrier, with respect to motor vehicles engaged in driveaway-towaway operations, shall comply with the requirements of this part. Exception: Maintenance records required by §396.3, the vehicle inspection report required by §396.11, and the periodic inspection required by §396.17 of this part shall not be required for any vehicle which is part of the shipment being delivered.

(b) **Pre-trip inspection.** Before the beginning of any driveaway-towaway operation of motor vehicles in combination, the motor carrier shall make a careful inspection and test to ascertain that:

(1) The towbar or saddle-mount connections are properly secured to the towed and towing vehicle;

(2) They function adequately without cramping or binding of any of the parts; and

(3) The towed motor vehicle follows substantially in the path of the towing vehicle without whipping or swerving.

(c) **Post-trip inspection.** Motor carriers shall maintain practices to ensure that following completion of any trip in driveaway-towaway operation of motor vehicles in combination, and before they are used again, the towbars and saddle-mounts are disassembled and inspected for worn, bent, cracked, broken, or missing parts. Before reuse, suitable repair or replacement shall be made of any defective parts and the devices shall be properly reassembled.

§396.17 Periodic inspection.

(a) Every commercial motor vehicle shall be inspected as required by this section. The inspection shall include, at a minimum, the parts and accessories set forth in Appendix G of this subchapter.[1]

Note: The term commercial motor vehicle includes each vehicle in a combination vehicle. For example, for a tractor semitrailer, fulltrailer combination, the tractor, semitrailer, and the fulltrailer (including the converter dolly if so equipped) shall each be inspected.

(b) Except as provided in §396.23, a motor carrier shall inspect or cause to be inspected all motor vehicles subject to its control.

(c) A motor carrier shall not use a commercial motor vehicle unless each component identified in Appendix G has passed an inspection in accordance with the terms of this section at least once during the preceding 12 months and documentation of such inspection is on the vehicle. The documentation may be:

(1) The inspection report prepared in accordance with paragraph 396.21(a), or

(2) Other forms of documentation, based on the inspection report (e.g., sticker or decal), which contains the following information:

(i) The date of inspection;

(ii) Name and address of the motor carrier or other entity where the inspection report is maintained;

(iii) Information uniquely identifying the vehicle inspected if not clearly marked on the motor vehicle; and

(iv) A certification that the vehicle has passed an inspection in accordance with §396.17.

(d) A motor carrier may perform the required annual inspection for vehicles under the carrier's control which are not subject to an inspection under §396.23(b)(1).

(e) In lieu of the self inspection provided for in paragraph (d) of this section, a motor carrier may choose to have a commercial garage, fleet leasing company, truck stop, or other similar commercial business perform the inspection as its agent, provided that business operates and maintains facilities appropriate for commercial vehicle inspections and it employs qualified inspectors, as required by §396.19.

---

[1] EDITOR'S NOTE: Appendix G begins on page 465 in this Pocketbook.

(f) Vehicles passing roadside or periodic inspections performed under the auspices of any State government or equivalent jurisdiction or the FHWA, meeting the minimum standards contained in Appendix G of this subchapter, will be considered to have met the requirements of an annual inspection for a period of 12 months commencing from the last day of the month in which the inspection was performed, except as provided in §396.23(b)(1).

(g) It shall be the responsibility of the motor carrier to ensure that all parts and accessories not meeting the minimum standards set forth in Appendix G to this subchapter are repaired promptly.

(h) Failure to perform properly the annual inspection set forth in this section shall cause the motor carrier to be subject to the penalty provisions provided by 49 U.S.C.521(b).

§396.19 Inspector qualifications.

(a) It shall be the motor carrier's responsibility to ensure that the individual(s) performing an annual inspection under §396.17(d) or (e) is qualified as follows:

(1) Understands the inspection criteria set forth in 49 CFR Part 393 and Appendix G of this subchapter and can identify defective components;

(2) Is knowledgeable of and has mastered the methods, procedures, tools and equipment used when performing an inspection; and

(3) Is capable of performing an inspection by reason of experience, training, or both as follows:

(i) Successfully completed a State or Federal-sponsored training program or has a certificate from a State or Canadian Province which qualifies the person to perform commercial motor vehicle safety inspections, or

(ii) Have a combination of training and/or experience totaling at least 1 year. Such training and/or experience may consist of:

(A) Participation in a truck manufacturer-sponsored training program or similar commercial training program designed to train students in truck operation and maintenance;

(B) Experience as a mechanic or inspector in a motor carrier maintenance program;

(C) Experience as a mechanic or inspector in truck maintenance at a commercial garage, fleet leasing company, or similar facility; or

(D) Experience as a commercial vehicle inspector for a State, Provincial or Federal Government.

(b) Evidence of that individual's qualifications under this section shall be retained by the motor carrier for the period during which that individual is performing annual motor vehicle inspections for the motor carrier, and for one year thereafter. However, motor carriers do not have to maintain documentation of inspector qualifications for those inspections performed either as part of a State periodic inspection program or at the roadside as part of a random roadside inspection program.

§396.21 Periodic inspection recordkeeping requirements.

(a) The qualified inspector performing the inspection shall prepare a report which:

(1) Identifies the individual performing the inspection;

(2) Identifies the motor carrier operating the vehicle;

(3) Identifies the date of the inspection;

(4) Identifies the vehicle inspected;

(5) Identifies the vehicle components inspected and describes the results of the inspection, including the identification of those components not meeting the minimum standards set forth in Appendix G to this subchapter; and

(6) Certifies the accuracy and completeness of the inspection as complying with all the requirements of this section.

(b)(1) The original or a copy of the inspection report shall be retained by the motor carrier or other entity who is responsible for the inspection for a period of fourteen months from the date of the inspection report. The original or a copy of the inspection report shall be retained where the vehicle is either housed or maintained.

(2) The original or a copy of the inspection report shall be available for inspection upon demand of an authorized Federal, State or local official.

(3) **Exception.** Where the motor carrier operating the commercial motor vehicles did not perform the commercial motor vehicle's last annual inspection, the motor carrier shall be responsible for obtaining the original or a copy of the last annual inspection report upon demand of an authorized Federal, State,

or local official.

§396.23 Equivalent to periodic inspection.

(a) The motor carrier may meet the requirements of §396.17 through a State or other jurisdiction's roadside inspection program. The inspection must have been performed during the preceding 12 months. In using the roadside inspection, the motor carrier would need to retain a copy of an annual inspection report showing that the inspection was performed in accordance with the minimum periodic inspection standards set forth in appendix G to this subchapter. When accepting such an inspection report, the motor carrier must ensure that the report complies with the requirements of §396.21(a).

(b)(1) If a commercial motor vehicle is subject to a mandatory State inspection program which is determined by the Administrator to be as effective as §396.17, the motor carrier shall meet the requirement of §396.17 through that State's inspection program. Commercial motor vehicle inspections may be conducted by State personnel, at State authorized commercial facilities, or by the motor carrier under the auspices of a State authorized self-inspection program.

(2) Should the FHWA determine that a State inspection program, in whole or in part, is not as effective as §396.17, the motor carrier must ensure that the periodic inspection required by §396.17 is performed on all commercial motor vehicles under its control in a manner specified in §396.17.

§396.25 Qualifications of brake inspectors.

(a) The motor carrier shall ensure that all inspections, maintenance, repairs or service to the brakes of its commercial motor vehicles, are performed in compliance with the requirements of this section.

Editor's Note: A vehicle will meet the Federal requirements if inspected under a state mandatory inspection program in Alabama, California, Connecticut, Hawaii, Louisiana, Maine, Maryland, Michigan, Minnesota, New Hampshire, New Jersey, New York, Ohio, Pennsylvania, Rhode Island, Texas, Utah, Vermont, Virginia, West Virginia, Wisconsin, and the District of Columbia. Of the above states, Alabama, California, Connecticut, Michigan, Minnesota, New Jersey, New York, Ohio, and Wisconsin have inspection programs that do not cover all commercial motor vehicles. There are three other states — Arkansas, Illinois, and Oklahoma — where the inspection is not mandatory but where the inspection will satisfy Federal requirements. The Federal Highway Administration has also determined that all of the Canadian Provinces and the Yukon Territory have periodic inspection programs that are as effective as the Federal requirements.

(b) For purposes of this section, "brake inspector" means any employee of a motor carrier who is responsible for ensuring all brake inspections, maintenance, service, or repairs to any commercial motor vehicle, subject to the motor carrier's control, meet the applicable Federal standards.

(c) No motor carrier shall require or permit any employee who does not meet the minimum brake inspector qualifications of §396.25(d) to be responsible for the inspection, maintenance, service or repairs of any brakes on its commercial motor vehicles.

(d) The motor carrier shall ensure that each brake inspector is qualified as follows:

(1) Understands the brake service or inspection task to be accomplished and can perform that task; and

(2) Is knowledgeable of and has mastered the methods, procedures, tools and equipment used when performing an assigned brake service or inspection task; and

(3) Is capable of performing the assigned brake service or inspection by reason of experience, training or both as follows:

(i) Has successfully completed an apprenticeship program sponsored by a State, a Canadian Province, a Federal agency or a labor union, or a training program approved by a State, Provincial or Federal agency, or has a certificate from a State or Canadian Province which qualifies the person to perform the assigned brake service or inspection task (including passage of Commercial Driver's License air brake tests in the case of a brake inspection); or

(ii) Has brake-related training or experience or a combination thereof totaling at least one year. Such training or experience may consist of:

(A) Participation in a training program sponsored by a brake or vehicle manufacturer or similar commercial training program designed to train students in brake maintenance or inspection similar to the assigned brake service or inspection tasks; or

(B) Experience performing brake maintenance or inspection similar to the assigned brake service or inspection task in a motor carrier maintenance program; or

(C) Experience performing brake maintenance or inspection similar to the assigned brake service or inspection task at a commercial garage, fleet leasing company, or similar facility.

(e) No motor carrier shall employ any person as a brake inspector unless the evidence of the inspector's qualifications, required under this section is maintained by the motor carrier at its principal place of business, or at the location at which the brake inspector is employed. The evidence must be maintained for the period during which the brake inspector is employed in that capacity and for one year thereafter. However, motor carriers do not have to maintain evidence of qualifications to inspect air brake systems for such inspections performed by persons who have passed the air brake knowledge and skills test for a Commercial Driver's License.

PART 397 — TRANSPORTATION OF HAZARDOUS MATERIALS; DRIVING AND PARKING RULES

Subpart A — General

Subpart B — Reserved

Subpart C — Routing of Non-Radioactive Hazardous Materials

Subpart D — Routing of Class 7 (Radioactive) Materials

Subpart E — Preemption Procedures

AUTHORITY: 49 U.S.C. 322; 49 CFR 1.48. Subpart A also issued under 49 U.S.C. 31136, 31502. Subparts C, D, and E also issued under 49 U.S.C. 5112, 5125.

Subpart A — General

§397.1 Application of the rules in this part.

(a) The rules in this part apply to each motor carrier engaged in the transportation of hazardous materials by a motor vehicle which must be marked or placarded in accordance with §177.823 of this title and to—

(1) Each officer or employee of the motor carrier who performs supervisory duties related to the transportation of hazardous materials; and

(2) Each person who operates or who is in charge of a motor vehicle containing hazardous materials.

(b) Each person designated in paragraph (a) of this section must know and obey the rules in this part.

§397.2 Compliance with Federal motor carrier safety regulations.

A motor carrier or other person to whom this part is applicable must comply with the rules in Part 390 through 397, inclusive, of this subchapter when he/she is transporting hazardous materials by a motor vehicle which must be marked or placarded in accordance with §177.823 of this title.

§397.3 State and local laws, ordinances and regulations.

Every motor vehicle containing hazardous materials must be driven and parked in compliance with the laws, ordinances, and regulations of the jurisdiction in which it is being operated, unless they are at variance with specific regulations of the Department of Transportation which are applicable to the operation of that vehicle and which impose a more stringent obligation or restraint.

§397.5 Attendance and surveillance of motor vehicles.

(a) Except as provided in paragraph (b) of this section, a motor vehicle which contains a Division 1.1, 1.2, or 1.3 (explosive) material must be attended at all times by its driver or a qualified representative of the motor carrier that operates it.

(b) The rules in paragraph (a) of this section do not apply to a motor vehicle which contains Division 1.1, 1.2, or 1.3 material if all the following conditions exist—

(1) The vehicle is located on the property of a motor carrier, on the property of a shipper or consignee of the explosives, in a safe haven, or, in the case of a vehicle containing 50 pounds or less of a Division 1.1, 1.2, or 1.3 material, on a construction or survey site; and

(2) The lawful bailee of the explosives is aware of the nature of the explosives the vehicle contains and has been instructed in the procedures which must be followed in emergencies; and

(3) The vehicle is within the bailee's unobstructed field of view or is located in a safe haven.

(c) A motor vehicle which contains hazardous materials other than Division 1.1, 1.2, or 1.3, materials, and which is located on a public street or highway, or the shoulder of a public highway, must be attended by its driver. However, the vehicle need not be attended while its driver is performing duties which are incident and necessary to the driver's duties as the operator of the vehicle.

(d) For purposes of this section—

(1) A motor vehicle is attended when the person in charge of the vehicle is on the vehicle, awake, and not in a sleeper berth, or is within 100 feet of the vehicle and has it within his/her unobstructed field of view.

(2) A qualified representative of a motor carrier is a person who—

(i) Has been designated by the carrier to attend the vehicle;

(ii) Is aware of the nature of the hazardous materials contained in the vehicle he/she attends;

(iii) Has been instructed in the procedures he/she must follow in emergencies; and

(iv) Is authorized to move the vehicle and has the means and ability to do so.

(3) A safe haven in an area specifically approved in writing by local, State, or Federal governmental authorities for the parking of unattended vehicles containing Division 1.1, 1.2, or 1.3 materials.

(e) The rules in this section do not relieve the driver from any obligation imposed by law relating to the placing of warning devices when a motor vehicle is stopped on a public street or highway.

§397.7 Parking.

(a) A motor vehicle which contains Division 1.1, 1.2, or 1.3 materials must not be parked under any of the following circumstances —

(1) On or within 5 feet of the traveled portion of a public street or highway;

(2) On private property (including premises of a fueling or eating facility) without the knowledge and consent of the person who is in charge of the property and who is aware of the nature of the hazardous materials the vehicle contains; or

(3) Within 300 feet of a bridge, tunnel, dwelling, or place where people work, congregate, or assemble, except for brief periods when the necessities of operation require the vehicle to be parked and make it impracticable to park the vehicle in any other place.

(b) A motor vehicle which contains hazardous materials other than Division 1.1, 1.2, or 1.3 materials must not be parked on or within five feet of the traveled portion of public street or highway except for brief periods when the necessities of operation require the vehicle to be parked and make it impracticable to park the vehicle in any other place.

§397.9 [Removed and reserved.]

§397.11 Fires.

(a) A motor vehicle containing hazardous materials must not be operated near an open fire unless its driver has first taken precautions to ascertain that the vehicle can safely pass the fire without stopping.

(b) A motor vehicle containing hazardous materials must not be parked within 300 feet of an open fire.

§397.13 Smoking.

No person may smoke or carry a lighted cigarette, cigar, or pipe on or within 25 feet of—

(a) A motor vehicle which contains Class 1 materials, Class 5 materials, or flammable materials classified as Division 2.1, Class 3, Divisions 4.1 and 4.2; or

(b) An empty tank motor vehicle which has been used to transport Class 3, flammable materials, or Division 2.1 flammable gases, which, when so used, was required to be marked or placarded in accordance with the rules in §177.823 of this title.

§397.15 Fueling.

When a motor vehicle which contains hazardous materials is being fueled—

(a) Its engine must not be operating; and

(b) A person must be in control of the fueling process at the point where the fuel tank is filled.

§397.17 Tires.

(a) If a motor vehicle which contains hazardous materials is equipped with dual tires on any axle, its driver must stop the vehicle in a safe location at least once during each 2 hours or 100 miles of travel, whichever is less, and must examine its tires. The driver must also examine the vehicle's tires at the beginning of each trip and each time the vehicle is parked.

(b) If, as the result of an examination pursuant to paragraph (a) of this section, or otherwise, a tire is found to be flat, leaking, or improperly inflated, the driver must cause the tire to be repaired, replaced, or properly inflated before the vehicle is driven. However, the vehicle may be driven to the nearest safe place to perform the required repair, replacement, or inflation.

(c) If, as the result of an examination pursuant to paragraph (a) of this section, or otherwise, a tire is found to be overheated, the driver shall immediately cause the overheated tire to be removed and placed at a safe distance from the vehicle. The driver shall not operate the vehicle until the cause of the overheating is corrected.

(d) Compliance with the rules in this section does not relieve a driver from the duty to comply with the rules in §§397.5 and 397.7.

§397.19 Instructions and documents.

(a) A motor carrier that transports Division 1.1, 1.2, or 1.3 (explosive) materials must furnish the driver of each motor vehicle in which the explosives are transported with the following documents:

(1) A copy of the rules in this part;

(2) [Reserved]

(3) A document containing instructions on procedures to be followed in the event of accident or delay. The documents must include the names and telephone numbers of persons (including representatives of carriers or shippers) to be contracted, the nature of the explosives being transported, and the precautions to be taken in emergencies such as fires, accidents, or leakages.

(b) A driver who receives documents in accordance with paragraph (a) of this section must sign a receipt for them. The motor carrier shall maintain the receipt for a period of 1 year from the date of signature.

(c) A driver of a motor vehicle which contains Division 1.1, 1.2, or 1.3 materials must be in possession of, be familiar with, and be in compliance with

(1) The documents specified in paragraph (a) of this section;

(2) The documents specified in §177.817 of this title; and

(3) The written route plan specified in §397.67.

Subpart C — Routing of Non-Radioactive Hazardous Materials

§397.61 Purpose and scope.

This subpart contains routing requirements and procedures that States and Indian tribes are required to follow if they establish, maintain, or enforce routing designations over which a non-radioactive hazardous material (NRHM) in a quantity which requires placarding may or may not be transported by a motor vehicle. It also provides regulations for motor carriers transporting placarded or marked NRHM and procedures for dispute resolutions regarding NRHM routing designations.

§397.63 Applicability.

The provisions of this subpart apply to any State or Indian tribe that establishes, maintains, or enforces any routing designations over which NRHM may or may not be transported by motor vehicle. They also apply to any motor carrier that transports or causes to be transported placarded or marked NRHM in commerce.

§397.65 Definitions.

For purposes of this subpart, the following definitions apply:

Administrator. The Federal Highway Administrator, who is the chief executive of the Federal Highway Administration, an agency within the United States Department of Transportation, or his/her designate.

Commerce. Any trade, traffic, or transportation in the United States which:

(1) is between a place under the jurisdiction of a State or Indian tribe and any place outside of such jurisdiction; or

(2) is solely within a place under the jurisdiction of a State or Indian tribe but which affects trade, traffic, or transportation described in subparagraph (a).

FHWA. The Federal Highway Administration, an agency within the Department of Transportation.

Hazardous material. A substance or material, including a hazardous substance, which has been determined by the Secretary of Transportation to be capable of posing an unreasonable risk to health, safety, or property when transported in commerce, and which has been so designated.

Indian tribe. Has the same meaning as contained in §4 of the Indian Self-Determination and Education Act, 25 U.S.C. 450b.

Motor carrier. A for-hire motor carrier or a private motor carrier of property. The term includes a motor carrier's agents, officers and representatives as well as employees responsible for hiring, supervising, training, assigning, or dispatching of drivers.

Motor vehicle. Any vehicle, machine, tractor, trailer, or semitrailer propelled or drawn by mechanical power and used upon the highways in the transportation of passengers or property, or any combination thereof.

NRHM. A non-radioactive hazardous material transported by motor vehicle in types and quantities which require placarding, pursuant to Table 1 or 2 of 49 CFR 172.504.

Political subdivision. A municipality, public agency or other instrumentality of one or more States, or a public corporation, board, or commission established under the laws of one or more States.

Radioactive material. Any material having a specific activity greater than 0.002 microcuries per gram (uCi/g), as defined in 49 CFR 173.403.

Routing agency. The State highway agency or other State agency designated by the Governor of that State, or an agency designated by an Indian tribe, to supervise, coordinate, and approve the NRHM routing designations for that State or Indian tribe.

Routing designations. Any regulation, limitation, restriction, curfew, time of travel restriction, lane restriction, routing ban, port-of-entry designation, or route weight restriction, applicable to the highway transportation of NRHM over a specific highway route or portion of a route.

Secretary. The Secretary of Transportation.

State. A State of the United States, the District of Columbia, the Commonwealth of Puerto Rico, the Commonwealth of the Northern Mariana Islands, the Virgin Islands, American Samoa or Guam.

§397.67 Motor carrier responsibility for routing.

(a) A motor carrier transporting NRHM shall comply with NRHM routing designations of a State or Indian tribe pursuant to this subpart.

(b) A motor carrier carrying hazardous materials required to be placarded or marked in accordance with 49 CFR 177.823 and not subject to a NRHM routing designations pursuant to this subpart, shall operate the vehicle over routes which do not go through or near heavily populated areas, places where crowds are assembled, tunnels, narrow streets, or alleys, except where the motor carrier determines that:

(1) There is no practicable alternative;

(2) A reasonable deviation is necessary to reach terminals, points of loading and unloading, facilities for food, fuel, repairs, rest, or a safe haven; or

(3) A reasonable deviation is required by emergency conditions, such as a detour that has been established by a highway authority, or a situation exists where a law enforcement official requires the driver to take an alternative route.

(c) Operating convenience is not a basis for determining whether it is practicable to operate a motor vehicle in accordance with paragraph (b) of this section.

(d) Before a motor carrier requires or permits a motor vehicle containing explosives in Class 1, Divisions 1.1, 1.2, 1.3, as defined in 49 CFR 173.50 and 173.53 respectively, to be operated, the carrier or its agent shall prepare a written route plan that complies with this section and shall furnish a copy to the driver. However, the driver may prepare the written plan as agent for the motor carrier when the trip begins at a location other than the carrier's terminal.

§397.69 Highway routing designations; preemption.

(a) Any State or Indian tribe that establishes or modifies a highway routing designation over which NRHM may or may not be transported on or after November 14, 1994, and maintains or enforces such designation, shall comply with the highway routing standards set forth in §397.71 of this subpart. For purposes of this subpart, any highway routing designation affecting the highway transportation of NRHM, made by a political subdivision of a State is considered as one made by that State, and all requirements of this subpart apply.

(b) Except as provided in §§397.75 and 397.219, a NRHM route designation made in violation of paragraph (a) of this section is preempted pursuant to section 105(b)(4) of the Hazardous Materials Transportation Act (49 U.S.C. app. 1804(b)(4)). This provision shall become effective after November 14, 1996.

(c) A highway routing designation established by a State, political subdivision, or Indian tribe before November 14, 1994 is subject to preemption in accordance with the preemption standards in paragraphs (a)(1) and (a)(2) of §397.203 of this subpart.

(d) A State, political subdivision, or Indian tribe may petition for a waiver of preemption in accordance with §397.213 of this part.

§397.71 Federal standards.

(a) A State or Indian tribe shall comply with the Federal standards under paragraph (b) of this section when establishing, maintaining or enforcing specific NRHM routing designations over which NRHM may or may not be transported.

(b) The Federal standards are as follows:

(1) **Enhancement of public safety.** The State or Indian tribe shall make a finding, supported by the record to be developed in accordance with paragraphs (b)(2)(ii) and (b)(3)(iv) of this section, that any NRHM routing designation enhances public safety in the areas subject to its jurisdiction and in other areas which are directly affected by such highway routing designation. In making such a finding, the State or Indian tribe shall consider:

(i) The factors listed in paragraph (b)(9) of this section; and

(ii) The DOT "Guidelines for Applying Criteria to Designate Routes for Transporting Hazardous Materials," DOT/RSPA/OHMT-89-02, July 1989[1] or its most current version; or an equivalent routing analysis which adequately considers overall risk to the public.

(2) **Public participation.** Prior to the establishment of any NRHM routing designation, the State or Indian tribe shall undertake the following actions to ensure participation by the public in the routing process:

(i) The State or Indian tribe shall provide the public with notice of any proposed NRHM routing designation and a 30-day period in which to comment. At any time during this period or following review of the comments received, the State or Indian tribe shall decide whether to hold a public hearing on the proposed NRHM route designation. The public shall be given 30 days prior notice of the public hearing which shall be conducted as described in paragraph (b)(2)(ii) of this section. Notice for both the comment period and the public hearing, if one is held, shall be given by publication in at least two newspapers of general circulation in the affected area or areas and shall contain a complete description of the proposed routing designation, together with the date, time, and location of any public hearings. Notice for both the comment period and any public hearing may also be published in the official register of the State.

(ii) If it is determined that a public hearing is necessary, the State or Indian tribe shall hold at least one public hearing on the record during which the public will be afforded the opportunity to present their views and any information or data related to the proposed NRHM routing designation. The State shall make available to the public, upon payment of prescribed costs,

---

[1] This document may be obtained from Safety Technology and Information Management Division, HHS-10, Federal Highway Administration, U.S. Department of Transportation, 400 7th Street, SW., Washington, D.C. 20590-0001.

copies of the transcript of the hearing, which shall include all exhibits and documents presented during the hearing or submitted for the record.

(3) **Consultation with others**. Prior to the establishment of any NRHM routing designation, the State or Indian tribe shall provide notice to, and consult with, officials of affected political subdivisions, States and Indian tribes, and any other affected parties. Such actions shall include the following:

(i) At least 60 days prior to establishing a routing designation, the State or Indian tribe shall provide notice, in writing, of the proposed routing designation to officials responsible for highway routing in all other affected States or Indian tribes. A copy of this notice may also be sent to all affected political subdivisions. This notice shall request approval, in writing, by those States or Indian tribes, of the proposed routing designations. If no response is received within 60 days from the day of receipt of the notification of the proposed routing designation, the routing designation shall be considered approved by the affected State or Indian tribe.

(ii) The manner in which consultation under this paragraph is conducted is left to the discretion of the State or Indian tribe.

(iii) The State or Indian tribe shall attempt to resolve any concern or disagreement expressed by any consulted official related to the proposed routing designation.

(iv) The State or Indian tribe shall keep a record of the names and addresses of the officials notified pursuant to this section and of any consultation or meeting conducted with these officials or their representatives. Such record shall describe any concern or disagreement expressed by the officials and any action undertaken to resolve such disagreement or address any concern.

(4) **Through routing.** In establishing any NRHM routing designation, the State or Indian tribe shall ensure through highway routing for the transportation of NRHM between adjacent areas. The term "through highway routing" as used in this paragraph means that the routing designation must ensure continuity of movement so as to not impede or unnecessarily delay the transportation of NRHM. The State or Indian tribe shall utilize the procedures established in paragraphs (b)(2) and (b)(3) of this section in meeting these requirements. In addition, the State or Indian tribe shall make a finding, supported by a risk analysis conducted in accordance with para-

graph (b)(1) of this section, that the routing designation enhances public safety. If the risk analysis shows—

(i) That the current routing presents at least 50 percent more risk to the public than the deviation under the proposed routing designation, then the proposed routing designation may go into effect.

(ii) That the current routing presents a greater risk but less than 50 percent more risk to the public than the deviation under the proposed routing restriction, then the proposed routing restriction made by a State or Indian tribe shall only go into effect if it does not force a deviation of more than 25 miles or result in an increase of more than 25 percent of that part of a trip affected by the deviation, whichever is shorter, from the most direct route through a jurisdiction as compared to the intended deviation.

(iii) That the current route has the same or less risk to the public than the deviation resulting from the proposed routing designation, then the routing designation shall not be allowed.

(5) **Agreement of other States; burden on commerce.** Any NRHM routing designation which affects another State or Indian tribe shall be established, maintained, or enforced only if:

(i) It does not unreasonably burden commerce, and

(ii) It is agreed to by the affected State or Indian tribe within 60 days of receipt of the notice sent pursuant to paragraph (b)(3)(i) of this section, or it is approved by the Administrator pursuant to §397.75.

(6) **Timeliness.** The establishment of a NRHM routing designation by any State or Indian tribe shall be completed within 18 months of the notice given in either paragraph (b)(2) or (b)(3) of this section, whichever occurs first.

(7) **Reasonable routes to terminals and other facilities.** In establishing or providing for reasonable access to and from designated routes, the State or Indian tribe shall use the shortest practicable route considering the factors listed in paragraph (b)(9) of this section. In establishing any NRHM routing designation, the State or Indian tribe shall provide reasonable access for motor vehicles transporting NRHM to reach:

(i) Terminals,

(ii) Points of loading, unloading, pickup and delivery, and

(iii) Facilities for food, fuel, repairs, rest, and safe havens.

(8) **Responsibility for local compliance.** The States shall be responsible for ensuring that all of their political subdivisions comply with the provisions of this subpart. The States shall be responsible for resolving all disputes between such political subdivisions within their jurisdictions. If a State or any political subdivision thereof, or an Indian tribe chooses to establish, maintain, or enforce any NRHM routing designation, the Governor, or Indian tribe, shall designate a routing agency for the State or Indian tribe, respectively. The routing agency shall ensure that all NRHM routing designations within its jurisdiction comply with the Federal standards in this section. The State or Indian tribe shall comply with the public information and reporting requirements contained in §397.73.

(9) **Factors to consider.** In establishing any NRHM routing designation, the State or Indian tribe shall consider the following factors:

(i) **Population density.** The population potentially exposed to a NRHM release shall be estimated from the density of the residents, employees, motorists, and other persons in the area, using United States census tract maps or other reasonable means for determining the population within a potential impact zone along a designated highway route. The impact zone is the potential range of effects in the event of a release. Special populations such as schools, hospitals, prisons, and senior citizen homes shall, among other things, be considered when determining the potential risk to the populations along a highway routing. Consideration shall be given to the amount of time during which an area will experience a heavy population density.

(ii) **Type of highway.** The characteristics of each alternative NRHM highway routing designation shall be compared. Vehicle weight and size limits, underpass and bridge clearances, roadway geometrics, number of lanes, degree of access control, and median and shoulder structures are examples of characteristics which a State or Indian tribe shall consider.

(iii) **Types and quantities of NRHM.** An examination shall be made of the type and quantity of NRHM normally transported along highway routes which are included in a proposed NRHM routing designation, and consideration shall be given to the relative impact zone and risks of each type and quantity.

(iv) **Emergency response capabilities.** In consultation with the proper fire, law enforcement, and highway safety agencies, consideration shall be given to the emergency response capabilities which may be needed as a result of a NRHM routing designation. The analysis of the emergency response capabilities shall be based upon the proximity of the emergency response facilities and their capabilities to contain and suppress NRHM releases within the impact zones.

(v) **Results of consultation with affected persons.** Consideration shall be given to the comments and concerns of all affected persons and entities provided during public hearings and consultations conducted in accordance with this section.

(vi) **Exposure and other risk factors.** States and Indian tribes shall define the exposure and risk factors associated with any NRHM routing designations. The distance to sensitive areas shall be considered. Sensitive areas include, but are not limited to, homes and commercial buildings; special populations in hospitals, schools, handicapped facilities, prisons and stadiums; water sources such as streams and lakes; and natural areas such as parks, wetlands, and wildlife reserves.

(vii) **Terrain considerations.** Topography along and adjacent to the proposed NRHM routing designation that may affect the potential severity of an accident, the dispersion of the NRHM upon release and the control and clean up of NRHM if released shall be considered.

(viii) **Continuity of routes.** Adjacent jurisdictions shall be consulted to ensure routing continuity for NRHM across common borders. Deviations from the most direct route shall be minimized.

(ix) **Alternative routes.** Consideration shall be given to the alternative routes to, or resulting from, any NRHM route designation. Alternative routes shall be examined, reviewed, or evaluated to the extent necessary to demonstrate that the most probable alternative routing resulting from a routing designation is safer than the current routing.

(x) **Effects on commerce.** Any NRHM routing designation made in accordance with this subpart shall not create an unreasonable burden upon interstate or intrastate commerce.

(xi) **Delays in transportation.** No NRHM routing designations may create unnecessary delays in the transportation of NRHM.

(xii) **Climatic conditions.** Weather conditions unique to a highway route such as snow, wind, ice, fog, or other climatic conditions that could affect the safety of a route, the dispersion of the NRHM upon release, or increase the difficulty of controlling it and cleaning it up shall be given appropriate consideration.

(xiii) **Congestion and accident history.** Traffic conditions unique to a highway routing such as: traffic congestion; accident experience with motor vehicles, traffic considerations that could affect the potential for an accident, exposure of the public to any release, ability to perform emergency response operations, or the temporary closing of a highway for cleaning up any release shall be given appropriate consideration.

§397.73 Public information and reporting requirements.

(a) **Public information.** Information on NRHM routing designations must be made available by the States and Indian tribes to the public in the form of maps, lists, road signs or some combination thereof. If road signs are used, those signs and their placements must comply with the provisions of the Manual on Uniform Traffic Control Devices,[1] published by the FHWA, particularly the Hazardous Cargo signs identified as R14-2 and R14-3 shown in Section 2B-43 of that Manual.

(b) **Reporting and publishing requirements.** Each State or Indian tribe, through its routing agency, shall provide information identifying all NRHM routing designations which exist within their jurisdictions on November 14, 1994 to the FHWA, HHS-30, 400 7th St., SW., Washington, D.C. 20590-0001 by March 13, 1995. The State or Indian tribe shall include descriptions of these routing designations, along with the dates they were established. This information may also be published in each State's official register of State regulations. Information on any subsequent changes or new NRHM routing designations shall be furnished within 60 days after establishment to the FHWA. This information will be available from the FHWA, consolidated by the FHWA, and published annually in whole or as updates in the *Federal Register*. Each State may also publish this information in its official register of State regulations.

(Approved by the Office of Management and Budget under control number 2125-0554)

---

[1]This publication may be purchased from the Superintendent of Documents, U.S. Government Printing Office (GPO), Washington, D.C. 20402 and has Stock No. 050-001-81001-8. It is available for inspection and copying as prescribed in 49 CFR part 7, appendix D. See 23 CFR 655, subpart F.

§397.75 Dispute resolution.

(a) **Petition.** One or more States or Indian tribes may petition the Administrator to resolve a dispute relating to an agreement on a proposed NRHM routing designation. In resolving a dispute under these provisions, the Administrator will provide the greatest level of safety possible without unreasonably burdening commerce, and ensure compliance with the Federal standards established at §397.71 of this subpart.

(b) **Filing.** Each petition for dispute resolution filed under this section must:

(1) Be submitted to the Administrator, Federal Highway Administration, U.S. Department of Transportation, 400 7th Street, SW., Washington, DC 20590-0001. Attention: HCC-10 Docket Room, Hazardous Materials Routing Dispute Resolution Docket.

(2) Identify the State or Indian tribe filing the petition and any other State, political subdivision, or Indian tribe whose NRHM routing designation is the subject of the dispute.

(3) Contain a certification that the petitioner has complied with the notification requirements of paragraph (c) of this section, and include a list of the names and addresses of each State, political subdivision, or Indian tribe official who was notified of the filing of the petition.

(4) Clearly set forth the dispute for which resolution is sought, including a complete description of any disputed NRHM routing designation and an explanation of how the disputed routing designation affects the petitioner or how it impedes through highway routing. If the routing designation being disputed results in alternative routing, then a comparative risk analysis for the designated route and the resulting alternative routing shall be provided.

(5) Describe any actions taken by the State or Indian tribe to resolve the dispute.

(6) Explain the reasons why the petitioner believes that the Administrator should intervene in resolving the dispute.

(7) Describe any proposed actions that the Administrator should take to resolve the dispute and how these actions would provide the greatest level of highway safety without unreasonably burdening commerce and would ensure compliance with the Federal standards established in this subpart.

(c) **Notice.**

(1) Any State or Indian tribe that files a petition for dispute

resolution under this subpart shall mail a copy of the petition to any affected State, political subdivision, or Indian tribe, accompanied by a statement that the State, political subdivision, or Indian tribe may submit comments regarding the petition to the Administrator within 45 days.

(2) By serving notice on any other State, political subdivision, or Indian tribe determined by the Administrator to be possibly affected by the issues in dispute or the resolution sought, or by publication in the *Federal Register*, the Administrator may afford those persons an opportunity to file written comments on the petition.

(3) Any affected State, political subdivision, or Indian tribe submitting written comments to the Administrator with respect to a petition filed under this section shall send a copy of the comments to the petitioner and certify to the Administrator as to having complied with this requirement. The Administrator may notify other persons participating in the proceeding of the comments and provide an opportunity for those other persons to respond.

(d) **Court actions.** After a petition for dispute resolution is filed in accordance with this section, no court action may be brought with respect to the subject matter of such dispute until a final decision has been issued by the Administrator or until the last day of the one-year period beginning on the day the Administrator receives the petition, whichever occurs first.

(e) **Hearings; alternative dispute resolution.** Upon receipt of a petition filed pursuant to paragraph (a) of this section, the Administrator may schedule a hearing to attempt to resolve the dispute and, if a hearing is scheduled, will notify all parties to the dispute of the date, time, and place of the hearing. During the hearing the parties may offer any information pertinent to the resolution of the dispute. If an agreement is reached, it may be stipulated by the parties, in writing, and, if the Administrator agrees, made part of the decision in paragraph (f) of this section. If no agreement is reached, the Administrator may take the matter under consideration and announce his or her decision in accordance with paragraph (f) of this section. Nothing in this section shall be construed as prohibiting the parties from settling the dispute or seeking other methods of alternative dispute resolution prior to the final decision by the Administrator.

(f) **Decision.** The Administrator will issue a decision based on the petition, the written comments submitted by the parties, the record of the hearing, and any other information in the record. The decision will include a written statement setting forth the relevant facts and the legal basis for the decision.

(g) **Record.** The Administrator will serve a copy of the decision upon the petitioner and any other party who participated in the proceedings. A copy of each decision will be placed on file in the public docket. The Administrator may publish the decision or notice of the decision in the *Federal Register*.

§397.77 Judicial review of dispute decision.

Any State or Indian tribe adversely affected by the Administrator's decision under §397.75 of this subpart may seek review by the appropriate district court of the United States under such proceeding only by filing a petition with such court within 90 days after such decision becomes final.

Subpart D — Routing of Class 7 (Radioactive) Materials

§397.101 Requirements for motor carriers and drivers.

(a) Except as provided in paragraph (b) of this section or in circumstances when there is only one practicable highway route available, considering operating necessity and safety, a carrier or any person operating a motor vehicle that contains a Class 7 (radioactive) material, as defined in 49 CFR 172.403, for which placarding is required under 49 CFR part 172 shall:

(1) Ensure that the motor vehicle is operated on routes that minimize radiological risk;

(2) Consider available information on accident rates, transit time, population density and activities, and the time of day and the day of week during which transportation will occur to determine the level of radiological risk; and

(3) Tell the driver which route to take and that the motor vehicle contains Class 7 (radioactive) materials.

(b) Except as otherwise permitted in this paragraph and in paragraph (f) of this section, a carrier or any person operating a motor vehicle containing a highway route controlled quantity of Class 7 (radioactive) materials, as defined in 49 CFR 173.403(l), shall operate the motor vehicle only over preferred routes.

(1) For purposes of this subpart, a preferred route is an Interstate System highway for which an alternative route is not

designated by a State routing agency; a State-designated route selected by a State routing agency pursuant to §397.103; or both of the above.

(2) The motor carrier or the person operating a motor vehicle containing a highway route controlled quantity of Class 7 (radioactive) materials, as defined in 49 CFR 173.403(l) and (y), shall select routes to reduce time in transit over the preferred route segment of the trip. An Interstate System bypass or Interstate System beltway around a city, when available, shall be used in place of a preferred route through a city, unless a State routing agency has designated an alternative route.

(c) A motor vehicle may be operated over a route, other than a preferred route, only under the following conditions:

(1) The deviation from the preferred route is necessary to pick up or deliver a highway route controlled quantity of Class 7 (radioactive) materials, to make necessary rest, fuel or motor vehicle repair stops, or because emergency conditions make continued use of the preferred route unsafe or impossible;

(2) For pickup and delivery not over preferred routes, the route selected must be the shortest-distance route from the pickup location to the nearest preferred route entry location, and the shortest-distance route to the delivery location from the nearest preferred route exit location. Deviation from the shortest-distance pickup or delivery route is authorized if such deviation:

(i) Is based upon the criteria in paragraph (a) of this section to minimize the radiological risk; and

(ii) Does not exceed the shortest-distance pickup or delivery route by more than 25 miles and does not exceed 5 times the length of the shortest-distance pickup or delivery route.

(iii) Deviations from preferred routes, or pickup or delivery routes other than preferred routes, which are necessary for rest, fuel, or motor vehicle repair stops or because of emergency conditions, shall be made in accordance with the criteria in paragraph (a) of this section to minimize radiological risk, unless due to emergency conditions, time does not permit use of those criteria.

(d) A carrier (or a designated agent) who operates a motor vehicle which contains a package of highway route controlled quantity of Class 7 (radioactive) materials, as defined in 49 CFR 173.403(l), shall prepare a written route plan and supply a copy before departure to the motor vehicle driver and a copy to the shipper (before departure for exclusive use shipments, as defined in 49 CFR 173.403(i), or within fifteen working days following departure for all other shipments). Any variation between the route plan and routes actually used, and the reason for it, shall be reported in an amendment to the route plan delivered to the shipper as soon as practicable but within 30 days following the deviation. The route plan shall contain:

(1) A statement of the origin and destination points, a route selected in compliance with this section, all planned stops, and estimated departure and arrival times; and

(2) Telephone numbers which will access emergency assistance in each State to be entered.

(e) No person may transport a package of highway route controlled quantity of Class 7 (radioactive) materials on a public highway unless:

(1) The driver has received within the two preceding years, written training on:

(i) Requirements in 49 CFR parts 172, 173, and 177 pertaining to the Class 7 (radioactive) materials transported;

(ii) The properties and hazards of the Class 7 (radioactive) materials being transported; and

(iii) Procedures to be followed in case of an accident or other emergency.

(2) The driver has in his or her immediate possession a certificate of training as evidence of training required by this section, and a copy is placed in his or her qualification file (see §391.51 of this subchapter), showing:

(i) The driver's name and operator's license number;

(ii) The dates training was provided;

(iii) The name and address of the person providing the training;

(iv) That the driver has been trained in the hazards and characteristics of highway route controlled quantity of Class 7 (radioactive) materials; and

(v) A statement by the person providing the training that information on the certificate is accurate.

(3) The driver has in his or her immediate possession the route plan required by paragraph (d) of this section and operates the motor vehicle in accordance with the route plan.

(f) A person may transport irradiated reactor fuel only in compliance with a plan if required under 49 CFR 173.22(c) that will ensure the physical security of the material. Variation for security purposes from the requirements of this section is permitted so far as necessary to meet the requirements imposed under such a plan, or otherwise imposed by the U.S. Nuclear Regulatory Commission in 10 CFR part 73.

(g) Expect for packages shipped in compliance with the physical security requirements of the U.S. Nuclear Regulatory Commission in 10 CFR part 73, each carrier who accepts for transportation a highway route controlled quantity of Class 7 (radioactive) material (see 49 CFR 173.401 (l)), shall, within 90 days following the acceptance of the package, file the following information concerning the transportation of each such package with the Associate Administrator for Safety and System Applications, Federal Highway Administration, Attn: Traffic Control Division, HHS-32, room 3419, 400 Seventh Street, SW., Washington, DC 20590-0001:

(1) The route plan required under paragraph (d) of this section including all required amendments reflecting the routes actually used;

(2) A statement identifying the names and addresses of the shipper, carrier and consignee; and

(3) A copy of the shipping paper or the description of the Class 7 (radioactive) material in the shipment required by 49 CFR 172.202 and 172.203.

§397.103 Requirements for State routing designations.

(a) The State routing agency, as defined in §397.201(c), shall select routes to minimize radiological risk using "Guidelines for Selecting Preferred Highway Routes for Highway Route Controlled Quantity Shipments of Radioactive Materials," or an equivalent routing analysis which adequately considers overall risk to the public. Designations must be preceded by substantive consultation with affected local jurisdictions and with any other affected States to ensure consideration of all impacts and continuity of designated routes.

(b) State routing agencies may designate preferred routes as an alternative to, or in addition to, one or more Interstate System highways, including interstate system bypasses, or Interstate System beltways.

(c) A State-designated route is effective when—

(1) The State gives written notice by certified mail, return receipt requested, to the Associated Administrator for Safety and System Applications, Federal Highway Administration, Attn:

Traffic Control Division, HHS-32, Room 3419, Registry of State-designated routes, at the address above; and

(2) Receipt thereof is acknowledged in writing by the Associate Administrator.

(d) Upon request, the Office of Highway Safety, Traffic Control Division, HHS-32, room 3419, at the address above, will provide a list of State-designated preferred routes and a copy of the "Guidelines for Selecting Preferred Highway Routes for Highway Route Controlled Quantity Shipments of Radioactive Materials."

Subpart E — Preemption Procedures

§397.201 Purpose and scope of the procedures.

(a) This subpart prescribes procedures by which:

(1) Any person, including a State, political subdivision thereof, or Indian tribe, directly affected by any highway routing designation for hazardous materials may apply to the Administrator for a determination as to whether that highway routing designation is preempted under 49 U.S.C. §5125, or §397.69 or §397.203 of this part; and

(2) A State, political subdivision thereof, or Indian tribe may apply to the Administrator for a waiver of preemption with respect to any highway routing designation that the State, political subdivision thereof, or Indian tribe acknowledges to be preempted by 49 U.S.C. §5125, or §397.69 or §397.203 of this part, or that has been determined by a court of competent jurisdiction to be so preempted.

(b) Unless otherwise ordered by the Administrator, an application for a preemption determination which includes an application for a waiver of preemption will be treated and processed solely as an application for a preemption determination.

(c) For purposes of this subpart:

Act means 49 U.S.C. §5101 *et seq.*, formerly known as the Hazardous Materials Transportation Act.

Administrator means the Federal Highway Administrator, who is the chief executive of the Federal Highway Administration, an agency of the United States Department of Transportation, or his/her designate.

Hazardous material means a substance or material, including a hazardous substance, which has been determined by the Secretary of Transportation to be capable of posing an unreasonable risk to health, safety, or property, when transported in commerce, and which has been so designated.

Indian tribe has the same meaning as contained in §4 of the Indian Self-Determination and Education Act, 25 U.S.C. 450b.

Person means an individual, firm, copartnership, corporation, company, association, joint-stock association, including any trustee, receiver, assignee, or similar representative thereof, or government, Indian tribe, or agency or instrumentality of any government or Indian tribe when it offers hazardous materials for transportation in commerce or transports hazardous materials in furtherance of a commercial enterprise, but such term does not include the United States Postal Service.

Political subdivision includes a municipality; a public agency or other instrumentality of one or more States, or a public corporation, board, or commission established under the laws of one or more States.

Routing agency means the State highway agency or other State agency designated by the Governor of a State, or an agency designated by an Indian tribe, to supervise, coordinate, and approve the highway routing designations for that State or Indian tribe. Any highway routing designation made by a political subdivision of a State shall be considered a designation made by that State.

Routing designation includes any regulation, limitation, restriction, curfew, time of travel restriction, lane restriction, routing ban, port-of-entry designation, or route weight restriction applicable to the highway transportation of hazardous materials over a specific highway route or portion of a route.

State means a State of the United States, the District of Columbia, the Commonwealth of Puerto Rico, the Commonwealth of the Northern Mariana Islands, the Virgin Islands, American Samoa, Guam, or any other territory of possession of the United States designated by the Secretary.

§397.203 Standards for determining preemption.

(a) Any highway routing designation established, maintained, or enforced by a State, political subdivision thereof, or Indian tribe is preempted if—

(1) Compliance with both the highway routing designation and any requirement under the Act or of a regulation issued under the Act is not possible;

(2) The highway routing designation as applied or enforced creates an obstacle to the accomplishment and execution of the Act or the regulations issued under the Act; or

(3) The highway routing designation is preempted pursuant to §397.69(b) of this part.

(b) [Reserved]

§397.205 Preemption application.

(a) Any person, including a State, political subdivision thereof, or Indian tribe directly affected by any highway routing designation of another State, political subdivision, or Indian tribe, may apply to the Administrator for a determination of whether that highway routing designation is preempted by the Act or §397.203 of this subpart. The Administrator shall publish notice of the application in the *Federal Register.*

(b) Each application filed under this section for a determination must:

(1) Be submitted to the Administrator, Federal Highway Administration, U.S. Department of Transportation, Washington, DC 20590-0001. Attention: HCC-10 Docket Room, Hazardous Materials Preemption;

(2) Set forth a detailed description of the highway routing designation of the State, political subdivision thereof, or Indian tribe for which the determination is sought;

(3) If applicable, specify the provisions of the Act or the regulations issued under the Act under which the applicant seeks preemption of the highway routing designation of the State, political subdivision thereof, or Indian tribe;

(4) Explain why the applicant believes the highway routing designation of the State, political subdivision thereof, or Indian tribe should or should not be preempted under the standards of §397.203; and

(5) State how the applicant is affected by the highway routing designation of the State, political subdivision thereof, or Indian tribe.

(c) The filing of an application for a determination under this section does not constitute grounds for noncompliance with any requirement of the Act or any regulation issued under the Act.

(d) Once the Administrator has published notice in the *Federal Register* of an application received under paragraph (a) of this section, no applicant for such determination may seek relief with respect to the same or substantially the same issue in any court until final action has been taken on the application or until 180 days after filing of the application, whichever occurs first. Nothing in this section shall be construed as prohibiting any person, including a State, political subdivision thereof, or Indian tribe, directly affected by any highway routing designation from seeking a determination of preemption in any court of competent jurisdiction in lieu of applying to the Administrator under paragraph (a) of this section.

§397.207 Preemption notice.

(a) If the applicant is other than a State, political subdivision thereof, or Indian tribe, the applicant shall mail a copy of the application to the State, political subdivision thereof, or Indian tribe concerned, accompanied by a statement that comments may be submitted regarding the application to the Administrator within 45 days. The application filed with the Administrator must include a certification that the applicant has complied with this paragraph and must include the names and addresses of each official to whom a copy of the application was sent.

(b) The Administrator may afford interested persons an opportunity to file written comments on the application by serving notice on any persons readily identifiable by the Administrator as persons who will be affected by the ruling sought or by publication in the *Federal Register*.

(c) Each person submitting written comments to the Administrator with respect to an application filed under this section shall send a copy of the comments to the applicant and certify to the Administrator that he or she has complied with this requirement. The Administrator may notify other persons participating in the proceeding of the comments and provide an opportunity for those other persons to respond.

§397.209 Preemption processing.

(a) The Administrator may initiate an investigation of any statement in an application and utilize in his or her evaluation any relevant facts obtained by that investigation. The Administrator may solicit and accept submissions from third persons relevant to an application and will provide the applicant an opportunity to respond to all third person submissions. In evaluating an application, the Administrator may consider any other source of information. The Administrator may convene a hearing or conference, if a hearing or conference will advance the evaluation of the application.

(b) The Administrator may dismiss the application without prejudice if:

(1) He or she determines that there is insufficient information upon which to base a determination; or

(2) He or she requests additional information from the applicant and it is not submitted.

§397.211 Preemption determination.

(a) Upon consideration of the application and other relevant information received, the Administrator issued a determination.

(b) Notwithstanding that an application for a determination has not been filed under §397.205, the Administrator, on his or her own initiative, may issue a determination as to whether a particular highway routing designation of a State, political subdivision thereof, or Indian tribe is preempted under the Act or the regulations issued under the Act.

(c) The determination includes a written statement setting forth the relevant facts and the legal basis for the determination, and provides that any person aggrieved thereby may file a petition for reconsideration within 20 days in accordance with §397.223.

(d) Unless the determination is issued pursuant to paragraph (b) of this section, the Administrator serves a copy of the determination upon the applicant. In all preemption determinations, the Administrator serves a copy of the determination upon any other person who participated in the proceeding or who is readily identifiable by the Administrator as affected by the determination. A copy of each determination is placed on file in the public docket. The Administrator may publish the determination or notice of the determination in the *Federal Register*.

(e) If no petition for reconsideration is filed within 20 days in accordance with §397.223, a determination issued under this section constitutes the final agency decision as to whether a particular highway routing designation of a State, political subdivision thereof, or Indian tribe is preempted under the Act or regulations issued thereunder. The fact that a determination has not been issued under this section with respect to a particular highway routing designation of a State, political subdivision thereof, or Indian tribe carries no implication as to whether the requirement is preempted under the Act or regulations issued thereunder.

§397.213 Waiver of preemption application.

(a) Any State, political subdivision thereof, or Indian tribe may apply to the Administrator for a waiver of preemption with respect to any highway routing designation that the State, political subdivision thereof, or Indian tribe acknowledges to be preempted by the Act, §397.203 of this subpart, or a court of competent jurisdiction. The Administrator may waive preemption with respect to such requirement upon a determination that such requirement—

(1) Affords an equal or greater level of protection to the public than is afforded by the requirements of the Act or regulations issued under the Act, and

(2) Does not unreasonably burden commerce.

(b) Each application filed under this section for a waiver of preemption determination must:

(1) Be submitted to the Administrator, Federal Highway Administration, U.S. Department of Transportation, Washington, DC 20590-0001. Attention: HCC-10 Docket Room, Hazardous Materials Preemption Docket;

(2) Set forth a detailed description of the highway routing designation of the State, political subdivision thereof, or Indian tribe for which the determination is being sought;

(3) Include a copy of any relevant court order or determination issued pursuant to §397.211;

(4) Contain an express acknowledgment by the applicant that the highway routing designation of the State, political subdivision thereof, or Indian tribe is preempted under the Act or the regulations issued under the Act, unless it has been so determined by a court of competent jurisdiction or in a determination issued under this subpart;

(5) Specify each provision of the Act or the regulations issued under the Act that preempts the highway routing designation of the State, political subdivision thereof, or Indian tribe;

(6) State why the applicant believes that the highway routing designation of the State, political subdivision thereof, or Indian tribe affords an equal or greater level of protection to the public than is afforded by the requirements of the Act or the regulations issued under the Act;

(7) State why the applicant believes that the highway routing designation of the State, political subdivision thereof, or In-

dian tribe does not unreasonably burden commerce; and

(8) Specify what steps the State, political subdivision thereof, or Indian tribe is taking to administer and enforce effectively the preempted requirement.

§397.215 Waiver notice.

(a) The applicant State, political subdivision thereof, or Indian tribe shall mail a copy of the application and any subsequent amendments or other documents relating to the application to each person whom the applicant reasonably ascertains will be affected by the determination sought. The copy of the application must be accompanied by a statement that the person may submit comments regarding the application to the Administrator within 45 days. The application filed with the Administrator must include a certification with the application has complied with this paragraph and must include the names and addresses of each person to whom the application was sent.

(b) Notwithstanding the provisions of paragraph (a) of this section, if the State, political subdivision thereof, or Indian tribe determines that compliance with paragraph (a) of this section would be impracticable, the applicant shall:

(1) Comply with the requirements of paragraph (a) of this section with regard to those persons whom it is reasonable and practicable to notify; and

(2) Include with the application filed with the Administrator a description of the persons or class or classes of persons to whom notice was not sent.

(c) The Administrator may require the applicant to provide notice in addition to that required by paragraphs (a) and (b) of this section, or may determine that the notice required by paragraph (a) of this section is not impracticable, or that notice should be published in the *Federal Register*.

(d) The Administrator may serve notice on any other persons readily identifiable by the Administrator as persons who will be affected by the determination sought and may afford those persons an opportunity to file written comments on the application.

(e) Any person submitting written comments to the Administrator with respect to an application filed under this section shall send a copy of the comments to the applicant. The person shall certify to the Administrator that he or she has complied with the requirements of this paragraph. The Administrator may notify other persons participating in the proceeding of the comments and provide an opportunity for those persons to respond.

§397.217 Waiver processing.

(a) The Administrator may initiate an investigation of any statement in an application and utilize any relevant facts obtained by that investigation. The Administrator may solicit and accept submissions from third persons relevant to an application and will provide the applicant an opportunity to respond to all third person submissions. In evaluating an application, the Administrator may convene a hearing or conference, if a hearing or conference will advance the evaluation of the application.

(b) The Administrator may dismiss the application without prejudice if:

(1) He or she determines that there is insufficient information upon which to base a determination;

(2) Upon his or her request, additional information is not submitted by the applicant; or

(3) The applicant fails to provide the notice required by this subpart.

(c) Except as provided in this subpart, the Administrator will only consider an application for a waiver of preemption determination if:

(1) The applicant expressly acknowledges in its application that the highway routing designation of the State, political subdivision thereof, or Indian tribe for which the determination is sought is preempted by the Act or the regulations thereunder; or

(2) The highway routing designation of the State, political subdivision thereof, or Indian tribe has been determined by a court of competent jurisdiction or in a determination issued pursuant to §397.211 to be preempted by the Act or the regulations issued thereunder.

(d) When the Administrator has received all substantive information necessary to process an application for a waiver of preemption determination, notice of that fact will be served upon the applicant. Additional notice to all other persons who received notice of the proceeding may be served by publishing a notice in the *Federal Register.*

§397.219 Waiver determination and order.

(a) Upon consideration of the application and other relevant information received or obtained during the proceeding, the Administrator issued an order setting forth his or her determination.

(b) The Adminshe finds that the requirement of the State, political subdivision thereof, or Indian tribe affords the public a level of safety at least equistrator may issue a waiver of pre-emption order only if he or al to that afforded by the requirements of the Act and the regulations issued under the Act and does not unreasonably burden commerce. In determining whether the requirement of the State, political subdivision thereof, or Indian tribe unreasonably burdens commerce, the Administrator may consider the following factors:

(1) The extent to which increased costs and impairment of efficiency result from the highway routing designation of the State, political subdivision thereof, or Indian tribe;

(2) Whether the highway routing designation of the State, political subdivision thereof, or Indian tribe has a rational basis;

(3) Whether the highway routing designation of the State, political subdivision thereof, or Indian tribe achieves its stated purpose; and

(4) Whether there is need for uniformity with regard to the subject concerned and if so, whether the highway routing designation of the State, political subdivision thereof, or Indian tribe competes or conflicts with those of other States, political subdivisions thereof, or Indian tribes.

(c) The order includes a written statement setting forth the relevant facts and the legal basis for the determination, and provides that any person aggrieved by the order may file a petition for reconsideration in accordance with §397.223.

(d) The Administrator serves a copy of the order upon the applicant, any other person who participated in the proceeding and upon any other person readily identifiable by the Administrator as one who may be affected by the order. A copy of each order is placed on file in the public docket. The Administrator may publish the order or notice of the order in the *Federal Register*.

(e) If no petition for reconsideration is filed within 20 days in accordance with §397.223, an order issued under this section constitutes the final agency decision regarding whether a particular requirement of a State, political subdivision thereof, or Indian tribe is preempted under the Act or any regulations issued thereunder, or whether preemption is waived.

§397.221 Timeliness.

If the Administrator fails to take action on the application within 90 days of serving the notice required by §397.217(d), the applicant may treat the application as having been denied in all respects.

§397.223 Petition for reconsideration.

(a) Any person aggrieved by an order issued under §397.211 or §397.219 may file a petition for reconsideration with the Administrator. The petition must be filed within 20 days of service of the determination or order issued under the above sections.

(b) The petition must contain a concise statement of the basis for seeking reconsideration, including any specific factual or legal errors, or material information not previously available.

(c) The petitioner shall mail a copy of the petition to each person who participated, either as an applicant or routing, in the waiver of preemption proceeding, accompanied by a statement that the person may submit comments concerning the petition to the Administrator within 20 days. The petition filed with the Administrator must contain a certification that the petitioner has complied with this paragraph and include the names and addresses of all persons to whom a copy of the petition was sent.

(d) The Administrator's decision under this section constitutes the final agency decision. If no petition for reconsideration is filed under this section, then the determination issued under §397.211 or §397.219 becomes the final agency decision at the end of the 20 day period.

§397.225 Judicial review.

A party to a proceeding under §397.205(a), §397.213(a), or §397.223(a) may seek review by the appropriate district court of the United States of the decision of the Administrator under such proceeding only by filing a petition with such court within 60 days after the final agency decision.

PART 399 — EMPLOYEE SAFETY AND HEALTH STANDARDS

Subparts A Through K [Reserved]

Subpart L — Step, Handhold, and Deck Requirements for Commercial Motor Vehicles

Sec.
399.201 Purpose and scope.
399.203 Applicability.
399.205 Definitions.
399.207 Truck and truck-tractor access requirements.
399.209 Test procedures.
399.211 Maintenance.

AUTHORITY: 49 U.S.C. 304; 1655; 49 CFR 1.48 and 301.60.

Subparts A — K [Reserved]

Subpart L — Step, Handhold, and Deck Requirements for Commercial Motor Vehicles

§399.201 Purpose and scope.

This subpart prescribes step, handhold, and deck requirements on commercial motor vehicles. These requirements are intended to enhance the safety of motor carrier employees.

§399.203 Applicability.

This subpart applies to all trucks and truck-tractors, having a high profile cab-over-engine (COE) configuration, for entrance, egress and back of cab access, manufactured on and after September 1, 1982.

§399.205 Definitions.

Cab-over-engine (COE) — A truck or truck-tractor having all, or the front portion, of the engine under the cab.

COE - High profile — A COE having the door sill step above the height of the front tires.

Deck plate — A horizontal surface designed to provide a person with stable footing for the performance of work such as the connection and disconnection of air and electrical lines, gaining access to permanently-mounted equipment or machinery or for similar needs.

Door sill step — Any step normally protected from the elements by the cab door when closed.

Effective peripheral grip — Any shaped surface, free of sharp edges, in which a full grasp can be made to secure a handhold by a person.

Fingertip grasp — A handhold surface which provides a person contact restricted to finger segments 1 and/or 2 only; or which limits wrap-around closure of finger segment 1 with the palm of the hand to 90 degrees as shown in Illustration I.

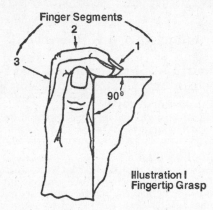

**Illustration I
Fingertip Grasp**

Full grasp — A handhold surface which provides a person contact with finger segments 2 and 3 and which provides space for finger segment 1 to wrap around toward the palm of the hand beyond the 90-degree surface restriction shown in Illustration I. The handhold need not require contact between fingers and thumb. For example, the hand position shown in Illustration II qualifies as full grasp.

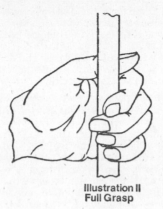

**Illustration II
Full Grasp**

Ground — The flat horizontal surface on which the tires of a motor vehicle rest.

Handhold — That which qualifies as providing full grasp if a person is able to find a hand position on the handhold which allows more than fingertip grasp.

Handprint — The surface area contacted by the hand when grasping a handhold. The size of this area is the width of the hand across the metacarpal and half the circumference of the handhold. The hand breadth of the typical person is 88.9 millimeters (3.5 inches).

Person — Any individual within the 5th percentile female adult through the 95th percentile male adult of anthropometric measures as described by the 1962 Health Examination Survey, "Weight, Height and Selected Body Dimensions of Adults, United States 1960-1962" which is incorporated by reference. It is Public Health Service publication No. 1000-Series 11-No. 8 and is for sale from the U.S. Department of Commerce, National Technical Information Service, 5285 Port Royal Road, Springfield, Virginia 22161. When ordering use NTIS Accession No. PB 267174. It is also available for inspection at the Office of the Federal Register Library, Room 8301, 1100 L Street, NW, Washington, D.C. 20408. This incorporation by reference was approved by the Director of the Federal Register on July 17, 1979. These materials are incorporated as they exist on the date of the approval and a notice of any change in these materials will be published in the *Federal Register*.

Slip resistant material — Any material designed to minimize the accumulation of grease, ice, mud and other debris and afford protection from accidental slipping.

§399.207 Truck and truck-tractor access requirements.

(a) **General rule.** Any person entering or exiting the cab or accessing the rear portion of a high profile COE truck or truck-tractor shall be afforded sufficient steps and handholds, and/or deck plates to allow the user to have at least 3 limbs in contact with the truck or truck-tractor at any time. This rule applies to intermediate positions as well as transition between intermediate positions. To allow for changes in climbing sequence, the step design shall include, as a minimum, one intermediate step of sufficient size to accommodate two feet. **Exception.** If air and electrical connections necessary to couple or uncouple a truck-tractor from a trailer are accessible from the ground, no step, handholds, or deck plates are required to permit access to the rear of the cab.

(b) **Performance requirements.** All high profile COE trucks or truck-tractors shall be equipped on each side of the vehicle where a seat is located, with a sufficient number of steps and handholds to conform with the requirements of paragraph (a) of this section and shall meet the performance requirements:

(1) **Vertical height.** All measurements of vertical height shall be made from ground level with the vehicle at unladen weight.

(2) **Distance between steps.** The distance between steps, up to and including the door sill step, shall provide any person a stable resting position which can be sustained without body motion and by exerting no more arm force than 35 percent of the person's body weight per grasp during all stages of entry and exit. This criterion applies to intermediate positions as well as transition between intermediate positions above ground level.

(i) When the ground provides the person foot support during entry or is the final step in the sequence during exit, and the step is 508 millimeters (20 inches) or more above ground, the stable resting position shall be achievable by the person using both hands to grasp the handhold(s) and requiring no more arm force than 35 percent of body weight per grasp.

(ii) The vertical height of the first step shall be no more than 609 millimeters (24 inches) from ground level.

(3) **Construction.** Each step or deck plate shall be of a slip resistant design which minimizes the accumulation of foreign material. Wherever practicable, a self-cleaning material should be used.

(4) **Foot accommodation.** Step depth or clearance and step width necessary to accommodate a climbing person are defined by using a minimum 127 millimeter (5 inch) diameter disc as shown in Illustration III.

(i) **Single foot accomodation.** The disc shall fit on a tread rung, or in a step recess, with no exterior overhang.

(ii) **Two-foot accommodations.** Two discs shall fit on a tread rung, or in a step recess, with no exterior overhang.

Single - foot Accommodation

Two - foot Accommodation

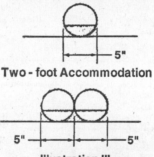

**Illustration III
Foot Accommodation**

Note: The 127 millimeter (5 inch) disc is only intended to test for a minimum depth and width requirement. The step need not retain the disc at rest.

(5) **Step strength.** Each step must withstand a vertical static load of at least 204 kilograms (450 pounds) uniformly distributed over any 127 millimeter (5 inch) increment of step width.

(6) **Handhold location.** A handhold must be located within

the reach of any person entering or exiting the vehicle.

(7) **Exterior mounting specifications for handholds.** Each handhold, affixed to the exterior of the vehicle, shall have at least 38 millimeters (1.5 inches) clearance between the handhold and the surface to which it is mounted for the distance between its mounting points.

(8) **Handhold size and shape.** Each handhold shall be free of sharp edges (minimum 1 millimeter [0.04 inch] radius) and have an effective peripheral grip length that permits full grasp by any person.

(9) **Handhold strength.** Each handhold shall withstand a horizontal static load of at least 114 kilograms (250 pounds) uniformly distributed over the area of a hand print and applied away from the mounting surface.

(10) **Deck plates.** Deck plates shall be on the rear of a truck-tractor as necessary to couple or uncouple air and/or electrical connections.

(11) **Deck plate strength.** Each deck plate shall be capable of withstanding the vertical static load of a least 205 kilograms (450 pounds) uniformly distributed over a 127 millimeter (5 inch) diameter disc.

§399.209 Test procedures.

(a) The force exerted on a handhold will be measured using a handheld spring scale or force transducer which can be attached to the vehicle and is free to rotate into alignment with a person's hand position.

(b) Hand grasp will be evaluated by observing the handgrip of any individual who conforms with the definition of "person" appearing in §399.205 of this subpart.

§399.211 Maintenance.

All steps, handholds, and/or deck plates required by this subpart shall be adequately maintained to serve their intended function.

PART 40
PROCEDURES FOR TRANSPORTATION WORKPLACE DRUG AND ALCOHOL TESTING PROGRAMS

Subpart A — General

Subpart B — Drug Testing

Subpart C — Alcohol Testing

Authority: 49 U.S.C. 102, 301, 322, 5331, 20140, 31306, and 45101 *et. seq.*

Subpart A — General

§40.1 Applicability.

This part applies, through regulations that reference it issued by agencies of the Department of Transportation, to transportation employers, including self-employed individuals, required to conduct drug and/or alcohol testing programs by DOT agency regulations and to such transportation employers' officers, employees, agents and contractors (including, but not limited to, consortia). Employers are responsible for the compliance of their officers, employees, agents, consortia and/or contractors with the requirements of this part.

§40.3 Definitions.

The following definitions apply to this part:

Air blank. A reading by an EBT of ambient air containing no alcohol. (In EBTs using gas chromatography technology, a reading of the device's internal standard.)

Alcohol. The intoxicating agent in beverage alcohol, ethyl alcohol or other low molecular weight alcohols including methyl or isopropyl alcohol.

Alcohol concentration. The alcohol in a volume of breath expressed in terms of grams of alcohol per 210 liters of breath as indicated by a breath test under this part.

Alcohol use. The consumption of any beverage, mixture or preparation, including any medication, containing alcohol.

Aliquot. A portion of a specimen used for testing.

Blind sample or blind performance test specimen. A urine specimen submitted to a laboratory for quality control testing purposes, with a fictitious identifier, so that the laboratory cannot distinguish it from employee specimens, and which is spiked with known quantities of specific drugs or which is blank, containing no drugs.

Breath Alcohol Technician (BAT). An individual who instructs and assists individuals in the alcohol testing process and operates an EBT.

Canceled or invalid test. In drug testing, a drug test that has been declared invalid by a Medical Review Officer. A canceled test is neither a positive nor a negative test. For purposes of this part, a sample that has been rejected for testing by a laboratory is treated the same as a canceled test. In alcohol testing, a test that is deemed to be invalid under §40.79. It is neither a positive nor a negative test.

Chain of custody. Procedures to account for the integrity of each urine or blood specimen by tracking its handling and storage from point of specimen collection to final disposition of the specimen. With respect to drug testing, these procedures shall require that an appropriate drug testing custody form (see §40.23(a)) be used from time of collection to receipt by the laboratory and that upon receipt by the laboratory an appropriate laboratory chain of custody form(s) account(s) for the sample or sample aliquots within the laboratory.

Collection container. A container into which the employee urinates to provide the urine sample used for a drug test.

Collection site. A place designated by the employer where individuals present themselves for the purpose of providing a specimen of their urine to be analyzed for the presence of drugs.

Collection site person. A person who instructs and assists individuals at a collection site and who receives and makes a screening examination of the urine specimen provided by those individuals.

Confirmation (or confirmatory) test. In drug testing, a second analytical procedure to identify the presence of a specific drug or metabolite that is independent of the screening test and that uses a different technique and chemical principle from that of the screening test in order to ensure reliability and accuracy. (Gas chromatography/mass spectrometry (GC/MS) is the only authorized confirmation method for cocaine, marijuana, opiates, amphetamines, and phencyclidine.) In alcohol testing, a second test, following a screening test with a result of 0.02 or greater, that provides quantitative data of alcohol concentration.

DHHS. The Department of Health and Human Services or any designee of the Secretary, Department of Health and Human Services.

DOT agency. An agency of the United States Department of Transportation administering regulations related to drug or alcohol testing, including the United States Coast Guard (for drug testing purposes only), the Federal Aviation Administration, the Federal Railroad Administration, the Federal Highway Administration, the Federal Transit Administration, the Research and Special Programs Administration, and the Office of the Secretary.

Employee. An individual designated in a DOT agency regulation as subject to drug testing and/or alcohol testing. As used in this part "employee" includes an applicant for employment. "Employee" and "individual" or "individual to be tested" have the same meaning for purposes of this part.

Employer. An entity employing one or more employees that is subject to DOT agency regulations requiring compliance with this part. As used in this part, **employer** includes an industry consortium or joint enterprise comprised of two or more employing entities.

EBT (or evidential breath testing device). An EBT approved by the National Highway Traffic Safety Administration (NHTSA) for the evidential testing of breath and placed on NHTSA's "Conforming Products List of Evidential Breath Measurement Devices" (CPL), and identified on the CPL as conforming with the model specifications available from the National Highway Traffic Safety Administration, Office of Alcohol and State Programs.

Medical Review Officer (MRO). A licensed physician (medical doctor or doctor of osteopathy) responsible for receiving laboratory results generated by an employer's drug testing program who has knowledge of substance abuse disorders and has appropriate medical training to interpret and evaluate an individual's confirmed positive test result together with his or her medical history and any other relevant biomedical information.

Screening test (or initial test). In drug testing, an immunoassay screen to eliminate "negative" urine specimens from further analysis. In alcohol testing, an analytic procedure to determine whether an employee may have a prohibited concentration of alcohol in a breath specimen.

Secretary. The Secretary of Transportation or the Secretary's designee.

Shipping container. A container capable of being secured with a tamper-evident seal that is used for transfer of one or more urine specimen bottle(s) and associated documentation from the collection site to the laboratory.

Specimen bottle. The bottle that, after being labeled and sealed according to the procedures in this part, is used to transmit a urine sample to the laboratory.

Substance abuse professional. A licensed physician (Medical Doctor or Doctor of Osteopathy); or a licensed or certified psychologist, social worker, or employee assistance professional; or an addiction counselor (certified by the National Association of Alcoholism and Drug Abuse Counselors Certification Commission or by the International Certification Reciprocity Consortium/Alcohol & Other Drug Abuse). All must have knowledge of and clinical experience in the diagnosis and treatment of alcohol and controlled substances-related disorders.

§§40.5 - 40.19 [Reserved]

Subpart B — Drug Testing

§40.21 The drugs.

(a) DOT agency drug testing programs require that employers test for marijuana, cocaine, opiates, amphetamines and phencyclidine.

(b) An employer may include in its testing protocols other controlled substances or alcohol only pursuant to a DOT agency approval, if testing for those substances is authorized under agency regulations and if the DHHS has established an approved testing protocol and positive threshold for each such substance.

(c) Urine specimens collected under DOT agency regulations requiring compliance with this part may only be used to test for controlled substances designated or approved for testing as described in this section and shall not be used to conduct any other analysis or test unless otherwise specifically authorized by DOT agency regulations.

(d) This section does not prohibit procedures reasonably incident to analysis of the specimen for controlled substance (e.g., determination of pH or tests for specific gravity, creatinine concentration or presence of adulterants).

§40.23 Preparation for testing.

The employer and certified laboratory shall develop and maintain a clear and well-documented procedure for collection, shipment, and accessioning of urine specimens under this part. Such a procedure shall include, at a minimum, the following:

(a)(1) Except as provided in paragraph (a)(2) of this section, use of the drug testing form prescribed under this part.

(i) This form is found in Appendix A to this part.

(ii) Employers and other participants in the DOT drug testing program may not modify or revise this form, except that the drug testing custody and control form may include such additional information as may be required for billing or other legitimate purposes necessary to the collection, provided that personal identifying information on the donor (other than the social security number or other employee ID number) may not be provided to the laboratory.

(iii) Donor medical information may appear only on the copy provided the donor.

(2) Notwithstanding the requirement of paragraph (a)(1)(ii) of this section, employers and other participants may use existing forms that were in use in the DOT drug testing program prior to February 16, 1995, until June 1, 1995.

(b)(1) Use of a clean, single-use specimen bottle that is securely wrapped until filled with the specimen. A clean, single-use collection container (e.g., disposable cup or sterile urinal) that is securely wrapped until used may also be employed. *If urination is directly into the specimen bottle*, the specimen bottle shall be provided to the employee still sealed in its wrapper or shall be unwrapped in the employee's presence immediately prior to its being provided. *If a separate collection container is used for urination,* the collection container shall be provided to the employee still sealed in its wrapper or shall be unwrapped in the employee's presence immediately prior to its being provided; and the collection site person shall unwrap the specimen bottle in the presence of the employee at the time the urine specimen is presented.

(2) Use of a tamperproof sealing system, designed in a manner such to ensure against undetected opening. The specimen bottle shall be identified with a unique identifying number identical to that appearing on the urine custody and control form, and space shall be provided to initial the bottle affirming its identity. For purposes of clarity, this part assumes use of a system made up of one or more preprinted labels and seals (or a unitary label/seal), but use of other, equally effective technologies is authorized.

(c) Use of a shipping container in which the specimen and associated paperwork may be transferred and which can be sealed and initialled to prevent undetected tampering. If the split specimen option is exercised, the split specimen and associated paperwork shall be sealed in a shipping (or storage) container and initialled to prevent undetected tampering.

(d) Written procedures, instructions and training shall be provided as follows:

(1) Employer collection procedures and training shall clearly emphasize that the collection site person is responsible for maintaining the integrity of the specimen collection and transfer process, carefully ensuring the modesty and privacy of the donor, and is to avoid any conduct or remarks that might be construed as accusatorial or otherwise offensive or inappropriate.

(2) A collection site person shall have successfully completed training to carry out this function or shall be a licensed medical professional or technician who is provided instructions for collection under this part and certifies completion as required in this part.

(i) A non-medical collection site person shall receive training in compliance with this part and shall demonstrate proficiency in the application of this part prior to serving as a collection site person. A medical professional, technologist or technician licensed or otherwise approved to practice in the jurisdiction in which the collection takes place is not required to receive such training if that person is provided instructions described in this part and performs collections in accordance with those instructions.

(ii) Collection site persons shall be provided with detailed, clear instructions on the collection of specimens in compliance with this part. Employer representatives and donors subject to testing shall also be provided standard written instructions setting forth their responsibilities.

(3) Unless it is impracticable for any other individual to perform this function, a direct supervisor of an employee shall not serve as the collection site person for a test of the employee. If the rules of a DOT agency are more stringent than this provision regarding the use of supervisors as collection site personnel, the DOT agency rules shall prevail with respect to testing to which they apply.

(4) In any case where a collection is monitored by non-medical personnel or is directly observed, the collection site person shall be of the same gender as the donor. A collection is monitored for this purpose if the enclosure provides less than complete privacy for the donor (e.g., if a restroom stall is used and the collection site person remains in the restroom, or if the collection site person is expected to listen for use of unsecured sources of water.)

§40.25 Specimen collection procedures.

(a) **Designation of collection site.** (1) Each employer drug testing program shall have one or more designated collection sites which have all necessary personnel, materials, equipment, facilities and supervision to provide for the collection, security, temporary storage, and shipping or transportation of urine specimens to a certified drug testing laboratory. An independent medical facility may also be utilized as a collection site provided the other applicable requirements of this part are met.

(2) A designated collection site may be any suitable location where a specimen can be collected under conditions set forth in this part, including a properly equipped mobile facility. A designated collection site shall be a location having an enclosure within which private urination can occur, a toilet for completion of urination (unless a single-use collector is used with sufficient capacity to contain the void), and a suitable clean surface for writing. The site must also have a source of water for washing hands, which, if practicable, should be external to the enclosure where urination occurs.

(b) **Security.** The purpose of this paragraph is to prevent unauthorized access which could compromise the integrity of the collection process or the specimen.

(1) Procedures shall provide for the designated collection site

to be secured. If a collection site facility is dedicated solely to urine collection, it shall be secure at all times. If a facility cannot be dedicated solely to drug testing, the portion of the facility used for testing shall be secured during drug testing.

(2) A facility normally used for other purposes, such as a public rest room or hospital examining room, may be secured by visual inspection to ensure other persons are not present and undetected access (e.g., through a rear door not in the view of the collection site person) is not possible. Security during collection may be maintained by effective restriction of access to collection materials and specimens. In the case of a public rest room, the facility must be posted against access during the entire collection procedure to avoid embarrassment to the employee or distraction of the collection site person.

(3) If it is impractical to maintain continuous physical security of a collection site from the time the specimen is presented until the sealed mailer is transferred for shipment, the following minimum procedures shall apply. The specimen shall remain under the direct control of the collection site person from delivery to its being sealed in the mailer. The mailer shall be immediately mailed, maintained in secure storage, or remain until mailed under the personal control of the collection site person.

(c) **Chain of custody**. The chain of custody block of the drug testing custody and control form shall be properly executed by authorized collection site personnel upon receipt of specimens. Handling and transportation of urine specimens from one authorized individual or place to another shall always be accomplished through chain of custody procedures. Since specimens and documentation are sealed in shipping containers that would indicate any tampering during transit to the laboratory and couriers, express carriers, and postal service personnel do not have access to the chain of custody forms, there is no requirement that such personnel document chain of custody for the shipping container during transit. Nor is there a requirement that there be a chain of custody entry when a specimen which is sealed in such a shipping container is put into or taken out of secure storage at the collection site prior to pickup by such personnel. This means that the chain of custody is not broken, and a test shall not be canceled, because couriers, express carriers, postal service personnel, or similar persons involved solely with the transportation of a specimen to a laboratory, have not documented their participation in the chain of custody documentation or because the chain of custody does not contain entries related to putting the specimen into or removing it from secure temporary storage at the collection site. Every effort shall be made to minimize the number of persons handling specimens.

(d) **Access to authorized personnel only.** No unauthorized personnel shall be permitted in any part of the designated collection site where urine specimens are collected or stored. Only the collection site person may handle specimens prior to their securement in the mailing container or monitor or observe specimen collection (under the conditions specified in this part). In order to promote security of specimens, avoid distraction of the collection site person and ensure against any confusion in the identification of specimens, the collection site person shall have only one donor under his or her supervision at any time. For this purpose, a collection procedure is complete when the urine bottle has been sealed and initialled, the drug testing custody and control form has been executed, and the employee has departed the site (or, in the case of an employee who was unable to provide a complete specimen, has entered a waiting area).

(e) **Privacy.** (1) Procedures for collecting urine specimens shall allow individual privacy unless there is a reason to believe that a particular individual may alter or substitute the specimen to be provided, as further described in this paragraph.

(2) For purposes of this part, the following circumstances are the exclusive grounds constituting a reason to believe that the individual may alter or substitute the specimen.

(i) The employee has presented a urine specimen that falls outside the normal temperature range (32°—38°C/90°—100°F), and

(A) The employee declines to provide a measurement of body temperature (taken by a means other than use of a rectal thermometer), as provided in paragraph (f)(14) of the part; or

(B) Body temperature varies by more than 1°C/1.8°F from the temperature of the specimen;

(ii) The last urine specimen provided by the employee (i.e., on a previous occasion) was determined by the laboratory to have a specific gravity of less than 1.003 and a creatinine concentration below .2g/L;

(iii) The collection site person observes conduct clearly and unequivocally indicating an attempt to substitute or adulterate the sample (e.g., substitute urine in plain view, blue dye in specimen presented, etc.); or

(iv) The employee has previously been determined to have used a controlled substance without medical authorization and the particular test was being conducted under a DOT agency regulation providing for follow-up testing upon or after return to service.

(3) A higher-level supervisor of the collection site person, or a designated employer representative, shall review and concur in advance with any decision by a collection site person to obtain a specimen under the direct observation of a same gender collection site person based upon the circumstances described in subparagraph (2) of this paragraph.

(f) **Integrity and identity of specimen.** Employers shall take precautions to ensure that a urine specimen is not adulterated or diluted during the collection procedure and that information on the urine bottle and on the urine custody and control form can identify the individual from whom the specimen was collected. The following minimum precautions shall be taken to ensure that unadulterated specimens are obtained and correctly identified:

(1) To deter the dilution of specimens at the collection site, toilet bluing agents shall be placed in toilet tanks wherever possible, so the reservoir of water in the toilet bowl always remains blue. Where practicable, there shall be no other source of water (e.g., shower or sink) in the enclosure where urination occurs. If there is another source of water in the enclosure it shall be effectively secure or monitored to ensure it is not used as a source for diluting the specimen.

(2) When an individual arrives at the collection site, the collection site person shall ensure that the individual is positively identified as the employee selected for testing (e.g., through presentation of photoidentification or identification by the employer's representative). If the individual's identity cannot be established, the collection site person shall not proceed with the collection. If the employee requests, the collection site person shall show his/her identification to the employee.

(3) If the individual fails to arrive at the assigned time, the collection site person shall contact the appropriate authority to obtain guidance on the action to be taken.

(4) The collection site person shall ask the individual to remove any unnecessary outer garments such as a coat or jacket that might conceal items or substances that could be used to

tamper with or adulterate the individual's urine specimen. The collection site person shall ensure that all personal belongings such as a purse or briefcase remain with the outer garments. The individual may retain his or her wallet. If the employee requests it, the collection site personnel shall provide the employee a receipt for any personal belongings.

(5) The individual shall be instructed to wash and dry his or her hands prior to urination.

(6) After washing hands, the individual shall remain in the presence of the collection site person and shall not have access to any water fountain, faucet, soap dispenser, cleaning agent or any other materials which could be used to adulterate the specimen.

(7) The individual may provide his/her specimen in the privacy of a stall or otherwise partitioned area that allows for individual privacy. The collection site person shall provide the individual with a specimen bottle or collection container, if applicable, for this purpose.

(8) The collection site person shall note any unusual behavior or appearance on the urine custody and control form.

(9) In the exceptional event that an employer-designated collection site is not accessible and there is an immediate requirement for specimen collection (e.g., circumstances require a post-accident test), a public rest room may be used according to the following procedures: A collection site person of the same gender as the individual shall accompany the individual into the public restroom which shall be made secure during the collection procedure. If possible, a toilet bluing agent shall be placed in the bowl and any accessible toilet tank. The collection site person shall remain in the rest room, but outside the stall, until the specimen is collected. If no bluing agent is available to deter specimen dilution, the collection site person shall instruct the individual not to flush the toilet until the specimen is delivered to the collection site person. After the collection site person has possession of the specimen, the individual will be instructed to flush the toilet and to participate with the collection site person in completing the chain of custody procedures.

(10) The collection site person shall instruct the employee to provide at least 45 ml of urine under the split sample method of collection or 30 ml of urine under the single sample method of collection.

(i)(A) Employers with employees subject to drug testing only under the drug testing rules of the Research and Special Programs Administration and/or Coast Guard may use the "split sample" method of collection or may collect a single sample for those employees.

(B) Employers with employees subject to drug testing under the drug testing rules of the Federal Highway Administration, Federal Railroad Administration, Federal Transit Administration, or Federal Aviation Administration shall use the "split sample" method of collection for those employees.

(ii) Employers using the split sample method of collection shall follow the procedures in this paragraph (f)(10)(ii):

(A) The donor shall urinate into a collection container or a specimen bottle capable of holding at least 60 ml.

(B)(1) If a collection container is used, the collection site person, in the presence of the donor, pours the urine into two specimen bottles. Thirty (30) ml shall be poured into one specimen bottle, to be used as the primary specimen. At least 15 ml shall be poured into the other bottle, to be used as the split specimen.

(2) If a single specimen bottle is used as a collection container, the collection site person, in the presence of the donor, shall pour 15 ml of urine from the specimen bottle into a second specimen bottle (to be used as the split specimen) and retain the remainder (at least 30 ml) in the collection bottle (to be used as the primary specimen).

(C) Nothing in this section precludes the use of a collection method or system that does not involve the physical pouring of urine from one container or bottle to another by the collection site person, provided that the method or system results in the subdivision of the specimen into a primary (30 ml) and a split (at least 15 ml) specimen that can be transmitted to the laboratory and tested in accordance with the requirements of this Subpart.

(D) Both bottles shall be shipped in a single shipping container, together with copies 1,2, and the split specimen copy of the chain of custody form, to the laboratory.

(E) If the test result of the primary specimen is positive, the employee may request that the MRO direct that the split specimen be tested in a different DHHS-certified laboratory for presence of the drug(s) for which a positive result was obtained in the test of the primary specimen. The MRO shall honor such a request if it is made within 72 hours of the employee having been notified of a verified positive test result.

(F) When the MRO informs the laboratory in writing that the employee has requested a test of the split specimen, the laboratory shall forward, to a different DHHS-approved laboratory, the split specimen bottle, with seal intact, a copy of the MRO request, and the split specimen copy of the chain of custody form with appropriate chain of custody entries.

(G) The result of the test of the split specimen is transmitted by the second laboratory to the MRO.

(H) Action required by DOT agency regulations as the result of a positive drug test (e.g., removal from performing a safety-sensitive function) is not stayed pending the result of the test of the split specimen.

(I) If the result of the test of the split specimen fails to reconfirm the presence of the drug(s) or drug metabolite(s) found in the primary specimen, the MRO shall cancel the test, and report the cancellation and the reasons for it to the DOT, the employer, and the employee.

(iii) Employers using the single sample collection method shall follow the procedures in paragraph:

(A) The collector may choose to direct the employee to urinate either directly into a specimen bottle or into a separate collection container.

(B) If a separate collection container is used, the collection site person shall pour at least 30 ml of the urine from the collection container into the specimen bottle in the presence of the employee.

(iv)(A)(1) In either collection methodology, upon receiving the specimen from the individual, the collection site person shall determine if the specimen has at least 30 milliliters of urine for a single specimen collection or 45 milliliters of urine for a split specimen collection.

(2) If the individual has not provided the required quantity of urine, the specimen shall be discarded. The collection site person shall direct the individual to drink up to 40 ounces of fluid, distributed reasonably through a period of up to three hours, or until the individual has provided a new urine specimen, whichever occurs first. If the employee refuses to drink fluids as directed or to provide a new urine specimen, the collection site person shall terminate the collection and notify the employer that the employee has refused to submit to testing.

(3) If the employee has not provided a sufficient specimen within three hours of the first unsuccessful attempt to provide

the specimen, the collection site person shall discontinue the collection and notify the employer.

(B) The employer shall direct any employee who does not provide a sufficient urine specimen (see paragraph (f)(10)(iv)(A)(3) of this section) to obtain, as soon as possible after the attempted provision of urine, an evaluation from a licensed physician who is acceptable to the employer concerning the employee's ability to provide an adequate amount of urine.

(1) If the physician determines, in his or her reasonable medical judgment, that a medical condition has, or with a high degree of probability, could have, precluded the employee from providing an adequate amount of urine, the employee's failure to provide an adequate amount of urine shall not be deemed a refusal to take a test. For purposes of this paragraph, a medical condition includes an ascertainable physiological condition (e.g., a urinary system dysfunction) or a documented pre-existing psychological disorder, but does not include unsupported assertions of "situational anxiety" or dehydration. The physician shall provide to the MRO a brief written statement setting forth his or her conclusion and the basis for it, which shall not include detailed information on the medical condition of the employee. Upon receipt of this statement, the MRO shall report his or her conclusions to the employer in writing.

(2) If the physician, in his or her reasonable medical judgment, is unable to make the determination set forth in paragraph (f)(10)(iv)(B)(1) of this section, the employee's failure to provide an adequate amount of urine shall be regarded as a refusal to take a test. The physician shall provide to the MRO a brief written statement setting forth his or her conclusion and the basis for it, which shall not include detailed information on the medical condition of the employee. Upon receipt of this statement, the MRO shall report his or her conclusions to the employer in writing.

(11) After the specimen has been provided and submitted to the collection site person, the individual shall be allowed to wash his or her hands.

(12) Immediately after the specimen is collected, the collection site person shall measure the temperature of the specimen. The temperature measuring device used must accurately reflect the temperature of the specimen and not contaminate the specimen. The time from urination to temperature measure is critical and in no case shall exceed 4 minutes.

(13) A specimen temperature outside the range of 32°—38° C/90°—100°F constitutes a reason to believe that the individual has altered or substituted the specimen(see paragraph (e)(2)(i) of this section). In such cases, the individual supplying the specimen may volunteer to have his or her oral temperature taken to provide evidence to counter the reason to believe the individual may have altered or substituted the specimen.

(14) Immediately after the specimen is collected, the collection site person shall also inspect the specimen to determine its color and look for any signs of contaminants. Any unusual findings shall be noted on the urine custody and control form.

(15) All specimens suspected of being adulterated shall be forwarded to the laboratory for testing.

(16) Whenever there is reason to believe that a particular individual has altered or substituted the specimen as described in paragraph (e)(2)(i) or (iii) of this section, a second specimen shall be obtained as soon as possible under the direct observation of a same gender collection site person.

(17) Both the individual being tested and the collection site person shall keep the specimen in view at all times prior to its being sealed and labeled. As provided below, the specimen shall be sealed (by placement of a tamperproof seal over the bottle cap and down the sides of the bottle) and labeled in the presence of the employee. If the specimen is transferred to a second bottle, the collection site person shall request the individual to observe the transfer of the specimen and the placement of the tamperproof seal over the bottle cap and down the sides of the bottle.

(18) The collection site person and the individual being tested shall be present at the same time during procedures outlined in paragraphs (f)(19) - (f)(22) of this section.

(19) The collection site person shall place securely on the bottle an identification label which contains the date, the individual's specimen number, and any other identifying information provided or required by the employer. If separate from the label, the tamperproof seal shall also be applied.

(20) The individual shall initial the identification label on the specimen bottle for the purpose of certifying that it is the specimen collected from him or her.

(21) The collection site person shall enter on the drug testing custody and control form all information identifying the specimen. The collection site person shall sign the drug testing cus-

tody and control form certifying that the collection was accomplished according to the applicable Federal requirements.

(22)(i) The individual shall be asked to read and sign a statement on the drug testing custody and control form certifying that the specimen identified as having been collected from him or her is in fact the specimen he or she provided.

(ii) When specified by DOT agency regulation or required by the collection site (other than an employer site) or by the laboratory, the employee may be required to sign a consent or release form authorizing the collection of the specimen, analysis of the specimen for designated controlled substances, and release of the results to the employer. The employee may not be required to waive liability with respect to negligence on the part of any person participating in the collection, handling or analysis of the specimen or to indemnify any person for the negligence of others.

(23) The collection site person shall complete the chain of custody portion of the drug testing custody and control form to indicate receipt of the specimen from the employee and shall certify proper completion of the collection.

(24) The urine specimen and chain of custody form are now ready for shipment. If the specimen is not immediately prepared for shipment, the collection site person shall ensure that it is appropriately safeguarded during temporary storage.

(25)(i) While any part of the above chain of custody procedures is being performed, it is essential that the urine specimen and custody documents be under the control of the involved collection tsite person. If the involved collection site person leaves his or her work station momentarily, the collection site person shall take the specimen and drug testing custody and control form with him or her or shall secure them. After the collection site person returns to the work station, the custody process will continue. If the collection site person is leaving for an extended period of time, he or she shall package the specimen for mailing before leaving the site.

(ii) The collection site person shall not leave the collection site in the interval between presentation of the specimen by the employee and securement of the sample with an identifying label bearing the employee's specimen identification number (shown on the urine custody and control form) and seal initialed by the employee. If it becomes necessary for the collection site person to leave the site during this interval, the collection shall be nullified and (at the election of the employer) a new collection begun.

(g) **Collection control**. To the maximum extent possible, collection site personnel shall keep the individual's specimen bottle within sight both before and after the individual has urinated. After the specimen is collected, it shall be properly sealed and labeled.

(h) **Transportation to laboratory**. Collection site personnel shall arrange to ship the collected specimen to the drug testing laboratory. The specimens shall be placed in shipping containers designed to minimize the possibility of damage during shipment (e.g., specimen boxes and/or padded mailers); and those containers shall be securely sealed to eliminate the possibility of undetected tampering with the specimen and/or the form. On the tape sealing the shipping container, the collection site person shall sign and enter the date specimens were sealed in the shipping container for shipment. The collection site person shall ensure that the chain of custody documentation is enclosed in each container sealed for shipment to the drug testing laboratory. Since specimens and documentation are sealed in shipping containers that would indicate any tampering during transit to the laboratory and couriers, express carriers, and postal service personnel do not have access to the chain of custody forms, there is no requirement that such personnel document chain of custody for the shipping container during transit. Nor is there a requirement that there be a chain of custody entry when a specimen which is sealed in such a shipping container is put into or taken out of secure storage at the collection site prior to pickup by such personnel. This means that the chain of custody is not broken, and a test shall not be canceled, because couriers, express carriers, postal service personnel, or similar persons involved solely with the transportation of a specimen to a laboratory, have not documented their participation in the chain of custody documentation or because the chain of custody does not contain entries related to putting the specimen into or removing it from secure temporary storage at the collection site.

(i) **Failure to cooperate**. If the employee refuses to cooperate with the collection process, the collection site person shall inform the employer representative and shall document the non-cooperation on the drug testing custody and control form.

(j) **Employee requiring medical attention**. If the sample

is being collected from an employee in need of medical attention (e.g., as part of a post-accident test given in an emergency medical facility), necessary medical attention shall not be delayed in order to collect the specimen.

(k) **Use of chain of custody form**. A chain of custody form (and a laboratory internal chain of custody document, where applicable), shall be used for maintaining control and accountability of each specimen from the point of collection to final disposition of the specimen. The date and purpose shall be documented on the form each time a specimen is handled or transferred and every individual in the chain of custody shall be identified. Since specimens and documentation are sealed in shipping containers that would indicate any tampering during transit to the laboratory and couriers, express carriers, and postal service personnel do not have access to the chain of custody forms, there is no requirement that such personnel document chain of custody for the shipping container during transit. Nor is there a requirement that there be a chain of custody entry when a specimen which is sealed in such a shipping container is put into or taken out of secure storage at the collection site prior to pickup by such personnel. This means that the chain of custody is not broken, and a test shall not be canceled, because couriers, express carriers, postal service personnel, or similar persons involved solely with the transportation of a specimen to a laboratory, have not documented their participation in the chain of custody documentation or because the chain of custody does not contain entries related to putting the specimen into or removing it from secure temporary storage at the collection site. Every effort shall be made to minimize the number of persons handling specimens.

§40.27 Laboratory personnel.

(a) **Day-to-day management**. (1) The laboratory shall have a qualified individual to assume professional, organizational, educational, and administrative responsibility for the laboratory's urine drug testing facility.

(2) This individual shall have documented scientific qualifications in analytical forensic toxicology. Minimum qualifications are:

(i) Certification as a laboratory director by a State in forensic or clinical laboratory toxicology; or

(ii) A Ph.D. in one of the natural sciences with an adequate undergraduate and graduate education in biology, chemistry, and pharmacology or toxicology; or

(iii) Training and experience comparable to a Ph.D. in one of the natural sciences, such as a medical or scientific degree with additional training and laboratory/research experience in biology, chemistry, and pharmacology or toxicology; and

(iv) In addition to the requirements in paragraph (a)(2)(i),(ii), or (iii) of this section, minimum qualifications also require;

(A) Appropriate experience in analytical forensic toxicology including experience with the analysis of biological material for drugs of abuse, and

(B) Appropriate training and/or experience in forensic applications of analytical toxicology, e.g., publications, court testimony, research concerning analytical toxicology of drugs of abuse, or other factors which qualify the individual as an expert witness in forensic toxicology.

(3) This individual shall be engaged in and responsible for the day-to-day management of the drug testing laboratory even where another individual has overall responsibility for an entire multi-specialty laboratory.

(4) This individual shall be responsible for ensuring that there are enough personnel with adequate training and experience to supervise and conduct the work of the drug testing laboratory. He or she shall assure the continued competency of laboratory personnel by documenting their in-service training, reviewing their work performance, and verifying their skills.

(5) This individual shall be responsible for the laboratory's having a procedure manual which is complete, up-to-date, available for personnel performing tests, and followed by those personnel. The procedure manual shall be reviewed, signed, and dated by this responsible individual whenever procedures are first placed into use or changed or when a new individual assumes responsibility for management of the drug testing laboratory. Copies of all procedures and dates on which they are in effect shall be maintained. (Specific contents of the procedure manual are described in §40.29 (n)(1).)

(6) This individual shall be responsible for maintaining a quality assurance program to assure the proper performance and reporting of all test results; for maintaining acceptable analytical performance for all controls and standards; for maintaining quality control testing; and for assuring and documenting the validity, reliability, accuracy, precision, and performance

characteristics of each test and test system.

(7) This individual shall be responsible for taking all remedial actions necessary to maintain satisfactory operation and performance of the laboratory in response to quality control systems not being within performance specifications, errors in result reporting or in analysis of performance testing results. This individual shall ensure that sample results are not reported until all corrective actions have been taken and he or she can assure that the tests results provided are accurate and reliable.

(b) **Test validation**. The laboratory's urine drug testing facility shall have a qualified individual(s) who reviews all pertinent data and quality control results in order to attest to the validity of the laboratory's test reports. A laboratory may designate more than one person to perform this function. This individual(s) may be any employee who is qualified to be responsible for day-to-day management or operation of the drug testing laboratory.

(c) **Day-to-day operations and supervision of analysts**. The laboratory's urine drug testing facility shall have an individual to be responsible for day-to-day operations and to supervise the technical analysts. This individual(s) shall have at least a bachelor's degree in the chemical or biological sciences or medical technology or equivalent. He or she shall have training and experience in the theory and practice of the procedures used in the laboratory, resulting in his or her thorough understanding of quality control practices and procedures; the review, interpretation, and reporting of test results; maintenance of chain of custody; and proper remedial actions to be taken in response to test systems being out of control limits or detecting aberrant test or quality control results.

(d) **Other personnel**. Other technicians or nontechnical staff shall have the necessary training and skills for the tasks assigned.

(e) **Training**. The laboratory's urine drug testing program shall make available continuing education programs to meet the needs of laboratory personnel.

(f) **Files**. Laboratory personnel files shall include: resume of training and experience, certification or license if any; references; job descriptions; records of performance evaluation and advancement; incident reports; and results of tests which establish employee competency for the position he or she holds, such as a test for color blindness, if appropriate.

§40.29 Laboratory analysis procedures.

(a) **Security and chain of custody**. (1) Drug testing laboratories shall be secure at all times. They shall have in place sufficient security measures to control access to the premises and to ensure that no unauthorized personnel handle specimens or gain access to the laboratory process or to areas where records are stored. Access to these secured areas shall be limited to specifically authorized individuals whose authorization is documented. With the exception of personnel authorized to conduct inspections on behalf of Federal agencies for which the laboratory is engaged in urine testing or on behalf of DHHS, all authorized visitors and maintenance and service personnel shall be escorted at all times. Documentation of individuals accessing these areas, dates, and time of entry and purpose of entry must be maintained.

(2) Laboratories shall use chain of custody procedures to maintain control and accountability of specimens from receipt through completion of testing, reporting of results during storage, and continuing until final disposition of specimens. The date and purpose shall be documented on an appropriate chain of custody form each time a specimen is handled or transferred and every individual in the chain shall be identified. Accordingly, authorized technicians shall be responsible for each urine specimen or aliquot in their possession and shall sign and complete chain of custody forms for those specimens or aliquots as they are received.

(b) **Receiving**. (1)(i) When a shipment of specimens is received, laboratory personnel shall inspect each package for evidence of possible tampering and compare information on specimen bottles within each package to the information on the accompanying chain of custody forms. Any direct evidence of tampering or discrepancies in the information on specimen bottles and the employer's chain of custody forms attached to the shipment shall be immediately reported to the employer and shall be noted on the laboratory's chain of custody form which shall accompany the specimens while they are in the laboratory's possession.

(ii) Where the employer has used the split sample method, and the laboratory observes that the split specimen is untestable, inadequate, or unavailable for testing, the laboratory shall nevertheless test the primary specimen. The laboratory does not inform the MRO or the employer of the untestability, inadequacy, or unavailability of the split specimen until and unless the primary specimen is a verified positive test and the MRO has informed the laboratory that the employee has requested a test of the split specimen.

(2) In situations where the employer uses the split sample collection method, the laboratory shall log in the split specimen, with the split specimen bottle seal remaining intact. The laboratory shall store this sample securely (see paragraph (c) of this section). If the result of the test of the primary specimen is negative, the laboratory may discard the split specimen. If the result of the test of the primary specimen is positive, the laboratory shall retain the split specimen in frozen storage for 60 days from the date on which the laboratory acquires it (see paragraph (h) of this section). Following the end of the 60-day period, if not informed by the MRO that the employee has requested a test of the split specimen, the laboratory may discard the split specimen.

(3) When directed in writing by the MRO to forward the split specimen to another DHHS-certified laboratory for analysis, the second laboratory shall analyze the split specimen by GC/MS to reconfirm the presence of the drug(s) or drug metabolite(s) found in the primary specimen. Such GC/MS confirmation shall be conducted without regard to the cutoff levels of §40.29(f). The split specimen shall be retained in long-term storage for one year by the laboratory conducting the analysis of the split specimen (or longer if litigation concerning the test is pending).

(c) **Short-term refrigerated storage**. Specimens that do not receive an initial test within 7 days of arrival at the laboratory shall be placed in secure refrigeration units. Temperatures shall not exceed 6°C. Emergency power equipment shall be available in case of prolonged power failure.

(d) **Specimen processing**. Laboratory facilities for urine drug testing will normally process specimens by grouping them into batches. The number of specimens in each batch may vary significantly depending on the size of the laboratory and its workload. When conducting either initial or confirmatory tests, every batch shall contain an appropriate number of standards for calibrating the instrumentation and a minimum of 10 percent controls. Both quality control and blind performance test samples shall appear as ordinary samples to laboratory analysts.

(e) **Initial test**. (1) The initial test shall use an immunoassay which meets the requirements of the Food and Drug Administration for commercial distribution. The following initial cutoff levels shall be used when screening specimens to determine whether they are negative for these five drugs or classes of drugs:

	Initial test cutoff levels (ng/ml)
Marijuana metabolites	50
Cocaine metabolites	300
Opiate metabolites	2000
Phencyclidine	25
Amphetamines	1,000

(2) These cutoff levels are subject to change by the Department of Health and Human Services as advances in technology or other considerations warrant identification of these substances at other concentrations.

(f) **Confirmatory test**. (1) All specimens identified as positive on the initial test shall be confirmed using gas chromatography/mass spectrometry (GC/MS) techniques at the cutoff levels listed in this paragraph for each drug. All confirmations shall be by quantitative analysis. Concentrations that exceed the linear region of the standard curve shall be documented in the laboratory record as "greater than highest standard curve value."

	Confirmatory test cutoff levels (ng/ml)
Marijuana metabolite[1]	15
Cocaine metabolite[2]	150
Opiates:	
Morphine	2000
Codeine	2000
6-Acetylmorphine[4]	10 ng/ml
Phencyclidine	25
Amphetamines:	
Amphetamine	500
Methamphetamine[3]	500

[1] Delta-9-tetrahydrocannabinol-9-carboxylic acid.
[2] Benzoylecgonine.
[3] Specimen must also contain amphetamine at a concentration greater than or equal to 200 ng/ml.
[4] Test for 6-AM when morphine concentration exceeds 2,000 ng/ml.

(2) These cutoff levels are subject to change by the Department of Health and Human Services as advances in technology or other considerations warrant identification of these substances at other concentrations.

(g) **Reporting results**. (1) The laboratory shall report test results to the employer's Medical Review Officer within an average of 5 working days after receipt of the specimen by the laboratory. Before any test result is reported(the results of initial tests, confirmatory tests, or quality control data), it shall be reviewed and the test certified as an accurate report by the responsible individual. The report shall identify the drugs/metabolites tested for, whether positive or negative, the specimen number assigned by the employer, and the drug testing laboratory specimen identification number(accession number).

(2) The laboratory shall report as negative all specimens that are negative on the initial test or negative on the confirmatory test. Only specimens confirmed positive shall be reported positive for a specific drug.

(3) The Medical Review Officer may request from the laboratory and the laboratory shall provide quantitation of test results. The MRO shall report whether the test is positive or negative, and may report the drug(s) for which there was a positive test, but shall not disclose the quantitation of test results to the employer. *Provided*, that the MRO may reveal the quantitation of a positive test result to the employer, the employee, or the decisionmaker in a lawsuit, grievance, or other proceeding initiated by or on behalf of the employee and arising from a verified positive drug test.

(4) The laboratory may transmit results to the Medical Review Officer by various electronic means (for example, teleprinters, facsimile, or computer) in a manner designed to ensure confidentiality of the information. Results may not be provided verbally by telephone. The laboratory and employer must ensure the security of the data transmission and limit access to any data transmission, storage, and retrieval system.

(5) The laboratory shall send only to the Medical Review Officer the original or a certified true copy of the drug testing custody and control form(part 2), which, in the case of a report positive for drug use, shall be signed(after the required certification block) by the individual responsible for day-to-day management of the drug testing laboratory or the individual responsible for attesting to the validity of the test reports, and attached to

which shall be a copy of the test report.

(6) The laboratory shall provide the employer an aggregate quarterly statistical summary of urinalysis testing of the employer's employees. Laboratories may provide the report to a consortium provided that the laboratory provides employer-specific data and the consortium forwards the employer-specific data to the respective employers within 14 days of receipt of the laboratory report. The laboratory shall provide the report to the employer or consortium not more than 14 calendar days after the end of the quarter covered by the summary. Laboratory confirmation data only shall be included from test results reported within that quarter. The summary shall contain only the following information:

(i) Number of specimens received for testing;

(ii) Number of specimens confirmed positive for—

(A) Marijuana metabolite

(B) Cocaine metabolite

(C) Opiates

(D) Phencyclidine

(E) Amphetamine;

(iii) Number of specimens for which a test was not performed.

Quarterly reports shall not contain personal identifying information or other data from which it is reasonably likely that information about individuals' tests can be readily inferred. If necessary, in order to prevent disclosure of such data, the laboratory shall not send such a report until data are sufficiently aggregated to make such an inference unlikely. In any quarter in which a report is withheld for this reason, or because no testing was conducted, the laboratory shall so inform the consortium/employer in writing.

(7) The laboratory shall make available copies of all analytical results for employer drug testing programs when requested by DOT or any DOT agency with regulatory authority over the employer.

(8) Unless otherwise instructed by the employer in writing, all records pertaining to a given urine specimen shall be retained by the drug testing laboratory for a minimum of 2 years.

(h) **Long-term storage**. Long-term frozen storage (-20°C or less) ensures that positive urine specimens will be available for any necessary retest during administrative or disciplinary proceedings. Drug testing laboratories shall retain and place in properly secured long-term frozen storage for a minimum of 1 year all specimens confirmed positive, in their original labeled specimen bottles. Within this 1-year period, an employer (or other person designated in a DOT agency regulation) may request the laboratory to retain the specimen for an additional period of time, but if no such request is received the laboratory may discard the specimen after the end of 1 year, except that the laboratory shall be required to maintain any specimens known to be under legal challenge for an indefinite period.

(i) **Retesting specimens**. Because some analytes deteriorate or are lost during freezing and/or storage, quantitation for a retest is not subject to a specific cutoff requirement but must provide data sufficient to confirm the presence of the drug or metabolite.

(j) **Subcontracting**. Drug testing laboratories shall not subcontract and shall perform all work with their own personnel and equipment. The laboratory must be capable of performing testing for the five classes of drugs (marijuana, cocaine, opiates, phencyclidine and amphetamines) using the initial immunoassay and confirmatory GC/MS methods specified in this part. This paragraph does not prohibit subcontracting of laboratory analysis if specimens are sent directly from the collection site to the subcontractor, the subcontractor is a laboratory certified by DHHS as required in this part, the subcontractor performs all analysis and provides storage required under this part, and the subcontractor is responsible to the employer for compliance with this part and applicable DOT agency regulations as if it were the prime contractor.

(k) **Laboratory facilities**. (1) Laboratory facilities shall comply with applicable provisions of any State licensing requirements.

(2) Laboratories certified in accordance with DHHS Guidelines shall have the capability, at the same laboratory premises, of performing initial and confirmatory tests for each drug or metabolite for which service is offered.

(l) **Inspections**. The Secretary, a DOT agency, any employer utilizing the laboratory, DHHS or any organization performing laboratory certification on behalf of DHHS reserves the right to inspect the laboratory at any time. Employer contracts with laboratories for drug testing, as well as contracts for collection site services, shall permit the employer and the DOT agency of jurisdiction (directly or through an agent) to conduct unannounced inspections.

(m) **Documentation**. The drug testing laboratories shall maintain and make available for at least 2 years documentation of all aspects of the testing process. This 2-year period may be extended upon written notification by a DOT agency or by any employer for which laboratory services are being provided. The required documentation shall include personnel files on all individuals authorized to have access to specimens; chain of custody documents; quality assurance/quality control records; procedure manuals; all test data (including calibration curves and any calculations used in determining test results); reports; performance records on performance testing; performance on certification inspections; and hard copies of computer-generated data. The laboratory shall maintain documents for any specimen known to be under legal challenge for an indefinite period.

(n) **Additional requirements for certified laboratories.** — (1) **Procedure manual**. Each laboratory shall have a procedure manual which includes the principles of each test preparation of reagents, standards and controls, calibration procedures, derivation of results, linearity of methods, sensitivity of methods, cutoff values, mechanisms for reporting results, controls criteria for unacceptable specimens and results, remedial actions to be taken when the test systems are outside of acceptable limits, reagents and expiration dates, and references. Copies of all procedures and dates on which they are in effect shall be maintained as part of the manual.

(2) **Standards and controls**. Laboratory standards shall be prepared with pure drug standards which are properly labeled as to content and concentration. The standards shall be labeled with the following dates: when received; when prepared or opened; when placed in service; and expiration date.

(3) **Instruments and equipment**. (i) Volumetric pipettes and measuring devices shall be certified for accuracy or be checked by gravimetric, colorimetric, or other verification procedure. Automatic pipettes and dilutors shall be checked for accuracy and reproducibility before being placed in service and checked periodically thereafter.

(ii) There shall be written procedures for instrument set-up and normal operation, a schedule for checking critical operating characteristics for all instruments, tolerance limits for acceptable function checks and instructions for major trouble shooting and repair. Records shall be available on preventive maintenance.

(4) **Remedial actions**. There shall be written procedures for the actions to be taken when systems are out of acceptable limits or errors are detected. There shall be documentation that these procedures are followed and that all necessary corrective actions are taken. There shall also be in place systems to verify all stages of testing and reporting and documentation that these procedures are followed.

(5) **Personnel available to testify at proceedings**. A laboratory shall have qualified personnel available to testify in an administrative or disciplinary proceeding against an employee when that proceeding is based on positive urinalysis results reported by the laboratory.

(6) The laboratory shall not enter into any relationship with an employer's MRO that may be construed as a potential conflict of interest or derive any financial benefit by having an employer use a specific MRO.

§40.31 Quality assurance and quality control.

(a) **General**. Drug testing laboratories shall have a quality assurance program which encompasses all aspects of the testing process including but not limited to specimen acquisition, chain of custody security and reporting of results, initial and confirmatory testing and validation of analytical procedures. Quality assurance procedures shall be designed, implemented and reviewed to monitor the conduct of each step of the process of testing for drugs.

(b) **Laboratory quality control requirements for initial tests**. Each analytical run of specimens to be screened shall include:

(1) Urine specimens certified to contain no drug;

(2) Urine specimens fortified with known standards; and

(3) Positive controls with the drug or metabolite at or near the cutoff level.

In addition, with each batch of samples a sufficient number of standards shall be included to ensure and document the linearity of the assay method over time in the concentration area of the cutoff. After acceptable values are obtained for the known standards, those values will be used to calculate sample data. Implementation of procedures to ensure the carryover does not contaminate the testing of an individual's specimen shall be documented. A minimum of 10 percent of all test samples shall be quality control specimens. Laboratory quality control samples, prepared from spiked urine samples of determined concentration shall be included in the run and should appear as normal samples to laboratory analysts. One percent of each run, with a minimum of at least one sample, shall be the laboratory's own quality control samples.

(c) **Laboratory quality control requirements for confirmation tests**. Each analytical run of specimens to be confirmed shall include:

(1) Urine specimens certified to contain no drug;

(2) Urine specimens fortified with known standards; and

(3) Positive controls with the drug or metabolite at or near the cutoff level. The linearity and precision of the method shall be periodically documented. Implementation of procedures to ensure that carryover does not contaminate the testing of an individual's specimen shall also be documented.

(d) **Employer blind performance test procedures**.

(1) Each employer covered by DOT agency drug testing regulations shall use blind testing quality control procedures as provided in this paragraph.

(2) Each employer shall submit three blind performance test specimens for each 100 employee specimens it submits, up to a maximum of 100 blind performance test specimens submitted per quarter. A DOT agency may increase this per quarter maximum number of samples if doing so is necessary to ensure adequate quality control of employers or consortiums with very large numbers of employees.

(3) For employers with 2000 or more covered employees, approximately 80 percent of the blind performance test samples shall be blank (i.e., containing no drug or otherwise as approved by a DOT agency) and the remaining samples shall be positive for one or more drugs per sample in a distribution such that all the drugs to be tested are included in approximately equal frequencies of challenge. The positive samples shall be spiked only with those drugs for which the employer is testing. This paragraph shall not be construed to prohibit spiking of other (potentially interfering) compounds, as technically appropriate, in order to verify the specificity of a particular assay.

(4) Employers with fewer than 2000 covered employees may submit blind performance test specimens as provided in paragraph (d)(3) of this section. Such employers may also submit only blank samples or may submit two separately labeled portions of a specimen from the same non-covered employee.

(5) Consortiums shall be responsible for the submission of blind samples on behalf of their members. The blind sampling rate shall apply to the total number of samples submitted by the consortium.

(6) The DOT agency concerned shall investigate, or shall refer to DHHS for investigation, any unsatisfactory performance testing result and, based on this investigation, the laboratory shall take action to correct the cause of the unsatisfactory performance test result. A record shall be made of the investigative findings and the corrective action taken by the laboratory, and that record shall be dated and signed by the individual responsible for the day-to-day management and operation of the drug testing laboratory. Then the DOT agency shall send the document to the employer as a report of the unsatisfactory performance testing incident. The DOT agency shall ensure notification of the finding to DHHS.

(7) Should a false positive error occur on a blind performance test specimen and the error is determined to be an administrative error (clerical, sample mixup, etc.), the employer shall promptly notify the DOT agency concerned. The DOT agency and the employer shall require the laboratory to take corrective action to minimize the occurrence of the particular error in the future, and, if there is reason to believe the error could have been systemic, the DOT agency may also require review and reanalysis of previously run specimens.

(8) Should a false positive error occur on a blind performance test specimen and the error is determined to be a technical or methodological error, the employer shall instruct the laboratory to submit all quality control data from the batch of specimens which include the false positive specimen to the DOT agency concerned. In addition, the laboratory shall retest all specimens analyzed positive for that drug or metabolite from the time of fitnal resolution of the error back to the time of the last satisfactory performance test cycle. This retesting shall be documented by a statement signed by the individual responsible for day-to-day management of the laboratory's urine drug testing. The DOT agency concerned may require an on-site review of the laboratory which may be conducted unannounced during any hours of operation of the laboratory. Based on information provided by the DOT agency, DHHS has the option of revoking or suspending the laboratory's certification or recommending that no further action be taken if the case is one of less serious error

in which corrective action has already been taken, thus reasonably assuring that the error will not occur again.

§40.33 Reporting and review of results.

(a) **Medical review officer shall review confirmed positive results**. (1) An essential part of the drug testing program is the final review of confirmed positive results from the laboratory. A positive test result does not automatically identify an employee/applicant as having used drugs in violation of a DOT agency regulation. An individual with a detailed knowledge of possible alternate medical explanations is essential to the review of results. This review shall be performed by the Medical Review Officer (MRO) prior to the transmission of the results to employer administrative officials. The MRO review shall include review of the chain of custody to ensure that it is complete and sufficient on its face.

(2) The duties of the MRO with respect to negative results are purely administrative.

(b) **Medical review officer—qualifications and responsibilities**. (1) The MRO shall be a licensed physician with knowledge of substance abuse disorders and may be an employee of a transportation employer or a private physician retained for this purpose.

(2) [Removed and reserved.]

(3) The role of the MRO is to review and interpret confirmed positive test results obtained through the employer's testing program. In carrying out this responsibility, the MRO shall examine alternate medical explanations for any positive test result. This action may include conducting a medical interview and review of the individual's medical history, or review of any other relevant biomedical factors. The MRO shall review all medical records made available by the tested individual when a confirmed positive test could have resulted from legally prescribed medication. The MRO shall not, however, consider the results or urine samples that are not obtained or processed in accordance with this part.

(c) **Positive test result**. (1) Prior to making a final decision to verify a positive test result for an individual, the MRO shall give the individual an opportunity to discuss the test result with him or her.

(2) The MRO shall contact the individual directly, on a confidential basis, to determine whether the employee wishes to dis-

cuss the test result. A staff person under the MRO's supervision may make the initial contact, and a medically licensed or certified staff person may gather information from the employee. Except as provided in paragraph (c)(5) of this section, the MRO shall talk directly with the employee before verifying a test as positive.

(3) If, after making all reasonable efforts and documenting them, the MRO is unable to reach the individual directly, the MRO shall contact a designated management official who shall direct the individual to contact the MRO as soon as possible. If it becomes necessary to reach the individual through the designated management official, the designated management official shall employ procedures that ensure, to the maximum extent practicable, the requirement that the employee contact the MRO is held in confidence.

(4) If, after making all reasonable efforts, the designated management official is unable to contact the employee, the employer may place the employee on temporary medically unqualified status or medical leave.

(5) The MRO may verify a test as positive without having communicated directly with the employee about the test in three circumstances:

(i) The employee expressly declines the opportunity to discuss the test;

(ii) Neither the MRO nor the designated employer representative, after making all reasonable efforts, has been able to contact the employee within 14 days of the date on which the MRO receives the confirmed positive test result from the laboratory;

(iii) The designated employer representative has successfully made and documented a contact with the employee and instructed the employee to contact the MRO (see paragraphs (c)(3) and (c)(4) of this section), and more than five days have passed since the date the employee was successfully contacted by the designated employer representative.

(6) If a test is verified positive under the circumstances specified in paragraph (c)(5) (ii) or (iii) of this section, the employee may present to the MRO information documenting that serious illness, injury, or other circumstances unavoidably prevented the employee from being contacted by the MRO or designated employer representative (paragraph (c)(5)(ii) of this section) or from contacting the MRO (paragraph (c)(5)(iii) of this section) within the times provided. The MRO, on the basis of such infor-

mation, may reopen the verification, allowing the employee to present information concerning a legitimate explanation for the confirmed positive test. If the MRO concludes that there is a legitimate explanation, the MRO declares the test to be negative.

(7) Following verification of a positive test result, the MRO shall, as provided in the employer's policy, refer the case to the employer's employee assistance or rehabilitation program, if applicable, to the management official empowered to recommend or take administrative action (or the official's designated agent), or both.

(d) **Verification for opiates; review for prescription medication**. Before the MRO verifies a confirmed positive result for opiates, he or she shall determine that there is clinical evidence — in addition to the urine test — of unauthorized use of any opium, opiate, or opium derivative (e.g., morphine/codeine). (This requirement does not apply if the employer's GC/MS confirmation testing for opiates confirms the presence of 6-monoacetylmorphine.)

(e) In a situation in which the employer has used the single sample method of collection, the MRO shall notify each employee who has a confirmed positive test that the employee has 72 hours in which to request a reanalysis of the original specimen, if the test is verified positive. If requested to do so by the employee within 72 hours of the employee's having been informed of a verified positive test, the Medical Review Officer shall direct, in writing, a reanalysis of the original sample. The MRO may also direct, in writing, such a reanalysis if the MRO questions the accuracy or validity of any test result. Only the MRO may authorize such a reanalysis, and such a reanalysis may take place only at laboratories certified by DHHS. If the reanalysis fails to reconfirm the presence of the drug or drug metabolite, the MRO shall cancel the test and report the cancellation and the reasons for it to the DOT, the employer and the employee.

(f)(1) In situations in which the employer uses the split sample method of collection, the MRO shall notify each employee who has a confirmed positive test that the employee has 72 hours in which to request a test of the split specimen, if the test is verified as positive. If the employee requests an analysis of the split specimen within 72 hours of having been informed of a verified positive test, the MRO shall direct, in writing, the laboratory to provide the split specimen to another DHHS-certified laboratory for analysis. If the analysis of the split specimen fails to reconfirm the presence of the drug(s) or drug metabolite(s) found in the primary specimen, or if the split specimen is unavailable, inadequate for testing or untestable, the MRO shall cancel the test and report cancellation and the reasons for it to the DOT, the employer, and the employee.

(2) If the analysis of the split specimen is reconfirmed by the second laboratory for the presence of the drug(s) or drug metabolites(s), the MRO shall notify the employer and employee of the results of the test.

(g) If an employee has not contacted the MRO within 72 hours, as provided in paragraphs (e) and (f) of this section, the employee may present to the MRO information documenting that serious illness, injury, inability to contact the MRO, lack of actual notice of the verified positive test, or other circumstances unavoidably prevented the employee from timely contacting the MRO. If the MRO concludes that there is a legitimate explanation for the employee's failure to contact the MRO within 72 hours, the MRO shall direct that the reanalysis of the primary specimen or analysis of the split specimen, as applicable, be performed.

(h) When the employer uses the split sample method of collection, the employee is not authorized to request a reanalysis of the primary specimen as provided in paragraph(e) of this section.

(i) **Disclosure of information**. Except as provided in this paragraph, the MRO shall not disclose to any third party medical information provided by the individual to the MRO as a part of the testing verification process.

(1) The MRO may disclose such information to the employer, a DOT agency or other Federal safety agency, or a physician responsible for determining the medical qualification of the employee under an applicable DOT agency regulation, as applicable, only if—

(i) An applicable DOT regulation permits or requires such disclosure;

(ii) In the MRO's reasonable medical judgment, the information could result in the employee being determined to be medically unqualified under an applicable DOT agency rule; or

(iii) In the MRO's reasonable medical judgment, in a situation in which there is no DOT agency rule establishing physical qualification standards applicable to the employee, the information indicates that continued performance by the employee of his or her safety-sensitive function could pose a significant safety risk.

(2) Before obtaining medical information from the employee as part of the verification process, the MRO shall inform the employee that information may be disclosed to third parties as provided in this paragraph and the identity of any parties to whom information may be disclosed.

§40.35 Protection of employee records.

Employer contracts with laboratories shall require that the laboratory maintain employee test records in confidence, as provided in DOT agency regulations. The contracts shall provide that the laboratory shall disclose information related to a positive drug test of an individual to the individual, the employer, or the decisionmaker in a lawsuit, grievance, or other proceeding initiated by or on behalf of the individual and arising from a certified positive drug test.

§40.37 Individual access to test and laboratory certification results.

Any employee who is the subject of a drug test conducted under this part shall, upon written request, have access to any records relating to his or her drug test and any records relating to the results of any relevant certification, review, or revocation-of-certification proceedings.

§40.39 Use of certified laboratories.

(a) Except as provided in paragraph (b) of this section, employers subject to this part shall use only laboratories certified under the DHHS "Mandatory Guidelines for Federal Workplace Drug Testing Programs," April 11, 1988, and subsequent amendments thereto.

(b) Employers subject to this part may also use laboratories located outside the United States if—

(1) The Department of Transportation, based on a written recommendation from DHHS, has certified the laboratory as meeting DHHS laboratory certification standards or deemed the laboratory fully equivalent to a laboratory meeting DHHS laboratory certification standards; or

(2) The Department of Transportation, based on a written recommendation from DHHS, has recognized a foreign certifying organization as having equivalent laboratory certification

standards and procedures to those of DHHS, and the foreign certifying organization has certified the laboratory, pursuant to those equivalent standards and procedures.

Subpart C — Alcohol Testing

§40.51 The breath alcohol technician.

(a) The breath alcohol technician (BAT) shall be trained to proficiency in the operation of the EBT he or she is using and in the alcohol testing procedures of this part.

(1) Proficiency shall be demonstrated by successful completion of a course of instruction which, at a minimum, provides training in the principles of EBT methodology, operation, and calibration checks; the fundamentals of breath analysis for alcohol content; and the procedures required in this part for obtaining a breath sample, and interpreting and recording EBT results.

(2) Only courses of instruction for operation of EBTs that are equivalent to the Department of Transportation model course, as determined by the National Highway Traffic Safety Administration (NHTSA), may be used to train BATs to proficiency. On request, NHTSA will review a BAT instruction course for equivalency.

(3) The course of instruction shall provide documentation that the BAT has demonstrated competence in the operation of the specific EBT(s) he/she will use.

(4) Any BAT who will perform an external calibration check of an EBT shall be trained to proficiency in conducting the check on the particular model of EBT, to include practical experience and demonstrated competence in preparing the breath alcohol simulator or alcohol standard, and in maintenance and calibration of the EBT.

(5) The BAT shall receive additional training, as needed, to ensure proficiency, concerning new or additional devices or changes in technology that he or she will use.

(6) The employer or its agent shall establish documentation of the training and proficiency test of each BAT it uses to test employees, and maintain the documentation as provided in §40.83.

(b) A BAT-qualified supervisor of an employee may conduct the alcohol test for that employee only if another BAT is unavailable to perform the test in a timely manner. A supervisor shall not serve as a BAT for the employee in any circumstance prohibited by a DOT operating administration regulation.

(c) Law enforcement officers who have been certified by state or local governments to conduct breath alcohol testing are deemed to be qualified as BATs. In order for a test conducted by such an officer to be accepted under Department of Transportation alcohol testing requirements, the officer must have been certified by a state or local government to use the EBT or non-evidential alcohol screening device that was used for the test.

§40.53 Devices to be used for breath alcohol tests.

(a) For screening tests, employers shall use only EBTs. When the employer uses for a screening test an EBT that does not meet the requirements of paragraphs (b)(1) through (3) of this section, the employer shall use a log book in conjunction with the EBT (see §40.59(c)).

(b) For confirmation tests, employers shall use EBTs that meet the following requirements:

(1) EBTs shall have the capability of providing, independently or by direct link to a separate printer, a printed result in triplicate (or three consecutive identical copies) of each breath test and of the operations specified in paragraphs (b)(2) and (3) of this section.

(2) EBTs shall be capable of assigning a unique and sequential number to each completed test, with the number capable of being read by the BAT and the employee before each test and being printed out on each copy of the result.

(3) EBTs shall be capable of printing out, on each copy of the result, the manufacturer's name for the device, the device's serial number, and the time of the test.

(4) EBTs shall be able to distinguish alcohol from acetone at the 0.02 alcohol concentration level.

(5) EBTs shall be capable of the following operations:

(i) Testing an air blank prior to each collection of breath; and

(ii) Performing an external calibration check.

§40.55 Quality assurance plans for EBTs.

(a) In order to be used in either screening or confirmation alcohol testing subject to this part, an EBT shall have a quality assurance plan (QAP) developed by the manufacturer.

(1) The plan shall designate the method or methods to be used to perform external calibration checks of the device, using only calibration devices on the NHTSA "Conforming Products

List of Calibrating Units for Breath Alcohol Tests."

(2) The plan shall specify the minimum intervals for performing external calibration checks of the device. Intervals shall be specified for different frequencies of use, environmental conditions (e.g., temperature, altitude, humidity), and contexts of operation (e.g., stationary or mobile use).

(3) The plan shall specify the tolerances on an external calibration check within which the EBT is regarded to be in proper calibration.

(4) The plan shall specify inspection, maintenance, and calibration requirements and intervals for the device.

(5) For a plan to be regarded as valid, the manufacturer shall have submitted the plan to NHTSA for review and have received NHTSA approval of the plan.

(b) The employer shall comply with the NHTSA-approved quality assurance plan for each EBT it uses for alcohol screening or confirmation testing subject to this part.

(1) The employer shall ensure that external calibration checks of each EBT are performed as provided in the QAP.

(2) The employer shall take an EBT out of service if any external calibration check results in a reading outside the tolerances for the EBT set forth in the QAP. The EBT shall not again be used for alcohol testing under this part until it has been serviced and has had an external calibration check resulting in a reading within the tolerances for the EBT.

(3) The employer shall ensure that inspection, maintenance, and calibration of each EBT are performed by the manufacturer or a maintenance representative certified by the device's manufacturer or a state health agency or other appropriate state agency. The employer shall also ensure that each BAT or other individual who performs an external calibration check of an EBT used for alcohol testing subject to this part has demonstrated proficiency in conducting such a check of the model of EBT in question.

(4) The employer shall maintain records of the external calibration checks of EBTs as provided in §40.83.

(c) When the employer is not using the EBT at an alcohol testing site, the employer shall store the EBT in a secure space.

§40.57 Locations for breath alcohol testing.

(a) Each employer shall conduct alcohol testing in a location that affords visual and aural privacy to the individual being tested, sufficient to prevent unauthorized persons from seeing or hearing test results. All necessary equipment, personnel, and materials for breath testing shall be provided at the location where testing is conducted.

(b) An employer may use a mobile collection facility (*e.g.*, a van equipped for alcohol testing) that meets the requirements of paragraph (a) of this section.

(c) No unauthorized persons shall be permitted access to the testing location when the EBT remains unsecured or, in order to prevent such persons from seeing or hearing a testing result, at any time when testing is being conducted.

(d) In unusual circumstances (*e.g.*, when it is essential to conduct a test outdoors at the scene of an accident), a test may be conducted at a location that does not fully meet the requirements of paragraph (a) of this section. In such a case, the employer or BAT shall provide visual and aural privacy to the employee to the greatest extent practicable.

(e) The BAT shall supervise only one employee's use of the EBT at a time. The BAT shall not leave the alcohol testing location while the testing procedure for a given employee (see §§40.61 through 40.65) is in progress.

§40.59 The breath alcohol testing form.

(a) Each employer shall use the breath alcohol testing form prescribed under this part. The form is found in Appendix A to this subpart. Employers may not modify or revise this form, except that a form directly generated by an EBT may omit the space for affixing a separate printed result to the form.

(b) The form shall provide triplicate (or three consecutive identical) copies. Copy 1 (white) shall be transmitted to the employer. Copy 2 (green) shall be provided to the employee. Copy 3 (blue) shall be retained by the BAT. Except for a form generated by an EBT, the form shall be $8^1/2$ by 11 inches in size.

§40.61 Preparation for breath alcohol testing.

(a) When the employee enters the alcohol testing location, the BAT will require him or her to provide positive identification (*e.g.*, through use of a photo I.D. card or identification by an employer representative). On request by the employee, the BAT shall provide positive identification to the employee.

(b) The BAT shall explain the testing procedure to the employee.

§40.63 Procedures for screening tests.

(a) The BAT shall complete Step 1 on the Breath Alcohol Testing Form. The employee shall then complete Step 2 on the form, signing the certification. Refusal by the employee to sign this certification shall be regarded as a refusal to take the test.

(b) An individually-sealed mouthpiece shall be opened in view of the employee and BAT and attached to the EBT in accordance with the manufacturer's instructions.

(c) The BAT shall instruct the employee to blow forcefully into the mouthpiece for at least 6 seconds or until the EBT indicates that an adequate amount of breath has been obtained.

(d)(1) If the EBT does not meet the requirements of §40.53(b)(1) through (3), the BAT shall ensure, before a screening test is administered to each employee, that he or she and the employee read the sequential test number displayed on the EBT. The BAT shall record the displayed result, test number, testing device, serial number of the testing device, and time in Step # of the form.

(2) If the EBT does not meet the requirements of §40.53(b)(1) through (3), the BAT and the employee shall take the following steps:

(i) Show the employee the result displayed on the EBT. The BAT shall record the displayed result, test number, testing device, serial number of the testing device, time and quantified result in Step 3 of the form.

(ii) Record the test number, date of the test, name of the BAT, location, and quantified test result in the log book. The employee shall initial the log book entry.

(3) If the EBT provides a printed result, but does not print the results directly onto the form, the BAT shall show the employee the result displayed on the EBT. The BAT shall then affix the test result printout to the breath alcohol test form in the designated space, using a method that will provide clear evidence of removal (*e.g.*, tamper-evident tape).

(4) If the EBT prints the test results directly onto the form, the BAT shall show the employee the result displayed on the EBT.

(e)(1) In any case in which the result of the screening test is a breath alcohol concentration of less than 0.02, the BAT shall date the form and sign the certification in Step 3 of the form. The employee shall sign the certification and fill in the date in Step 4 of the form.

(2) No further testing is authorized. The BAT shall transmit the result of less than 0.02 to the employer in a confidential manner, and the employer shall receive and store the information so as to ensure that confidentiality is maintained as required by §40.81.

(3) If the employee does not sign the certification in Step 4 of the form for a test, it shall not be considered a refusal to be tested. In this event, the BAT shall note the employee's failure to sign in the "Remarks" section of the form.

(4) If a test result printed by the EBT (See paragraph (d)(3) or (d) (4) of this section) does not match the displayed result, or if a sequential test number printed by the EBT does not match the sequential test number displayed by the EBT prior to the screening test (see paragraph (d)(1) of this section), the BAT shall note the disparity in the "Remarks" section. Both the employee and the BAT shall initial and sign the notation. In accordance with §40.79, the test is invalid and the employee shall be so advised.

(f) If the result of the screening test is an alcohol concentration of 0.02 or greater, a confirmation test shall be performed as provided in §40.65.

(g) If the confirmation test will be conducted by a different BAT, the BAT who conducts the screening test shall complete and sign the form and log book entry. The BAT will provide the employee with Copy 2 of the form.

(h) If the confirmation test will be conducted at a different site from the screening test, the employer or its agent shall ensure that—

(1) The employee is advised against taking any of the actions mentioned in the first sentence of §40.65(b) of this Part;

(2) The employee is advised that he or she must not drive, perform safety-sensitive duties, or operate heavy equipment, as noted in Block 4 of the alcohol testing form; and

(3) The employee is under observation of a BAT, STT, or other employer personnel while in transit from the screening test site to the confirmation test site.

§40.65 Procedures for confirmation tests.

(a) If a BAT other than the one who conducted the screening test is conducting the confirmation test, the new BAT shall follow the procedures of §40.61.

(b) The BAT shall instruct the employee not to eat, drink, put any object or substance in his or her mouth, and, to the extent possible, not belch during a waiting period before the confirmation test. This time period begins with the completion of the screening test, and shall not be less than 15 minutes. The confirmation test shall be conducted within 30 minutes of the completion of the screening test. The BAT shall explain to the employee the reason for this requirement (*i.e.*, to prevent any accumulation of mouth alcohol leading to an artificially high reading) and the fact that it is for the employee's benefit. The BAT shall also explain that the test will be conducted at the end of the waiting period, even if the employee has disregarded the instruction. If the BAT becomes aware that the employee has not complied with this instruction, the BAT shall so note in the "Remarks" section of the form. If the BAT conducts the confirmation test more than 30 minutes after the result of the screening test has been obtained, the BAT shall note in the "Remarks" section of the form the time that elapsed between the screening and confirmation tests and the reason why the confirmation test could not be conducted within 30 minutes of the screening test.

(c)(1) If a BAT other than the one who conducted the screening test is conducting the confirmation test, the new BAT shall initiate a new Breath Alcohol Testing form. The BAT shall complete Step 1 on the form. The employee shall then complete Step 2 on the form, signing the certification. Refusal by the employee to sign this certification shall be regarded as a refusal to take the test. The BAT shall note in the "Remarks" section of the form that a different BAT conducted the screening test.

(2) In all cases, the procedures of §40.63 (a), (b), and (c) shall be followed. A new mouthpiece shall be used for the confirmation test.

(d) Before the confirmation test is administered for each employee, the BAT shall ensure that the EBT registers 0.00 on an air blank. If the reading is greater than 0.00, the BAT shall conduct one more air blank. If the reading is greater than 0.00, testing shall not proceed using that instrument, which shall be taken out of service. However, testing may proceed on another instrument. Any EBT taken out of service because of failure to perform an air blank accurately shall not be used for testing until a check of external calibration is completed and the EBT is found to be within tolerance limits.

(e) Before the confimation test is administered for each employee, the BAT shall ensure that he or she and the employee read the sequential test number displayed by the EBT.

(f) In the event that the screening and confirmation test results are not identical, the confirmation test result is deemed to be the final result upon which any action under operating administration rules shall be based.

(g)(1) If the EBT provides a printed result, but does not print the results directly onto the form, the BAT shall show the employee the result displayed on the EBT. The BAT shall then affix the test result printout to the breath alcohol test form in the designated space, using a method that will provide clear evidence of removal (*e.g.*, tamper-evident tape).

(2) If the EBT prints the test results directly onto the form, the BAT shall show the employee the result displayed on the EBT.

(h)(1) Following the completion of the test, the BAT shall date the form and sign the certification in Step 3 of the form. The employee shall sign the certification and fill in the date in Step 4 of the form.

(2) If the employee does not sign the certification in Step 4 of the form, it shall not be considered a refusal to be tested. In this event, the BAT shall note the employee's failure to sign in the "Remarks" section.

(3) If a test result printed by the EBT (see paragraph (g)(1) or (g)(2) of this section) does not match the displayed result, or if a sequential test number printed by the EBT does not match the sequential test number displayed by the EBT prior to the confirmation test (see paragraph (e) of this section), the BAT shall note the disparity in the "Remarks" section. Both the employee and the BAT shall initial and sign the notation. In accordance with §40.79, the test is invalid and the employee shall be so advised.

(i) The BAT shall transmit all results to the employer in a confidential manner.

(1) Each employer shall designate one or more employer representatives for the purpose of receiving and handling alcohol testing results in a confidential manner. All communications by BATs to the employer concerning the alcohol testing results of employees shall be to a designated employer representative.

(2) Such transmission may be in writing (the employer copy (Copy 1) of the breath alcohol testing form), in person or by telephone or electronic means, but the BAT shall ensure immediate

transmission to the employer of results that require the employer to prevent the employee from performing a safety-sensitive function.

(3) If the initial transmission is not in writing (e.g., by telephone), the employer shall establish a mechanism to verify the identity of the BAT providing the information.

(4) If the initial transmission is not in writing, the BAT shall follow the initial transmission by providing to the employer the employer's copy of the breath alcohol testing form. The employer shall store the information so as to ensure that confidentiality is maintained as required by §40.81.

§40.67 Refusals to test and uncompleted tests.

(a) Refusal by an employee to complete and sign the breath alcohol testing form (Step 2), to provide breath, to provide an adequate amount of breath, or otherwise to cooperate with the testing process in a way that prevents the completion of the test, shall be noted by the BAT in the remarks section of the form. The testing process shall be terminated and the BAT shall immediately notify the employer.

(b) If a screening or confirmation test cannot be completed, or if an event occurs that would invalidate the test, the BAT shall, if practicable, begin a new screening or confirmation test, as applicable, using a new breath alcohol testing form with a new sequential test number (in the case of a screening test conducted on an EBT that meets the requirements of §40.53(b) or in the case of a confirmation test).

§40.69 Inability to provide an adequate amount of breath.

(a) This section sets forth procedures to be followed in any case in which an employee is unable, or alleges that he or she is unable, to provide an amount of breath sufficient to permit a valid breath test because of a medical condition.

(b) The BAT shall again instruct the employee to attempt to provide an adequate amount of breath. If the employee refuses to make the attempt, the BAT shall immediately inform the employer.

(c) If the employee attempts and fails to provide an adequate amount of breath, the BAT shall so note in the "Remarks" section of the breath alcohol testing form and immediately inform the employer.

(d) If the employee attempts and fails to provide an adequate amount of breath, the employer shall proceed as follows:

(1) [Reserved]

(2) The employer shall direct the employee to obtain, as soon as practical after the attempted provision of breath, an evaluation from a licensed physician who is acceptable to the employer concerning the employee's medical ability to provide an adequate amount of breath.

(i) If the physician determines, in his or her reasonable medical judgment, that a medical condition has, or with a high degree of probability, could have, precluded the employee from providing an adequate amount of breath, the employee's failure to provide an adequate amount of breath shall not be deemed a refusal to take a test. The physician shall provide to the employer a written statement of the basis for his or her conclusion.

(ii) If the licensed physician, in his or her reasonable medical judgment, is unable to make the determination set forth in paragraph (d)(2)(i) of this section, the employee's failure to provide an adequate amount of breath shall be regarded as a refusal to take a test. The licensed physician shall provide a written statement of the basis for his or her conclusion to the employer.

§§40.71 - 40.77 [Reserved]

§40.79 Invalid tests.

(a) A breath alcohol test shall be invalid under the following circumstances:

(1) The next external calibration check of an EBT produces a result that differs by more than the tolerance stated in the QAP from the known value of the test standard. In this event, every test result of 0.02 or above obtained on the device since the last valid external calibration check shall be invalid;

(2) The BAT does not observe the minimum 15-minute waiting period prior to the confirmation test, as provided in §40.65 (b);

(3) The BAT does not perform an air blank of the EBT before a confirmation test, or an air blank does not result in a reading of 0.00 prior to the administration of the test, as provided in §40.65;

(4) The BAT does not sign the form as required by §§40.63 and 40.65;

(5) The BAT has failed to note on the remarks section of the form that the employee has failed or refused to sign the form following the recording or printing on or attachment to the form of the test result;

(6) An EBT fails to print a confirmation test result; or

(7) On a confirmation test and, where applicable, on a screening test, the sequential test number or alcohol concentration displayed on the EBT is not the same as the sequential test number or alcohol concentration on the printed result.

(b) [Reserved]

§40.81 Availability and disclosure of alcohol testing information about individual employees.

(a) Employers shall maintain records in a secure manner, so that disclosure of information to unauthorized persons does not occur.

(b) Except as required by law or expressly authorized or required in this section, no employer shall release covered employee information that is contained in the records required to be maintained by this part or by DOT agency alcohol misuse rules.

(c) An employee subject to testing is entitled, upon written request, to obtain copies of any records pertaining to the employee's use of alcohol, including any records pertaining to his or her alcohol tests. The employer shall promptly provide the records requested by the employee. Access to an employee's records shall not be contingent upon payment for records other than those specifically requested.

(d) Each employer shall permit access to all facilities utilized in complying with the requirements of this part and DOT agency alcohol misuse rules to the Secretary of Transportation, any DOT agency with regulatory authority over the employer, or a state agency with regulatory authority over the employer (as authorized by DOT agency regulations).

(e) When requested by the Secretary of Transportation, any DOT agency with regulatory authority over the employer, or a state agency with regulatory authority over the employer (as authorized by DOT agency regulations), each employer shall make available copies of all results for employer alcohol testing conducted under the requirements of this part and any other information pertaining to the employer's alcohol misuse prevention program. The information shall include name-specific alcohol test results, records and reports.

(f) When requested by the National Transportation Safety Board as part of an accident investigation, an employer shall disclose information related to the employer's administration of any post-accident alcohol tests administered following the accident under investigation.

(g) An employer shall make records available to a subsequent employer upon receipt of a written request from a covered employee. Disclosure by the subsequent employer is permitted only as expressly authorized by the terms of the employee's written request.

(h) An employer may disclose information required to be maintained under this part pertaining to a covered employee to that employee or to the decisionmaker in a lawsuit, grievance, or other proceeding initiated by or on behalf of the individual, and arising from the results of an alcohol test administered under the requirements of this part, or from the employer's determination that the employee engaged in conduct prohibited by a DOT agency alcohol misuse regulation (including, but not limited to, a worker's compensation, unemployment compensation, or other proceeding relating to a benefit sought by the employee).

(i) An employer shall release information regarding a covered employee's records as directed by the specific, written consent of the employee authorizing release of the information to an identified person. Release of such information is permitted only in accordance with the terms of the employee's consent.

§40.83 Maintenance and disclosure of records concerning EBTs and BATs.

(a) Each employer or its agent shall maintain the following records for two years:

(1) Records of the inspection and maintenance of each EBT used in employee testing;

(2) Documentation of the employer's compliance with the QAP for each EBT it uses for alcohol testing under this part;

(3) Records of the training and proficiency testing of each BAT used in employee testing;

(4) The log books required by §40.59(c).

(b) Each employer or its agent shall maintain for five years records pertaining to the calibration of each EBT used in alcohol testing under this part, including records of the results of external calibration checks.

(c) Records required to be maintained by this section shall be disclosed on the same basis as provided in §40.81.

Subpart D — Non-Evidential Alcohol Screening Devices

§40.91 Authorization for use of non-evidential alcohol screening devices.

Non-evidential alcohol screening tests, performed using screening devices included by the National Highway Traffic Safety Administration on its conforming products list for non-evidential screening devices, may be used in lieu of EBTs to perform screening tests required by operating administrations' alcohol testing regulations. Non-evidential screening devices may not be used for confirmation alcohol tests, which must be conducted using EBTs as provided in Subpart C of this Part.

§40.93 The screening test technician.

(a) Anyone meeting the requirements of this Part to be a BAT may act as a screening test technician (STT), provided that the individual has demonstrated proficiency in the operation of the non-evidential screening device he or she is using.

(b) Any other individual may act as an STT if he or she successfully completes a course of instruction concerning the procedures required by this Part for conducting alcohol screening tests. Only the Department of Transportation model course, or a course of instruction determined by the Department of Transportation's Office of Drug Enforcement and Program Compliance to be equivalent to it, may be used for this purpose.

(c) With respect to any non-evidential screening device involving changes, contrasts, or other readings that are indicated on the device in terms of color, STTs shall, in order to be regarded as proficient, be able to discern correctly these changes, contrasts or readings.

(d) The STT shall receive additional training, as needed, to ensure proficiency, concerning new or additional devices or changes in technology that he or she will use.

(e) The employer or its agent shall document the training and proficiency of each STT it uses to test employees and maintain the documentation as provided in §40.83.

(f) The provisions of §40.51(b) and (c); §40.57; §40.59; §40.61; §40.63 (e)(1)-(2), (f), (g), and (h); §40.69; and §40.81; and other provisions, as applicable, of this Part apply to STTs as well as to BATs.

§40.95 Quality assurance plans for non-evidential screening devices.

(a) In order to be used for alcohol screening tests subject to this part, a non-evidential screening device shall have an approved quality assurance plan (QAP) developed by the manufacturer and approved by the National Highway Traffic Safety Administration (NHTSA).

(1) The plan shall designate the method or methods to be used to perform quality control checks; the temperatures at which the non-evidential screening device shall be stored and used, as well as other environmental conditions (e.g., altitude, humidity) that may affect the performance of the device; and, where relevant, the shelf life of the device.

(2) The QAP shall prohibit the use of any device that does not pass the specified quality control checks or that has passed its expiration date.

(b) The manufacturers' instructions on or included in the package for each saliva testing device shall include directions on the proper use of the device, the time frame within which the device must be read and the manner in which the reading is made.

(c) The employer and its agents shall comply with the QAP and manufacturer's instructions for each non-evidential screening device it uses for alcohol screening tests subject to this Part.

§40.97 Locations for non-evidential alcohol screening tests.

(a) Locations for non-evidential alcohol screening tests shall meet the same requirements set forth for breath alcohol testing in §40.57 of this Part.

(b) The STT shall supervise only one employee's use of a non-evidential screening device at a time. The STT shall not leave the alcohol testing location while the screening test procedure for a given employee is in progress.

§40.99 Testing forms.

STTs conducting tests using a non-evidential screening device shall use the alcohol testing form as provided in §40.59 and Appendix B of this Part for the screening test.

§40.101 Screening test procedure.

(a) The steps for preparation for testing shall be the same as provided for breath alcohol testing in §40.61 of this Part.

(b) The STT shall complete Step 1 on the form required by §40.99. The employee shall then complete Step 2 on the form, signing the certification. Refusal by the employee to sign this certification shall be regarded as a refusal to take the test.

(c) If the employer is using a non-evidential breath testing device, the STT shall follow the same steps outlined for screening tests using EBTs in §40.63.

(d) If the employer is using a saliva testing device, the STT shall take the following steps:

(1) The STT shall explain the testing procedure to the employee.

(2) The STT shall check the expiration date of the saliva testing device, show the date to the employee, and shall not use a device at any time subsequent to the expiration date.

(3) The STT shall open an individually sealed package containing the device in the presence of the employee.

(4) The STT shall offer the employee the opportunity to use the swab. If the employee chooses to use the swab, the STT shall instruct the employee to insert the absorbent end of the swab into the employee's mouth, moving it actively throughout the mouth for a sufficient time to ensure that it is completely saturated, as provided in the manufacturer's instructions for the device.

(5) If the employee chooses not to use the swab, or in all cases in which a new test is necessary because the device did not activate (see paragraph (d)(8) of this section), the STT shall insert the absorbent end of the swab into the employee's mouth, moving it actively throughout the mouth for a sufficient time to ensure that it is completely saturated, as provided in the manufacturer's instructions for the device. The STT shall wear a surgical grade glove while doing so.

(6) The STT shall place the device on a flat surface or otherwise in a position in which the swab can be firmly placed into the opening provided in the device for this purpose. The STT shall insert the swab into this opening and maintain firm pressure on the device until the device indicates that it is activated.

(7) If the procedures of paragraph (d)(3)-(d)(5) of this section are not followed successfully (e.g., the swab breaks, the STT drops the swab on the floor or another surface, the swab is removed or falls from the device before the device is activated), the STT shall discard the device and swab and conduct a new test using a new device. The new device shall be one that has

been under the control of the employer or STT prior to the test The STT shall note in the remarks section of the form the reason for the new test. In this case, the STT shall offer the employee the choice of using the swab himself or herself or having the STT use the swab. If the procedures of paragraph (d)(3)-(d)(5) of this section are not followed successfully on the new test, the collection shall be terminated and an explanation provided in the remarks section of the form. A new test shall then be conducted, using an EBT for both the screening and confirmation tests.

(8) If the procedures of paragraph (d)(3)-(d)(5) of this section are followed successfully, but the device is not activated, the STT shall discard the device and swab and conduct a new test, in the same manner as provided in paragraph (d)(7) of this section. In this case, the STT shall place the swab into the employee's mouth to collect saliva for the new test.

(9) The STT shall read the result displayed on the device two minutes after inserting the swab into the device. The STT shall show the device and its reading to the employee and enter the result on the form.

(10) Devices, swabs, gloves and other materials used in saliva testing shall not be reused, and shall be disposed of in a sanitary manner following their use, consistent with applicable requirements.

(e) In the case of any screening test performed under this section, the STT, after determining the alcohol concentration result, shall follow the applicable provisions of §40.63 (e)(1)-(2), (f), (g), and (h). The STT shall also enter, in the "Remarks" section of the form, a notation that the screening test was performed using a non-evidential breath testing device or a saliva device, as applicable. Following completion of the screening test, the STT shall date the form and sign the certification in Step 3 of the form.

§40.103 Refusals to test and uncompleted tests.

(a) Refusal by an employee to complete and sign the alcohol testing form required by §40.99 (Step 2), to provide a breath or saliva sample, to provide an adequate amount of breath, or otherwise to cooperate in a way that prevents the completion of the testing process, shall be noted by the STT in the remarks section of the form. This constitutes a refusal to test. The testing process shall be terminated and the STT shall immediately notify the employer.

(b) If the screening test cannot be completed, for reasons other than a refusal by the employee, or if an event occurs that would invalidate the test, the STT shall, if practicable, immediately begin a new screening test, using a new testing form and, in the case of a test using a saliva screening device, a new device.

§40.105 Inability to provide an adequate amount of breath or saliva.

(a) If an employee is unable to provide sufficient breath to complete a test on a non-evidential breath testing device, the procedures of §40.69 apply.

(b) If an employee is unable to provide sufficient saliva to complete a test on a saliva screening device (e.g., the employee does not provide sufficient saliva to activate the device), the STT, as provided in §40.101 of this Part, shall conduct a new test using a new device. If the employee refuses to complete the new test, the STT shall terminate testing and immediately inform the employer. This constitutes a refusal to test.

(c) If the new test is completed, but there is an insufficient amount of saliva to activate the device, STT shall immediately inform the employer, which shall immediately cause an alcohol test to be administered to the employee using an EBT.

§40.107 Invalid tests.

An alcohol test using a non-evidential screening device shall be invalid under the following circumstances:

(a) With respect to a test conducted on a saliva device—

(1) The result is read before two minutes or after 15 minutes from the time the swab is inserted into the device;

(2) The device does not activate;

(3) The device is used for a test after the expiration date printed on its package; or

(4) The STT fails to note in the remarks section of the form that the screening test was conducted using a saliva device;

(b) With respect to a test conducted on any non-evidential alcohol testing device, the STT has failed to note on the remarks section of the form that the employee has failed or refused to sign the form following the recording on the form of the test result.

§40.109 Availability and disclosure of alcohol testing information about individual employees.

The provisions of §40.81 apply to records of non-evidential-alcohol screening tests.

§40.111 Maintenance and disclosure of records concerning non-evidential testing devices and STTs.

Records concerning STTs and non-evidential testing devices shall be maintained and disclosed following the same requirements applicable to BATs and EBTs under §40.81 of this Part.

Subpart E — Additional Administrative Provisions and Validity Testing

§40.201 Additional definitions.

The following definitions apply to the provisions of this subpart E and subpart F of this part:

Adulterated specimen. A specimen that contains a substance that is not expected to be present in human urine, or contains a substance expected to be present but is at a concentration so high that it is not consistent with human urine.

Affiliate. Persons are affiliates of one another if, directly or indirectly, one controls or has the power to control the other, or a third party controls or has the power to control both. Indicators of control include, but are not limited to: interlocking management or ownership; shared interest among family members; shared facilities or equipment; or common use of employees. Following the issuance of a public interest exclusion, an organization having the same or similar management, ownership, or principal employees as the service agent concerning whom a public interest exclusion is in effect is regarded as an affiliate. This definition is used in connection with the public interest exclusion procedures of Subpart F of this part.

Confirmation (or confirmatory) validity test. A second test performed on a urine specimen to further support a validity test result.

Dilute specimen. A specimen with creatinine and specific gravity values that are lower than expected for human urine.

Initial validity test. The first test used to determine if a specimen is adulterated, diluted, or substituted.

Office of Drug and Alcohol Policy and Compliance (ODAPC). The office in the Office of the Secretary, DOT, that is responsible for coordinating drug and alcohol testing program matters within the Department and providing information concerning the implementation of this part.

Split specimen. In drug testing, a part of the urine specimen that is sent to a first laboratory and retained unopened, and which is transported to a second laboratory in the event that the employee requests that it be tested following a verified positive test of the primary specimen or a verified adulterated or substituted test result.

Substituted specimen. A specimen with creatinine and specific gravity values that are so diminished that they are not consistent with human urine.

§40.203 Who issues authoritative interpretations of this regulation?

ODAPC and the DOT Office of General Counsel (OGC) provide written interpretations of the provisions of this part. These written DOT interpretations are the only official and authoritative interpretations concerning the provisions of this part. DOT agencies may incorporate ODAPC/OGC interpretations in written guidance they issue concerning drug and alcohol testing matters.

§40.205 What is validity testing, and are laboratories authorized to conduct it?

(a) Specimen validity testing is the evaluation of the specimen to determine if it is consistent with normal human urine. The purpose of validity testing is to determine whether certain adulterants or foreign substances were added to the urine, if the urine was diluted, or if the specimen was substituted.

(b) As a laboratory, you are authorized to conduct validity testing.

§40.207 What validity tests must laboratories conduct on primary specimens?

As a laboratory, if you conduct validity testing under the authorization of §40.205(b), you must conduct it in accordance with the requirements of this section.

(a) You must test each primary specimen for creatinine. You must also determine its specific gravity if you find that the creatinine concentration is less than 20 mg/dL.

(b) You must measure the pH of each primary specimen.

(c) You must test each primary specimen to determine if it contains substances that may be used to adulterate the specimen. Your tests must have the capability of determining whether any substance identified in current HHS requirements or specimen validity guidance is present in the specimen.

(d) If you suspect the presence of an interfering substance/adulterant that could make a test result invalid, but you are unable to identify it (*e.g.*, a new adulterant), you may, as the first laboratory, send the specimen to another HHS certified laboratory that has the capability of doing so.

(e) If you identify a substance in a specimen that appears to be an adulterant, but which is not listed in current HHS requirements or guidance, you must report the finding in writing to ODAPC and the Division of Workplace Programs, HHS, within three business days. You must also complete testing of the specimen for drugs, to the extent technically feasible.

(f) You must conserve as much as possible of the specimen for possible future testing.

§40.209 What criteria do laboratories use to establish that a specimen is dilute or substituted?

(a) As a laboratory you must consider the primary specimen to be dilute if the creatinine concentration is less than 20mg/dL *and* the specific gravity is less than 1.003, unless the criteria for a substituted specimen are met.

(b) As a laboratory you must consider the primary specimen to be substituted if the creatinine concentration is less than or equal to 5 mg/dL *and* the specific gravity is less than or equal to 1.001 or greater than or equal to 1.020.

§40.211 What criteria do laboratories use to establish that a specimen is adulterated?

(a) As a laboratory, you must consider the primary specimen to be adulterated if you determine that—

(1) A substance that is not expected to be present in human urine is identified in the specimen;

(2) A substance that is expected to be present in human urine is identified at a concentration so high that it is not consistent with human urine; or

(3) The physical characteristics of the specimen are outside the normal expected range for human urine.

(b) In making your determination under paragraph (a) of this section, you must apply the criteria in current HHS requirements or specimen validity guidance.

§40.213 How long does the laboratory retain specimens after testing?

(a) As a laboratory testing the primary specimen, you must retain a specimen that was reported with positive, adulterated, substituted, or invalid results for a minimum of one year.

(b) You must keep such a specimen in secure, long-term, frozen storage in accordance with HHS requirements.

(c) Within the one-year period, the MRO, the employee, the employer, or a DOT agency may request in writing that you retain a specimen for an additional period of time (*e.g.*, for the purpose of preserving evidence for litigation or a safety investigation). If you receive such a request, you must comply with it. If you do not receive such a request, you may discard the specimen at the end of the year.

(d) If you have not sent the split specimen to another laboratory for testing, you must retain the split specimen for an employee's test for the same period of time that you retain the primary specimen and under the same storage conditions.

(e) As the laboratory testing the split specimen, you must meet the requirements of paragraphs (a) through (c) of this section with respect to the split specimen.

§40.215 On what basis does the MRO verify test results involving adulteration or substitution?

(a) As an MRO, when you receive a laboratory report that a specimen is adulterated or substituted, you must treat that report in the same way you treat the laboratory's report of a confirmed positive test for a drug or drug metabolite.

(b) You must follow the same procedures used for verification of a confirmed positive test for a drug or drug except as otherwise provided in this section.

(c) In the verification interview, you must explain the laboratory findings to the employee and address technical questions or issues the employee may raise.

(d) You must offer the employee the opportunity to present a legitimate medical explanation for the laboratory findings with respect to presence of the adulterant in, or the creatinine and specific gravity findings for, the specimen.

(e) The employee has the burden of proof that there is a legitimate medical explanation.

(1) To meet this burden in the case of an adulterated specimen, the employee must demonstrate that the adulterant found by the laboratory entered the specimen through physiological means.

(2) To meet this burden in the case of a substituted specimen, the employee must demonstrate that he or she did produce or could have produced urine, through physiological means, meeting the creatinine and specific gravity criteria of §40.209(b).

(3) The employee must present information meeting this burden at the time of the verification interview. As the MRO, you have discretion to extend the time available to the employee for this purpose for up to five days before verifying the specimen, if you determine that there is a reasonable basis to believe that the employee will be able to produce relevant evidence supporting a legitimate medical explanation within that time.

(f) As the MRO or the employer, you are not responsible for arranging, conducting, or paying for any studies, examinations or analyses to determine whether a legitimate medical explanation exists.

(g) As the MRO, you must exercise your best professional judgment in deciding whether the employee has established a legitimate medical explanation.

(1) If you determine that the employee's explanation does not present a reasonable basis for concluding that there may be a legitimate medical explanation, you must report the test to the DER as averified refusal to test because of adulteration or substitution, as applicable.

(2) If you believe that the employee's explanation may present a reasonable basis for concluding that there is a legitimate medical explanation, you must direct the employee to obtain, within the five-day period set forth in paragraph (e)(3) of this section, a further medical evaluation. This evaluation must be performed by a licensed physician (the "referral physician"), acceptable to you, with expertise in the medical issues raised by the employee's explanation. (The MRO may perform this evaluation if the MRO has appropriate expertise.)

(i) As the MRO or employer, you are not responsible for finding or paying a referral physician. However, on request of the employee, you must provide reasonable assistance to the employee's efforts to find such a physician. The final choice of the referral physician is the employee's, as long as the physician is acceptable to you.

(ii) As the MRO, you must consult with the referral physician, providing guidance to him or her concerning his or her responsibilities under this section. As part of this consultation, you must provide the following information to the referral physician:

(A) That the employee was required to take a DOT drug test, but the laboratory reported that the specimen was adulterated or substituted, which is treated as a refusal to test;

(B) The consequences of the appropriate DOT agency regulation for refusing to take the required drug test;

(C) That the referral physician must agree to follow the requirements of paragraphs (g)(3) through (g)(4) of this section; and

(D) That the referral physician must provide you with a signed statement of his or her recommendations.

(3) As the referral physician, you must evaluate the employee and consider any evidence the employee presents concerning the employee's medical explanation. You may conduct additional tests to determine whether there is a legitimate medical explanation. Any additional urine tests must be performed in an HHS-certified laboratory.

(4) As the referral physician, you must then make a written recommendation to the MRO about whether the MRO should determine that there is a legitimate medical explanation. As the MRO, you must seriously consider and assess the referral physician's recommendation in deciding whether there is a legitimate medical explanation.

(5) As the MRO, if you determine that there is a legitimate medical explanation, you must cancel the test and inform ODAPC in writing of the determination and the basis for it (*e.g.,* referral physician's findings, evidence produced by the employee).

(6) As the MRO, if you determine that there is not a legitimate medical explanation, you must report the test to the DER as a verified refusal to test because of adulteration or substitution.

(h) The following are examples of types of evidence an employee could present to support an assertion of a legitimate medical explanation for a substituted result:

(1) Medically valid evidence demonstrating that the employee is capable of physiologically producing urine meeting the creatinine and specific gravity criteria of §40.209(b).

(i) To be regarded as medically valid, the evidence must have been gathered using appropriate methodology and controls to ensure its accuracy and reliability.

(ii) Assertion by the employee that his or her personal characteristics (*e.g.*, with respect to race, gender, weight, diet, working conditions) are responsible for the substituted result does not, in itself, constitute a legitimate medical explanation. To make a case that there is a legitimate medical explanation, the employee must present evidence showing that the cited personal characteristics actually result in the physiological production of urine meeting the creatinine and specific gravity criteria of §40.209 (b).

(2) Information from a medical evaluation under paragraph (g) of this section that the individual has a medical condition that has been demonstrated to cause the employee to physiologically produce urine meeting the creatinine and specific gravity criteria of §40.209(b).

(i) A finding or diagnosis by the physician that an employee has a medical condition, in itself, does not constitute a legitimate medical explanation.

(ii) To establish there is a legitimate medical explanation, the employee must demonstrate that the cited medical condition actually results in the physiological production of urine meeting the creatinine and specific gravity criteria of §40.209(b).

§40.217 What does the second laboratory do with the split specimen when it is tested to reconfirm an adulterated test result?

As the laboratory testing the split specimen, you must test the split specimen for the adulterant detected in the primary specimen using the same criteria that were used for the primary specimen or HHS guidance, as applicable. The result of the primary specimen is reconfirmed if the split specimen meets these criteria.

§40.219 What does the second laboratory do with the split specimen when it is tested to reconfirm a substituted test result?

As the laboratory testing the split specimen, you must test the split specimen using the criteria of §40.209(b), just as you would do for a primary specimen. The result of the primary specimen is reconfirmed if the split specimen meets these criteria.

§40.221 What information do laboratories report to MROs regarding split specimen results?

(a) As the laboratory responsible for testing the split specimen, and you are using the Federal Testing Custody and Control Form (CCF) issued by HHS on June 23, 2000, you must report split specimen test results in adulteration and substitution situations by checking the "Reconfirmed" box or the "Failed to Reconfirm" box (Step 5(b)) on Copy 1 of the CCF.

(b) If you check the "Failed to Reconfirm" box, one of the following statements must be included (as appropriate) on the "Reason" line (Step 5(b)):

(1) "Drug(s)/metabolite(s) not detected."

(2) "Adulterant not found within criteria."

(3) "Specimen not consistent with substitution criteria [specify creatinine, specific gravity, or both]"

(4) "Specimen not available for testing."

(c) If you are using the CCF issued by HHS prior to June 23, 2000, enter the information referenced in paragraph (b)(2), (3), or (4) of this section on the "remarks" line.

(d) As the laboratory certifying scientist, enter your name, sign, and date the CCF.

§40.223 What does the MRO do with split specimen laboratory results?

As an MRO, you must take the following actions when a laboratory reports the following results of split specimen tests concerning adulterated or substituted specimens:

(a) **Reconfirmed.** (1) In the case of a reconfirmed positive test for a drug or drug metabolite, report the reconfirmation to the DER and the employee.

(2) In the case of a reconfirmed adulterated or substituted result, report to the DER and the employee that the specimen was adulterated or substituted, either of which constitutes a refusal to test. Therefore, "refusal to test" is the final result.

(b) **Failed to Reconfirm: Drug(s)/Drug Metabolite(s) Not Detected.** (1) Report to the DER and the employee that both tests must be cancelled.

(2) Inform ODAPC of the failure to reconfirm.

(c) **Failed to Reconfirm: Adulterated or Substituted (as appropriate); Criteria Not Met.** (1) Report to the DER and the employee that both tests must be cancelled.

(2) Inform ODAPC of the failure to reconfirm.

(d) **Failed to Reconfirm: Specimen not Available for Testing.** (1) Report to the DER and the employee that both tests must be cancelled and the reason for cancellation.

(2) Direct the DER to ensure the immediate collection of another specimen from the employee under direct observation, with no notice given to the employee of this collection requirement until immediately before the collection.

(3) Inform ODAPC of the failure to reconfirm.

(e) Enter your name, sign and date the appropriate copy of the CCF.

(f) Send a legible copy of the appropriate copy of the CCF (or a signed and dated letter) to the employer and keep a copy for your records.

§40.225 What is a refusal to take a DOT drug test, and what are the consequences?

(a) [Reserved]

(b) As an employee, if the MRO reports that you have a verified adulterated or substituted test result, you have refused to take a drug test.

(c) As an employee, if you refuse to take a drug test, you incur the consequences specified under DOT agency regulations for a violation of those DOT agency regulations.

(d) [Reserved]

(e) [Reserved]

§40.227 Is the MRO required to review laboratory internal chain of custody documentation?

(a) As the MRO, you are not required to review laboratory internal chain of custody documentation.

(b) No one is permitted to cancel a test because you have not reviewed this documentation.

Subpart F — Public Interest Exclusions

§§40.301-40.359 [Reserved]

§40.361 What is the purpose of a public interest exclusion (PIE)?

(a) To protect the public interest, including protecting transportation employers and employees from serious noncompliance with DOT drug and alcohol testing rules, the Department's policy is to ensure that employers conduct business only with responsible service agents.

(b) The Department therefore uses PIEs to exclude from participation in DOT's drug and alcohol testing program any service agent who, by serious noncompliance with this part or other DOT agency drug and alcohol testing regulations, has shown that it is not currently acting in a responsible manner.

(c) A PIE is a serious action that the Department takes only to protect the public interest. We intend to use PIEs only to remedy situations of serious noncompliance. PIEs are not used for the purpose of punishment.

(d) Nothing in this subpart precludes a DOT agency or the Inspector General from taking other action authorized by its regulations with respect to service agents or employers that violate its regulations.

§40.363 On what basis may the Department issue a PIE?

(a) If you are a service agent, the Department may issue a PIE concerning you if we determine that you have failed or refused to provide drug or alcohol testing services consistent with the requirements of this part or a DOT agency drug and alcohol regulation.

(b) The Department also may issue a PIE if you have failed to cooperate with DOT agency representatives concerning inspections, complaint investigations, compliance and enforcement reviews, or requests for documents and other information about compliance with this part or DOT agency drug and alcohol regulations.

§40.365 What is the Department's policy concerning starting a PIE proceeding?

(a) It is the Department's policy to start a PIE proceeding only in cases of serious, uncorrected noncompliance with the provisions of this part, affecting such matters as safety, the outcomes of test results, privacy and confidentiality, due process and fairness for employees, the honesty and integrity of the testing program, and cooperation with or provision of information to DOT agency representatives.

(b) The following are examples of the kinds of serious noncompliance that, as a matter of policy, the Department views as appropriate grounds for starting a PIE proceeding. These examples are not intended to be an exhaustive or exclusive list of the grounds for starting a PIE proceeding. We intend them to illustrate the level of seriousness that the Department believes supports starting a PIE proceeding. The examples follow:

(1) For an MRO, verifying tests positive without interviewing the employees as required by this part or providing MRO services without meeting the qualifications for an MRO required by this part;

(2) For a laboratory, refusing to provide information to the Department, an employer, or an employee as required by this part; or a pattern or practice of testing errors that result in the cancellation of tests. (As a general matter of policy, the Department does not intend to initiate a PIE proceeding concerning a laboratory with respect to matters on which HHS initiates certification actions under its laboratory guidelines.);

(3) For a collector, a pattern or practice of directly observing collections when doing so is unauthorized, or failing or refusing to directly observe collections when doing so is mandatory;

(4) For collectors, BATs, or STTs, a pattern or practice of using forms, testing equipment, or collection kits that do not meet the standards in this part;

(5) For a collector, BAT, or STT, a pattern or practice of "fatal flaws" or other significant uncorrected errors in the collection process;

(6) For a laboratory, MRO or C/TPA, failing or refusing to report tests results as required by this part or DOT agency regulations;

(7) For a laboratory, falsifying, concealing, or destroying documentation concerning any part of the drug testing process, including, but not limited to, documents in a "litigation package";

(8) For SAPs, providing SAP services while not meeting SAP qualifications required by this part or performing evaluations without face-to-face interviews;

(9) For any service agent, maintaining a relationship with

another party that constitutes a conflict of interest under this part (*e.g.*, a laboratory that derives a financial benefit from having an employer use a specific MRO);

(10) For any service agent, representing falsely that the service agent or its activities is approved or certified by the Department or a DOT agency;

(11) For any service agent, disclosing an employee's test result information to any party this part or a DOT agency regulation does not authorize, including by obtaining a "blanket" consent from employees or by creating a data base from which employers or others can retrieve an employee's DOT test results without the specific consent of the employee;

(12) For any service agent, interfering or attempting to interfere with the ability of an MRO to communicate with the Department, or retaliating against an MRO for communicating with the Department;

(13) For any service agent, directing or recommending that an employer fail or refuse to implement any provision of this part; or

(14) With respect to noncompliance with a DOT agency regulation, conduct that affects important provisions of Department-wide concern (*e.g.*, failure to properly conduct the selection process for random testing).

§40.367 Who initiates a PIE proceeding?

The following DOT officials may initiate a PIE proceeding:

(a) The drug and alcohol program manager of a DOT agency;

(b) An official of ODAPC, other than the Director; or

(c) The designee of any of these officials.

§40.369 What is the discretion of an initiating official in starting a PIE proceeding?

(a) Initiating officials have broad discretion in deciding whether to start a PIE proceeding.

(b) In exercising this discretion, the initiating official must consider the Department's policy regarding the seriousness of the service agent's conduct (see §40.365) and all information he or she has obtained to this point concerning the facts of the case. The initiating official may also consider the availability of the resources needed to pursue a PIE proceeding.

(c) A decision not to initiate a PIE proceeding does not necessarily mean that the Department regards a service agent as being in compliance or that the Department may not use other applicable remedies in a situation of noncompliance.

§40.371 On what information does an initiating official rely in deciding whether to start a PIE proceeding?

(a) An initiating official may rely on credible information from any source as the basis for starting a PIE proceeding.

(b) Before sending a correction notice (see §40.373), the initiating official informally contacts the service agent to determine if there is any information that may affect the initiating official's determination about whether it is necessary to send a correction notice. The initiating official may take any information resulting from this contact into account in determining whether to proceed under this subpart.

§40.373 Before starting a PIE proceeding, does the initiating official give the service agent an opportunity to correct problems?

(a) If you are a service agent, the initiating official must send you a correction notice before starting a PIE proceeding.

(b) The correction notice identifies the specific areas in which you must come into compliance in order to avoid being subject to a PIE proceeding.

(c) If you make and document changes needed to come into compliance in the areas listed in the correction notice to the satisfaction of the initiating official within 60 days of the date you receive the notice, the initiating official does not start a PIE proceeding. The initiating official may conduct appropriate fact finding to verify that you have made and maintained satisfactory corrections. When he or she is satisfied that you are in compliance, the initiating official sends you a notice that the matter is concluded.

§40.375 How does the initiating official start a PIE proceeding?

(a) As a service agent, if your compliance matter is not correctable (see §40.373(a)), or if have not resolved compliance matters as provided in §40.373(c), the initiating official starts a PIE proceeding by sending you a notice of proposed exclusion (NOPE). The NOPE contains the initiating official's recommendations concerning the issuance of a PIE, but it is not a decision by the Department to issue a PIE.

(b) The NOPE includes the following information:

(1) A statement that the initiating official is recommending that the Department issue a PIE concerning you;

(2) The factual basis for the initiating official's belief that you are not providing drug and/or alcohol testing services to DOT-regulated employers consistent with the requirements of this part or are in serious noncompliance with a DOT agency drug and alcohol regulation;

(3) The factual basis for the initiating official's belief that your noncompliance has not been or cannot be corrected;

(4) The initiating official's recommendation for the scope of the PIE;

(5) The initiating official's recommendation for the duration of the PIE; and

(6) A statement that you may contest the issuance of the proposed PIE, as provided in §40.379.

(c) The initiating official sends a copy of the NOPE to the ODAPC Director at the same time he or she sends the NOPE to you.

§40.377 Who decides whether to issue a PIE?

(a) The ODAPC Director, or his or her designee, decides whether to issue a PIE. If a designee is acting as the decision maker, all references in this subpart to the Director refer to the designee.

(b) To ensure his or her impartiality, the Director plays no role in the initiating official's determination about whether to start a PIE proceeding.

(c) There is a "firewall" between the initiating official and the Director. This means that the initiating official and the Director are prohibited from having any discussion, contact, or exchange of information with one another about the matter, except for documents and discussions that are part of the record of the proceeding.

§40.379 How do you contest the issuance of a PIE?

(a) If you receive a NOPE, you may contest the issuance of the PIE.

(b) If you want to contest the proposed PIE, you must provide the Director information and argument in opposition to the proposed PIE in writing, in person, and/or through a representative. To contest the proposed PIE, you must take one or more of the steps listed in this paragraph (b) within 30 days after you receive the NOPE.

(1) You may request that the Director dismiss the proposed PIE without further proceedings, on the basis that it does not concern serious noncompliance with this part or DOT agency regulations, consistent with the Department's policy as stated in §40.365.

(2) You may present written information and arguments, consistent with the provisions of §40.381, contesting the proposed PIE.

(3) You may arrange with the Director for an informal meeting to present your information and arguments.

(c) If you do not take any of the actions listed in paragraph (b) of this section within 30 days after you receive the NOPE, the matter proceeds as an uncontested case. In this event, the Director makes his or her decision based on the record provided by the initiating official (*i.e.,* the NOPE and any supporting information or testimony) and any additional information the Director obtains.

§40.381 What information do you present to contest the proposed issuance of a PIE?

(a) As a service agent who wants to contest a proposed PIE, you must present at least the following information to the Director:

(1) Specific facts that contradict the statements contained in the NOPE (see §40.375(b)(2) and (3)). A general denial is insufficient to raise a genuine dispute over facts material to the issuance of a PIE;

(2) Identification of any existing, proposed or prior PIE; and

(3) Identification of your affiliates, if any.

(b) You may provide any information and arguments you wish concerning the proposed issuance, scope and duration of the PIE (see §40.375(b)(4) and (5)).

(c) You may provide any additional relevant information or arguments concerning any of the issues in the matter.

§40.383 What procedures apply if you contest the issuance of a PIE?

(a) DOT conducts PIE proceedings in a fair and informal manner. The Director may use flexible procedures to allow you to present matters in opposition. The Director is not required to follow formal rules of evidence or procedure in creating the record of the proceeding.

(b) The Director will consider any information or argument he or she determines to be relevant to the decision on the matter.

(c) You may submit any documentary evidence you want the Director to consider. In addition, if you have arranged an informal meeting with the Director, you may present witnesses and confront any person the initiating official presents as a witness against you.

(d) In cases where there are material factual issues in dispute, the Director or his or her designee may conduct additional fact-finding.

(e) If you have arranged a meeting with the Director, the Director will make a transcribed record of the meeting available to you on your request. You must pay the cost of transcribing and copying the meeting record.

§40.385 Who bears the burden of proof in a PIE proceeding?

(a) As the proponent of issuing a PIE, the initiating official bears the burden of proof.

(b) This burden is to demonstrate, by a preponderance of the evidence, that the service agent was in serious noncompliance with the requirements of this part for drug and/or alcohol testing-related services or with the requirements of another DOT agency drug and alcohol testing regulation.

§40.387 What matters does the Director decide concerning a proposed PIE?

(a) Following the service agent's response (see §40.379(b)) or, if no response is received, after 30 days have passed from the date on which the service agent received the NOPE, the Director may take one of the following steps:

(1) In response to a request from the service agent (see §40.379(b)(1)) or on his or her own motion, the Director may dismiss a PIE proceeding if he or she determines that it does not concern serious noncompliance with this part or DOT agency regulations, consistent with the Department's policy as stated in §40.365.

(i) If the Director dismisses a proposed PIE under this paragraph (a), the action is closed with respect to the noncompliance alleged in the NOPE.

(ii) The Department may initiate a new PIE proceeding against you on the basis of different or subsequent conduct that is in noncompliance with this part or other DOT drug and alcohol testing rules.

(2) If the Director determines that the initiating official's submission does not have complete information needed for a decision, the Director may remand the matter to the initiating official. The initiating official may resubmit the matter to the Director when the needed information is complete. If the basis for the proposed PIE has changed, the initiating official must send an amended NOPE to the service agent.

(b) The Director makes determinations concerning the following matters in any PIE proceeding that he or she decides on the merits:

(1) Any material facts that are in dispute;

(2) Whether the facts support issuing a PIE;

(3) The scope of any PIE that is issued; and

(4) The duration of any PIE that is issued.

§40.389 What factors may the Director consider?

This section lists examples of the kind of mitigating and aggravating factors that the Director may consider in determining whether to issue a PIE concerning you, as well as the scope and duration of a PIE. This list is not exhaustive or exclusive. The Director may consider other factors if appropriate in the circumstances of a particular case. The list of examples follows:

(a) The actual or potential harm that results or may result from your noncompliance;

(b) The frequency of incidents and/or duration of the noncompliance;

(c) Whether there is a pattern or prior history of noncompliance;

(d) Whether the noncompliance was pervasive within your organization, including such factors as the following:

(1) Whether and to what extent your organization planned, initiated, or carried out the noncompliance;

(2) The positions held by individuals involved in the noncompliance, and whether your principals tolerated their noncompliance; and

(3) Whether you had effective standards of conduct and control systems (both with respect to your own organization and any contractors or affiliates) at the time the noncompliance occurred;

(e) Whether you have demonstrated an appropriate compliance disposition, including such factors as the following:

(1) Whether you have accepted responsibility for the noncompliance and recognize the seriousness of the conduct that led to the cause for issuance of the PIE;

(2) Whether you have cooperated fully with the Department during the investigation. The Director may consider when the cooperation began and whether you disclosed all pertinent information known to you;

(3) Whether you have fully investigated the circumstances of the noncompliance forming the basis for the PIE and, if so, have made the result of the investigation available to the Director;

(4) Whether you have taken appropriate disciplinary action against the individuals responsible for the activity that constitutes the grounds for issuance of the PIE; and

(5) Whether your organization has taken appropriate corrective actions or remedial measures, including implementing actions to prevent recurrence;

(f) With respect to noncompliance with a DOT agency regulation, the degree to which the noncompliance affects matters common to the DOT drug and alcohol testing program;

(g) Other factors appropriate to the circumstances of the case.

§40.391 What is the scope of a PIE?

(a) The scope of a PIE is the Department's determination about the divisions, organizational elements, types of services, affiliates, and/or individuals (including direct employees of a service agent and its contractors) to which a PIE applies.

(b) If, as a service agent, the Department issues a PIE concerning you, the PIE applies to all your divisions, organizational elements, and types of services that are involved with or affected by the noncompliance that forms the factual basis for issuing the PIE.

(c) In the NOPE (see §40.375(b)(4)), the initiating official sets forth his or her recommendation for the scope of the PIE. The proposed scope of the PIE is one of the elements of the proceeding that the service agent may contest (see §40.381(b)) and about which the Director makes a decision (see §40.387(b)(3)).

(d) In recommending and deciding the scope of the PIE, the initiating official and Director, respectively, must take into account the provisions of paragraphs (e) through (j) of this section.

(e) The pervasiveness of the noncompliance within a service agent's organization (see §40.389(d)) is an important consideration in determining the scope of a PIE. The appropriate scope of a PIE grows broader as the pervasiveness of the noncompliance increases.

(f) The application of a PIE is not limited to the specific location or employer at which the conduct that forms the factual basis for issuing the PIE was discovered.

(g) A PIE applies to your affiliates, if the affiliate is involved with or affected by the conduct that forms the factual basis for issuing the PIE.

(h) A PIE applies to individuals who are officers, employees, directors, shareholders, partners, or other individuals associated with your organization in the following circumstances:

(1) Conduct forming any part of the factual basis of the PIE occurred in connection with the individual's performance of duties by or on behalf of your organization; or

(2) The individual knew of, had reason to know of, approved, or acquiesced in such conduct. The individual's acceptance of benefits derived from such conduct is evidence of such knowledge, acquiescence, or approval.

(i) If a contractor to your organization is solely responsible for the conduct that forms the factual basis for a PIE, the PIE does not apply to the service agent itself unless the service agent knew or should have known about the conduct and did not take action to correct it.

(j) PIEs do not apply to drug and alcohol testing that DOT does not regulate.

(k) The following examples illustrate how the Department intends the provisions of this section to work:

Example 1 to §40.391. Service Agent P provides a variety of drug testing services. P's SAP services are involved in a serious violation of this Part 40. However, P's other services fully comply with this part, and P's overall management did not plan or concur in the noncompliance, which in fact was contrary to P's articulated standards. Because the noncompliance was isolated in one area of the organization's activities, and did not pervade the entire organization, the scope of the PIE could be limited to

SAP services.

Example 2 to §40.391. Service Agent Q provides a similar variety of services. The conduct forming the factual basis for a PIE concerns collections for a transit authority. As in Example 1, the noncompliance is not pervasive throughout Q's organization. The PIE would apply to collections at all locations served by Q, not just the particular transit authority or not just in the state in which the transit authority is located.

Example 3 to §40.391. Service Agent R provides a similar array of services. One or more of the following problems exists: R's activities in several areas—collections, MROs, SAPs, protecting the confidentiality of information—are involved in serious noncompliance; DOT determines that R's management knew or should have known about serious noncompliance in one or more areas, but management did not take timely corrective action; or, in response to an inquiry from DOT personnel, R's management refuses to provide information about its operations. In each of these three cases, the scope of the PIE would include all aspects of R's services.

Example 4 to §40.391. Service Agent W provides only one kind of service (*e.g.*, laboratory or MRO services). The Department issues a PIE concerning these services. Because W only provides this one kind of service, the PIE necessarily applies to all its operations.

Example 5 to §40.391. Service Agent X, by exercising reasonably prudent oversight of its collection contractor, should have known that the contractor was making numerous "fatal flaws" in tests. Alternatively, X received a correction notice pointing out these problems in its contractor's collections. In neither case did X take action to correct the problem. X, as well as the contractor, would be subject to a PIE with respect to collections.

Example 6 to §40.391. Service Agent Y could not reasonably have known that one of its MROs was regularly failing to interview employees before verifying tests positive. When it received a correction notice, Y immediately dismissed the erring MRO. In this case, the MRO would be subject to a PIE but Y would not.

Example 7 to §40.391. The Department issues a PIE with respect to Service Agent Z. Z provides services for DOT-regulated transportation employers, a Federal agency under the HHS-regulated Federal employee testing program, and various private businesses and public agencies that DOT does not regulate. The PIE applies only to the DOT-regulated transportation employers with respect to their DOT-mandated testing, not to the Federal agency or the other public agencies and private businesses. The PIE does not prevent the non-DOT regulated entities from continuing to use Z's services.

§40.393 How long does a PIE stay in effect?

(a) In the NOPE (see §40.375(b)(5)), the initiating official proposes the duration of the PIE. The duration of the PIE is one of the elements of the proceeding that the service agent may contest (see §40.381(b)) and about which the Director makes a decision (see §40.387(b)(4)).

(b) In deciding upon the duration of the PIE, the Director considers the seriousness of the conduct on which the PIE is based and the continued need to protect employers and employees from the service agent's noncompliance. The Director considers factors such as those listed in §40.389 in making this decision.

(c) The duration of a PIE will be between one and five years, unless the Director reduces its duration under §40.407.

§40.395 Can you settle a PIE proceeding?

At any time before the Director's decision, you and the initiating official can, with the Director's concurrence, settle a PIE proceeding.

§40.397 When does the Director make a PIE decision?

The Director makes his or her decision within 60 days of the date when the record of a PIE proceeding is complete (including any meeting with the Director and any additional fact-finding that is necessary). The Director may extend this period for good cause for additional periods of up to 30 days.

§40.399 How does the Department notify service agents of its decision?

If you are a service agent involved in a PIE proceeding, the Director provides you written notice as soon as he or she makes a PIE decision. The notice includes the following elements:

(a) If the decision is not to issue a PIE, a statement of the reasons for the decision, including findings of fact with respect to any material factual issues that were in dispute.

(b) If the decision is to issue a PIE—

(1) A reference to the NOPE;

(2) A statement of the reasons for the decision, including findings of fact with respect to any material factual issues that were in dispute;

(3) A statement of the scope of the PIE; and

(4) A statement of the duration of the PIE.

§40.401 How does the Department notify employers and the public about a PIE?

(a) The Department maintains a document called the "List of Excluded Drug and Alcohol Service Agents." This document may be found on the Department's web site (http://www.dot.gov/ost/dapc). You may also request a copy of the document from ODAPC.

(b) When the Director issues a PIE, he or she adds to the List the name and address of the service agent, and any other persons or organizations, to whom the PIE applies and information about the scope and duration of the PIE.

(c) When a service agent ceases to be subject to a PIE, the Director removes this information from the List.

(d) The Department also publishes a *Federal Register* notice to inform the public on any occasion on which a service agent is added to or taken off the List.

§40.403 Must a service agent notify its clients when the Department issues a PIE?

(a) As a service agent, if the Department issues a PIE concerning you, you must notify each of your DOT-regulated employer clients, in writing, about the issuance, scope, duration, and effect of the PIE. You may meet this requirement by sending a copy of the Director's PIE decision or by a separate notice. You must send this notice to each client within three working days of receiving from the Department the notice provided for in §40.399(b).

(b) As part of the notice you send under paragraph (a) of this section, you must offer to transfer immediately all records pertaining to the employer and its employees to the employer or to any other service agent the employer designates. You must carry out this transfer as soon as the employer requests it.

§40.405 May the Federal courts review PIE decisions?

The Director's decision is a final administrative action of the Department. Like all final administrative actions of Federal agencies, the Director's decision is subject to judicial review under the Administrative Procedure Act (5 U.S.C. 551 *et seq.*).

§40.407 May a service agent ask to have a PIE reduced or terminated?

(a) Yes, as a service agent concerning whom the Department has issued a PIE, you may request that the Director terminate a PIE or reduce its duration and/or scope. This process is limited to the issues of duration and scope. It is not an appeal or reconsideration of the decision to issue the PIE.

(b) Your request must be in writing and supported with documentation.

(c) You must wait at least nine months from the date on which the Director issued the PIE to make this request.

(d) The initiating official who was the proponent of the PIE may provide information and arguments concerning your request to the Director.

(e) If the Director verifies that the sources of your noncompliance have been eliminated and that all drug or alcohol testing-related services you would provide to DOT-regulated employers will be consistent with the requirements of this part, the Director may issue a notice terminating or reducing the PIE.

§40.409 What does the issuance of a PIE mean to transportation employers?

(a) As an employer, you are deemed to have notice of the issuance of a PIE when it appears on the List mentioned in §40.401(a) or the notice of the PIE appears in the *Federal Register* as provided in §40.401(d). You should check this List to ensure that any service agents you are using or planning to use are not subject to a PIE.

(b) As an employer who is using a service agent concerning whom a PIE is issued, you must stop using the services of the service agent no later than 90 days after the Department has published the decision in the *Federal Register* or posted it on its web site. You may apply to the ODAPC Director for an extension of 30 days if you demonstrate that you cannot find a substitute service agent within 90 days.

(c) Except during the period provided in paragraph (b) of this section, you must not, as an employer, use the services of a service agent that are covered by a PIE that the Director has issued under this subpart. If you do so, you are in violation of the

Department's regulations and subject to applicable DOT agency sanctions (*e.g.*, civil penalties, withholding of Federal financial assistance).

(d) You also must not obtain drug or alcohol testing services through a contractor or affiliate of the service agent to whom the PIE applies.

Example to Paragraph (d). Service Agent R was subject to a PIE with respect to SAP services. As an employer, not only must you not use R's own SAP services, but you also must not use SAP services you arrange through R, such as services provided by a subcontractor or affiliate of R or a person or organization that receives financial gain from its relationship with R.

(e) This section's prohibition on using the services of a service agent concerning which the Director has issued a PIE applies to employers in all industries subject to DOT drug and alcohol testing regulations.

Example to Paragraph (e). The initiating official for a PIE was the FAA drug and alcohol program manager, and the conduct forming the basis of the PIE pertained to the aviation industry. As a motor carrier, transit authority, pipeline, railroad, or maritime employer, you are also prohibited from using the services of the service agent involved in connection with the DOT drug and alcohol testing program.

(f) The issuance of a PIE does not result in the cancellation of drug or alcohol tests conducted using the service agent involved before the issuance of the Director's decision or up to 90 days following its publication in the *Federal Register* or posting on the Department's web site, unless otherwise specified in the Director's PIE decision or the Director grants an extension as provided in paragraph (b) of this section.

Example to Paragraph (f). The Department issues a PIE concerning Service Agent N on September 1. All tests conducted using N's services before September 1, and through November 30, are valid for all purposes under DOT drug and alcohol testing regulations, assuming they meet all other regulatory requirements.

§40.411 What is the role of the DOT Inspector General's office?

(a) Any person may bring concerns about waste, fraud, or abuse on the part of a service agent to the attention of the DOT Office of Inspector General.

(b) In appropriate cases, the Office of Inspector General may pursue criminal or civil remedies against a service agent.

(c) The Office of Inspector General may provide factual information to other DOT officials for use in a PIE proceeding.

§40.413 How are notices sent to service agents?

(a) If you are a service agent, DOT sends notices to you, including correction notices, notices of proposed exclusion, decision notices, and other notices, in any of the ways mentioned in paragraph (b) or (c) of this section.

(b) DOT may send a notice to you, your identified counsel, your agent for service of process, or any of your partners, officers, directors, owners, or joint venturers to the last known street address, fax number, or e-mail address. DOT deems the notice to have been received by you if sent to any of these persons.

(c) DOT considers notices to be received by you—

(1) When delivered, if DOT mails the notice to the last known street address, or five days after we send it if the letter is undeliverable;

(2) When sent, if DOT sends the notice by fax or five days after we send it if the fax is undeliverable; or

(3) When delivered, if DOT sends the notice by e-mail or five days after DOT sends it if the e-mail is undeliverable.

Editor's Note: Appendixes A and B, which contain the Drug Testing Custody and Control Form and the Breath Alcohol Testing Form, are not included in this Pocketbook.

Appendix G to Subchapter B — Minimum Periodic Inspection Standards

A vehicle does not pass an inspection if it has one of the following defects or deficiencies:

1. **Brake System.**
   a. **Service Brakes.**
      (1) Absence of braking action on any axle required to have brakes upon application of the service brakes (such as missing brakes or brake shoe(s) failing to move upon application of a wedge. S-cam, cam, or disc brake).
      (2) Missing or broken mechanical components including: shoes, lining pads, springs, anchor pins, spiders, cam rollers, push-rods, and air chamber mounting bolts.
      (3) Loose brake components including air chambers, spiders, and cam shaft support brackets.
      (4) Audible air leak at brake chamber (Example-ruptured diaphragm, loose chamber clamp, etc.).
      (5) **Readjustment limits.** The maximum stroke at which brakes should be readjusted is given below. Any brake $1/4''$ or more past the readjustment limit or any two brakes less than $1/4''$ beyond the readjustment limit shall be cause for rejection. Stroke shall be measured with engine off and reservoir pressure of 80 to 90 psi with brakes fully applied.

BOLT TYPE BRAKE CHAMBER DATA

Type	Effective area (sq. in.)	Outside dia. (in.)	Maximum stroke at which brakes should be readjusted
A	12	$6\,^{15}/_{16}$	$1\,^{3}/_{8}$
B	24	$9\,^{3}/_{16}$	$1\,^{3}/_{4}$
C	16	$8\,^{1}/_{16}$	$1\,^{3}/_{4}$
D	6	$5\,^{1}/_{4}$	$1\,^{1}/_{4}$
E	9	$6\,^{3}/_{16}$	$1\,^{3}/_{8}$
F	36	11	$2\,^{1}/_{4}$
G	30	$9\,^{7}/_{8}$	2

ROTOCHAMBER DATA

Type	Effective area (sq. in.)	Outside dia. (in.)	Maximum stroke at which brakes should be readjusted
9	9	4 $9/32$	1 $1/2$
12	12	4 $13/16$	1 $1/2$
16	16	5 $13/32$	2
20	20	5 $15/16$	2
24	24	6 $13/32$	2
30	30	7 $1/16$	2 $1/4$
36	36	7 $5/8$	2 $3/4$
50	50	8 $7/8$	3

CLAMP TYPE BRAKE CHAMBER DATA

Type	Effective area (sq. in.)	Outside dia. (in.)	Maximum stroke at which brakes should be readjusted
6	6	4 $1/2$	1 $1/4$
9	9	5 $1/4$	1 $3/8$
12	12	5 $11/16$	1 $3/8$
16	16	6 $3/8$	1 $3/4$
20	20	6 $25/32$	1 $3/4$
24	24	7 $7/32$	1 $3/4$[1]
30	30	8 $3/32$	2
36	36	9	2 $1/4$

[1] (2″ for long stroke design).

WEDGE BRAKE DATA.—Movement of the scribe mark on the lining shall not exceed $1/16$ inch.

    (6) Brake linings or pads.
       (a) Lining or pad is not firmly attached to the shoe;
       (b) Saturated with oil, grease, or brake fluid; or
       (c) Non-steering axles: Lining with a thickness less than $1/4$ inch at the shoe center for air drum brakes, $1/16$ inch or less at the shoe center for hydraulic and electric drum brakes, and less than $1/8$ inch for air disc brakes.
       (d) Steering axles: Lining with a thickness less than $1/4$ inch at the shoe center for drum brakes, less than $1/8$ inch for air disc brakes and $1/16$ inch or less for

hydraulic disc and electric brakes.

(7) Missing brake on any axle required to have brakes.

(8) Mismatch across any power unit steering axle of:

    (a) Air chamber sizes.

    (b) Slack adjuster length.

b. **Parking Brake System.** No brakes on the vehicle or combination are applied upon actuation of the parking brake control, including driveline hand controlled parking brakes.

c. **Brake Drum or Rotors.**

(1) With any external crack or cracks that open upon brake application (do not confuse short hairline heat check cracks with flexural cracks).

(2) Any portion of the drum or rotor missing or in danger of falling away.

d. **Brake Hose.**

(1) Hose with any damage extending through the outer reinforcement ply. (Rubber impregnated fabric cover is not a reinforcement ply). (Thermoplastic nylon may have braid reinforcement or color difference between cover and inner tube. Exposure of second color is cause for rejection.

(2) Bulge or swelling when air pressure is applied.

(3) Any audible leaks.

(4) Two hoses improperly joined (such as a splice made by sliding the hose ends over a piece of tubing and clamping the hose to the tube).

(5) Air hose cracked, broken or crimped.

e. **Brake Tubing**

(1) Any audible leak.

(2) Tubing cracked, damaged by heat, broken or crimped.

f. **Low Pressure Warning Device** missing, inoperative, or does not operate at 55 psi and below, or $1/2$ the governor cut-out pressure, whichever is less.

g. **Tractor Protection Valve.** Inoperable or missing tractor protection valve(s) on power unit.

h. **Air Compressor.**

(1) Compressor drive belts in condition of impending or probable failure.

(2) Loose compressor mounting bolts.

(3) Cracked, broken or loose pulley.

(4) Cracked or broken mounting brackets, braces or adapters.

i. **Electric Brakes.**

(1) Absence of braking action on any wheel required to have brakes.

(2) Missing or inoperable breakaway braking device.

j. **Hydraulic Brakes. (Including Power Assist Over Hydraulic and Engine Drive Hydraulic Booster).**

(1) Master cylinder less than $1/4$ full.

(2) No pedal reserve with engine running except by pumping pedal.

(3) Power assist unit fails to operate.

(4) Seeping or swelling brake hose(s) under application of pressure.

(5) Missing or inoperative check valve.

(6) Has any visually observed leaking hydraulic fluid in the brake system.

(7) Has hydraulic hose(s) abraded (chafed) through outer cover-to-fabric layer.

(8) Fluid lines or connections leaking restricted, crimped, cracked or broken.

(9) Brake failure or low fluid warning light on and/or inoperative.

k. **Vacuum Systems.** Any vacuum system which:

(1) Has insufficient vacuum reserve to permit one full brake application after engine is shut off.

(2) Has vacuum hose(s) or line(s) restricted, abraded (chafed) through outer cover to cord ply, crimped, cracked, broken or has collapse of vacuum hose(s) when vacuum is applied.

(3) Lacks an operative low-vacuum warning device as required.

2. **Coupling Devices.**

a. **Fifth Wheels.**

(1) Mounting to frame.

(a) Any fasteners missing or ineffective.

(b) Any movement between mounting components.

(c) Any mounting angle iron cracked or broken.

(2) Mounting plates and pivot brackets.

    (a) Any fasteners missing or ineffective.

    (b) Any welds or parent metal cracked.

    (c) More than $3/8$ inch horizontal movement between pivot bracket pin and bracket.

    (d) Pivot bracket pin missing or not secured.

(3) Sliders.

    (a) Any latching fasteners missing or ineffective.

    (b) Any fore or aft stop missing or not securely attached.

    (c) Movement more than $3/8$ inch between slider bracket and slider base.

    (d) Any slider component cracked in parent metal or weld.

(4) Lower coupler.

    (a) Horizontal movement between the upper and lower fifth wheel halves exceeds $1/2$ inch.

    (b) Operating handle not in closed or locked position.

    (c) Kingpin not properly engaged.

    (d) Separation between upper and lower coupler allowing light to show through from side to side.

    (e) Cracks in the fifth wheel plate.

        Exceptions: Cracks in fifth wheel approach ramps and casting shrinkage cracks in the ribs of the body of a cast fifth wheel.

    (f) Locking mechanism parts missing, broken, or deformed to the extent the kingpin is not securely held.

b. Pintle Hooks.

(1) Mounting to frame.

    (a) Any missing or ineffective fasteners (a fastener is not considered missing if there is an empty hole in the device but no corresponding hole in the frame or vise versa).

    (b) Mounting surface cracks extending from point of attachment (*e.g.*, cracks in the frame at mounting bolt holes).

    (c) Loose mounting.

       (d) Frame crossmember providing pintle hook attachment cracked.

   (2) Integrity.

       (a) Cracks anywhere in pintle hook assembly.

       (b) Any welded repairs to the pintle hook.

       (c) Any part of the horn section reduced by more than 20%.

       (d) Latch insecure.

c. Drawbar/Towbar Eye.

   (1) Mounting.

       (a) Any cracks in attachment welds.

       (b) Any missing or ineffective fasteners.

   (2) Integrity.

       (a) Any cracks.

       (b) Any part of the eye reduced by more than 20%.

d. Drawbar/Towbar Tongue.

   (1) Slider (power or manual).

       (a) Ineffective latching mechanism.

       (b) Missing or ineffective stop.

       (c) Movement of more than $1/4$ inch between slider and housing.

       (d) Any leaking, air or hydraulic cylinders, hoses, or chambers (other than slight oil weeping normal with hydraulic seals).

   (2) Integrity.

       (a) Any cracks.

       (b) Movement of $1/4$ inch between subframe and drawbar at point of attachment.

e. Safety Devices.

   (1) Safety devices missing.

   (2) Unattached or incapable of secure attachment.

   (3) Chains and hooks.

       (a) Worn to the extent of a measurable reduction in link cross section.

       (b) Improper repairs including welding, wire, small bolts, rope and tape.

   (4) Cable.

       (a) Kinked or broken cable strands.

(b) Improper clamps or clamping

f. **Saddle-Mounts.**

  (1) Method of attachment.

    (a) Any missing or ineffective fasteners.

    (b) Loose mountings.

    (c) Any cracks or breaks in a stress or load bearing member.

    (d) Horizontal movement between upper and lower saddle-mount halves exceeds $1/4$ inch.

3. Exhaust System.

a. Any exhaust system determined to be leaking at a point forward of or directly below the driver/sleeper compartment.

b. A bus exhaust system leaking or discharging to the atmosphere:

  (1) **Gasoline powered** — excess of 6 inches forward of the rearmost part of the bus.

  (2) **Other than gasoline powered** — in excess of 15 inches forward of the rearmost part of the bus.

  (3) **Other than gasoline powered** — forward of a door or window designed to be opened. (**Exception:** emergency exits).

c. No part of the exhaust system of any motor vehicle shall be so located as would be likely to result in burning, charring, or damaging the electrical wiring, the fuel supply, or any combustible part of the motor vehicle.

4. Fuel System.

a. A fuel system with a visible leak at any point.

b. A fuel tank filler cap missing.

c. A fuel tank not securely attached to the motor vehicle by reason of loose, broken or missing mounting bolts or brackets (some fuel tanks use springs or rubber bushings to permit movement).

5. Lighting Devices.

All lighting devices and reflectors required by Section 393 shall be operable.

6. Safe loading.

a. Part(s) of vehicle or condition of loading such that the spare tire or any part of the load or dunnage can fall onto the roadway.

b. Protection Against Shifting Cargo—Any vehicle without a front-end structure or equivalent device as required.

7. **Steering Mechanism.**
   a. **Steering Wheel Free Play** (on vehicles equipped with power steering the engine must be running).

Steering wheel diameter	Manual steering system	Power steering system
16"	2"	4 $\frac{1}{2}$"
18"	2 $\frac{1}{4}$"	4 $\frac{3}{4}$"
20"	2 $\frac{1}{2}$"	5 $\frac{1}{4}$"
22"	2 $\frac{3}{4}$"	5 $\frac{3}{4}$"

   b. **Steering Column.**
      (1) Any absence or looseness of U-bolt(s) or positioning part(s).
      (2) Worn, faulty or obviously repair welded universal joint(s).
      (3) Steering wheel not properly secured.
   c. **Front Axle Beam and All Steering Components Other Than Steering Column.**
      (1) Any crack(s).
      (2) Any obvious welded repair(s).
   d. **Steering Gear Box.**
      (1) Any mounting bolt(s) loose or missing.
      (2) Any crack(s) in gear box or mounting brackets.
   e. **Pitman Arm.** Any looseness of the pitman arm on the steering gear output shaft.
   f. **Power Steering.** Auxiliary power assist cylinder loose.
   g. **Ball and Socket Joints.**
      (1) Any movement under steering load of a stud nut.
      (2) Any motion, other than rotational, between any linkage member and it's attachment point of more than $\frac{1}{4}$ inch.
   h. **Tie Rods and Drag Links.**
      (1) Loose clamp(s) or clamp bolt(s) on tie rods or drag links.
      (2) Any looseness in any threaded joint.
   i. **Nuts.** Nut(s) loose or missing on tie rods pitman arm, drag link, steering arm or tie rod arm.

j. **Steering System.** Any modification or other condition that interferes with free movement of any steering component.

8. **Suspension.**

a. Any U-bolt(s), spring hanger(s), or other axle positioning part(s) cracked, broken, loose or missing resulting in shifting of an axle from its normal position. (After a turn, lateral axle displacement is normal with some suspensions. Forward or rearward operation in a straight line will cause the axle to return to alignment).

b. **Spring Assembly.**

(1) Any leaves in a leaf spring assembly broken or missing.

(2) Any broken main leaf in a leaf spring assembly. (Includes assembly with more than one main spring).

(3) Coil spring broken.

(4) Rubber spring missing.

(5) One or more leaves displaced in a manner that could result in contact with a tire, rim, brake drum or frame.

(6) Broken torsion bar spring in a torsion bar suspension.

(7) Deflated air suspension, *i.e.*, system failure, leak, etc.

c. **Torque, Radius or Tracking Components.**
Any part of a torque, radius or tracking component assembly or any part used for attaching the same to the vehicle frame or axle that is cracked, loose, broken or missing. (Does not apply to loose bushings in torque or track rods.)

9. **Frame.**

a. **Frame Members.**

(1) Any cracked, broken, loose, or sagging frame member.

(2) Any loose or missing fasteners including fasteners attaching functional component such as engine, transmission, steering gear, suspension, body parts, and fifth wheel.

b. **Tire and Wheel Clearance.** Any condition, including loading, that causes the body or frame to be in contact with a tire or any part of the wheel assemblies.

c. (1) **Adjustable Axle Assemblies (Sliding Subframes).**
Adjustable axle assembly with locking pins missing or not engaged.

10. **Tires.**
   a. **Any tire on any steering axle of a power unit.**
      (1) With less than $4/32$ inch tread when measured at any point on a major tread groove.
      (2) Has body ply or belt material exposed through the tread or sidewall.
      (3) Has any tread or sidewall separation.
      (4) Has a cut where the ply or belt material is exposed.
      (5) Labeled "Not for Highway Use" or displaying other marking which would exclude use on steering axle.
      (6) A tube-type radial tire without radial tube stem markings. These markings include a red band around the tube stem, the word "radial" embossed in metal stems, or the word "radial" molded in rubber stems.
      (7) Mixing bias and radial tires on the same axle.
      (8) Tire flap protrudes through valve slot in rim and touches stem.
      (9) Regrooved tire except motor vehicles used solely in urban or suburban service (see exception in 393.75(e).
      (10) Boot, blowout patch or other ply repair.
      (11) Weight carried exceeds tire load limit. This includes overloaded tire resulting from low air pressure.
      (12) Tire is flat or has noticeable (*e.g.*, can be heard or felt) leak.
      (13) Any bus equipped with recapped or retreaded tire(s).
      (14) So mounted or inflated that it comes in contact with any part of the vehicle.
   b. **All tires other than those found on the steering axle of a power unit:**
      (1) Weight carried exceeds tire load limit. This includes overloaded tire resulting from low air pressure.
      (2) Tire is flat or has noticeable (*e.g.*, can be heard or felt) leak.
      (3) Has body ply or belt material exposed through the tread or sidewall.
      (4) Has any tread or sidewall separation.
      (5) Has a cut where ply or belt material is exposed.

(6) So mounted or inflated that it comes in contact with any part of the vehicle. (This includes a tire that contacts its mate.)

(7) Is marked "Not for highway use" or otherwise marked and having like meaning.

(8) With less than $^2/_{32}$ inch tread when measured at any point on a major tread groove.

11. Wheels and Rims.

a. **Lock or Side Ring.** Bent, broken, cracked, improperly seated, sprung or mismatched ring(s).

b. **Wheels and Rims.** Cracked or broken or has elongated bolt holes.

c. **Fasteners (both spoke and disc wheels).** Any loose, missing, broken, cracked, stripped or otherwise ineffective fasteners.

d. **Welds.**

(1) Any cracks in welds attaching disc wheel disc to rim.

(2) Any crack in welds attaching tubeless demountable rim to adapter.

(3) Any welded repair on aluminum wheel(s) on a steering axle.

(4) Any welded repair other than disc to rim attachment on steel disc wheel(s) mounted on the steering axle.

12. Windshield Glazing.

(Not including a 2 inch border at the top, a 1 inch border at each side and the area below the topmost portion of the steering wheel.) Any crack, discoloration or vision reducing matter except: (1) coloring or tinting applied at time of manufacture; (2) any crack not over $^1/_4$ inch wide, if not intersected by any other crack; (3) any damaged area not more than $^3/_4$ inch in diameter, if not closer than 3 inches to any other such damaged area; (4) labels, stickers, decalcomania, etc. (see 393.60 for exceptions).

13. Windshield Wipers.

Any power unit that has an inoperative wiper, or missing or damaged parts that render it ineffective.

Comparison of Appendix G, and the new North American Uniform Driver-Vehicle Inspection Procedure (North American Commercial Vehicle Critical Safety Inspection Items and Out-Of-Service Criteria)

The vehicle portion of the FHWA's North American Uniform Driver-Vehicle Inspection Procedure (NAUD-VIP) requirements, CVSA's North American Commercial Vehicle Critical Safety Inspection Items and Out-Of-Service Criteria and Appendix G of subchapter B are similar documents and follow the same inspection procedures. The same items are required to be inspected by each document. FHWA's and CVSA's out-of-service criteria are intended to be used in random roadside inspections to identify critical vehicle inspection items and provide criteria for placing a vehicle(s) out-of-service. A vehicle(s) is placed out-of-service only when by reason of its mechanical condition or loading it is determined to be so imminently hazardous as to likely cause an accident or breakdown, or when such condition(s) would likely contribute to loss of control of the vehicle(s) by the driver. A certain amount of flexibility is given to the inspecting official whether to place the vehicle out-of-service at the inspection site or if it would be less hazardous to allow the vehicle to proceed to a repair facility for repair. The distance to the repair facility must not exceed 25 miles. The roadside type of inspection, however, does not necessarily mean that a vehicle has to be defect-free in order to continue in service.

In contrast, the Appendix G inspection procedure requires that all items required to be inspected are in proper adjustment, are not defective and function properly prior to the vehicle being placed in service.

Differences Between the Out-Of-Service Criteria & FHWA's Annual Inspection

1. **Brake System.**
   The Appendix G criteria rejects vehicles with any defective brakes, any air leaks, etc. The out-of-service criteria allows 20% defective brakes on non-steering axles and a certain latitude on air leaks before placing a vehicle out-of-service.

2. **Coupling Devices.**
   Appendix G rejects vehicles with any fifth wheel mounting fastener missing or ineffective. The out-of-service criteria allows up to 20% missing or ineffective fasteners on frame mountings and pivot bracket mountings and 25% on slider-latching fasteners. The out-of-service criteria also allows some latitude on cracked welds.

3. **Exhaust System.**
   Appendix G follows Section 393.83 verbatim. The CVSA out-of-service criteria allows vehicles to exhaust forward of the dimensions given in Section 393.83 as long as the exhaust does not leak or exhaust under the chassis.

4. **Fuel System.**
   Same for Appendix G and the out-of-service criteria.

5. **Lighting Devices.**
   Appendix G requires all lighting devices required by section 393 to be operative at all times. The out-of-service criteria only requires one stop light and functioning turn signals on the rear most vehicle of a combination vehicle to be operative at all times. In addtion one operative head lamp and tail lamp are required during the hours of darkness.

6. **Safe Loading.**
   Same for both Appendix G and the out-of-service criteria.

7. **Steering Mechanism.**
   Steering lash requirements of Appendix G follows the new requirements of §393.209.

8. **Suspension.**
   Appendix G follows the new requirements of §393.207 which does not allow any broken leaves in a leaf spring assembly. The out-of-service criteria allows up to 25% broken or missing leaves before being placed out-of-service.

9. Frame.
The out-of-service criteria allows a certain latitude in frame cracks before placing a vehicle out-of-service. Appendix G follows the new requirements of 393.201 which does not allow any frame cracks.

10. Tires.
Appendix G follows the requirements of 393.75 which requires a tire tread depth of $^4/_{32}$ inch on power unit steering axles and $^2/_{32}$ inch on all other axles. The out-of-service criteria only requires $^2/_{32}$ inch tire tread depth on power unit steering axles and $^1/_{32}$ inch on all other axles.

11. Wheel and Rims.
The out-of-service criteria allows a certain amount latitude for wheel and rim cracks and missing or defective fasteners. Appendix G meets the requirements of the new 393.205 which does not allow defective wheels and rims non-effective nuts and bolts.

12. Windshield Glazing.
The out-of-service criteria places in a restricted service condition any vehicle that has a crack or discoloration in the windshield area lying within the sweep of the wiper on the drivers side and does not address the remaining area of the windshield. Appendix G addresses requirements for the whole windshield as specified in 393.60.

13. Windshield Wipers.
Appendix G requires windshield wipers to be operative at all times. The out-of-service criteria only requires that the windshield wiper on the driver's side to be inspected during inclement weather.

NOTES

NOTES